Teen Titans

THE FUTURE IS NOW

Dan DiDio VP-Executive Editor

Eddie Berganza Editor-original series

Tom Palmer, Jr. Associate Editor-original series

Robert Greenberger Senior Editor-collected edition

Robbin Brosterman Senior Art Director

Paul Levitz President & Publisher

Georg Brewer VP-Design & DC Direct Creative

Richard Bruning Senior VP-Creative Director

Patrick Caldon Senior VP-Finance & Operations

Chris Caramalis VP-Finance

Terri Cunningham VP-Managing Editor

Stephanie Fierman Senior VP-Sales & Marketing

Alison Gill VP-Manufacturing

Rich Johnson VP-Book Trade Sales

Hank Kanalz VP-General Manager, WildStorm

Lillian Laserson Senior VP & General Counsel

Jim Lee Editorial Director-WildStorm

Paula Lowitt Senior VP-Business & Legal Affairs

David McKillips VP-Advertising & Custom Publishing

John Nee VP-Business Development

Gregory Noveck Senior VP-Creative Affairs

Cheryl Rubin Senior VP-Brand Management

Jeff Trojan VP-Business Development, DC Direct

Bob Wayne VP-Sales

TEEN TITANS: THE FUTURE IS NOW

DC Comics, 1700 Broadway, New York, NY 10019
A Warner Bros. Entertainment Company
Printed in Canada. Second Printing.
ISBN: 1-4012-0475-9
ISBN 13: 978-1-4012-0475-4
Cover illustration by Mike McKone & Marlo Alquiza
Logo designed by Terry Marks

Teen Titans

THE FUTURE IS NOW

SUPERBOY & THE LEGION	TITANS TOMORROW	HIDING	LIGHTS OUT
Geoff Johns & Mark Waid Writers	Geoff Johns Writer	Geoff Johns Writer	Geoff Johns Writer
Mike McKone, Ivan Reis & Joe Prado Pencillers	Mike McKone Penciller	Tom Grummett Penciller	Mike McKone Penciller
Marlo Alquiza & Mark Campos Inkers	Marlo Alquiza Inker	Nelson Inker	Marlo Alquiza Inker
Comicraft & Rob Leigh Letterers	Comicraft Letterer	Comicraft Letterer	Comicraft Letterer
Jeromy Cox & Sno-Cone Colorists	Jeromy Cox Colorist	Jeromy Cox Colorist	Jeromy Cox Colorist

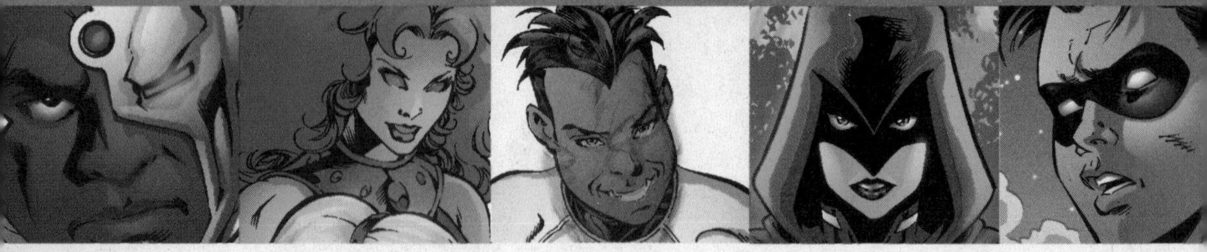

W H O ' S   W H O

THE TEEN TITANS

There has always been a next generation of hero to be trained. As much can be learned from fellow novices as from a mentor, so were born the Teen Titans. Over the years the lineup has changed, but the need for guidance remains as does the spirit of comradery and friendship.

CYBORG

Victor Stone's parents were research scientists for S.T.A.R. Labs, and during an experiment his mother accidentally unleashed a destructive force, killing her and destroying most of Vic's body. His father saved the youth's life with cybernetic components, making Vic feel like an outsider. He only came to accept his fate when he joined the Titans. Through many changes, Vic remains committed to the team. Currently, Cyborg has taken it upon himself to re-form the Titans and usher in today's teenaged superheroes at the new Titans Tower in San Francisco.

STARFIRE

Princess Koriand'r of Tamaran was sacrificed by her father to save their world. Subjected to horrendous experiments, she gained the ability to generate energy bolts in addition to her natural gift of flight. Escaping her tormentors, she made her way to Earth and found a new life as Starfire. Her world is now gone, a victim of Imperiex. Starfire tends to be impatient, and that, combined with her disinterest in being anyone's teacher, has made her uncomfortable about her role on the new team.

BEAST BOY

Garfield Logan was poisoned with sakutia, a rare African toxin. His geneticist parents used an experimental treatment to save his life, and in so doing imbued him with green skin and the ability to transform himself into any animal life form. When his parents died in an accident, he was adopted by Rita Farr and Steve Dayton of the Doom Patrol. Gar desperately wants to be an actor but is most comfortable serving with the various incarnations of the Titans. At age 19, Beast Boy finds himself acting as the mediator between the older and younger Titans, a role he readily accepts.

RAVEN

The daughter of a human and the demon Trigon, she has spent much of her life trying to escape her father's influence. Raven was warned to always keep her anger and frustrations in check, lest she give in to her father's demonic influence. When Trigon wanted to invade Earth, she preceded him, helping form one version of the Titans to stop him. Since then, she has opposed Trigon frequently, losing her mortal body in the process. Without a body to inhabit, Raven's soul-self wandered the world aimlessly until recently.

ROBIN

Perhaps the best prepared of the younger heroes, Tim Drake has been trained by the best – Batman and the first Robin, Dick Grayson. Tim wants to fight crime, but not forever, and uses his quick mind and strong body in addition to a veritable arsenal to stop crime. He has hated lying to his father about his costumed exploits and recently suffered the crushing dissolution of Young Justice, a team he led. Robin remains a mystery to those around him. Even when the Titans began to believe they could predict his next move, they found out they were mistaken.

SUPERBOY

In the wake of Superman's death, a clone was formed using DNA drawn not only from Superman, but from Lex Luthor. Being a hybrid human/Kryptonian, Superboy has a different set of abilities including flight, strength, speed, limited invulnerability and something he calls tactile telekinesis. Impulsive, the clone strives to do the right thing but acts without thinking. Superman recently asked his adoptive parents, the Kents, to help raise the teen. He also entrusted the youth, now called Conner, with Krypto's safekeeping.

KID FLASH

Bart Allen has quite a legacy to live up to. His grandfather was Barry Allen, the second Flash. Born in the 30th century, Bart was brought to the 21st century by his grandmother to be properly schooled in the use of his natural super-speed. For a time, he operated as Impulse, under the tutelage of Max Mercury, Zen master of speed. After recent events, Bart decided it was time to grow up, and toward that goal he has speed-read and memorized the contents of the San Francisco Public Library. He has the knowledge but now needs the experience to be worthy of the Flash mantle. Changing his name to Kid Flash was the first step in the process.

WONDER GIRL

Cassie Sandsmark was thrilled to befriend Diana, the Themysciran princess known as Wonder Woman — so much so that during a crisis, she borrowed the Sandals of Hermes and the Gauntlet of Atlas to aid Diana. She then boldly asked Zeus for additional powers. Amused, he granted her strength and flight and she adventured as Wonder Girl. She began training under Artemis until the death of Donna Troy, the first Wonder Girl. When her secret identity was exposed, Cassie enrolled in a private school. Cassie continues to grow into her heroic role, discovering new limits to her powers and finding new allies and enemies lurking among Ancient Myth, such as the war god Ares who recently gave her a golden lasso.

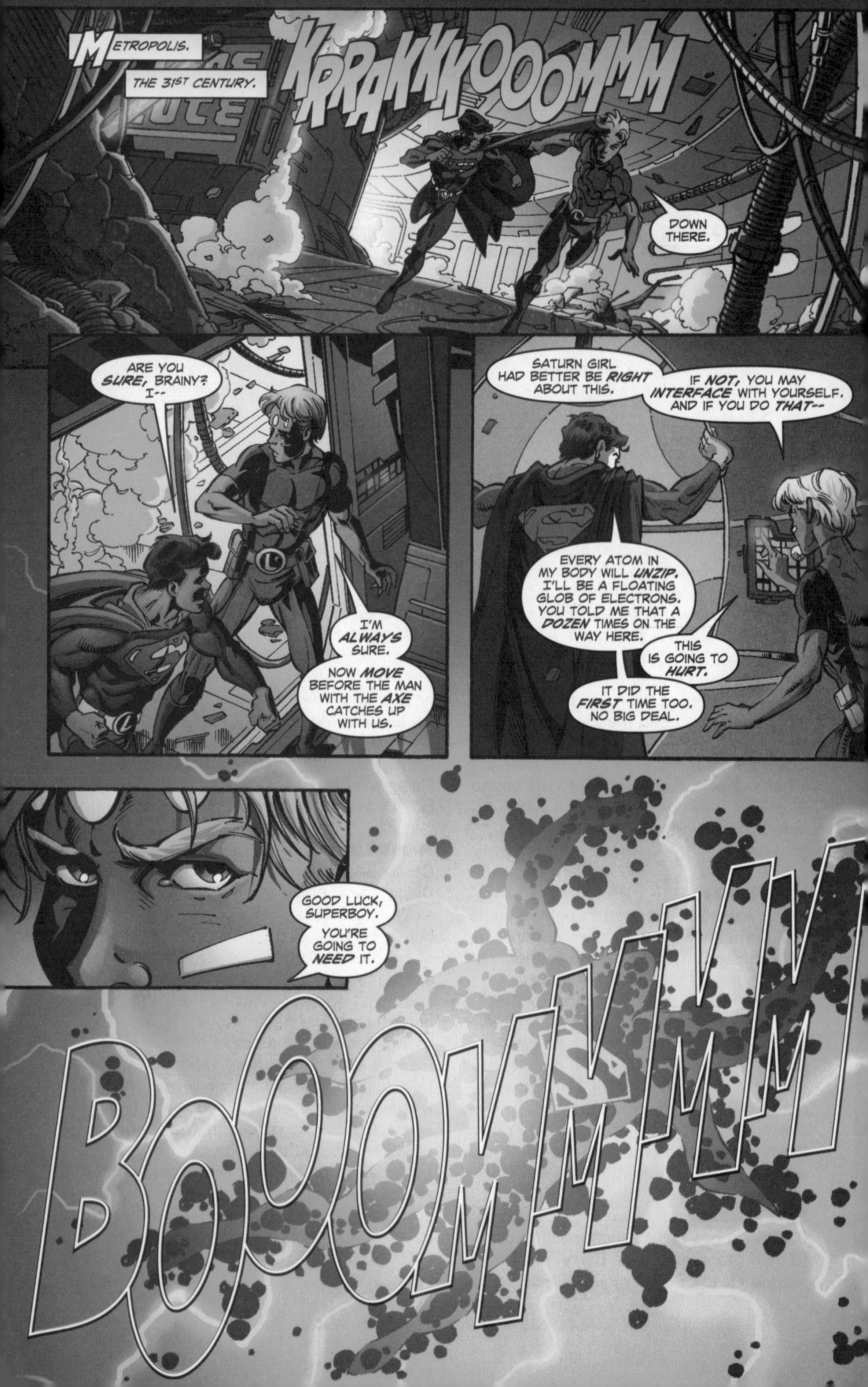
METROPOLIS.
THE 31ST CENTURY.
KRRAKKKOOOMMM
DOWN THERE.
ARE YOU SURE, BRAINY? I--
I'M ALWAYS SURE.
NOW MOVE BEFORE THE MAN WITH THE AXE CATCHES UP WITH US.
SATURN GIRL HAD BETTER BE RIGHT ABOUT THIS.
IF NOT, YOU MAY INTERFACE WITH YOURSELF. AND IF YOU DO THAT--
EVERY ATOM IN MY BODY WILL UNZIP. I'LL BE A FLOATING GLOB OF ELECTRONS. YOU TOLD ME THAT A DOZEN TIMES ON THE WAY HERE.
THIS IS GOING TO HURT.
IT DID THE FIRST TIME TOO. NO BIG DEAL.
GOOD LUCK, SUPERBOY.
YOU'RE GOING TO NEED IT.
BOOOMMMMMMM

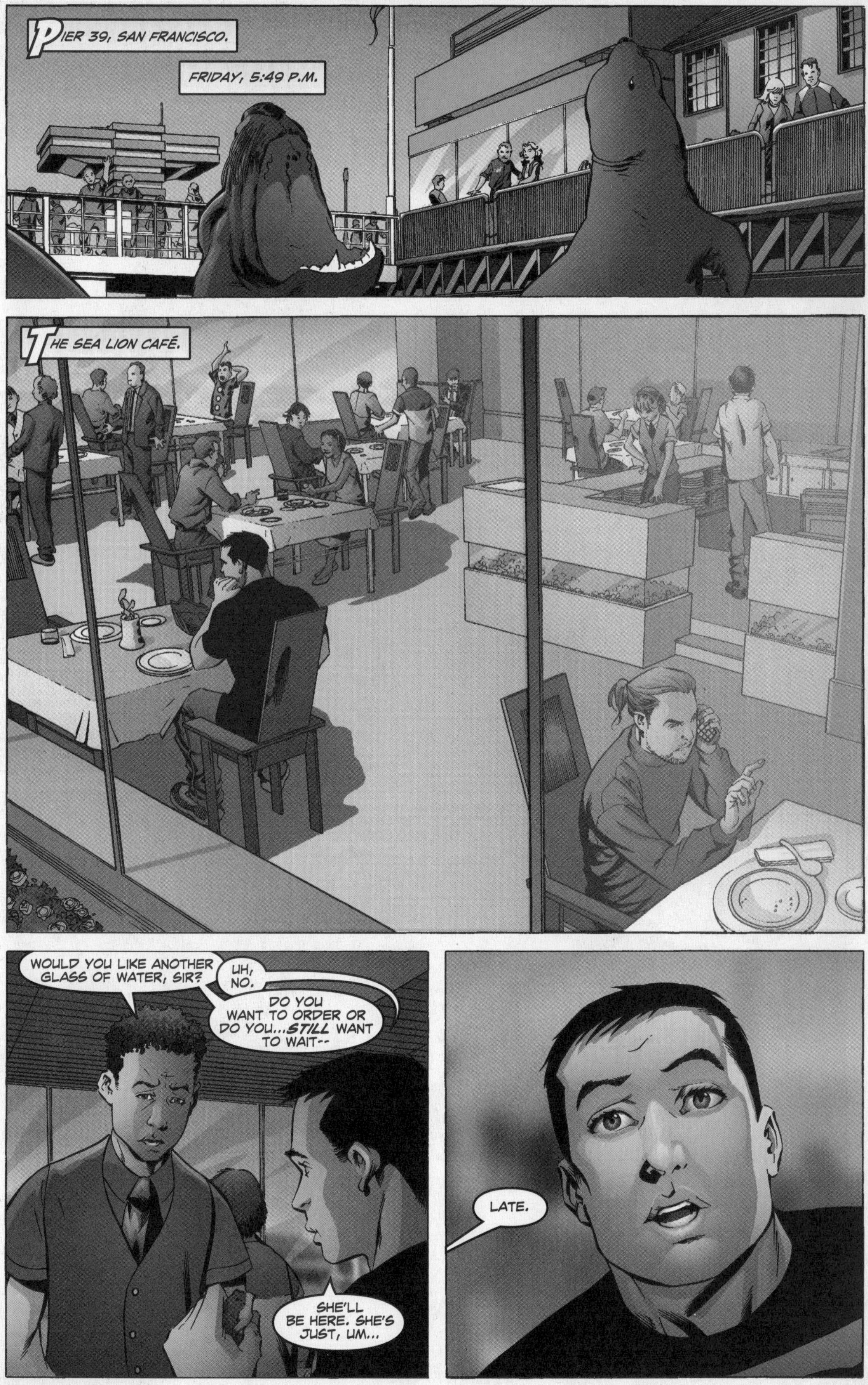
PIER 39, SAN FRANCISCO.
FRIDAY, 5:49 P.M.
THE SEA LION CAFÉ.
WOULD YOU LIKE ANOTHER GLASS OF WATER, SIR?
UH, NO.
DO YOU WANT TO ORDER OR DO YOU...STILL WANT TO WAIT--
SHE'LL BE HERE. SHE'S JUST, UM...
LATE.

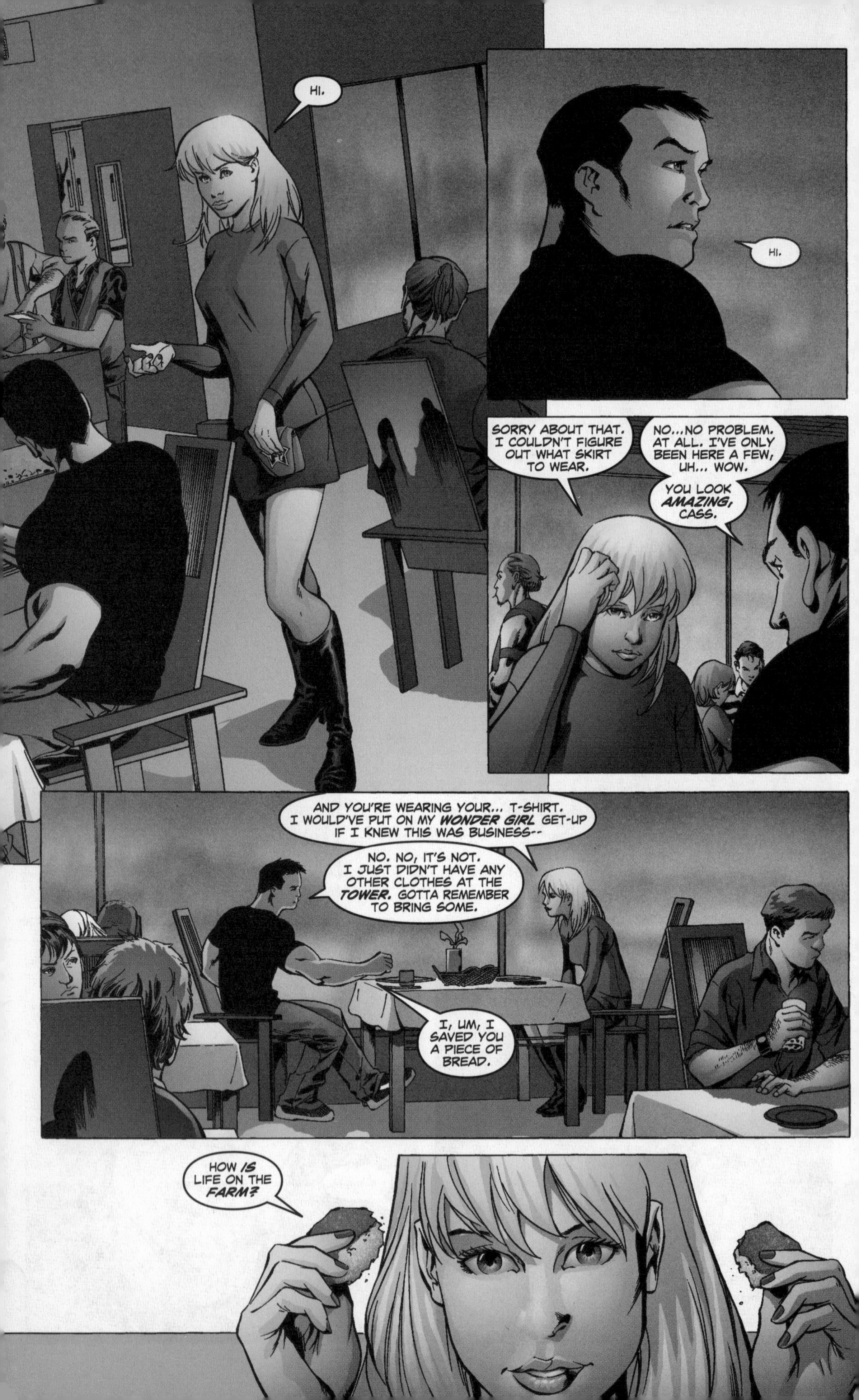
HI.
HI.
SORRY ABOUT THAT. I COULDN'T FIGURE OUT WHAT SKIRT TO WEAR.
NO...NO PROBLEM. AT ALL. I'VE ONLY BEEN HERE A FEW, UH... WOW.
YOU LOOK *AMAZING,* CASS.
AND YOU'RE WEARING YOUR... T-SHIRT. I WOULD'VE PUT ON MY *WONDER GIRL* GET-UP IF I KNEW THIS WAS BUSINESS--
NO. NO, IT'S NOT. I JUST DIDN'T HAVE ANY OTHER CLOTHES AT THE *TOWER.* GOTTA REMEMBER TO BRING SOME.
I, UM, I SAVED YOU A PIECE OF BREAD.
HOW *IS* LIFE ON THE *FARM?*

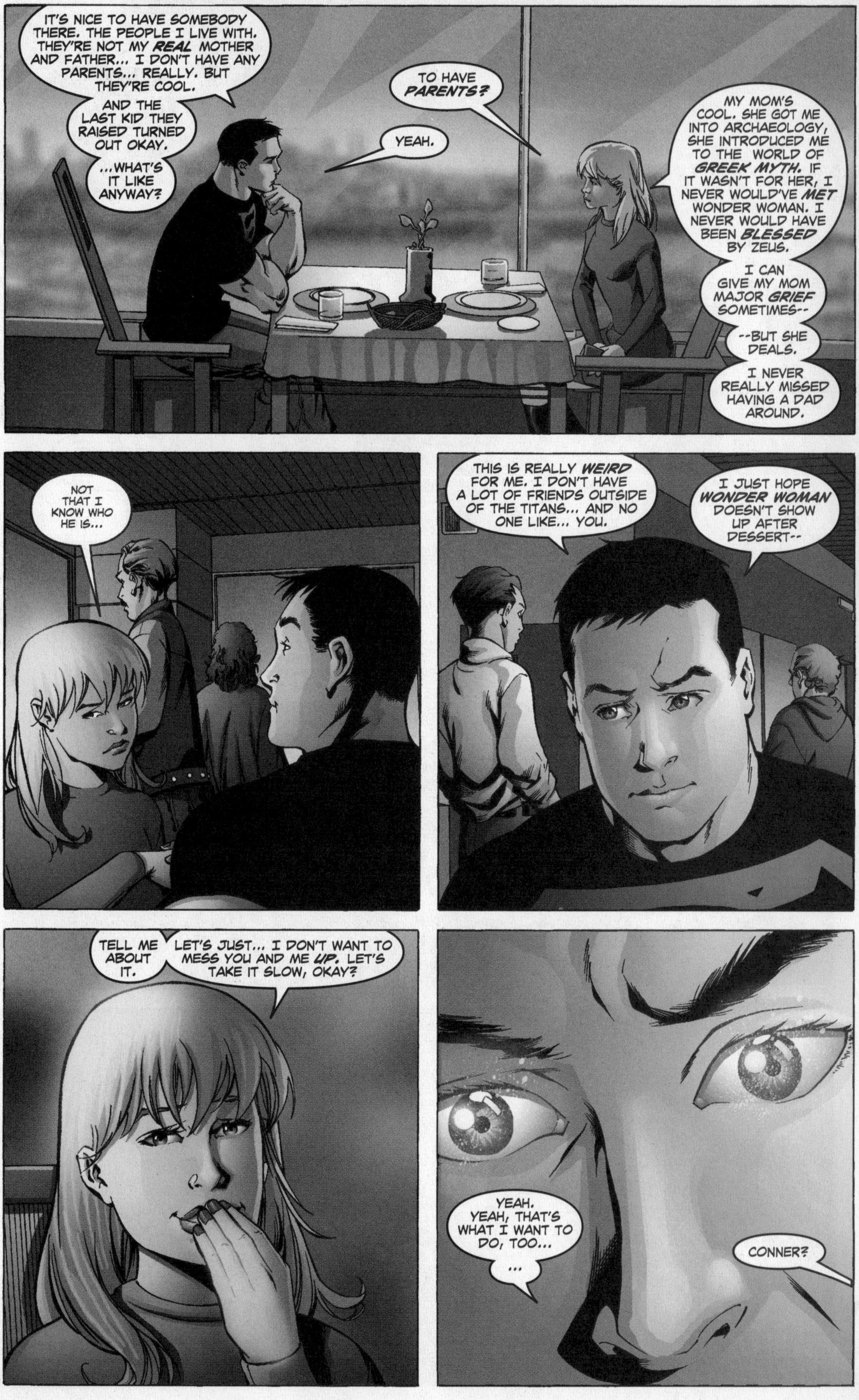
IT'S NICE TO HAVE SOMEBODY THERE. THE PEOPLE I LIVE WITH. THEY'RE NOT MY REAL MOTHER AND FATHER... I DON'T HAVE ANY PARENTS... REALLY. BUT THEY'RE COOL.
AND THE LAST KID THEY RAISED TURNED OUT OKAY.
...WHAT'S IT LIKE ANYWAY?
TO HAVE PARENTS?
YEAH.
MY MOM'S COOL. SHE GOT ME INTO ARCHAEOLOGY, SHE INTRODUCED ME TO THE WORLD OF GREEK MYTH. IF IT WASN'T FOR HER, I NEVER WOULD'VE MET WONDER WOMAN. I NEVER WOULD HAVE BEEN BLESSED BY ZEUS.
I CAN GIVE MY MOM MAJOR GRIEF SOMETIMES--
--BUT SHE DEALS.
I NEVER REALLY MISSED HAVING A DAD AROUND.
NOT THAT I KNOW WHO HE IS...
THIS IS REALLY WEIRD FOR ME. I DON'T HAVE A LOT OF FRIENDS OUTSIDE OF THE TITANS... AND NO ONE LIKE... YOU.
I JUST HOPE WONDER WOMAN DOESN'T SHOW UP AFTER DESSERT--
TELL ME ABOUT IT.
LET'S JUST... I DON'T WANT TO MESS YOU AND ME UP. LET'S TAKE IT SLOW, OKAY?
YEAH. YEAH, THAT'S WHAT I WANT TO DO, TOO...
...
CONNER?

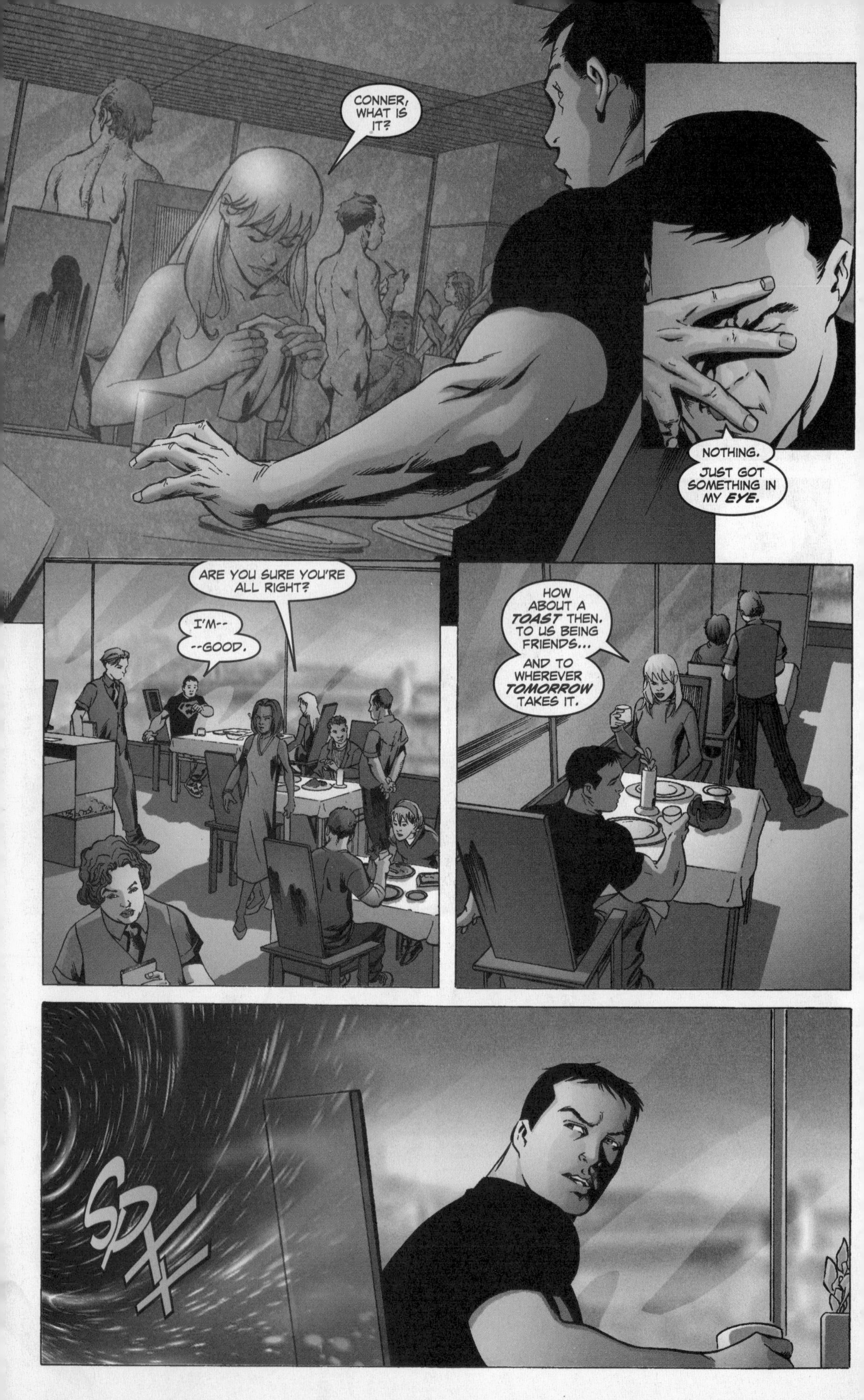
CONNER, WHAT IS IT?
NOTHING. JUST GOT SOMETHING IN MY *EYE.*
ARE YOU SURE YOU'RE ALL RIGHT?
I'M--
--GOOD.
HOW ABOUT A *TOAST* THEN. TO US BEING FRIENDS...
AND TO WHEREVER *TOMORROW* TAKES IT.
SPXX

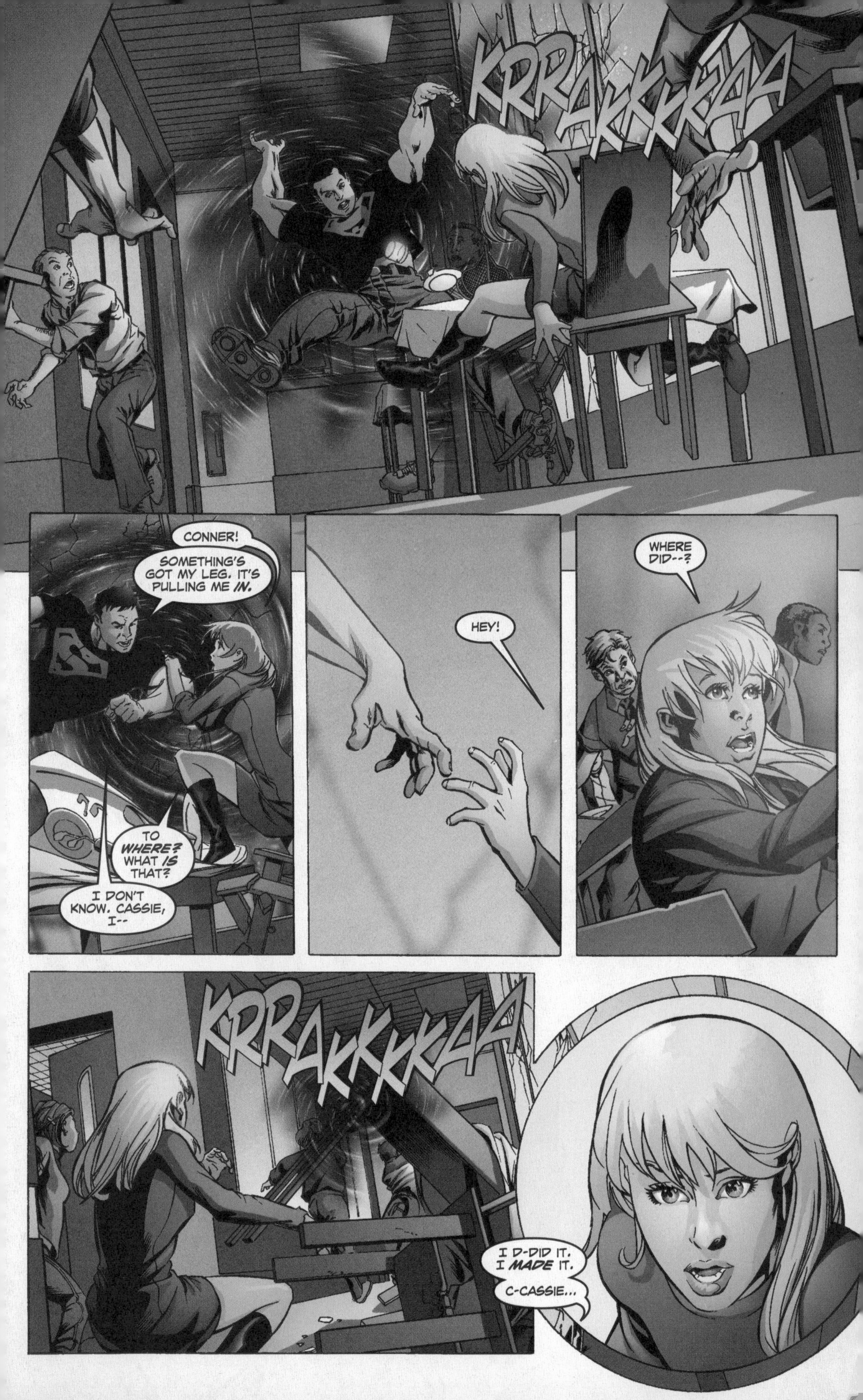
KRRAKKKKAA
CONNER! SOMETHING'S GOT MY LEG. IT'S PULLING ME *IN.*
TO *WHERE?* WHAT *IS* THAT?
I DON'T KNOW. CASSIE, I--
HEY!
WHERE DID--?
KRRAKKKKAA
I D-DID IT. I *MADE* IT.
C-CASSIE...

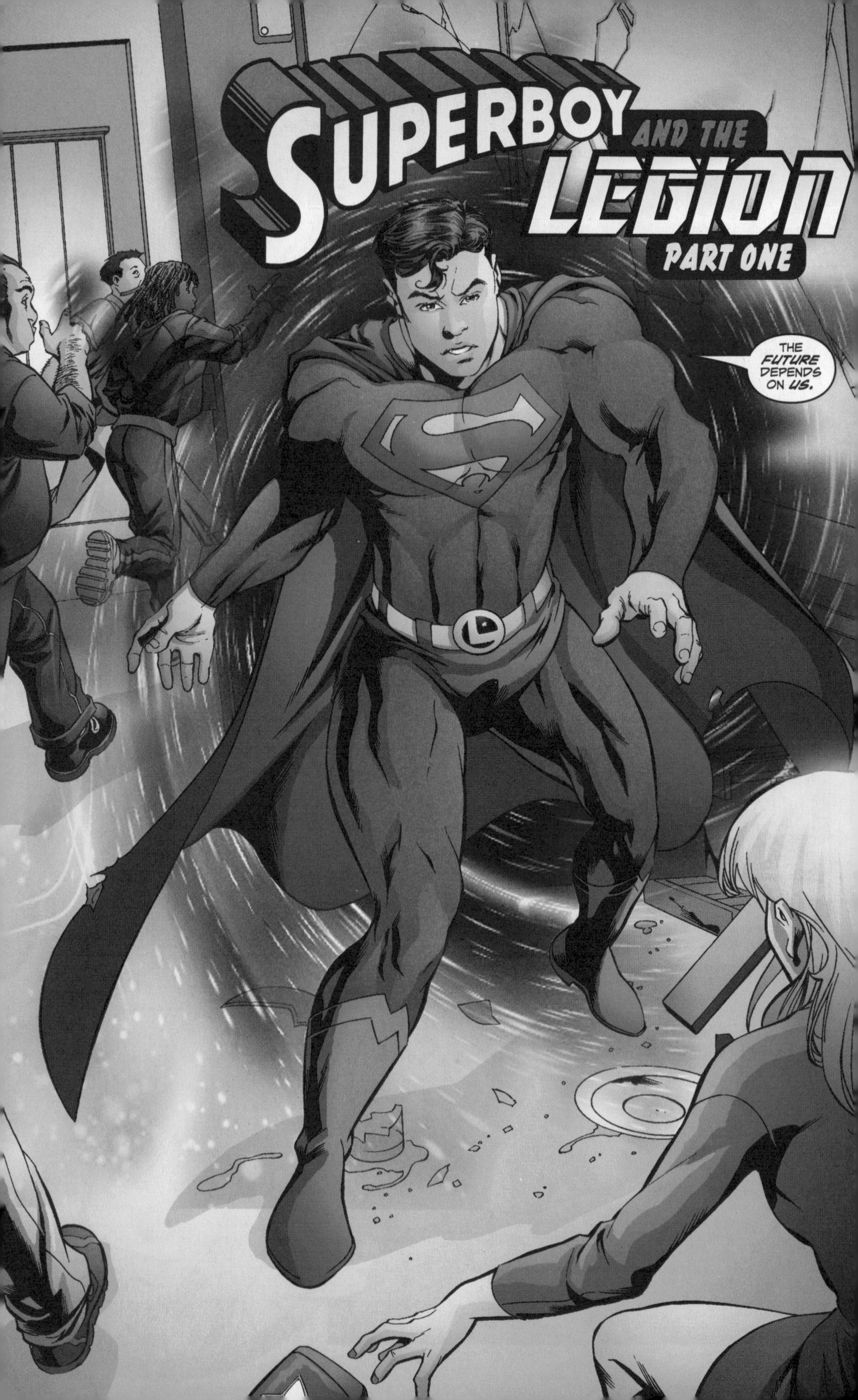
SUPERBOY AND THE LEGION
PART ONE
THE FUTURE DEPENDS ON US.

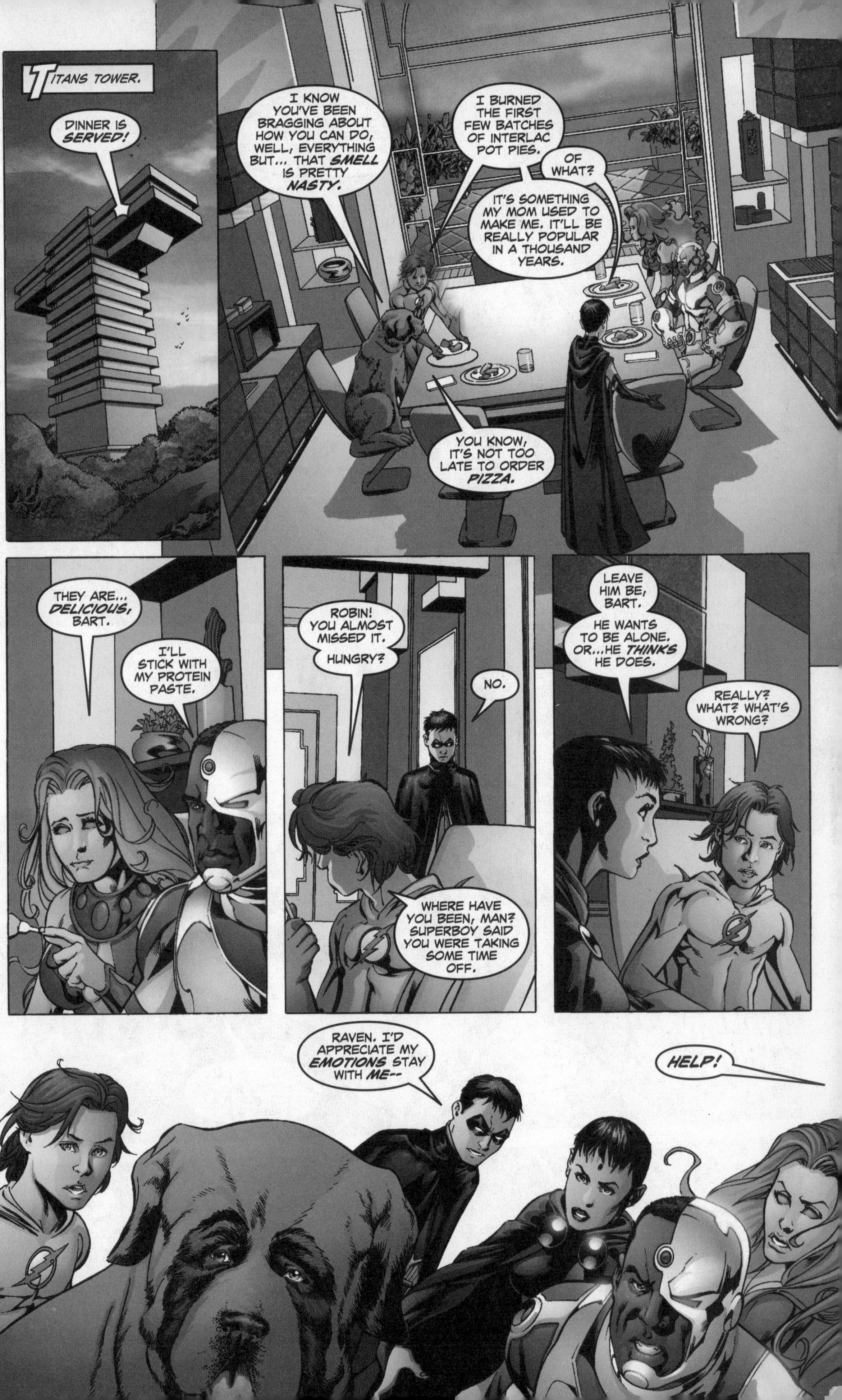
TITANS TOWER.
DINNER IS SERVED!
I KNOW YOU'VE BEEN BRAGGING ABOUT HOW YOU CAN DO, WELL, EVERYTHING BUT... THAT SMELL IS PRETTY NASTY.
I BURNED THE FIRST FEW BATCHES OF INTERLAC POT PIES.
OF WHAT?
IT'S SOMETHING MY MOM USED TO MAKE ME. IT'LL BE REALLY POPULAR IN A THOUSAND YEARS.
YOU KNOW, IT'S NOT TOO LATE TO ORDER PIZZA.
THEY ARE... DELICIOUS, BART.
I'LL STICK WITH MY PROTEIN PASTE.
ROBIN! YOU ALMOST MISSED IT.
HUNGRY?
NO.
WHERE HAVE YOU BEEN, MAN? SUPERBOY SAID YOU WERE TAKING SOME TIME OFF.
LEAVE HIM BE, BART.
HE WANTS TO BE ALONE. OR...HE THINKS HE DOES.
REALLY? WHAT? WHAT'S WRONG?
RAVEN. I'D APPRECIATE MY EMOTIONS STAY WITH ME--
HELP!

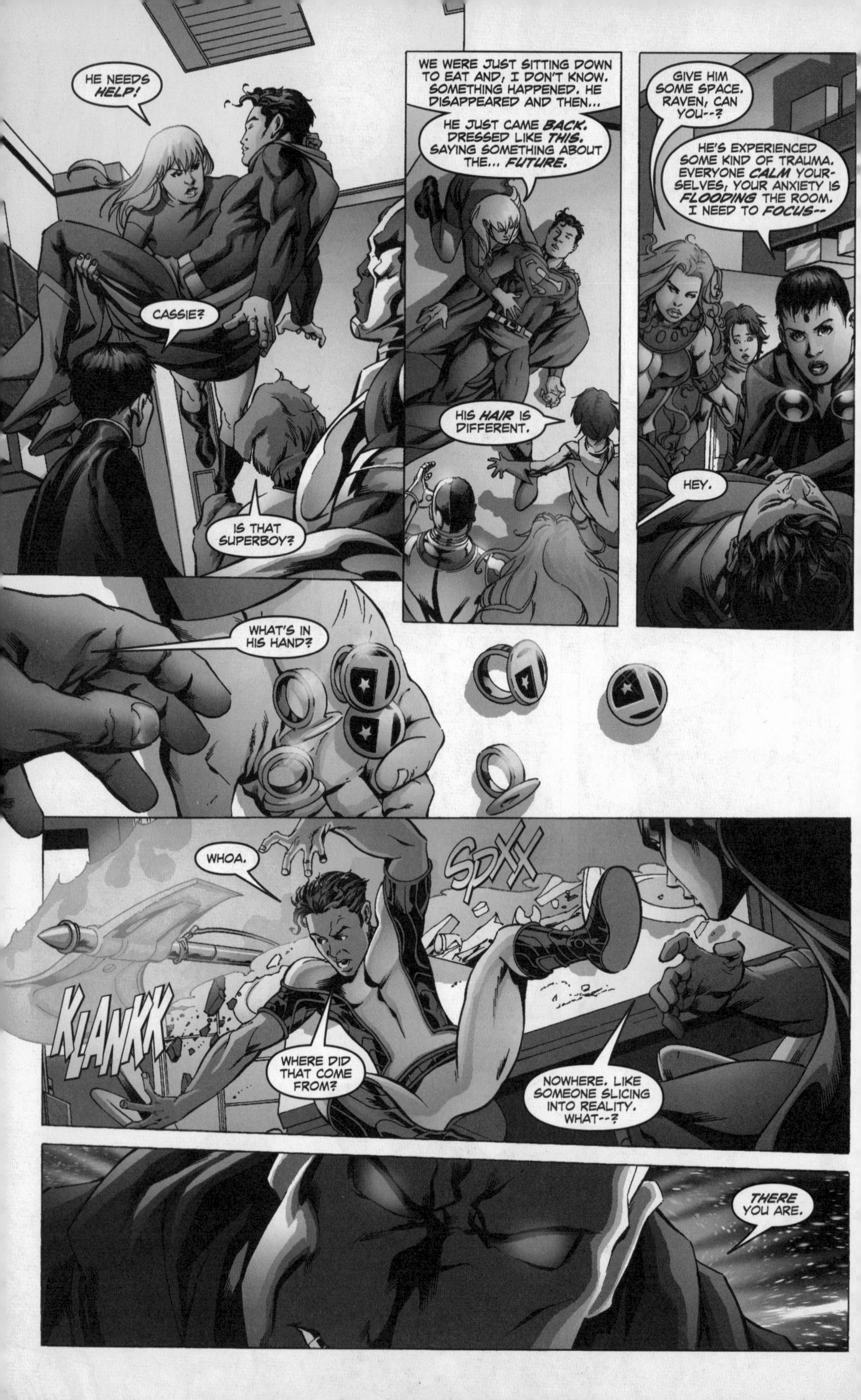
HE NEEDS HELP!
CASSIE?
IS THAT SUPERBOY?
WE WERE JUST SITTING DOWN TO EAT AND, I DON'T KNOW. SOMETHING HAPPENED. HE DISAPPEARED AND THEN...
HE JUST CAME BACK. DRESSED LIKE THIS. SAYING SOMETHING ABOUT THE... FUTURE.
HIS HAIR IS DIFFERENT.
GIVE HIM SOME SPACE. RAVEN, CAN YOU--?
HE'S EXPERIENCED SOME KIND OF TRAUMA. EVERYONE CALM YOUR-SELVES, YOUR ANXIETY IS FLOODING THE ROOM. I NEED TO FOCUS--
HEY.
WHAT'S IN HIS HAND?
WHOA.
SPXX
KLANKK
WHERE DID THAT COME FROM?
NOWHERE. LIKE SOMEONE SLICING INTO REALITY. WHAT--?
THERE YOU ARE.

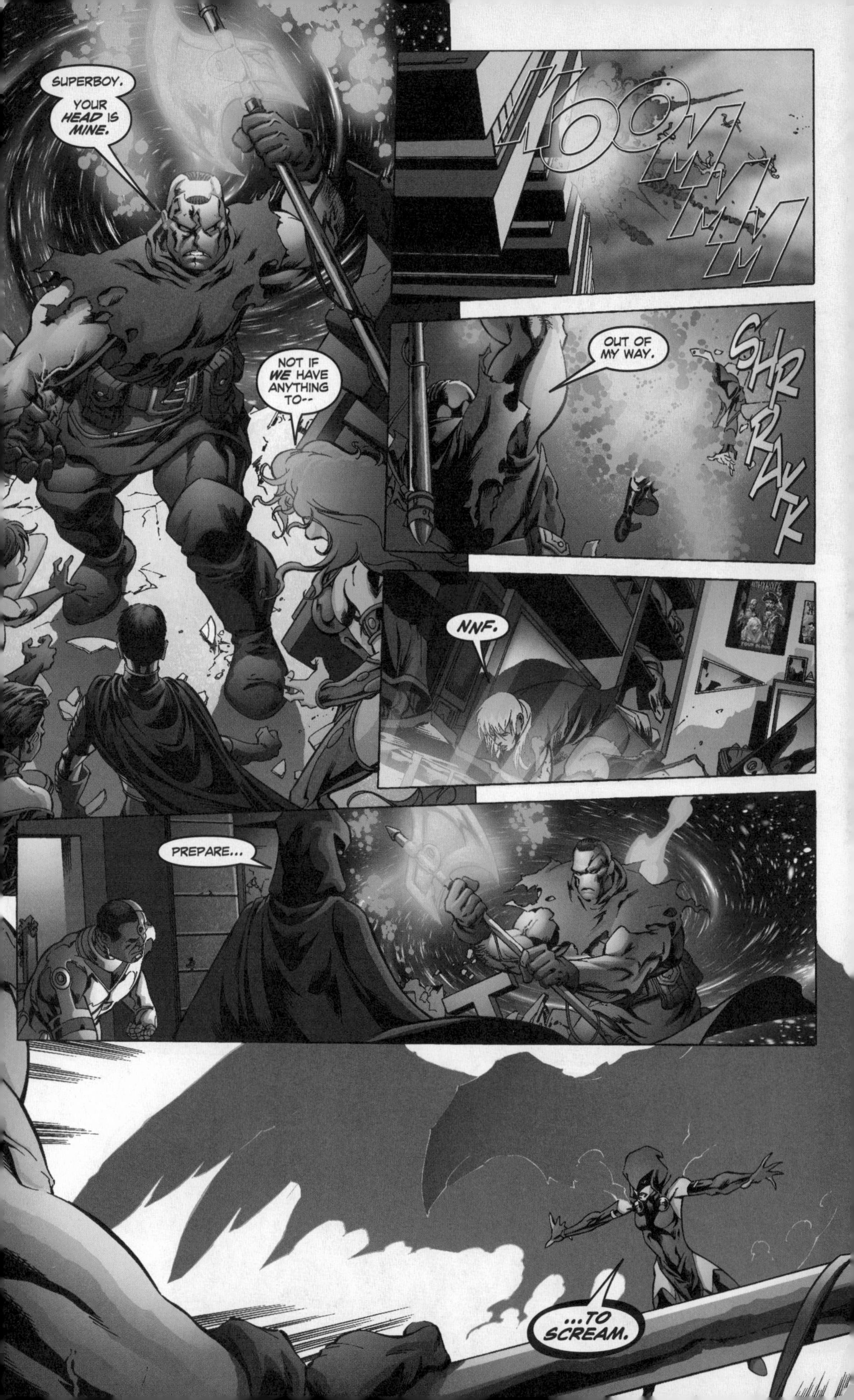
SUPERBOY. YOUR HEAD IS MINE.
WHOOOM
NOT IF WE HAVE ANYTHING TO--
OUT OF MY WAY.
SHRRAKK
NNF.
PREPARE...
...TO SCREAM.

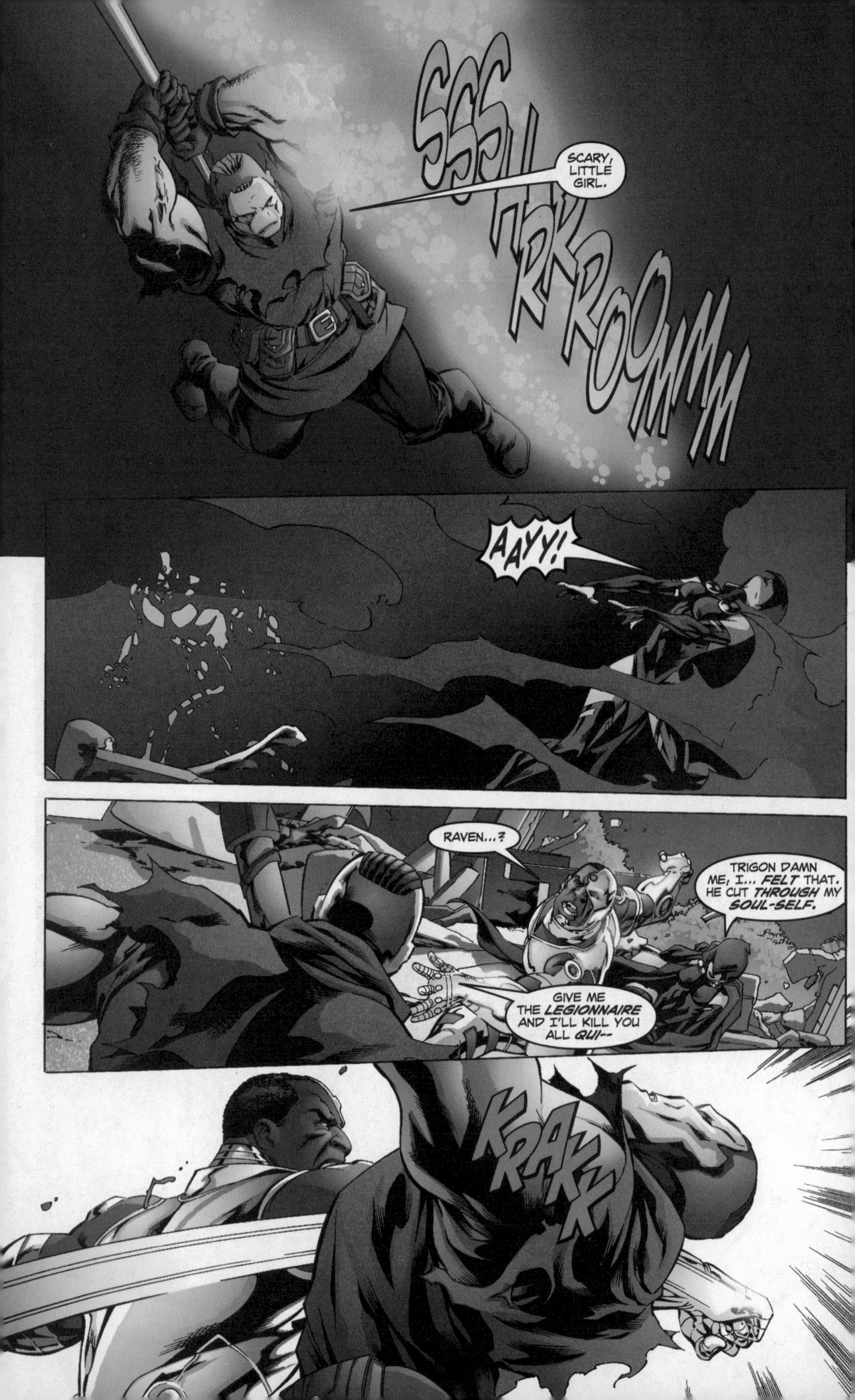
SSSHRK-ROOMMM
SCARY, LITTLE GIRL.
AAYY!
RAVEN...?
TRIGON DAMN ME, I... FELT THAT. HE CUT THROUGH MY SOUL-SELF.
GIVE ME THE LEGIONNAIRE AND I'LL KILL YOU ALL QUI--
KRAKK

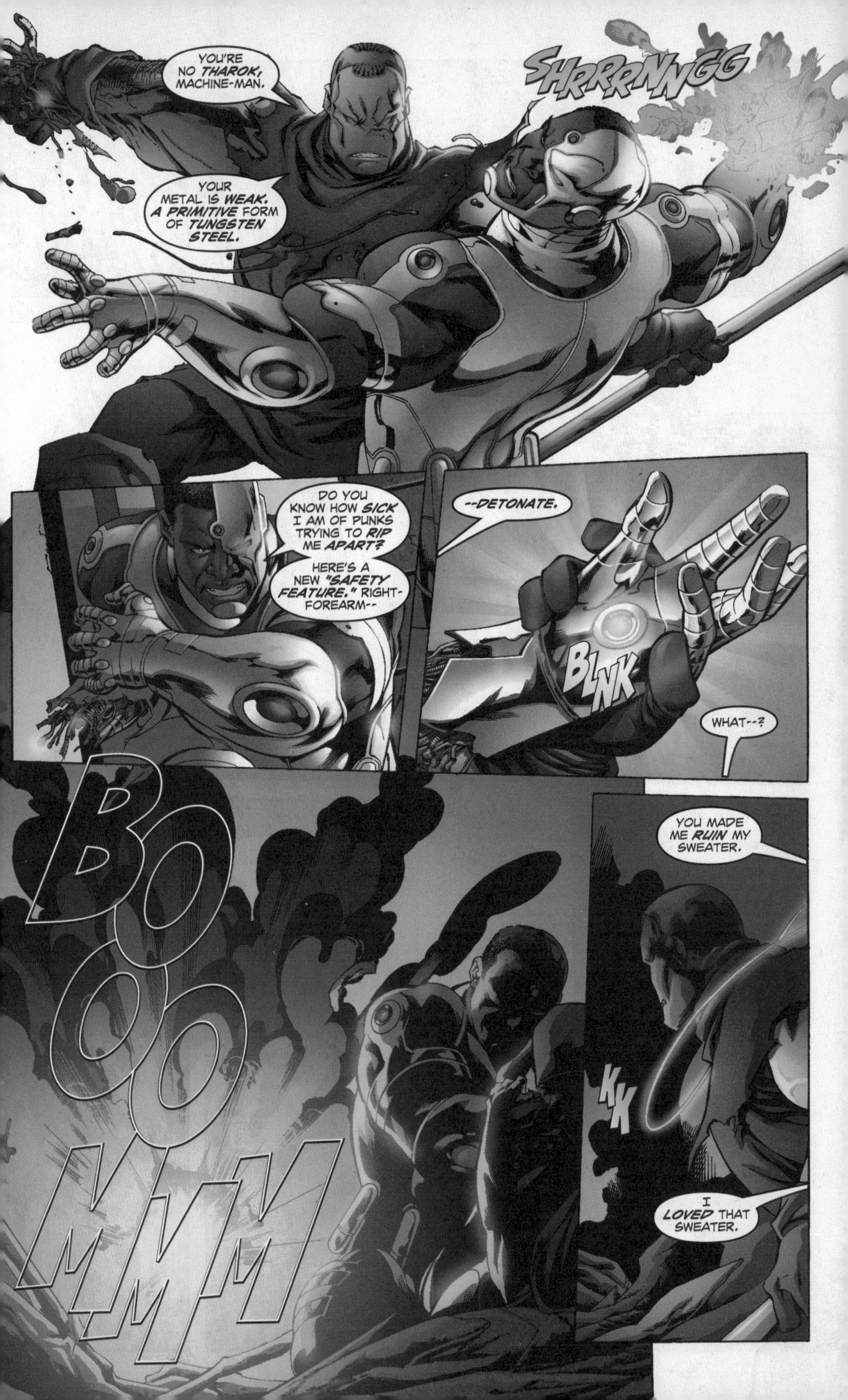
YOU'RE NO THAROK, MACHINE-MAN.
SHRRRNNGG
YOUR METAL IS WEAK. A PRIMITIVE FORM OF TUNGSTEN STEEL.
DO YOU KNOW HOW SICK I AM OF PUNKS TRYING TO RIP ME APART?
HERE'S A NEW "SAFETY FEATURE." RIGHT-FOREARM--
--DETONATE.
BLNK
WHAT--?
BOOOOMMMMM
YOU MADE ME RUIN MY SWEATER.
KK
I LOVED THAT SWEATER.

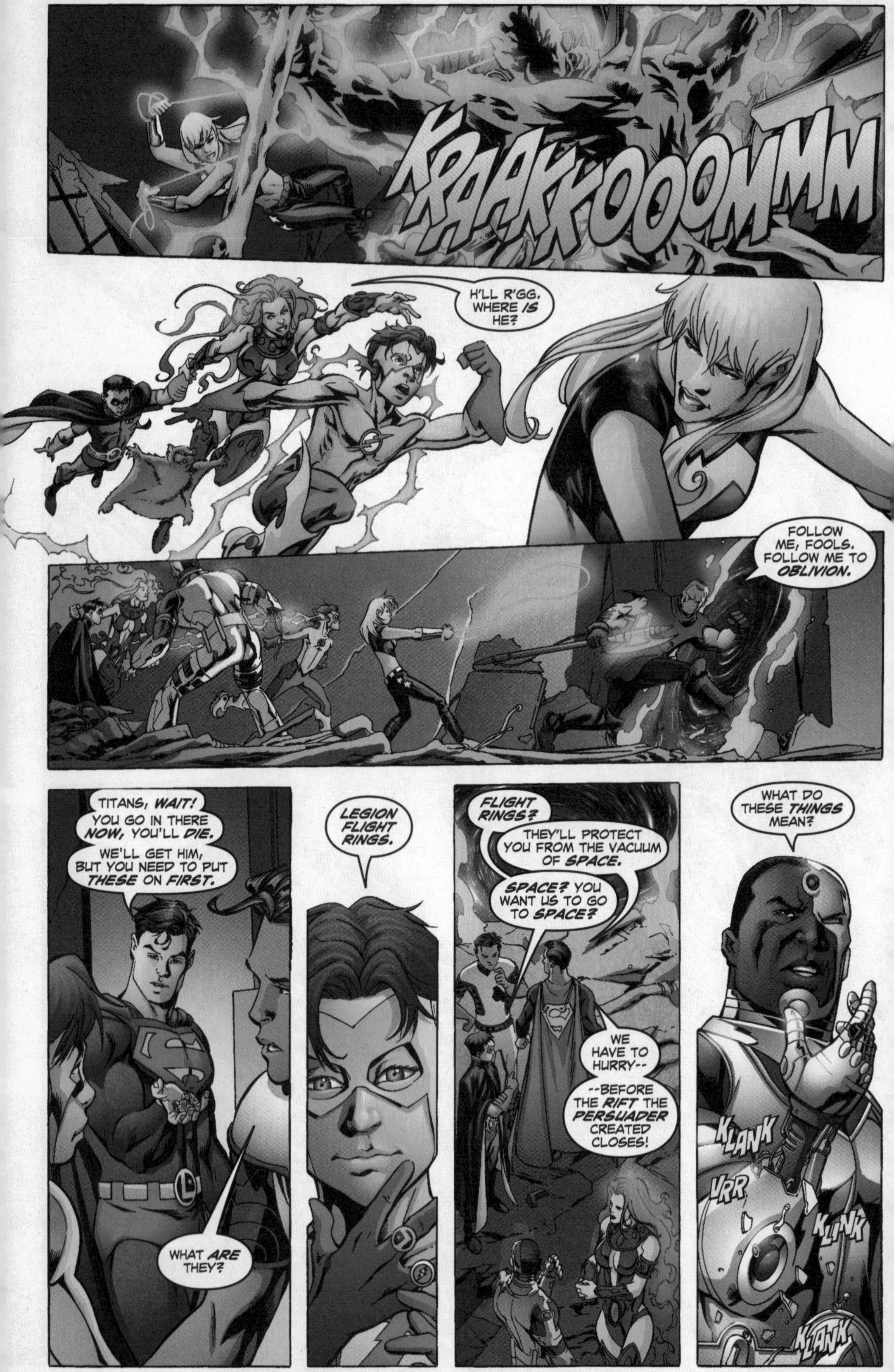

KRAKKOOOMMM
H'LL R'GG. WHERE *IS* HE?
FOLLOW ME, FOOLS. FOLLOW ME TO *OBLIVION.*
TITANS, *WAIT!* YOU GO IN THERE *NOW,* YOU'LL *DIE.*
WE'LL GET HIM, BUT YOU NEED TO PUT *THESE* ON *FIRST.*
WHAT *ARE* THEY?
LEGION FLIGHT RINGS.
FLIGHT RINGS?
THEY'LL PROTECT YOU FROM THE VACUUM OF *SPACE.*
SPACE? YOU WANT US TO GO TO *SPACE?*
WE HAVE TO HURRY--
--BEFORE THE *RIFT* THE *PERSUADER* CREATED CLOSES!
WHAT DO THESE *THINGS* MEAN?
KLANK
URR
KLINK
KLANK

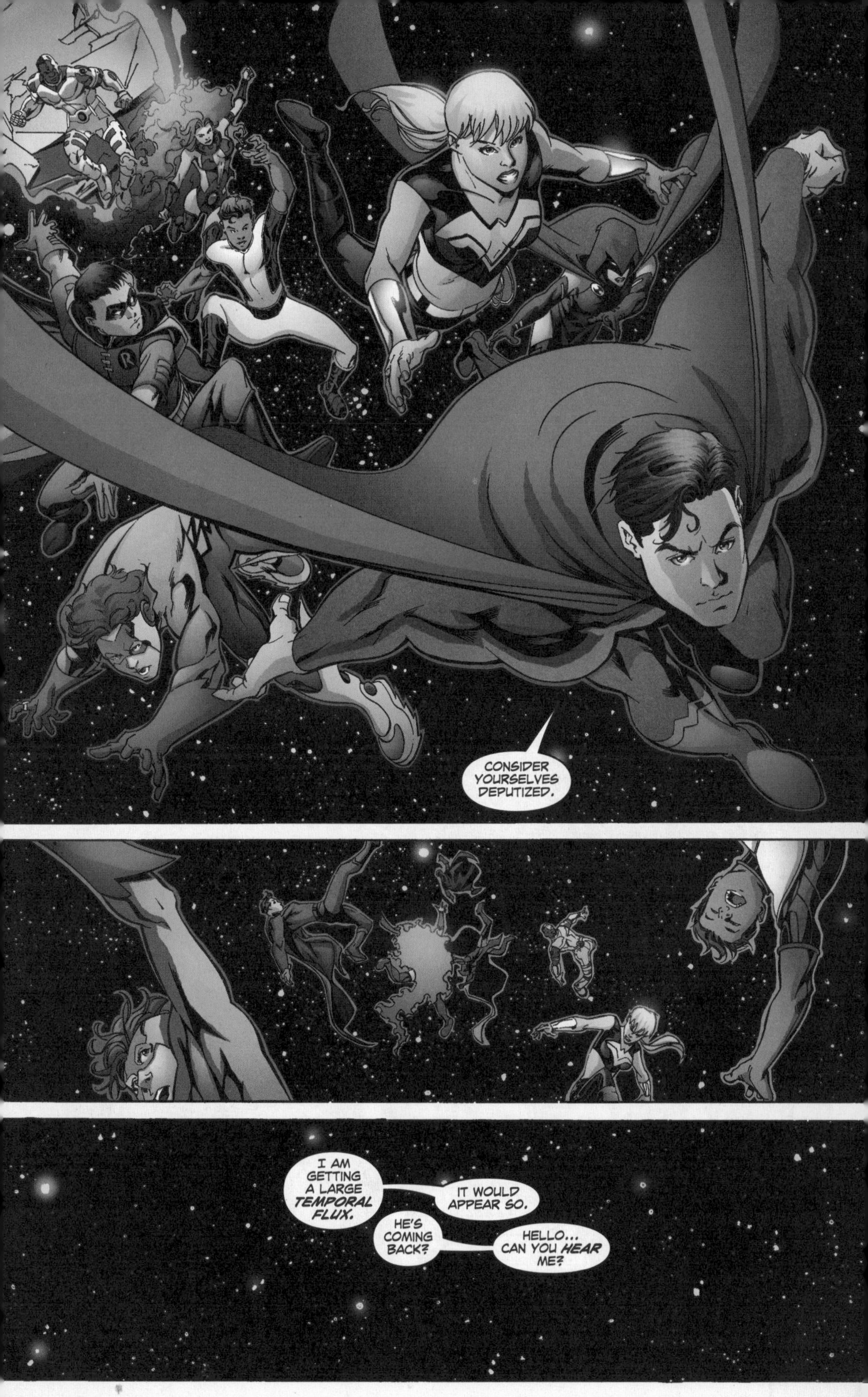
CONSIDER YOURSELVES DEPUTIZED.
I AM GETTING A LARGE *TEMPORAL FLUX.*
IT WOULD APPEAR SO.
HE'S COMING BACK?
HELLO... CAN YOU *HEAR* ME?

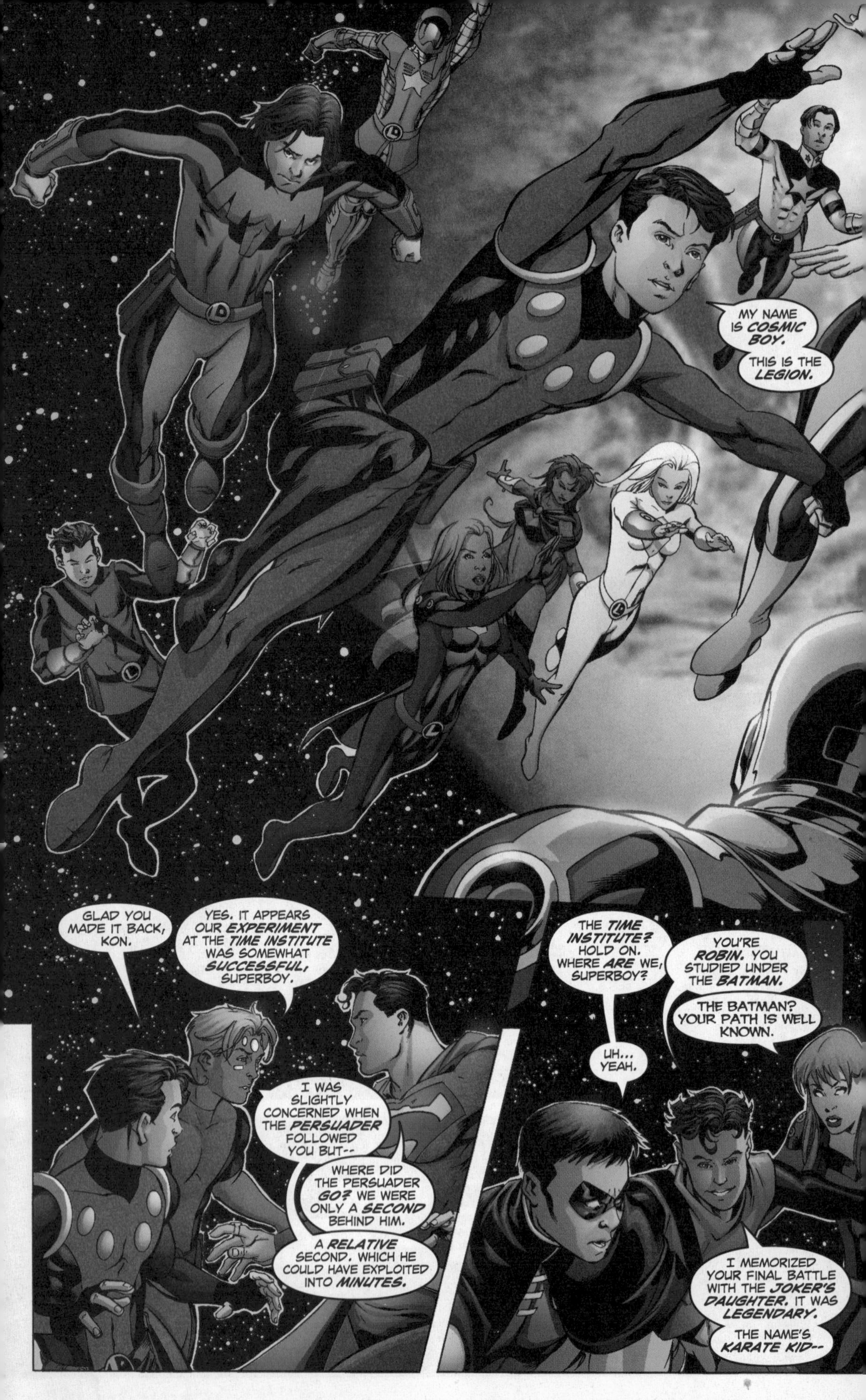
MY NAME IS COSMIC BOY.
THIS IS THE LEGION.
GLAD YOU MADE IT BACK, KON.
YES. IT APPEARS OUR EXPERIMENT AT THE TIME INSTITUTE WAS SOMEWHAT SUCCESSFUL, SUPERBOY.
I WAS SLIGHTLY CONCERNED WHEN THE PERSUADER FOLLOWED YOU BUT--
WHERE DID THE PERSUADER GO? WE WERE ONLY A SECOND BEHIND HIM.
A RELATIVE SECOND. WHICH HE COULD HAVE EXPLOITED INTO MINUTES.
THE TIME INSTITUTE? HOLD ON. WHERE ARE WE, SUPERBOY?
YOU'RE ROBIN. YOU STUDIED UNDER THE BATMAN.
THE BATMAN? YOUR PATH IS WELL KNOWN.
UH... YEAH.
I MEMORIZED YOUR FINAL BATTLE WITH THE JOKER'S DAUGHTER. IT WAS LEGENDARY.
THE NAME'S KARATE KID--

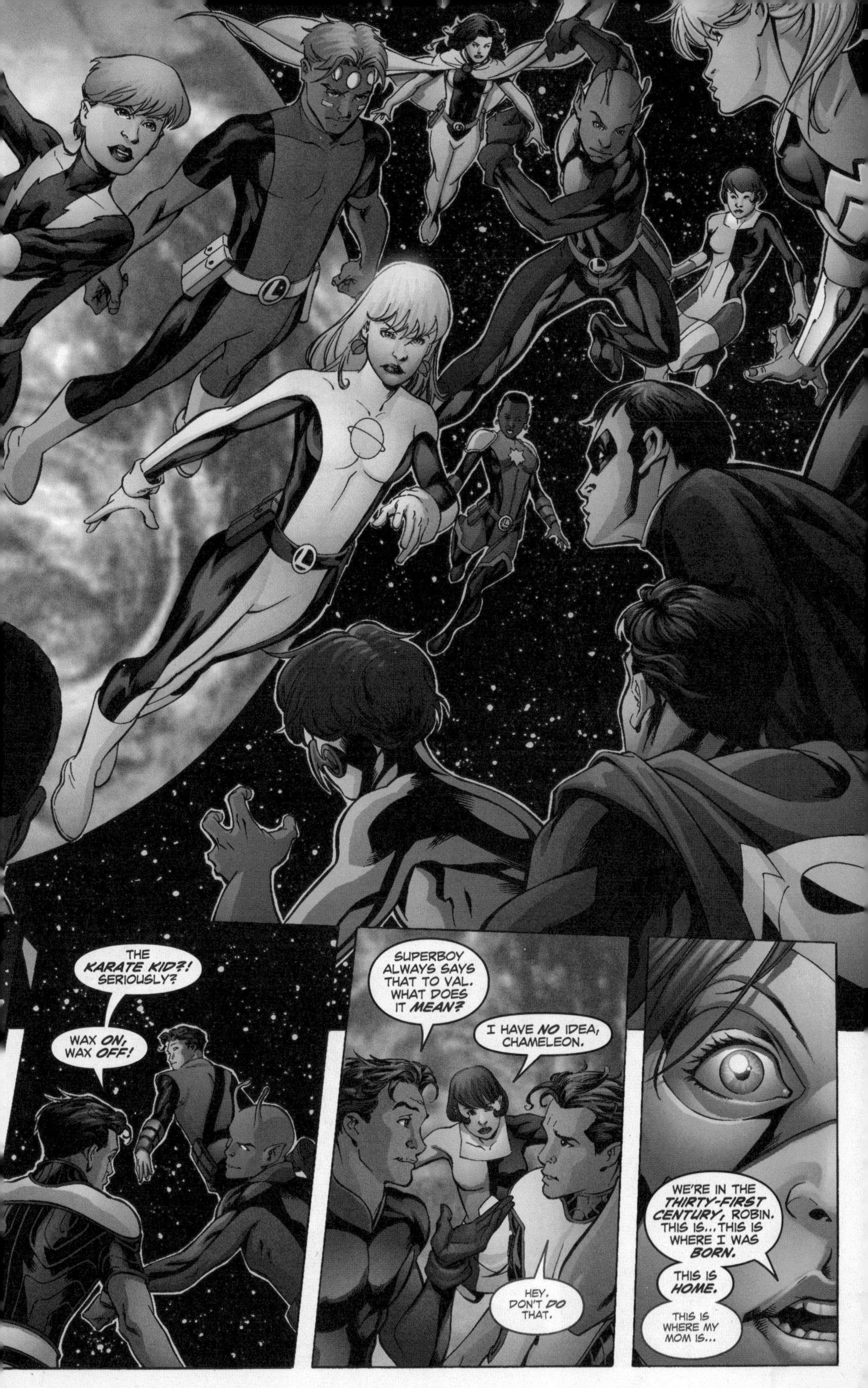
THE KARATE KID?! SERIOUSLY?
WAX ON, WAX OFF!
SUPERBOY ALWAYS SAYS THAT TO VAL. WHAT DOES IT MEAN?
I HAVE NO IDEA, CHAMELEON.
HEY. DON'T DO THAT.
WE'RE IN THE THIRTY-FIRST CENTURY, ROBIN. THIS IS... THIS IS WHERE I WAS BORN.
THIS IS HOME.
THIS IS WHERE MY MOM IS...

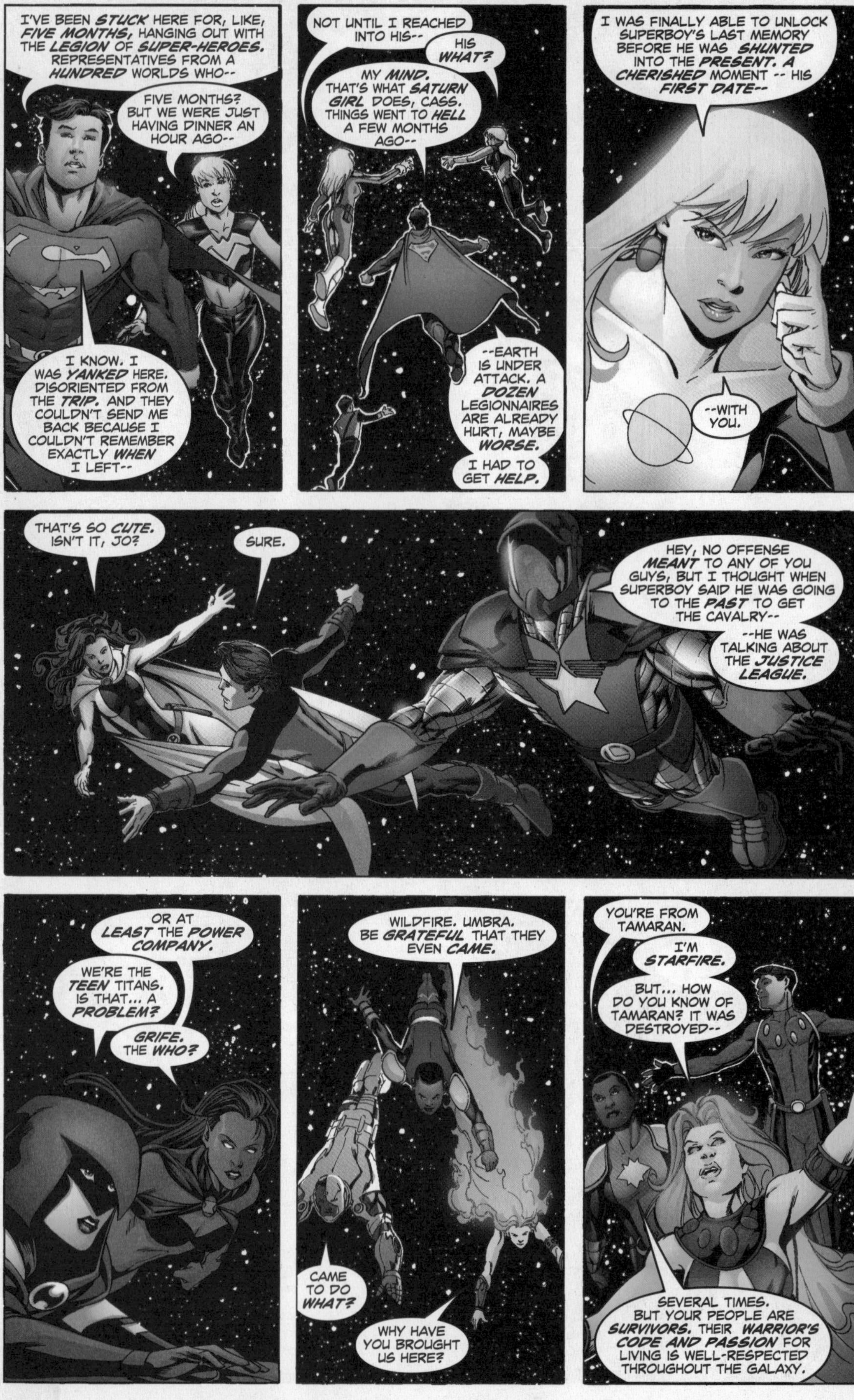
I'VE BEEN STUCK HERE FOR, LIKE, FIVE MONTHS, HANGING OUT WITH THE LEGION OF SUPER-HEROES. REPRESENTATIVES FROM A HUNDRED WORLDS WHO--
FIVE MONTHS? BUT WE WERE JUST HAVING DINNER AN HOUR AGO--
I KNOW. I WAS YANKED HERE. DISORIENTED FROM THE TRIP. AND THEY COULDN'T SEND ME BACK BECAUSE I COULDN'T REMEMBER EXACTLY WHEN I LEFT--
NOT UNTIL I REACHED INTO HIS--
HIS WHAT?
MY MIND. THAT'S WHAT SATURN GIRL DOES, CASS. THINGS WENT TO HELL A FEW MONTHS AGO--
--EARTH IS UNDER ATTACK. A DOZEN LEGIONNAIRES ARE ALREADY HURT, MAYBE WORSE.
I HAD TO GET HELP.
I WAS FINALLY ABLE TO UNLOCK SUPERBOY'S LAST MEMORY BEFORE HE WAS SHUNTED INTO THE PRESENT. A CHERISHED MOMENT -- HIS FIRST DATE--
--WITH YOU.
THAT'S SO CUTE. ISN'T IT, JO?
SURE.
HEY, NO OFFENSE MEANT TO ANY OF YOU GUYS, BUT I THOUGHT WHEN SUPERBOY SAID HE WAS GOING TO THE PAST TO GET THE CAVALRY--
--HE WAS TALKING ABOUT THE JUSTICE LEAGUE.
OR AT LEAST THE POWER COMPANY.
WE'RE THE TEEN TITANS. IS THAT... A PROBLEM?
GRIFE. THE WHO?
WILDFIRE. UMBRA. BE GRATEFUL THAT THEY EVEN CAME.
CAME TO DO WHAT?
WHY HAVE YOU BROUGHT US HERE?
YOU'RE FROM TAMARAN.
I'M STARFIRE.
BUT... HOW DO YOU KNOW OF TAMARAN? IT WAS DESTROYED--
SEVERAL TIMES. BUT YOUR PEOPLE ARE SURVIVORS. THEIR WARRIOR'S CODE AND PASSION FOR LIVING IS WELL-RESPECTED THROUGHOUT THE GALAXY.

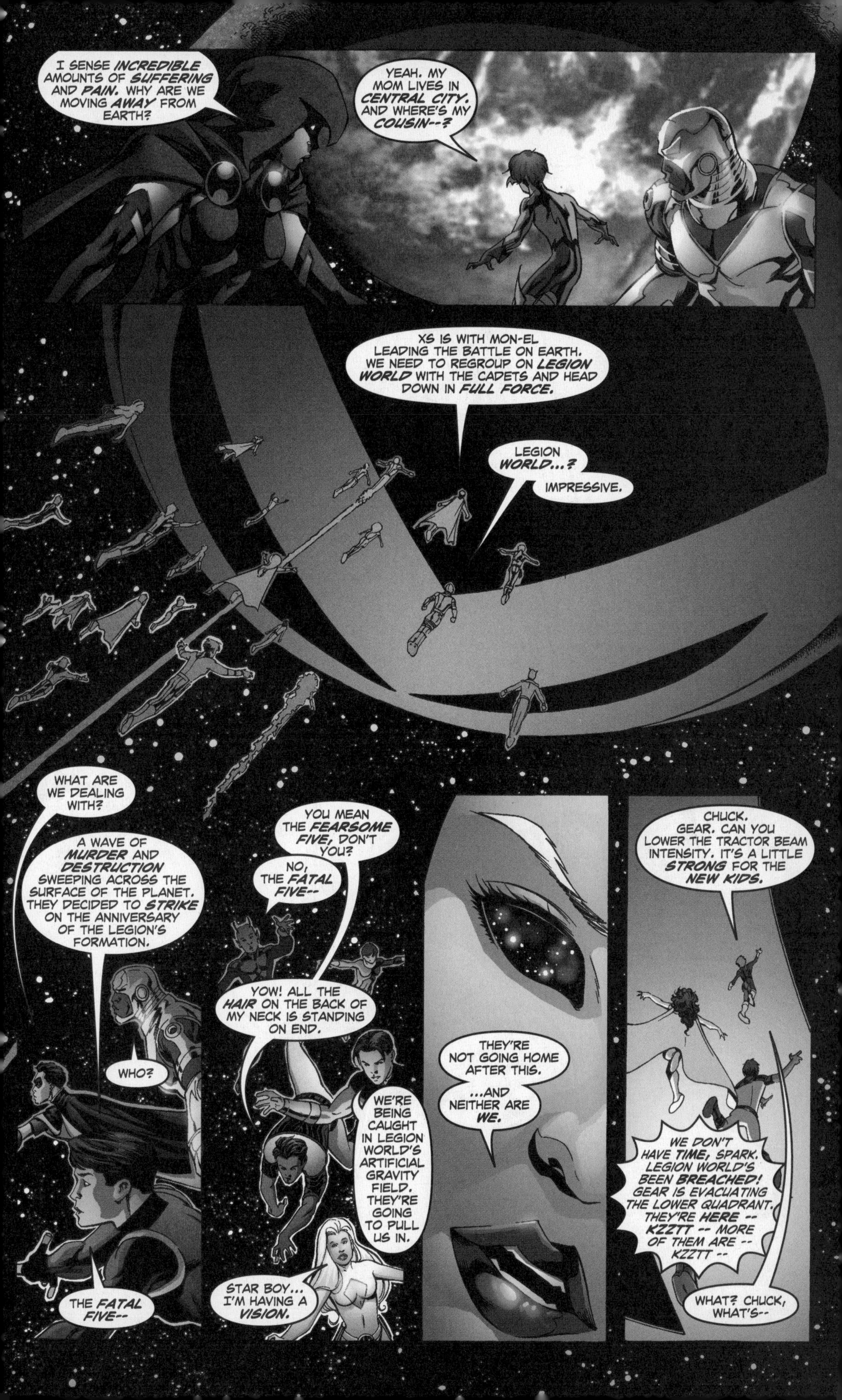
I SENSE INCREDIBLE AMOUNTS OF SUFFERING AND PAIN. WHY ARE WE MOVING AWAY FROM EARTH?
YEAH. MY MOM LIVES IN CENTRAL CITY. AND WHERE'S MY COUSIN--?
XS IS WITH MON-EL LEADING THE BATTLE ON EARTH. WE NEED TO REGROUP ON LEGION WORLD WITH THE CADETS AND HEAD DOWN IN FULL FORCE.
LEGION WORLD...?
IMPRESSIVE.
WHAT ARE WE DEALING WITH?
A WAVE OF MURDER AND DESTRUCTION SWEEPING ACROSS THE SURFACE OF THE PLANET. THEY DECIDED TO STRIKE ON THE ANNIVERSARY OF THE LEGION'S FORMATION.
WHO?
THE FATAL FIVE--
YOU MEAN THE FEARSOME FIVE, DON'T YOU?
NO, THE FATAL FIVE--
YOW! ALL THE HAIR ON THE BACK OF MY NECK IS STANDING ON END.
WE'RE BEING CAUGHT IN LEGION WORLD'S ARTIFICIAL GRAVITY FIELD. THEY'RE GOING TO PULL US IN.
STAR BOY... I'M HAVING A VISION.
THEY'RE NOT GOING HOME AFTER THIS.
...AND NEITHER ARE WE.
CHUCK. GEAR. CAN YOU LOWER THE TRACTOR BEAM INTENSITY. IT'S A LITTLE STRONG FOR THE NEW KIDS.
WE DON'T HAVE TIME, SPARK. LEGION WORLD'S BEEN BREACHED! GEAR IS EVACUATING THE LOWER QUADRANT. THEY'RE HERE -- KZZTT -- MORE OF THEM ARE -- KZZTT --
WHAT? CHUCK, WHAT'S--

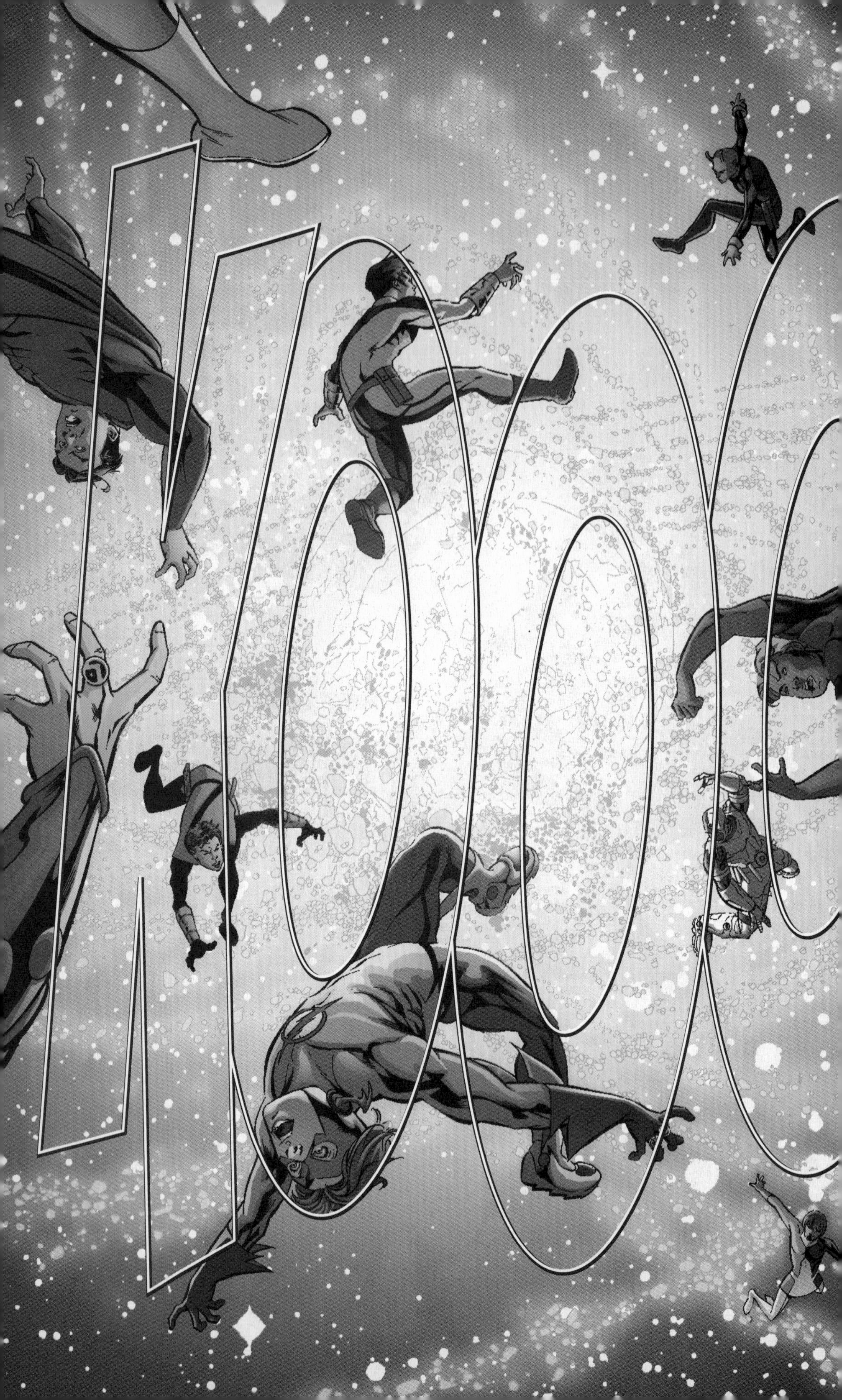

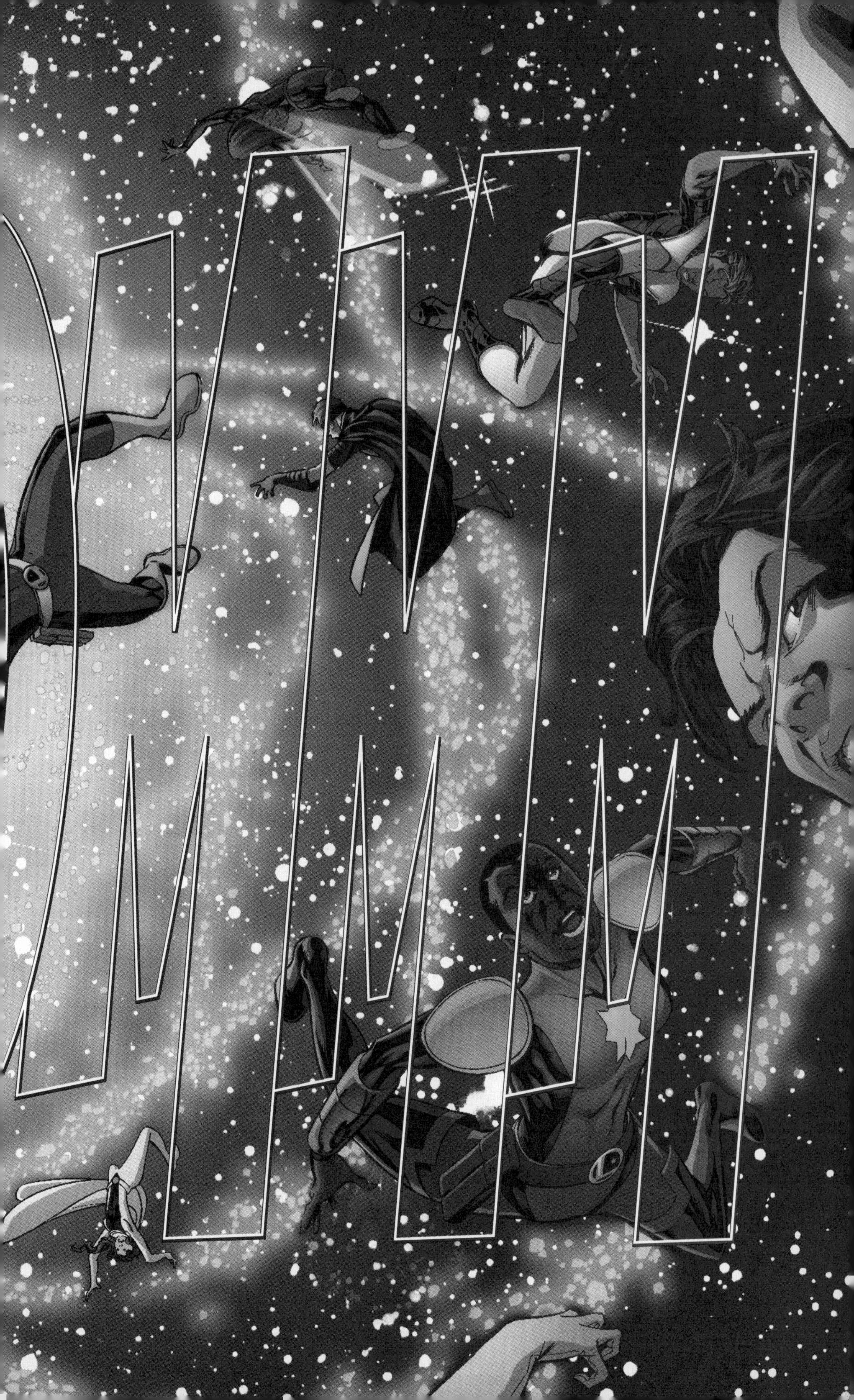

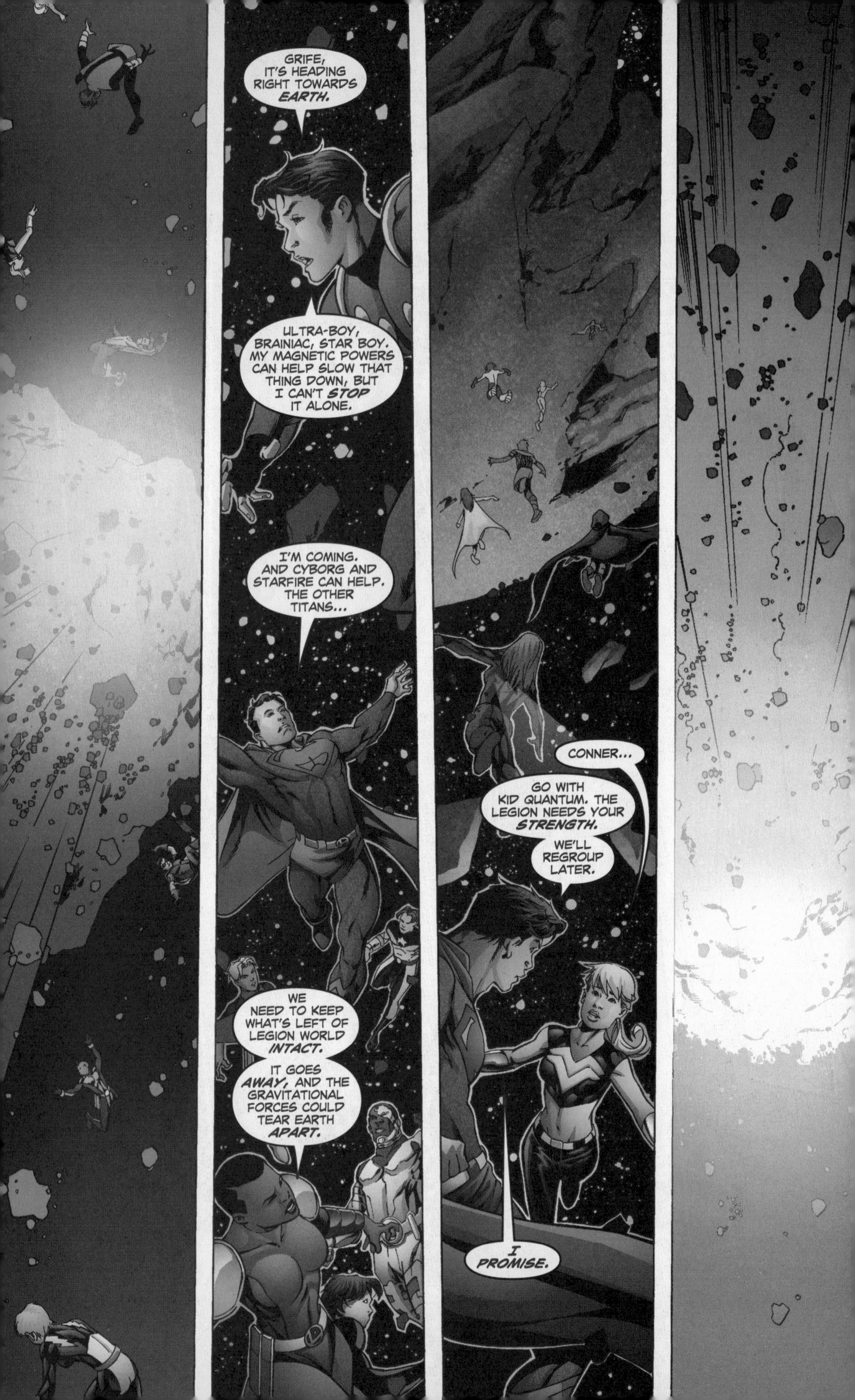
GRIFE, IT'S HEADING RIGHT TOWARDS EARTH.
ULTRA-BOY, BRAINIAC, STAR BOY. MY MAGNETIC POWERS CAN HELP SLOW THAT THING DOWN, BUT I CAN'T STOP IT ALONE.
I'M COMING. AND CYBORG AND STARFIRE CAN HELP. THE OTHER TITANS...
WE NEED TO KEEP WHAT'S LEFT OF LEGION WORLD INTACT.
IT GOES AWAY, AND THE GRAVITATIONAL FORCES COULD TEAR EARTH APART.
CONNER...
GO WITH KID QUANTUM. THE LEGION NEEDS YOUR STRENGTH.
WE'LL REGROUP LATER.
I PROMISE.

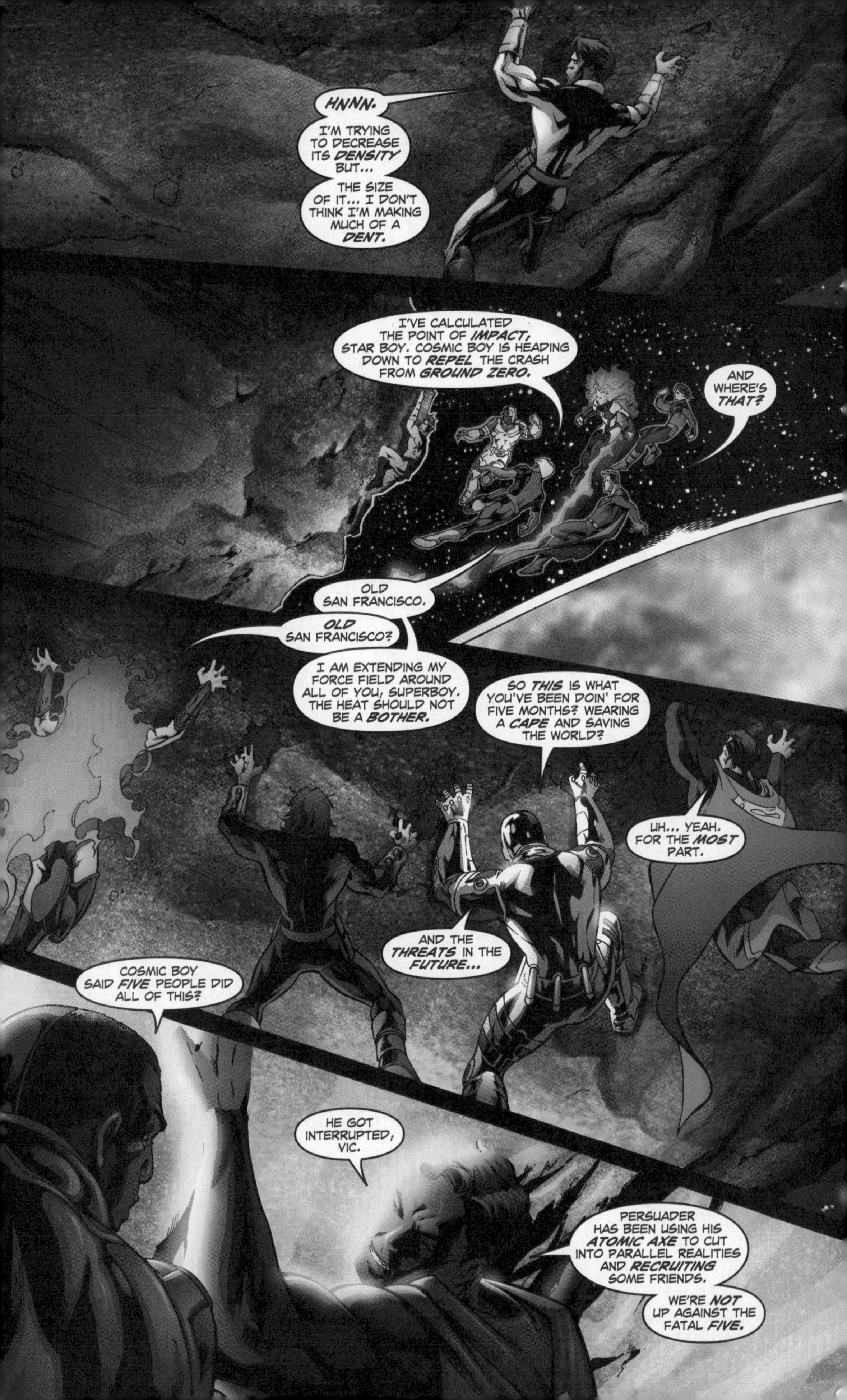
HNNN.
I'M TRYING TO DECREASE ITS DENSITY BUT...
THE SIZE OF IT... I DON'T THINK I'M MAKING MUCH OF A DENT.
I'VE CALCULATED THE POINT OF IMPACT, STAR BOY. COSMIC BOY IS HEADING DOWN TO REPEL THE CRASH FROM GROUND ZERO.
AND WHERE'S THAT?
OLD SAN FRANCISCO.
OLD SAN FRANCISCO?
I AM EXTENDING MY FORCE FIELD AROUND ALL OF YOU, SUPERBOY. THE HEAT SHOULD NOT BE A BOTHER.
SO THIS IS WHAT YOU'VE BEEN DOIN' FOR FIVE MONTHS? WEARING A CAPE AND SAVING THE WORLD?
UH... YEAH. FOR THE MOST PART.
AND THE THREATS IN THE FUTURE...
COSMIC BOY SAID FIVE PEOPLE DID ALL OF THIS?
HE GOT INTERRUPTED, VIC.
PERSUADER HAS BEEN USING HIS ATOMIC AXE TO CUT INTO PARALLEL REALITIES AND RECRUITING SOME FRIENDS.
WE'RE NOT UP AGAINST THE FATAL FIVE.

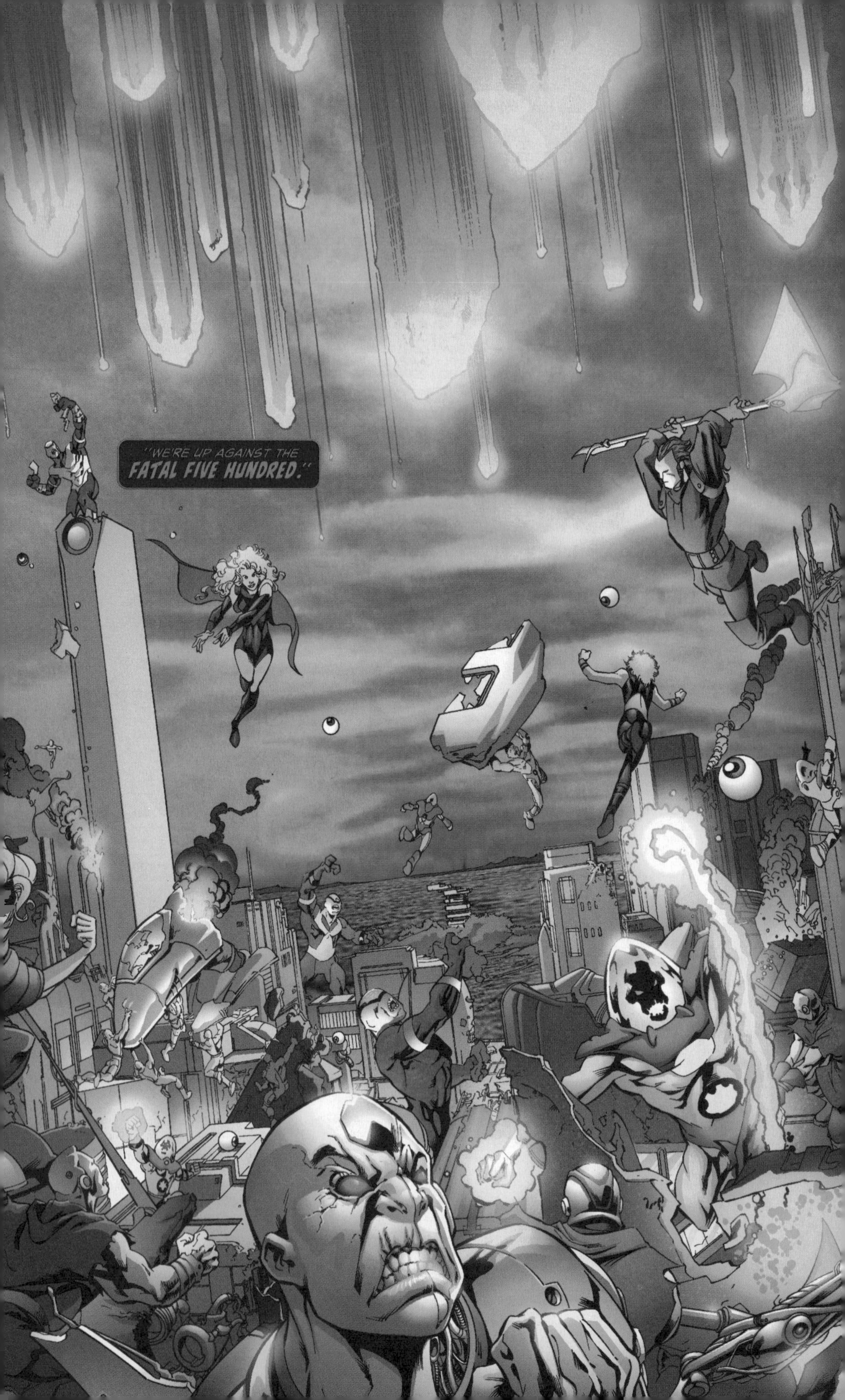
"WE'RE UP AGAINST THE FATAL FIVE HUNDRED."

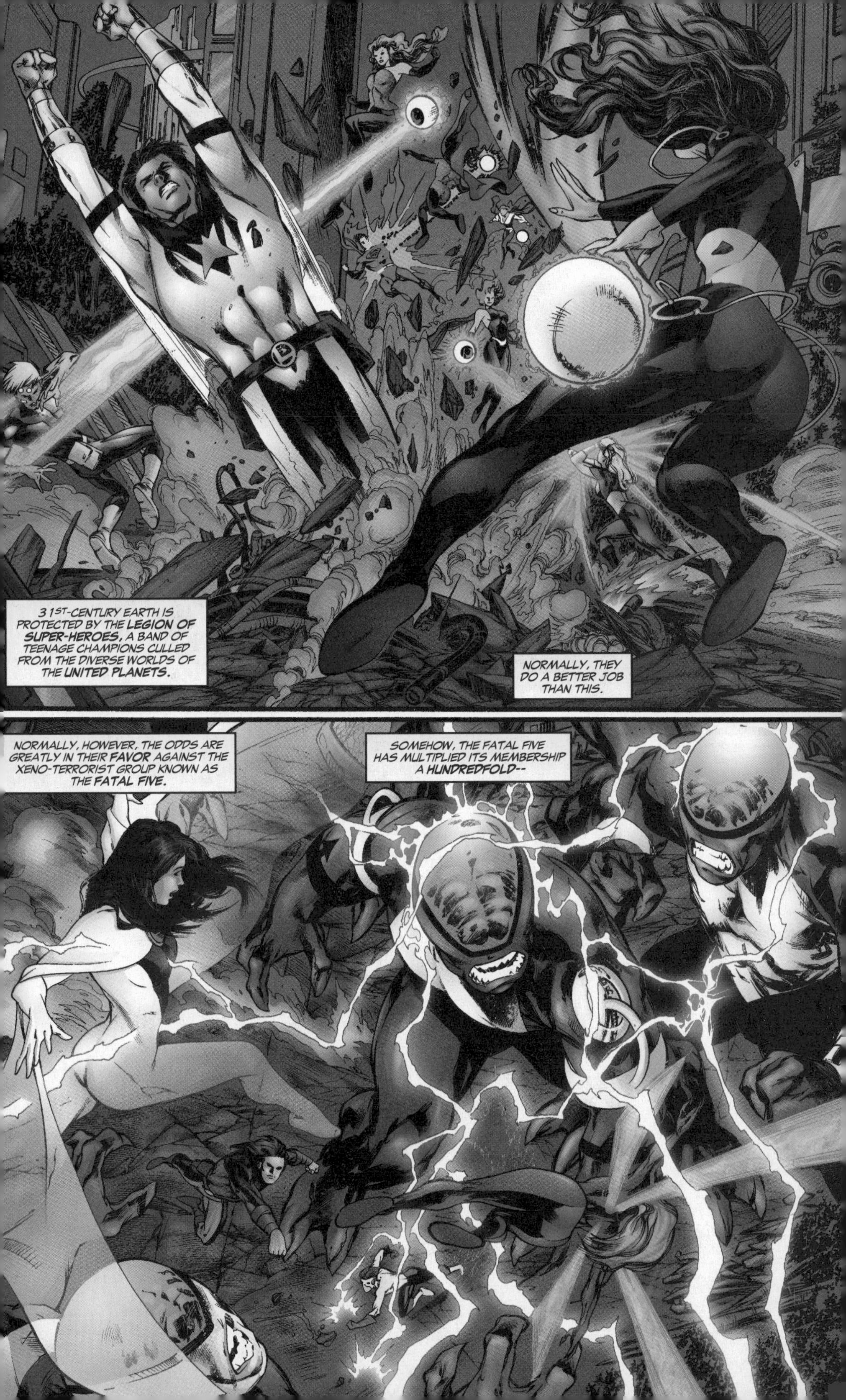

31ST-CENTURY EARTH IS PROTECTED BY THE LEGION OF SUPER-HEROES, A BAND OF TEENAGE CHAMPIONS CULLED FROM THE DIVERSE WORLDS OF THE UNITED PLANETS.
NORMALLY, THEY DO A BETTER JOB THAN THIS.
NORMALLY, HOWEVER, THE ODDS ARE GREATLY IN THEIR FAVOR AGAINST THE XENO-TERRORIST GROUP KNOWN AS THE FATAL FIVE.
SOMEHOW, THE FATAL FIVE HAS MULTIPLIED ITS MEMBERSHIP A HUNDREDFOLD--

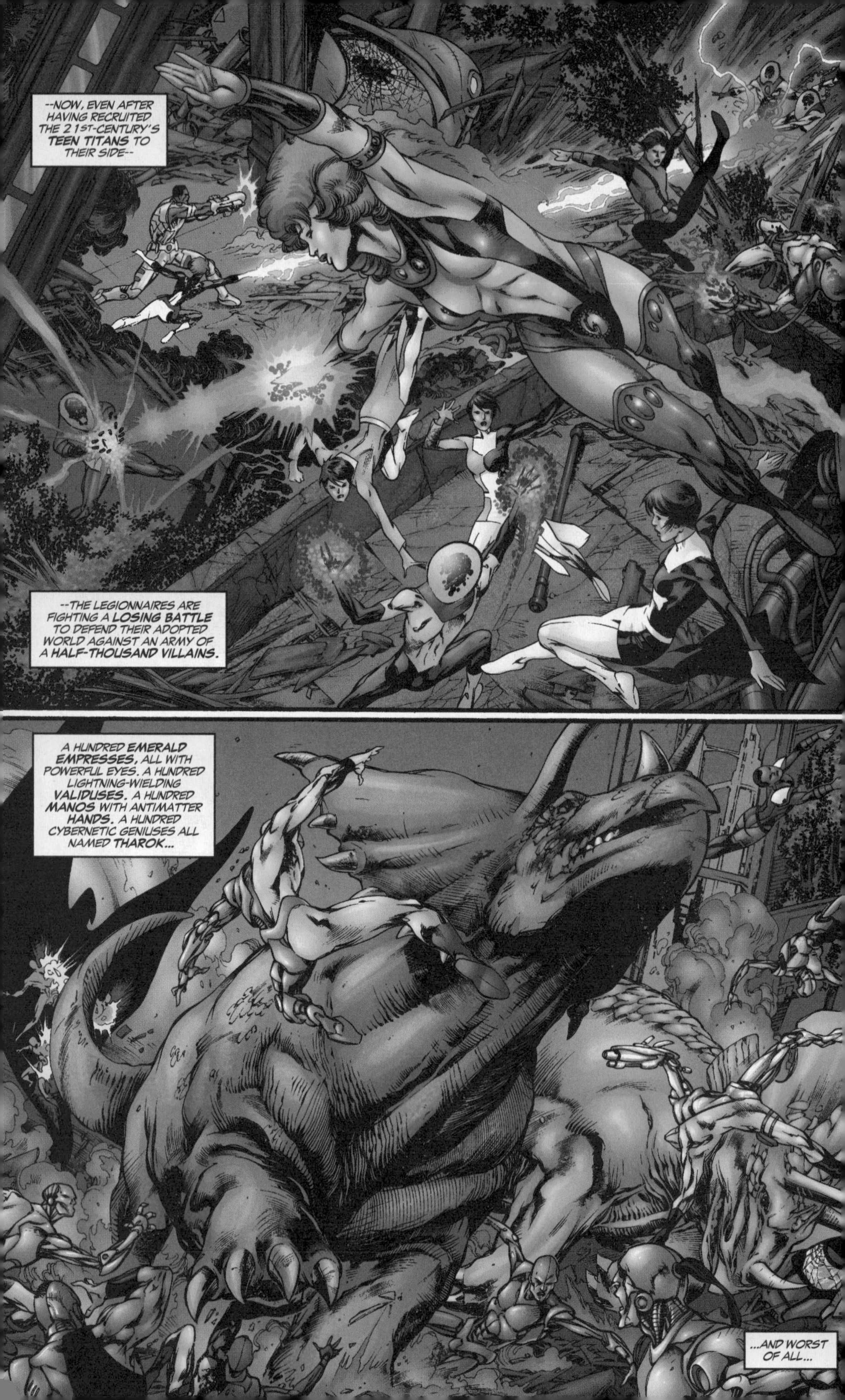
--NOW, EVEN AFTER HAVING RECRUITED THE 21ST-CENTURY'S TEEN TITANS TO THEIR SIDE--
--THE LEGIONNAIRES ARE FIGHTING A LOSING BATTLE TO DEFEND THEIR ADOPTED WORLD AGAINST AN ARMY OF A HALF-THOUSAND VILLAINS.
A HUNDRED EMERALD EMPRESSES, ALL WITH POWERFUL EYES. A HUNDRED LIGHTNING-WIELDING VALIDUSES. A HUNDRED MANOS WITH ANTIMATTER HANDS. A HUNDRED CYBERNETIC GENIUSES ALL NAMED THAROK...
...AND WORST OF ALL...

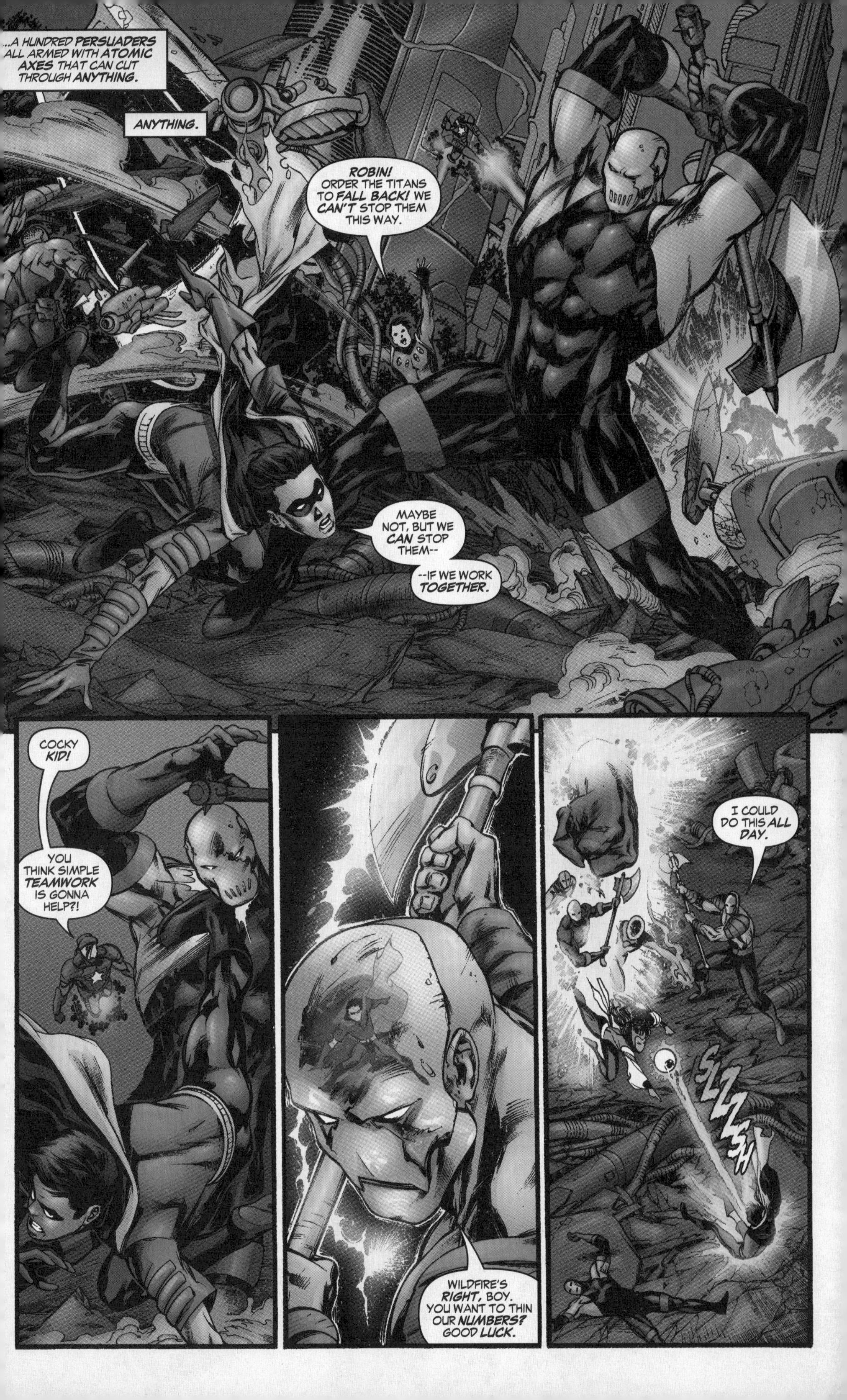
...A HUNDRED PERSUADERS ALL ARMED WITH ATOMIC AXES THAT CAN CUT THROUGH ANYTHING.
ANYTHING.
ROBIN! ORDER THE TITANS TO FALL BACK! WE CAN'T STOP THEM THIS WAY.
MAYBE NOT, BUT WE CAN STOP THEM--
--IF WE WORK TOGETHER.
COCKY KID!
YOU THINK SIMPLE TEAMWORK IS GONNA HELP?!
WILDFIRE'S RIGHT, BOY. YOU WANT TO THIN OUR NUMBERS? GOOD LUCK.
I COULD DO THIS ALL DAY.
SZZZSH

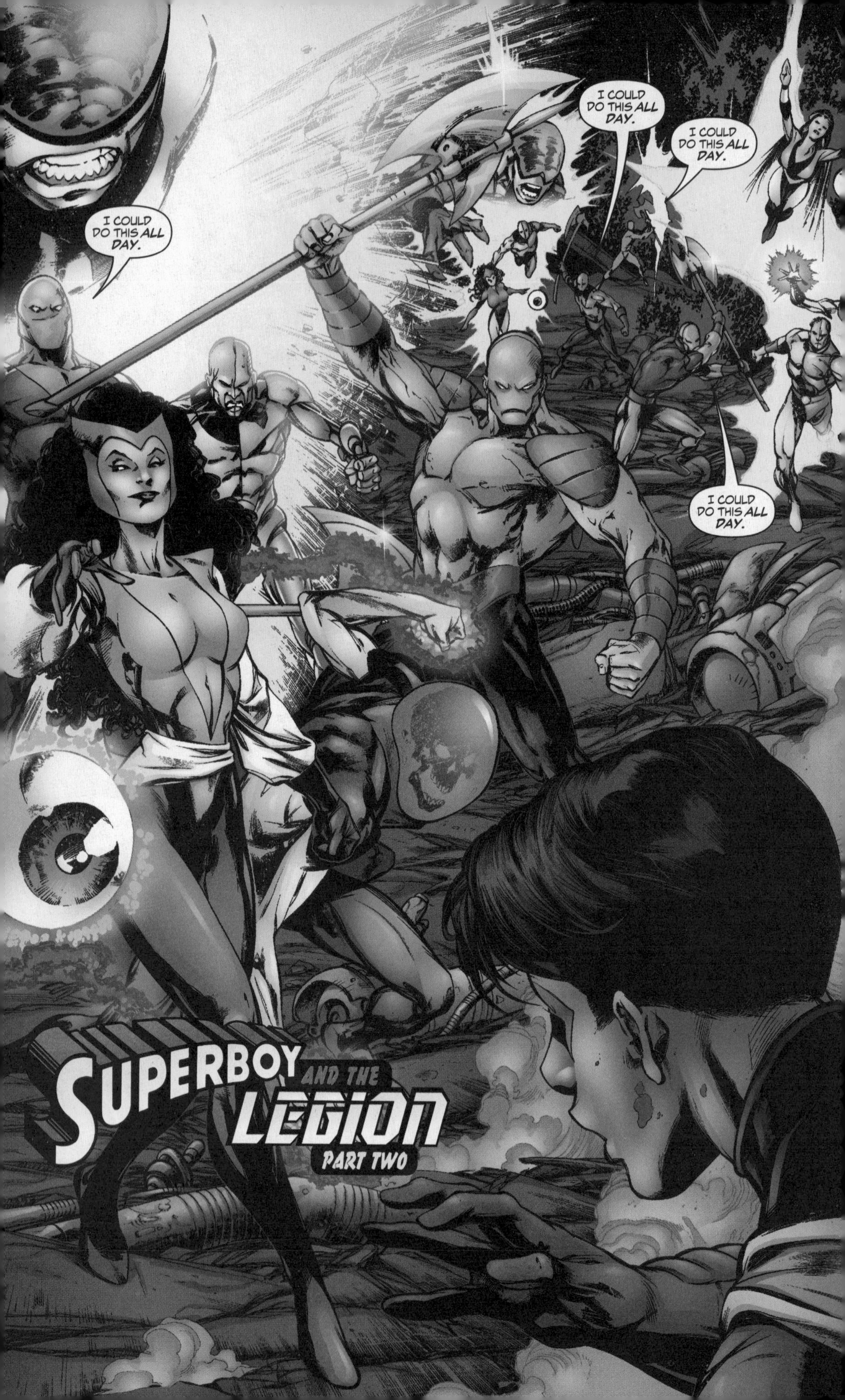
I COULD DO THIS ALL DAY.
I COULD DO THIS ALL DAY.
I COULD DO THIS ALL DAY.
I COULD DO THIS ALL DAY.
SUPERBOY AND THE LEGION
PART TWO

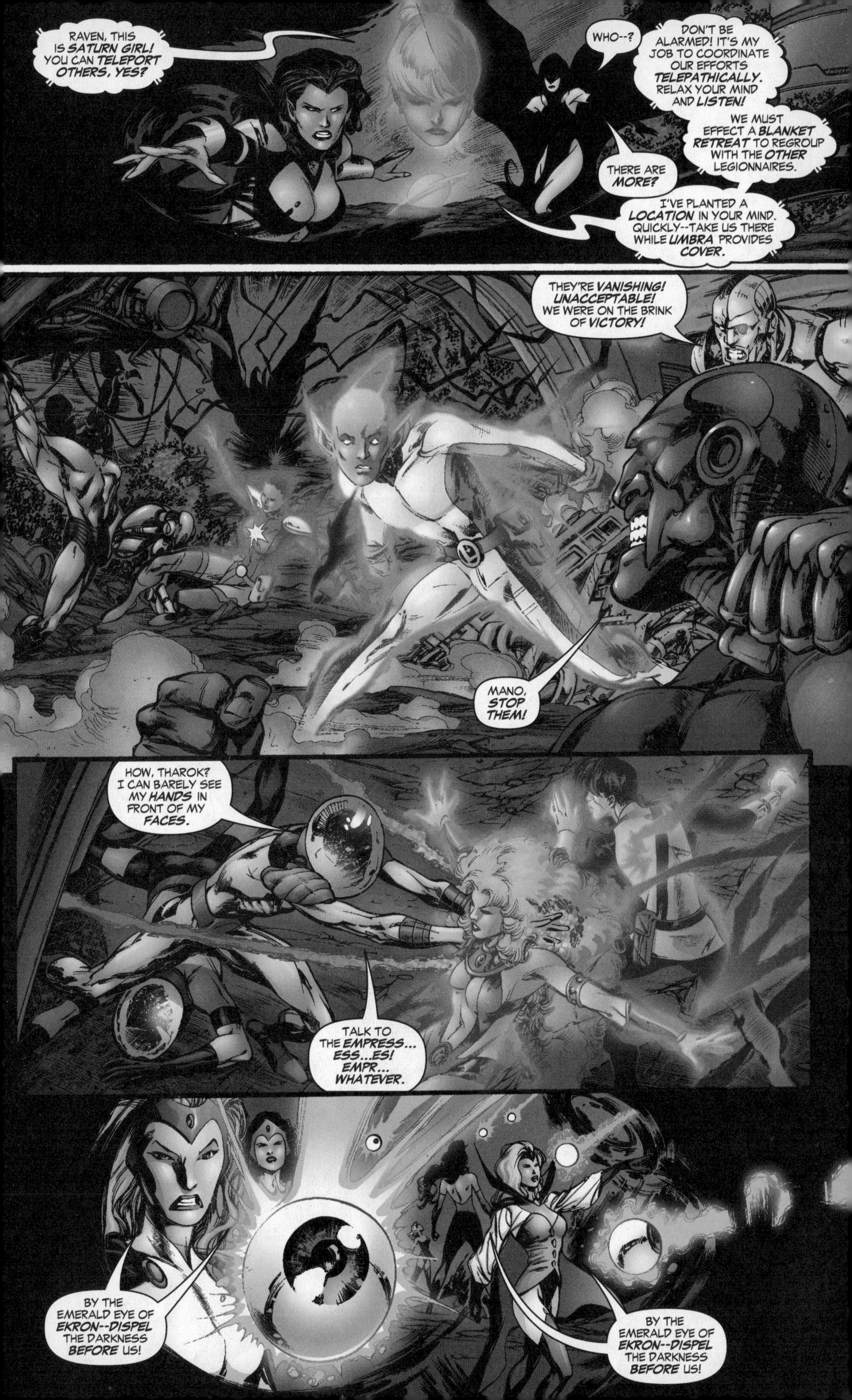
RAVEN, THIS IS SATURN GIRL! YOU CAN TELEPORT OTHERS, YES?
WHO--?
DON'T BE ALARMED! IT'S MY JOB TO COORDINATE OUR EFFORTS TELEPATHICALLY. RELAX YOUR MIND AND LISTEN!
WE MUST EFFECT A BLANKET RETREAT TO REGROUP WITH THE OTHER LEGIONNAIRES.
THERE ARE MORE?
I'VE PLANTED A LOCATION IN YOUR MIND. QUICKLY--TAKE US THERE WHILE UMBRA PROVIDES COVER.
THEY'RE VANISHING! UNACCEPTABLE! WE WERE ON THE BRINK OF VICTORY!
MANO, STOP THEM!
HOW, THAROK? I CAN BARELY SEE MY HANDS IN FRONT OF MY FACES.
TALK TO THE EMPRESS... ESS...ES! EMPR... WHATEVER.
BY THE EMERALD EYE OF EKRON--DISPEL THE DARKNESS BEFORE US!
BY THE EMERALD EYE OF EKRON--DISPEL THE DARKNESS BEFORE US!

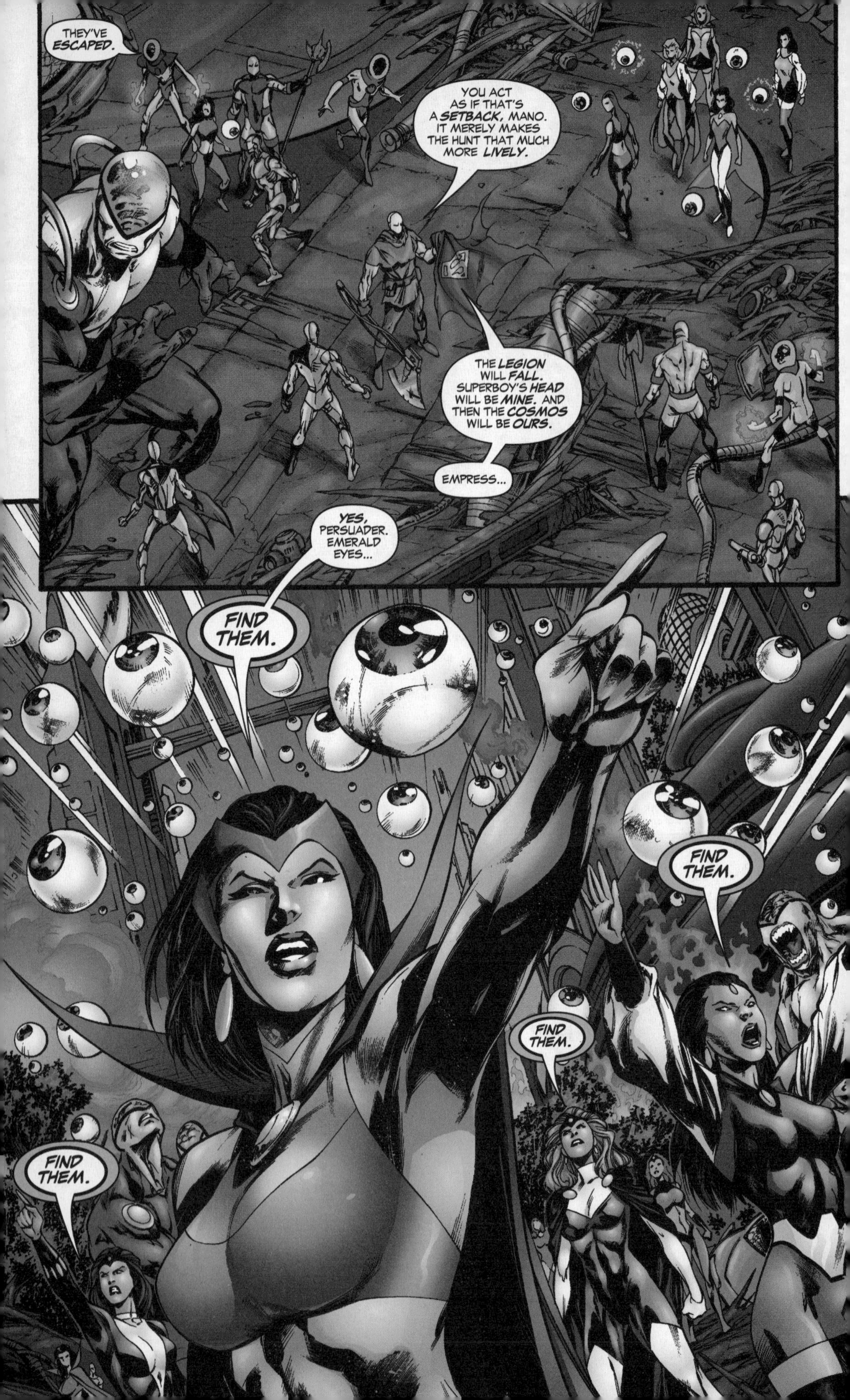
THEY'VE ESCAPED.
YOU ACT AS IF THAT'S A SETBACK, MANO. IT MERELY MAKES THE HUNT THAT MUCH MORE LIVELY.
THE LEGION WILL FALL. SUPERBOY'S HEAD WILL BE MINE. AND THEN THE COSMOS WILL BE OURS.
EMPRESS...
YES, PERSUADER. EMERALD EYES...
FIND THEM.
FIND THEM.
FIND THEM.
FIND THEM.

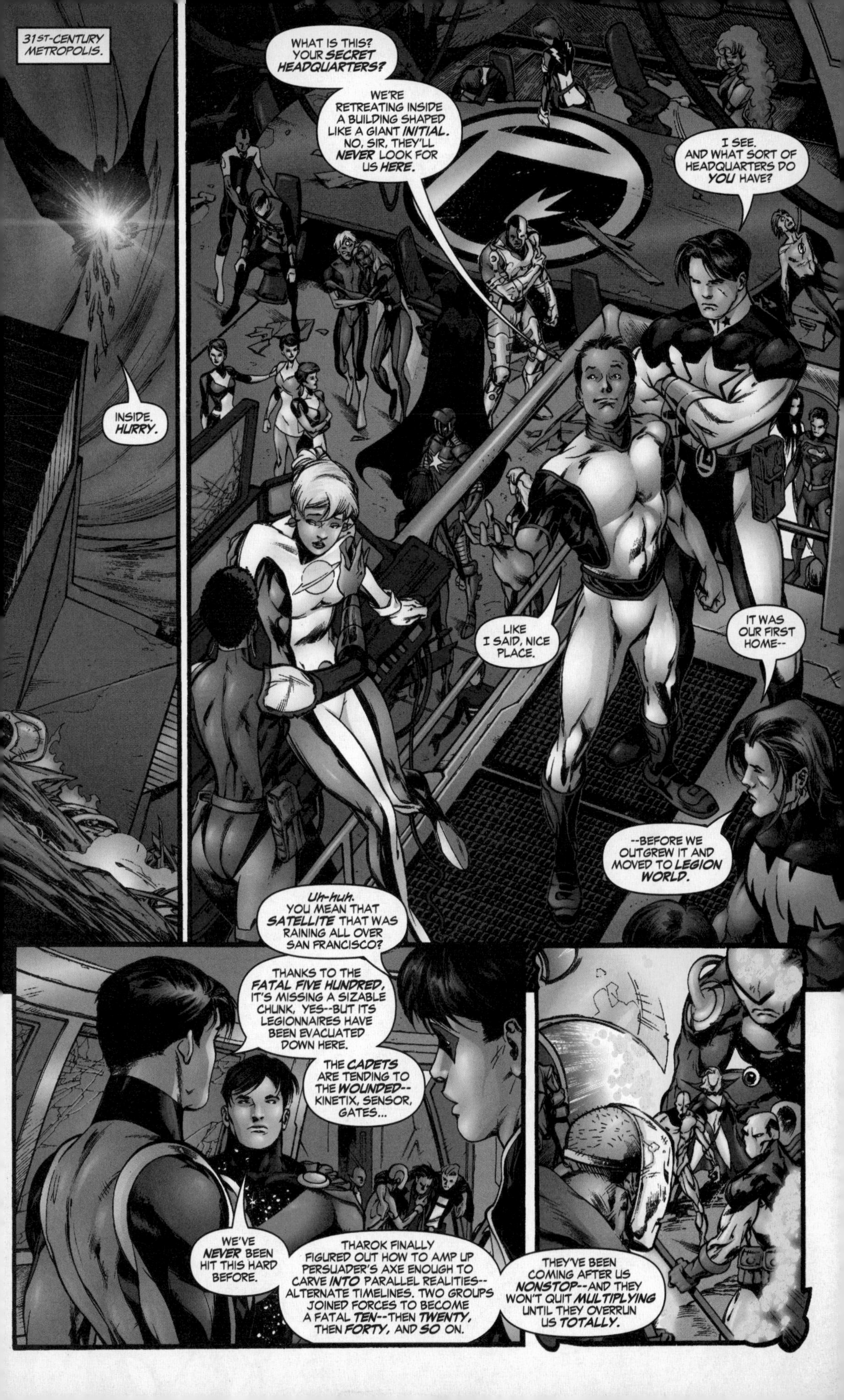

31ST-CENTURY METROPOLIS.
INSIDE. HURRY.
WHAT IS THIS? YOUR SECRET HEADQUARTERS?
WE'RE RETREATING INSIDE A BUILDING SHAPED LIKE A GIANT INITIAL. NO, SIR, THEY'LL NEVER LOOK FOR US HERE.
I SEE. AND WHAT SORT OF HEADQUARTERS DO YOU HAVE?
LIKE I SAID, NICE PLACE.
IT WAS OUR FIRST HOME--
--BEFORE WE OUTGREW IT AND MOVED TO LEGION WORLD.
Uh-huh. YOU MEAN THAT SATELLITE THAT WAS RAINING ALL OVER SAN FRANCISCO?
THANKS TO THE FATAL FIVE HUNDRED, IT'S MISSING A SIZABLE CHUNK, YES--BUT ITS LEGIONNAIRES HAVE BEEN EVACUATED DOWN HERE.
THE CADETS ARE TENDING TO THE WOUNDED-- KINETIX, SENSOR, GATES...
WE'VE NEVER BEEN HIT THIS HARD BEFORE.
THAROK FINALLY FIGURED OUT HOW TO AMP UP PERSUADER'S AXE ENOUGH TO CARVE INTO PARALLEL REALITIES-- ALTERNATE TIMELINES. TWO GROUPS JOINED FORCES TO BECOME A FATAL TEN--THEN TWENTY, THEN FORTY, AND SO ON.
THEY'VE BEEN COMING AFTER US NONSTOP--AND THEY WON'T QUIT MULTIPLYING UNTIL THEY OVERRUN US TOTALLY.

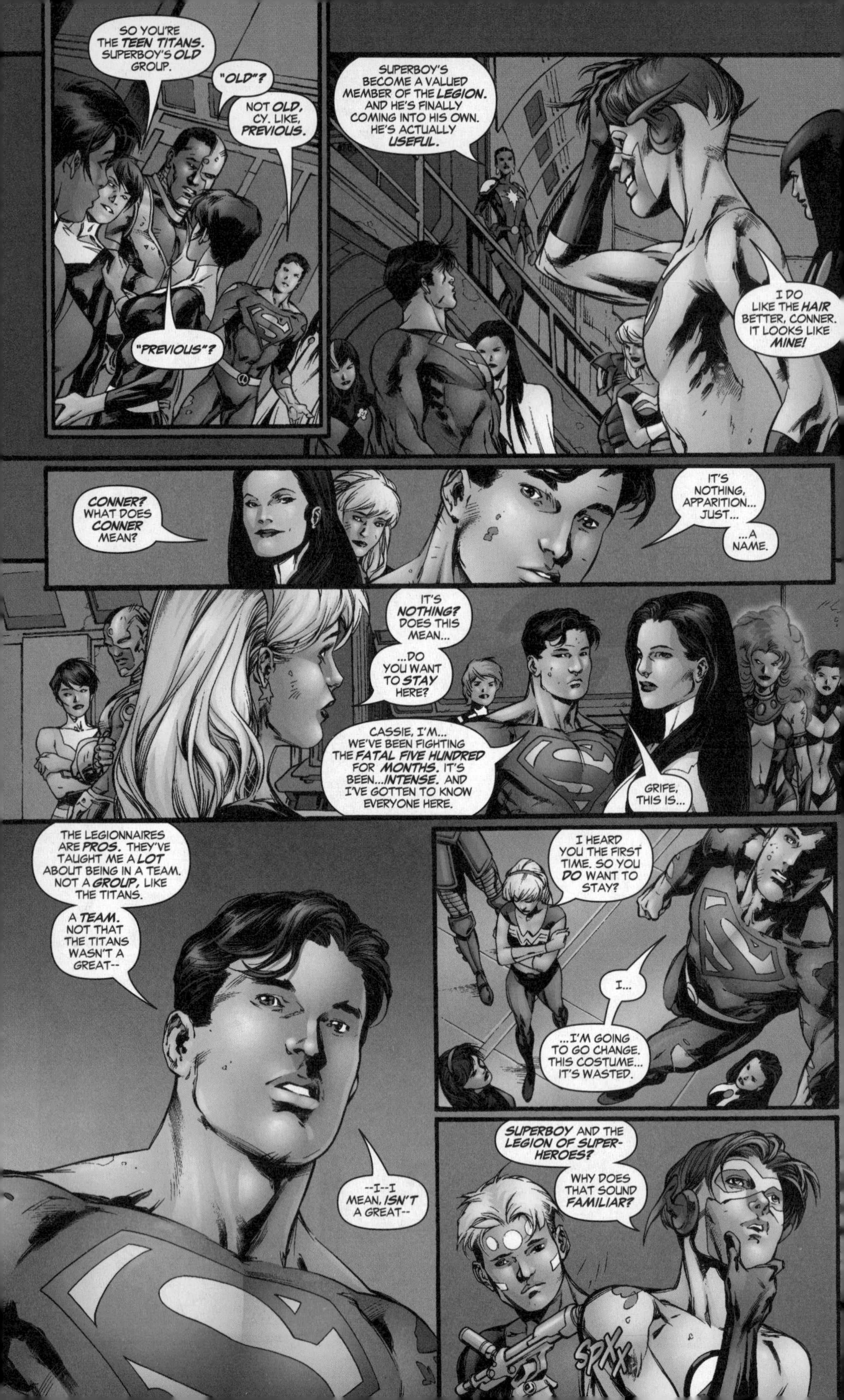
SO YOU'RE THE TEEN TITANS. SUPERBOY'S OLD GROUP.
"OLD"?
NOT OLD, CY. LIKE, PREVIOUS.
"PREVIOUS"?
SUPERBOY'S BECOME A VALUED MEMBER OF THE LEGION. AND HE'S FINALLY COMING INTO HIS OWN. HE'S ACTUALLY USEFUL.
I DO LIKE THE HAIR BETTER, CONNER. IT LOOKS LIKE MINE!
CONNER? WHAT DOES CONNER MEAN?
IT'S NOTHING, APPARITION... JUST...
...A NAME.
IT'S NOTHING? DOES THIS MEAN...
...DO YOU WANT TO STAY HERE?
CASSIE, I'M... WE'VE BEEN FIGHTING THE FATAL FIVE HUNDRED FOR MONTHS. IT'S BEEN...INTENSE. AND I'VE GOTTEN TO KNOW EVERYONE HERE.
GRIFE, THIS IS...
THE LEGIONNAIRES ARE PROS. THEY'VE TAUGHT ME A LOT ABOUT BEING IN A TEAM. NOT A GROUP, LIKE THE TITANS.
A TEAM. NOT THAT THE TITANS WASN'T A GREAT--
--I--I MEAN, ISN'T A GREAT--
I HEARD YOU THE FIRST TIME. SO YOU DO WANT TO STAY?
I...
...I'M GOING TO GO CHANGE. THIS COSTUME... IT'S WASTED.
SUPERBOY AND THE LEGION OF SUPER-HEROES?
WHY DOES THAT SOUND FAMILIAR?
SPXX

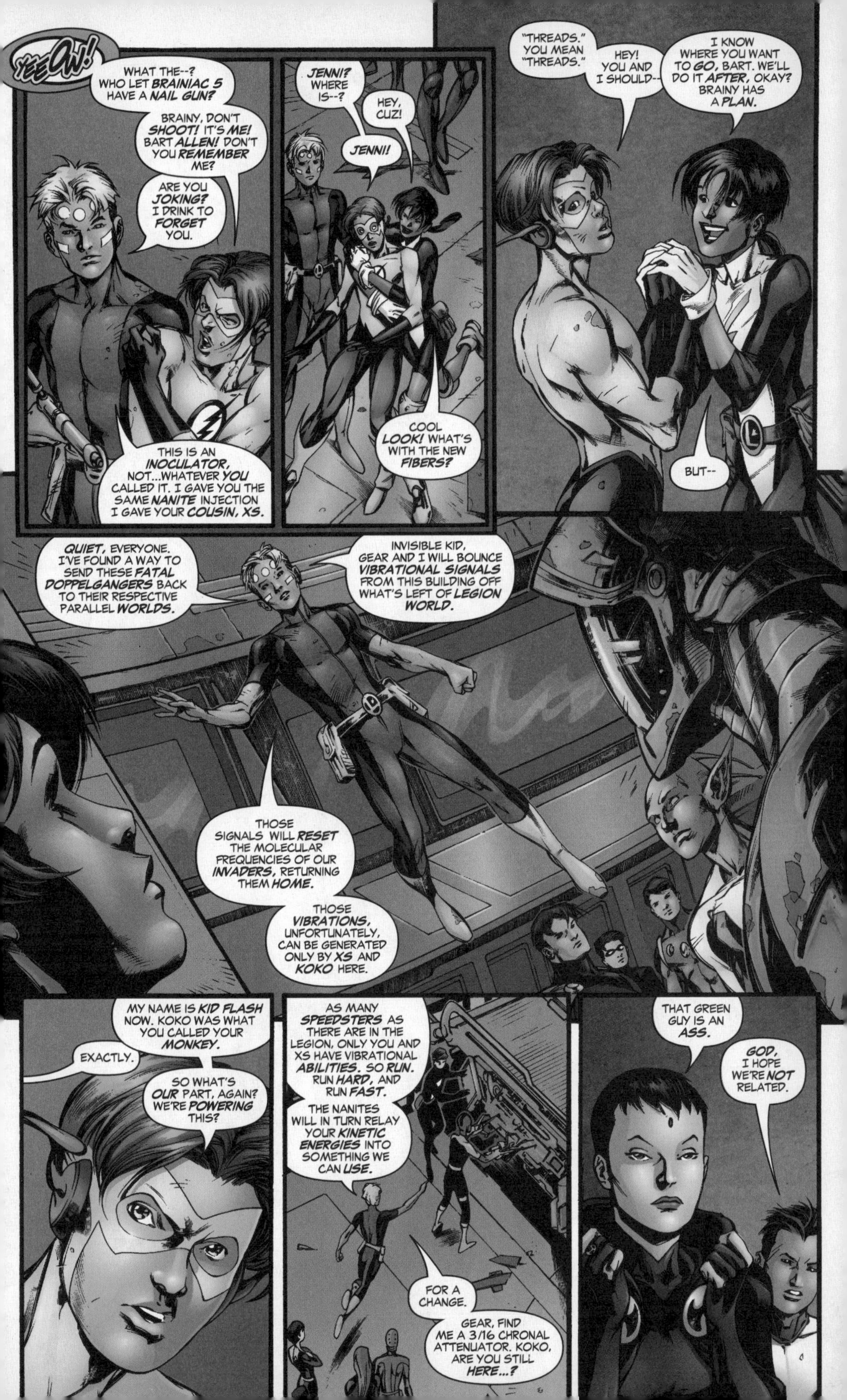
YEEOW!
WHAT THE--? WHO LET BRAINIAC 5 HAVE A NAIL GUN?
BRAINY, DON'T SHOOT! IT'S ME! BART ALLEN! DON'T YOU REMEMBER ME?
ARE YOU JOKING? I DRINK TO FORGET YOU.
THIS IS AN INOCULATOR, NOT...WHATEVER YOU CALLED IT. I GAVE YOU THE SAME NANITE INJECTION I GAVE YOUR COUSIN, XS.
JENNI? WHERE IS--?
HEY, CUZ!
JENNI!
COOL LOOK! WHAT'S WITH THE NEW FIBERS?
"THREADS." YOU MEAN "THREADS."
HEY! YOU AND I SHOULD--
I KNOW WHERE YOU WANT TO GO, BART. WE'LL DO IT AFTER, OKAY? BRAINY HAS A PLAN.
BUT--
QUIET, EVERYONE. I'VE FOUND A WAY TO SEND THESE FATAL DOPPELGANGERS BACK TO THEIR RESPECTIVE PARALLEL WORLDS.
INVISIBLE KID, GEAR AND I WILL BOUNCE VIBRATIONAL SIGNALS FROM THIS BUILDING OFF WHAT'S LEFT OF LEGION WORLD.
THOSE SIGNALS WILL RESET THE MOLECULAR FREQUENCIES OF OUR INVADERS, RETURNING THEM HOME.
THOSE VIBRATIONS, UNFORTUNATELY, CAN BE GENERATED ONLY BY XS AND KOKO HERE.
MY NAME IS KID FLASH NOW. KOKO WAS WHAT YOU CALLED YOUR MONKEY.
EXACTLY.
SO WHAT'S OUR PART, AGAIN? WE'RE POWERING THIS?
AS MANY SPEEDSTERS AS THERE ARE IN THE LEGION, ONLY YOU AND XS HAVE VIBRATIONAL ABILITIES. SO RUN. RUN HARD, AND RUN FAST.
THE NANITES WILL IN TURN RELAY YOUR KINETIC ENERGIES INTO SOMETHING WE CAN USE.
FOR A CHANGE.
GEAR, FIND ME A 3/16 CHRONAL ATTENUATOR. KOKO, ARE YOU STILL HERE...?
THAT GREEN GUY IS AN ASS.
GOD, I HOPE WE'RE NOT RELATED.

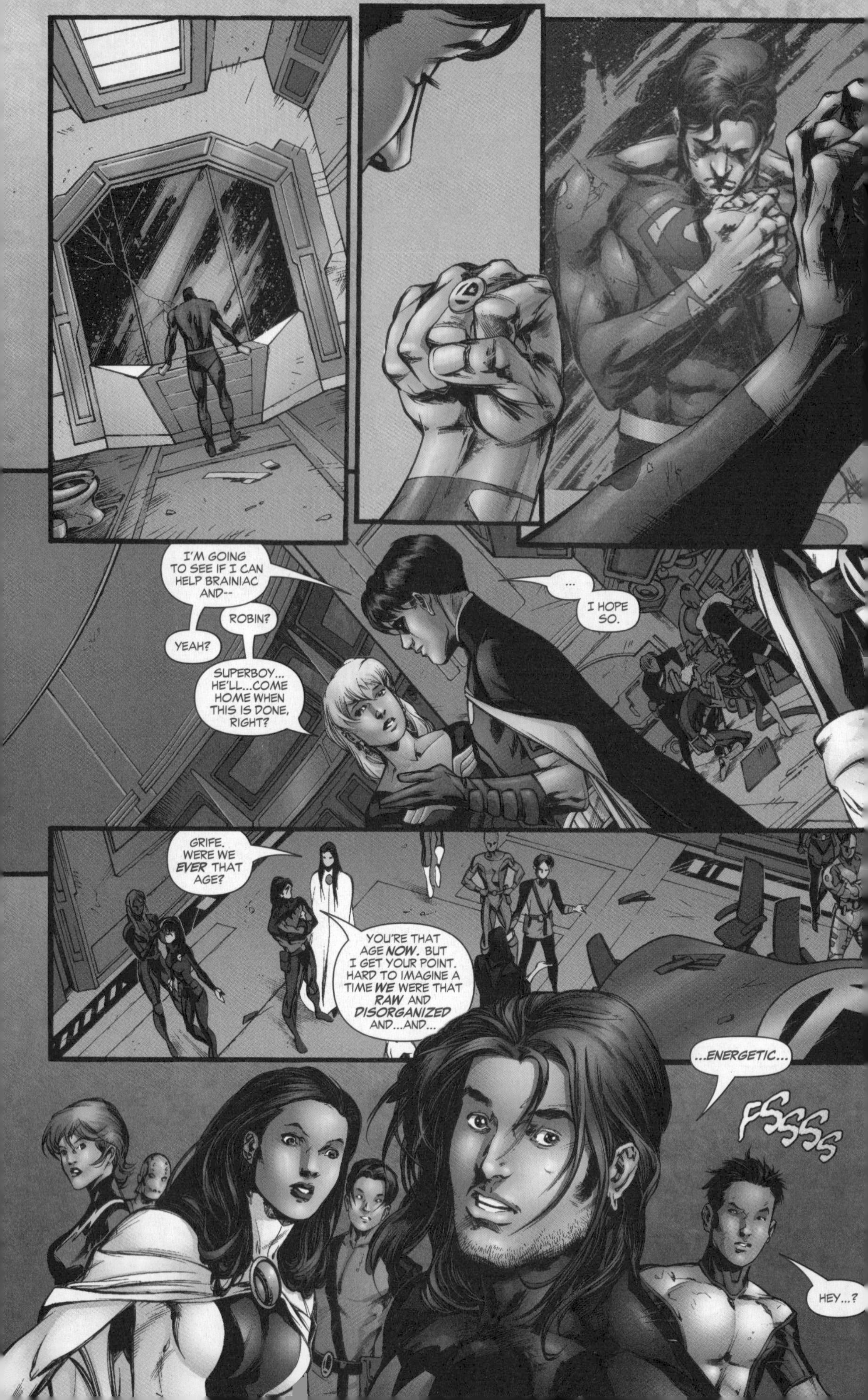
I'M GOING TO SEE IF I CAN HELP BRAINIAC AND--
ROBIN?
YEAH?
SUPERBOY... HE'LL...COME HOME WHEN THIS IS DONE, RIGHT?
...
I HOPE SO.
GRIFE. WERE WE EVER THAT AGE?
YOU'RE THAT AGE NOW. BUT I GET YOUR POINT. HARD TO IMAGINE A TIME WE WERE THAT RAW AND DISORGANIZED AND...AND...
...ENERGETIC...
FSSSS
HEY...?

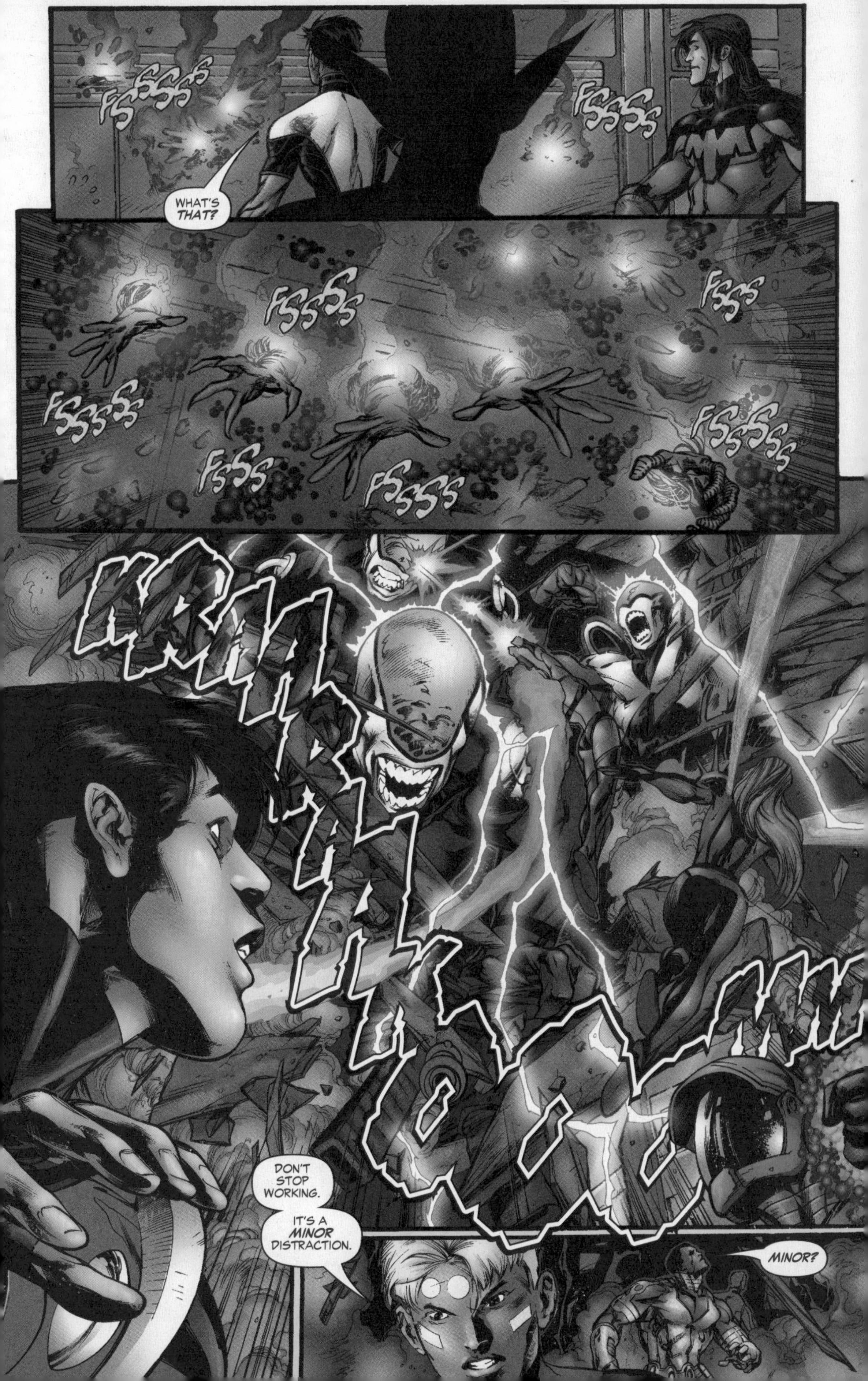
FSSSSSS
FSSSSS
WHAT'S THAT?
FSSSSS
FSSS
FSSSSS
FSSS
FSSSS
FSSSSSS
DON'T STOP WORKING.
IT'S A MINOR DISTRACTION.
MINOR?

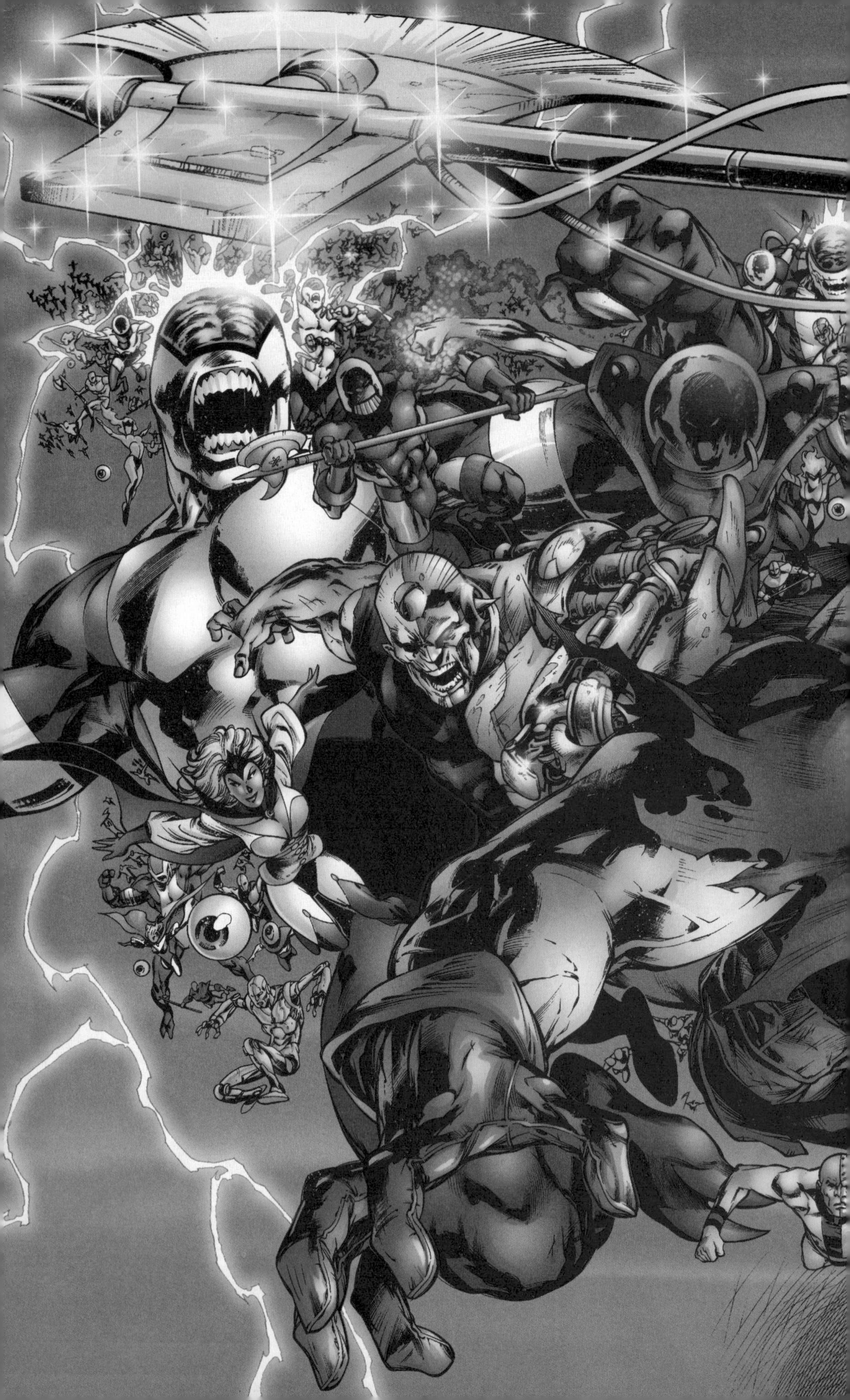

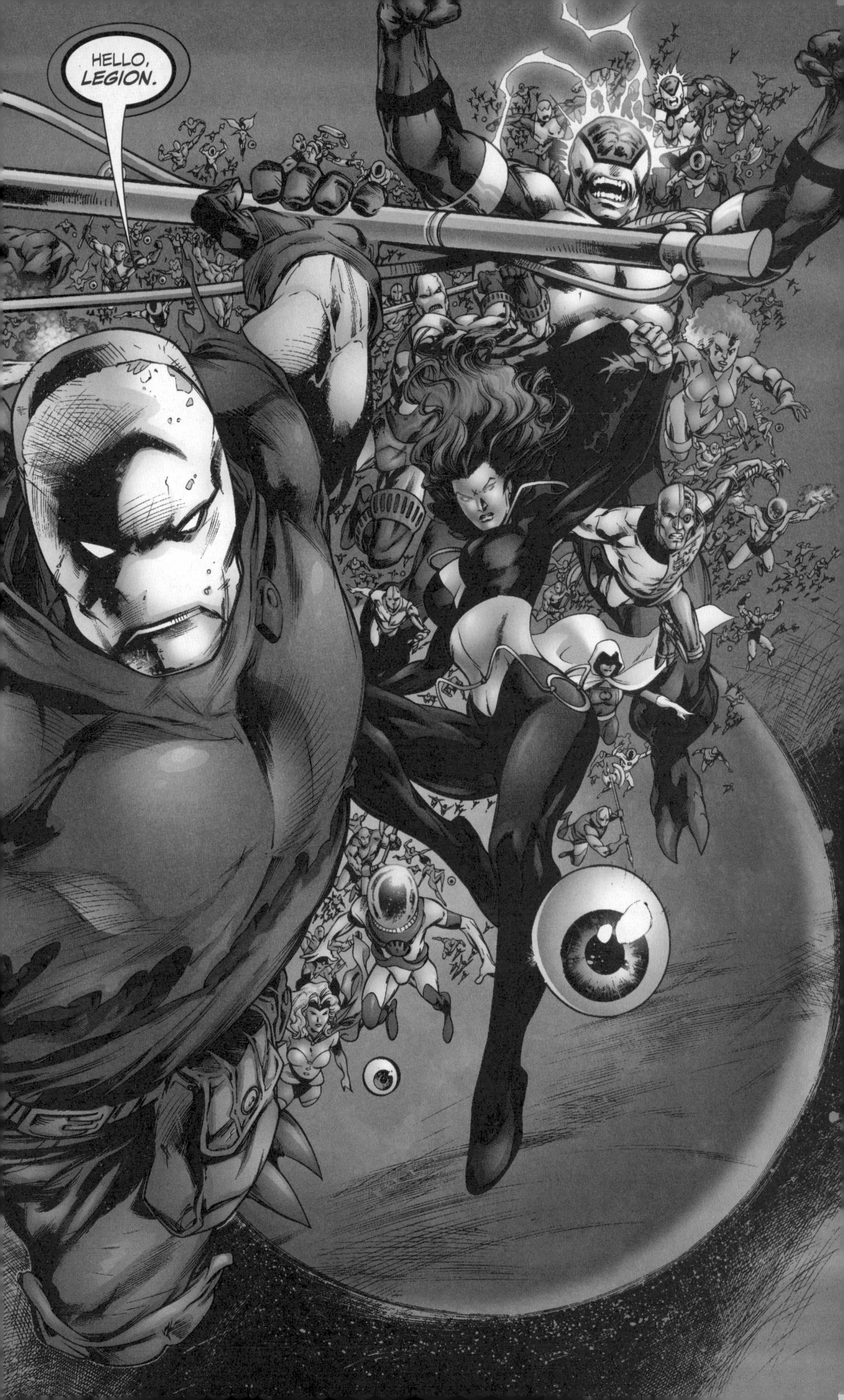
HELLO, LEGION.

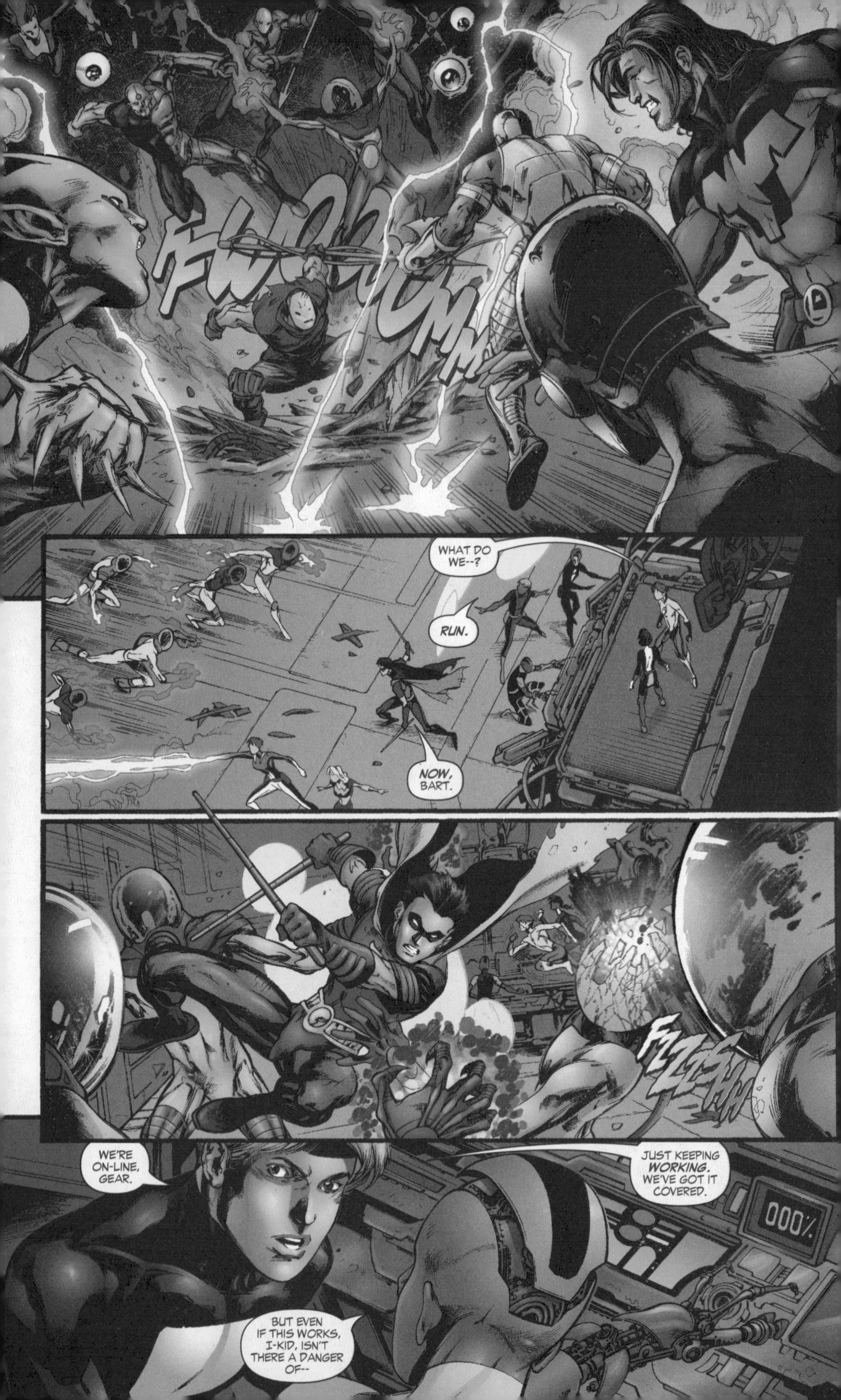

FWOOOOOMM
WHAT DO WE--?
RUN.
NOW, BART.
FZZZSHH
WE'RE ON-LINE, GEAR.
JUST KEEPING WORKING. WE'VE GOT IT COVERED.
000%
BUT EVEN IF THIS WORKS, I-KID, ISN'T THERE A DANGER OF--

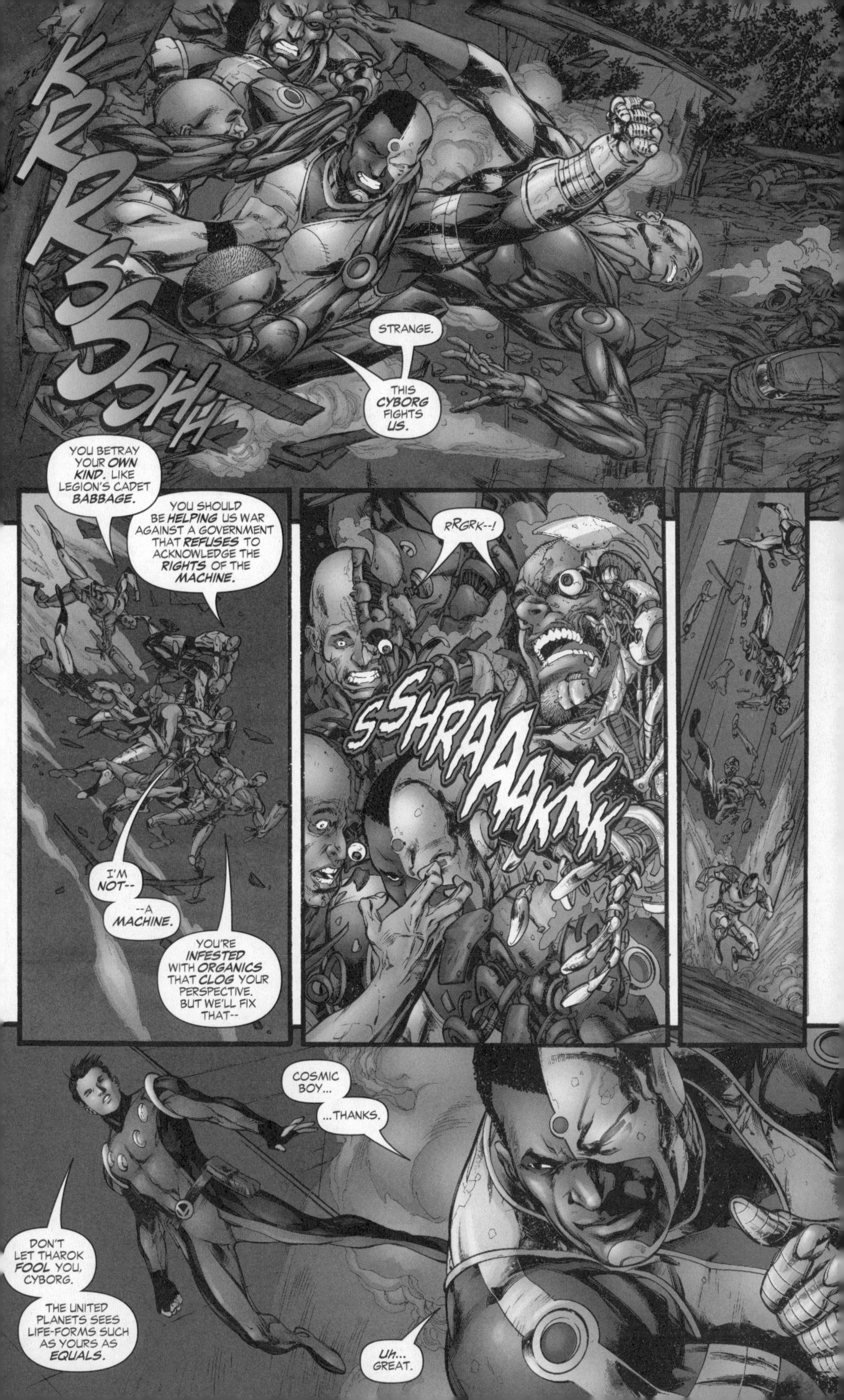
KRRSSSHHH
STRANGE.
THIS CYBORG FIGHTS US.
YOU BETRAY YOUR OWN KIND. LIKE LEGION'S CADET BABBAGE.
YOU SHOULD BE HELPING US WAR AGAINST A GOVERNMENT THAT REFUSES TO ACKNOWLEDGE THE RIGHTS OF THE MACHINE.
I'M NOT--
--A MACHINE.
YOU'RE INFESTED WITH ORGANICS THAT CLOG YOUR PERSPECTIVE. BUT WE'LL FIX THAT--
RRGRK--!
SSHRAAAKKK
COSMIC BOY...
...THANKS.
DON'T LET THAROK FOOL YOU, CYBORG.
THE UNITED PLANETS SEES LIFE-FORMS SUCH AS YOURS AS EQUALS.
UH... GREAT.

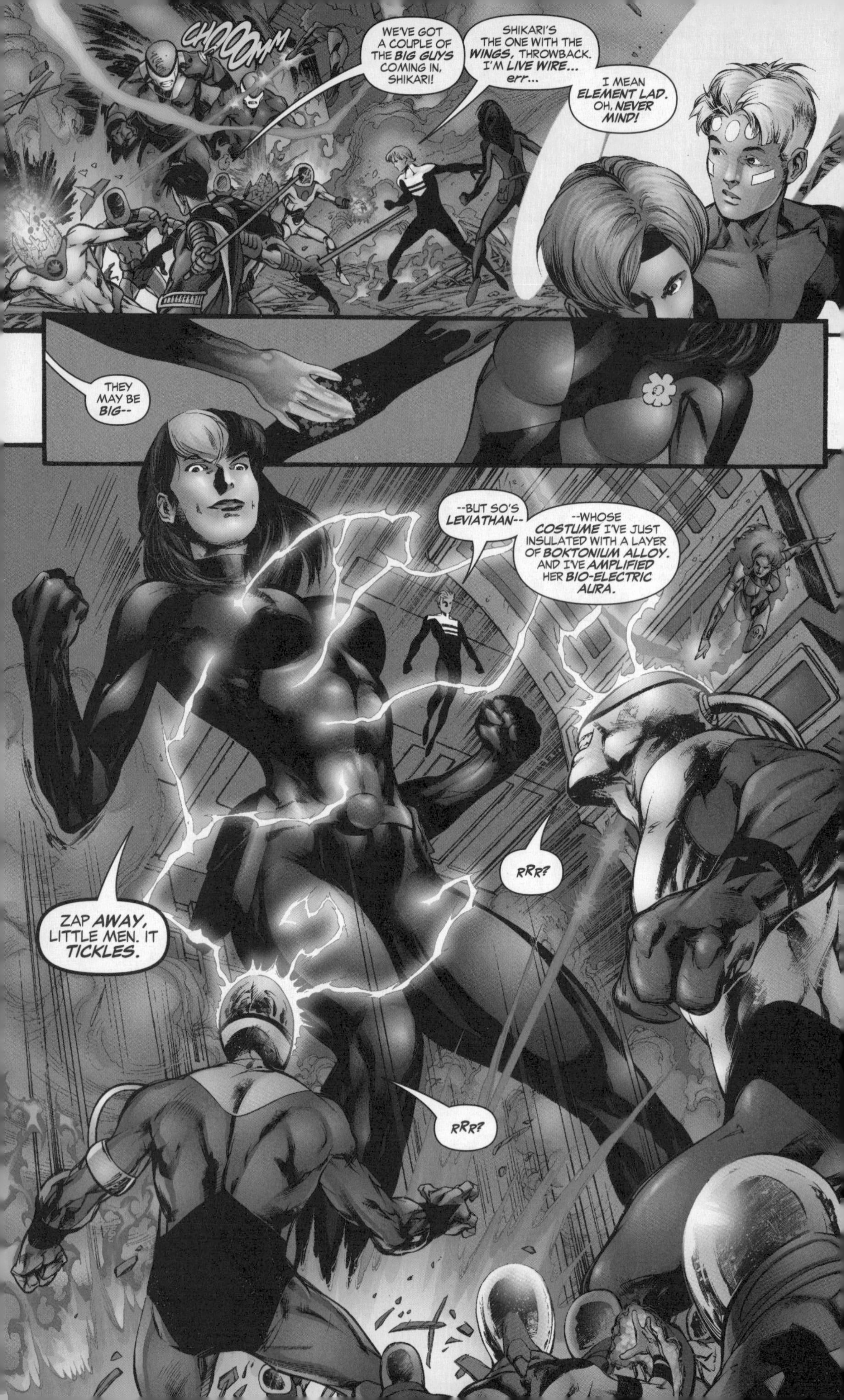
CHOOOMM
WE'VE GOT A COUPLE OF THE BIG GUYS COMING IN, SHIKARI!
SHIKARI'S THE ONE WITH THE WINGS, THROWBACK. I'M LIVE WIRE... err...
I MEAN ELEMENT LAD. OH, NEVER MIND!
THEY MAY BE BIG--
--BUT SO'S LEVIATHAN--
--WHOSE COSTUME I'VE JUST INSULATED WITH A LAYER OF BOKTONIUM ALLOY. AND I'VE AMPLIFIED HER BIO-ELECTRIC AURA.
RRR?
ZAP AWAY, LITTLE MEN. IT TICKLES.
RRR?

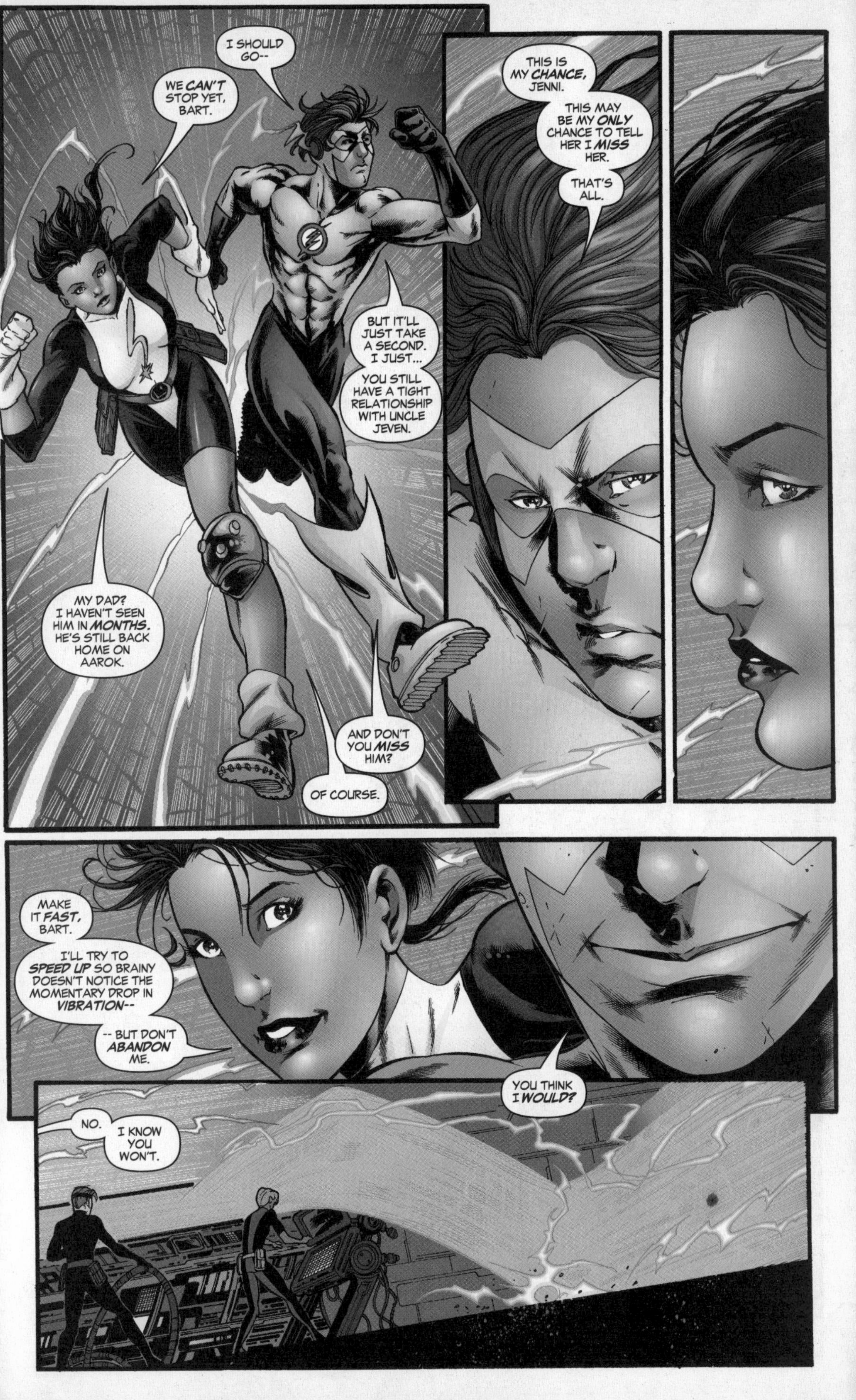

I SHOULD GO--
WE CAN'T STOP YET, BART.
BUT IT'LL JUST TAKE A SECOND. I JUST...
YOU STILL HAVE A TIGHT RELATIONSHIP WITH UNCLE JEVEN.
MY DAD? I HAVEN'T SEEN HIM IN MONTHS. HE'S STILL BACK HOME ON AAROK.
AND DON'T YOU MISS HIM?
OF COURSE.
THIS IS MY CHANCE, JENNI.
THIS MAY BE MY ONLY CHANCE TO TELL HER I MISS HER.
THAT'S ALL.
MAKE IT FAST, BART.
I'LL TRY TO SPEED UP SO BRAINY DOESN'T NOTICE THE MOMENTARY DROP IN VIBRATION--
-- BUT DON'T ABANDON ME.
YOU THINK I WOULD?
NO.
I KNOW YOU WON'T.

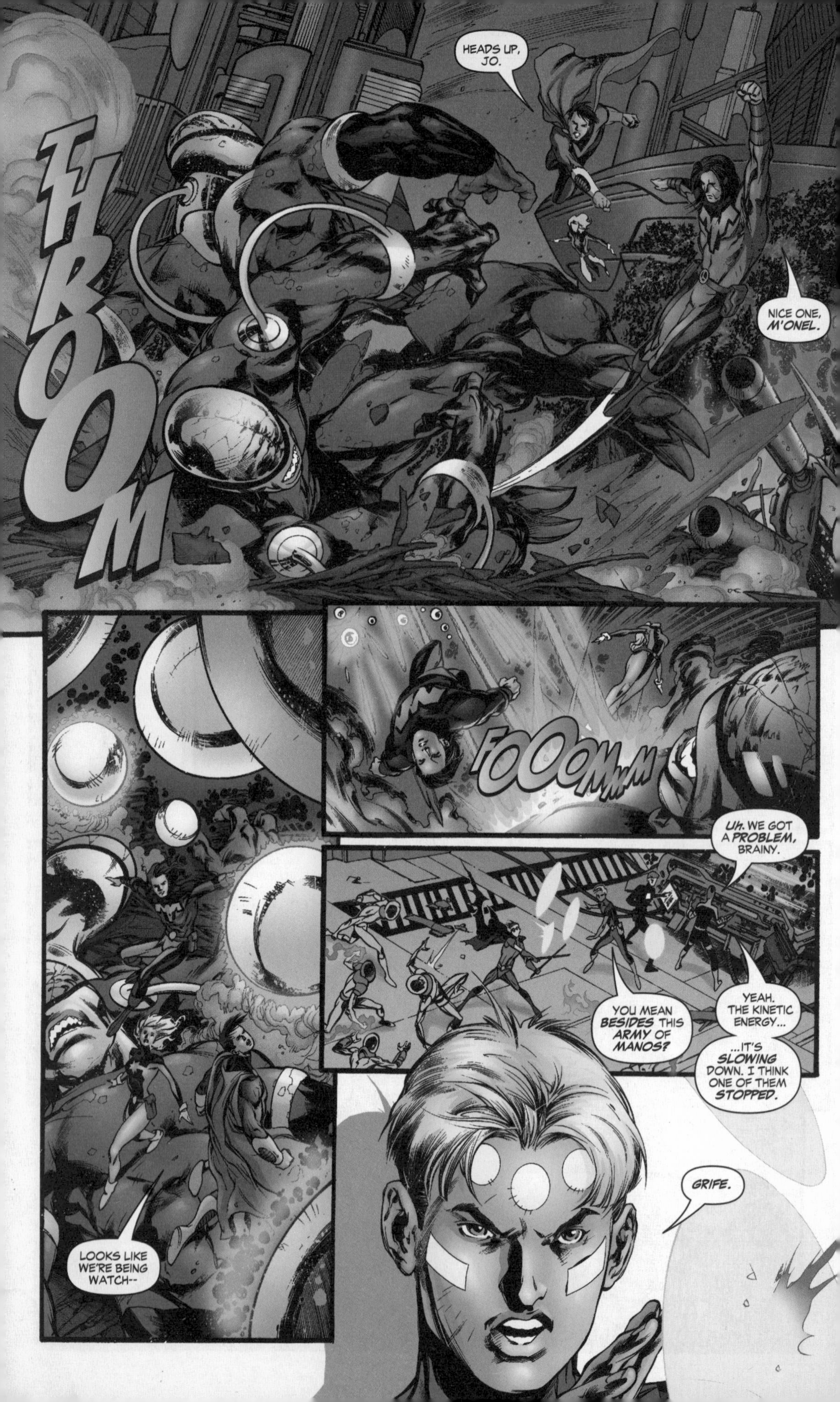

THROOOM
HEADS UP, JO.
NICE ONE, M'ONEL.
FOOOMMM
LOOKS LIKE WE'RE BEING WATCH--
Uh. WE GOT A PROBLEM, BRAINY.
YOU MEAN BESIDES THIS ARMY OF MANOS?
YEAH. THE KINETIC ENERGY...
...IT'S SLOWING DOWN. I THINK ONE OF THEM STOPPED.
GRIFE.

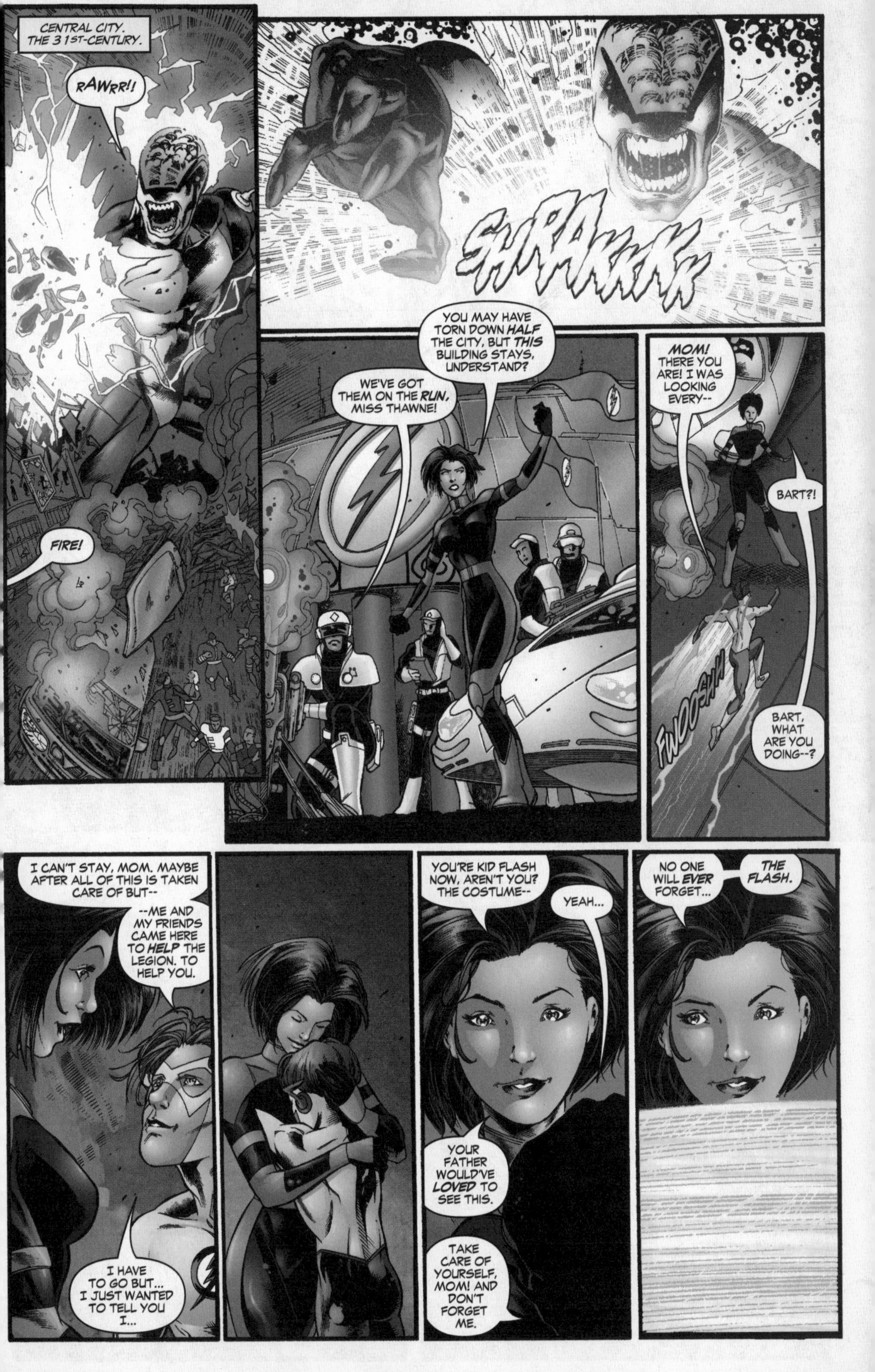
CENTRAL CITY. THE 31ST-CENTURY.
RAWRR!!
FIRE!
SHRAKKKK
YOU MAY HAVE TORN DOWN HALF THE CITY, BUT THIS BUILDING STAYS, UNDERSTAND?
WE'VE GOT THEM ON THE RUN, MISS THAWNE!
MOM! THERE YOU ARE! I WAS LOOKING EVERY--
BART?!
FWOOSHH
BART, WHAT ARE YOU DOING--?
I CAN'T STAY, MOM. MAYBE AFTER ALL OF THIS IS TAKEN CARE OF BUT--
--ME AND MY FRIENDS CAME HERE TO HELP THE LEGION. TO HELP YOU.
I HAVE TO GO BUT... I JUST WANTED TO TELL YOU I...
YOU'RE KID FLASH NOW, AREN'T YOU? THE COSTUME--
YEAH...
YOUR FATHER WOULD'VE LOVED TO SEE THIS.
TAKE CARE OF YOURSELF, MOM! AND DON'T FORGET ME.
NO ONE WILL EVER FORGET...
THE FLASH.

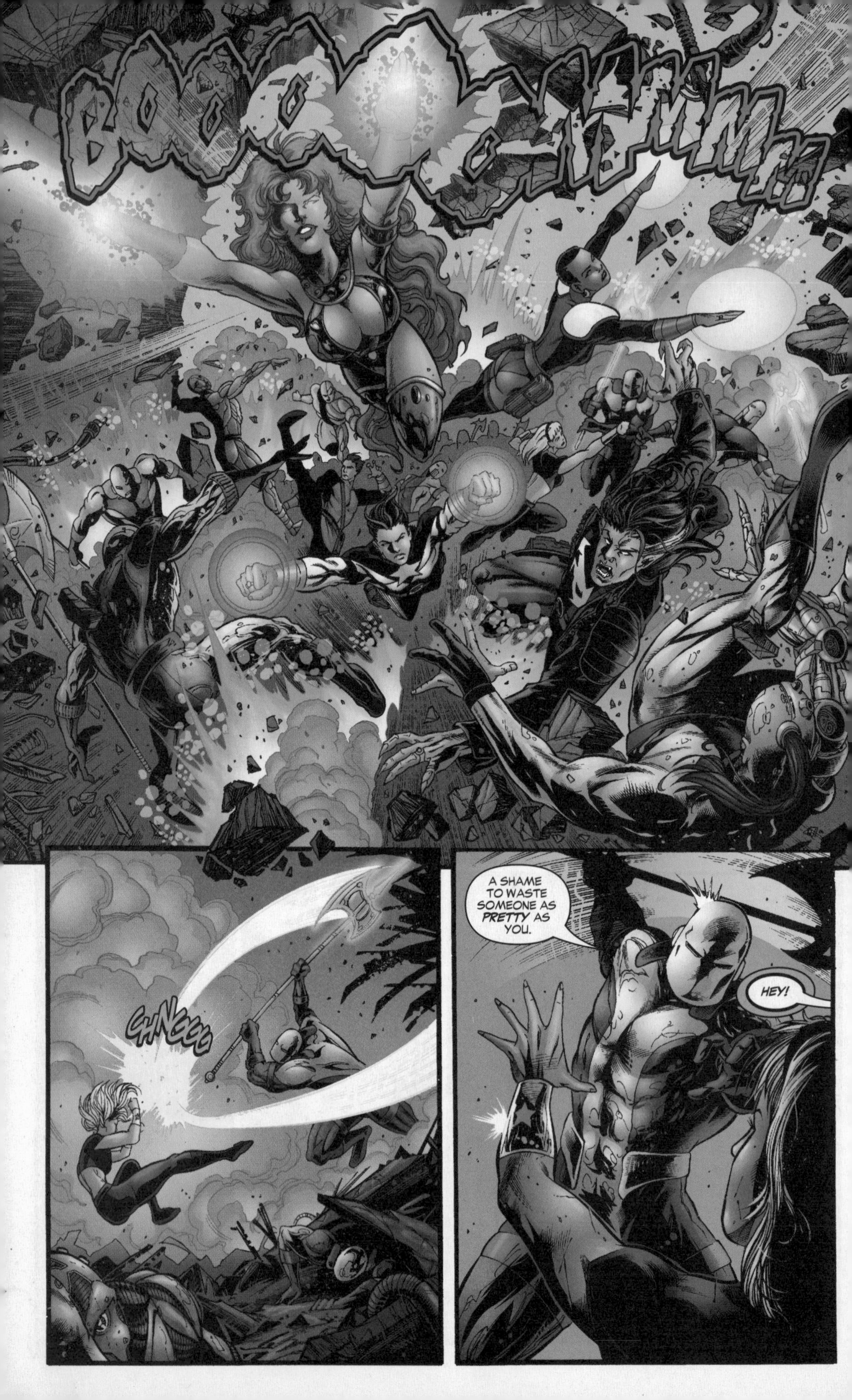
A SHAME TO WASTE SOMEONE AS *PRETTY* AS YOU.
HEY!

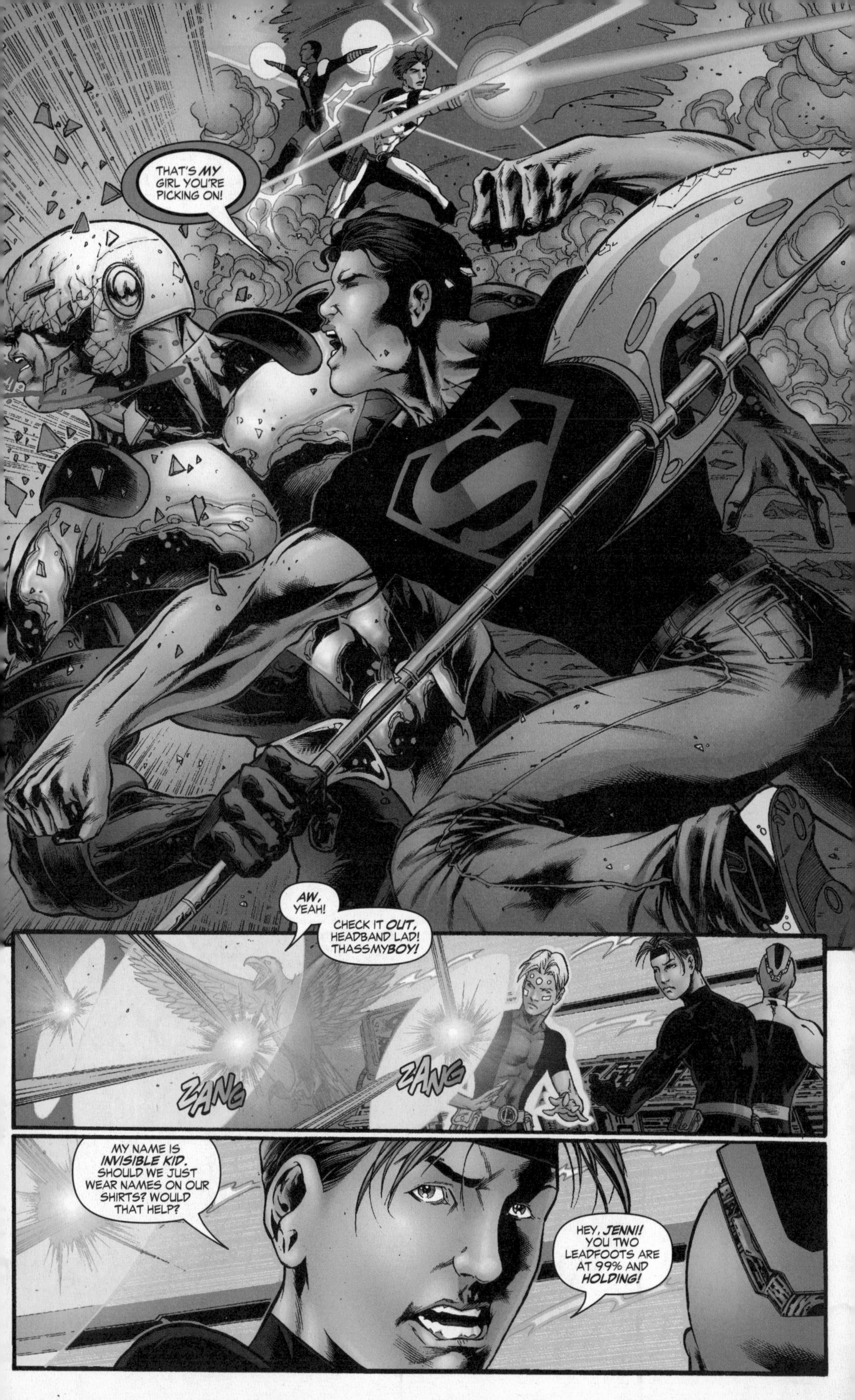
THAT'S MY GIRL YOU'RE PICKING ON!
AW, YEAH!
CHECK IT OUT, HEADBAND LAD! THASSMYBOY!
ZANG
ZANG
MY NAME IS INVISIBLE KID. SHOULD WE JUST WEAR NAMES ON OUR SHIRTS? WOULD THAT HELP?
HEY, JENNI! YOU TWO LEADFOOTS ARE AT 99% AND HOLDING!

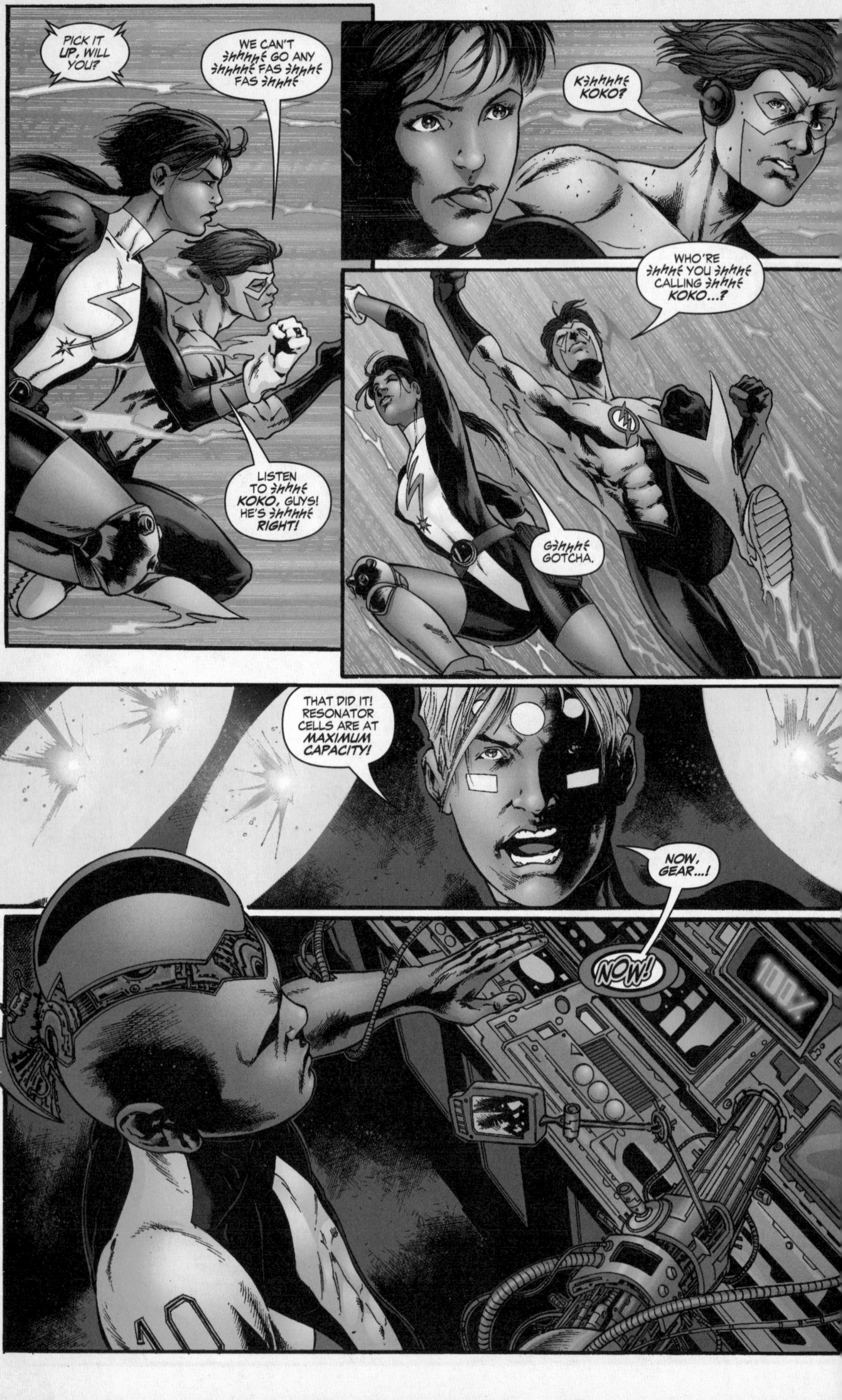
PICK IT UP, WILL YOU?
WE CAN'T hhhh GO ANY hhhh FAS hhhh FAS hhhh
LISTEN TO hhhh KOKO, GUYS! HE'S hhhh RIGHT!
Khhhh KOKO?
WHO'RE hhhh YOU hhhh CALLING hhhh KOKO...?
Ghhhh GOTCHA.
THAT DID IT! RESONATOR CELLS ARE AT MAXIMUM CAPACITY!
NOW, GEAR...!
NOW!
100%

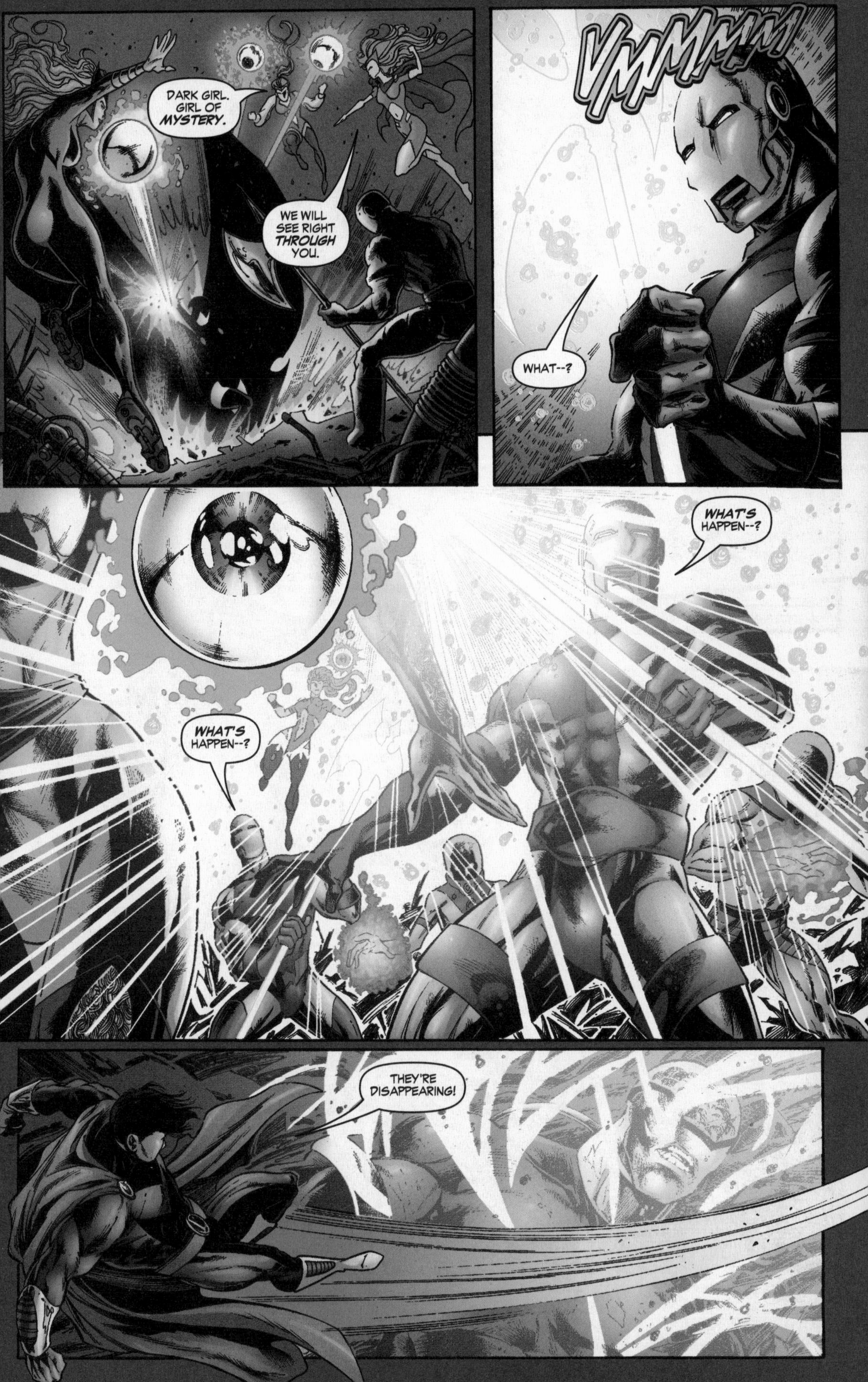
DARK GIRL. GIRL OF MYSTERY.
WE WILL SEE RIGHT THROUGH YOU.
VMMMMM
WHAT--?
WHAT'S HAPPEN--?
WHAT'S HAPPEN--?
THEY'RE DISAPPEARING!

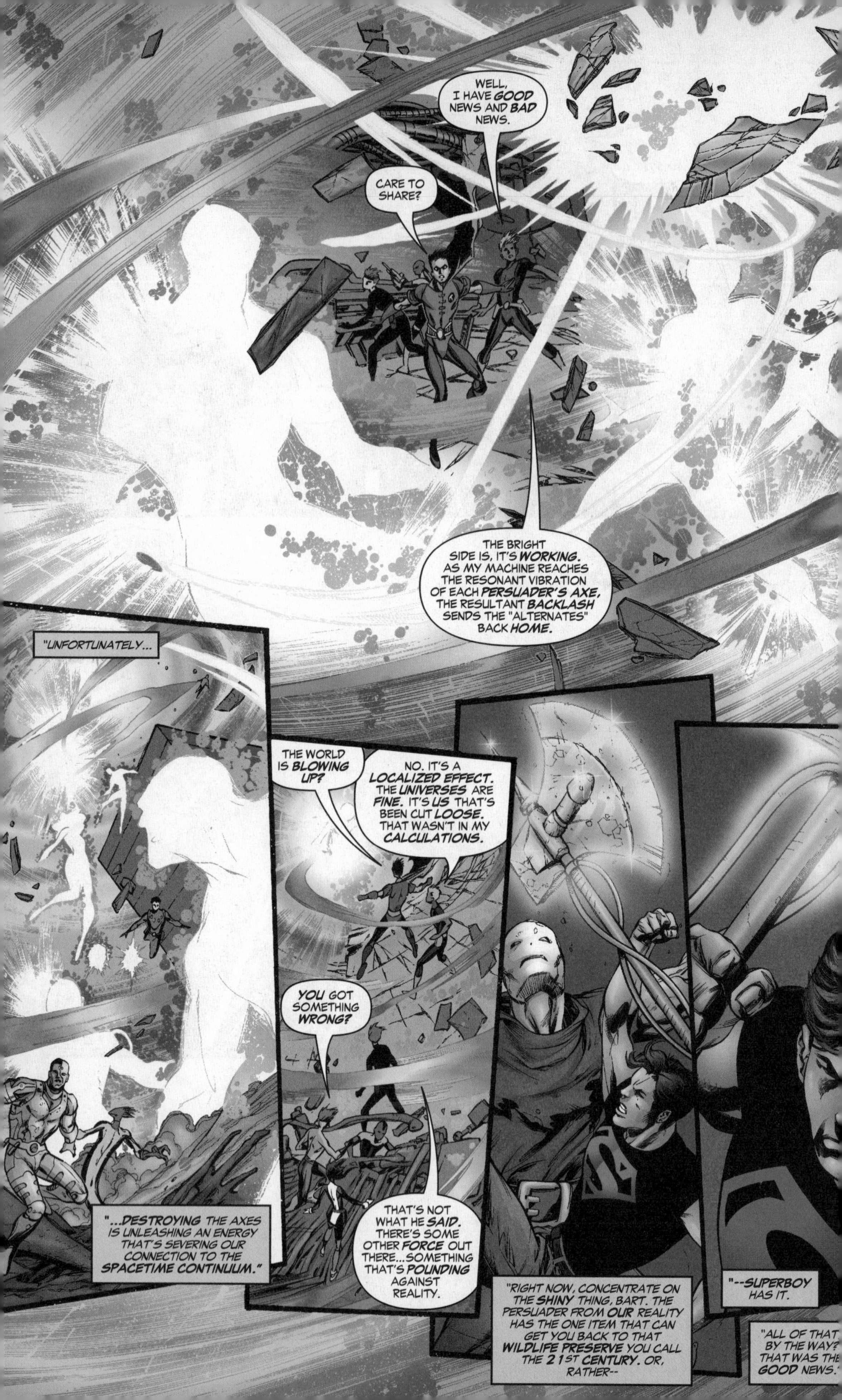
WELL, I HAVE GOOD NEWS AND BAD NEWS.
CARE TO SHARE?
THE BRIGHT SIDE IS, IT'S WORKING. AS MY MACHINE REACHES THE RESONANT VIBRATION OF EACH PERSUADER'S AXE, THE RESULTANT BACKLASH SENDS THE "ALTERNATES" BACK HOME.
"UNFORTUNATELY...
"...DESTROYING THE AXES IS UNLEASHING AN ENERGY THAT'S SEVERING OUR CONNECTION TO THE SPACETIME CONTINUUM."
THE WORLD IS BLOWING UP?
NO. IT'S A LOCALIZED EFFECT. THE UNIVERSES ARE FINE. IT'S US THAT'S BEEN CUT LOOSE. THAT WASN'T IN MY CALCULATIONS.
YOU GOT SOMETHING WRONG?
THAT'S NOT WHAT HE SAID. THERE'S SOME OTHER FORCE OUT THERE...SOMETHING THAT'S POUNDING AGAINST REALITY.
"RIGHT NOW, CONCENTRATE ON THE SHINY THING, BART. THE PERSUADER FROM OUR REALITY HAS THE ONE ITEM THAT CAN GET YOU BACK TO THAT WILDLIFE PRESERVE YOU CALL THE 21ST CENTURY. OR, RATHER--
"--SUPERBOY HAS IT.
"ALL OF THAT BY THE WAY? THAT WAS THE GOOD NEWS.

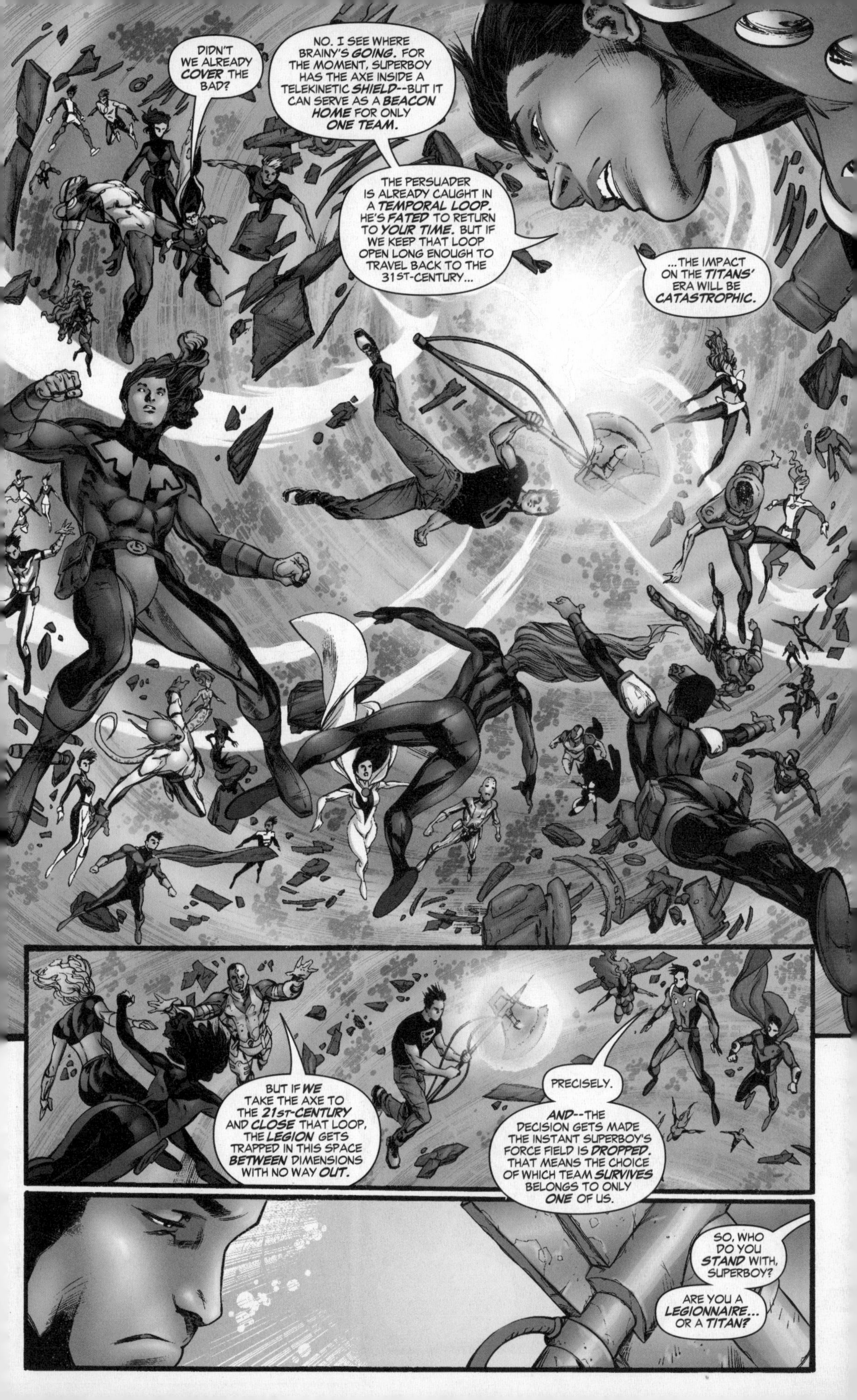

DIDN'T WE ALREADY COVER THE BAD?
NO. I SEE WHERE BRAINY'S GOING. FOR THE MOMENT, SUPERBOY HAS THE AXE INSIDE A TELEKINETIC SHIELD--BUT IT CAN SERVE AS A BEACON HOME FOR ONLY ONE TEAM.
THE PERSUADER IS ALREADY CAUGHT IN A TEMPORAL LOOP. HE'S FATED TO RETURN TO YOUR TIME. BUT IF WE KEEP THAT LOOP OPEN LONG ENOUGH TO TRAVEL BACK TO THE 31ST-CENTURY...
...THE IMPACT ON THE TITANS' ERA WILL BE CATASTROPHIC.
BUT IF WE TAKE THE AXE TO THE 21ST-CENTURY AND CLOSE THAT LOOP, THE LEGION GETS TRAPPED IN THIS SPACE BETWEEN DIMENSIONS WITH NO WAY OUT.
PRECISELY.
AND--THE DECISION GETS MADE THE INSTANT SUPERBOY'S FORCE FIELD IS DROPPED. THAT MEANS THE CHOICE OF WHICH TEAM SURVIVES BELONGS TO ONLY ONE OF US.
SO, WHO DO YOU STAND WITH, SUPERBOY?
ARE YOU A LEGIONNAIRE... OR A TITAN?

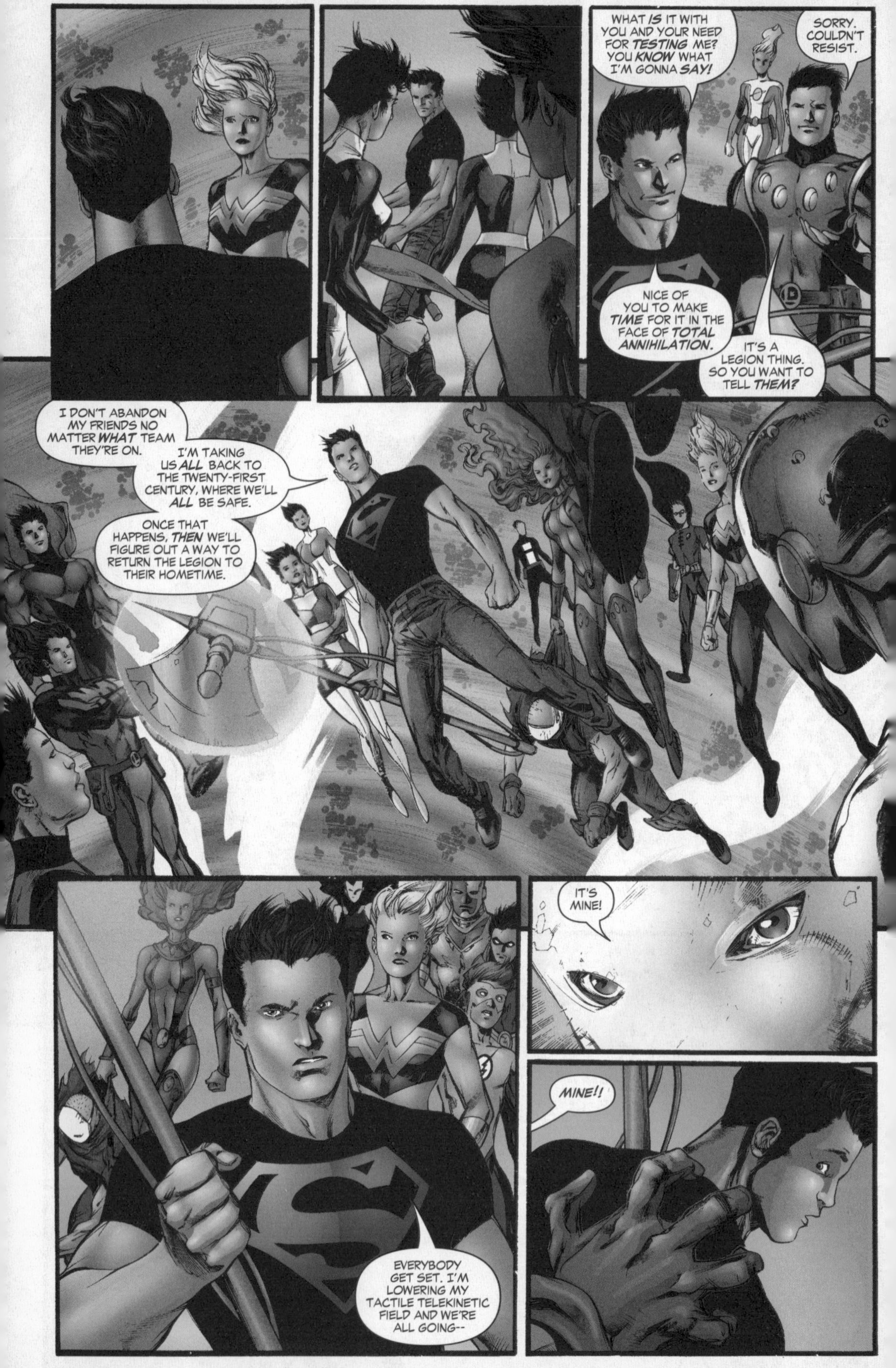
WHAT *IS* IT WITH YOU AND YOUR NEED FOR *TESTING* ME? YOU *KNOW* WHAT I'M GONNA *SAY!*
SORRY. COULDN'T RESIST.
NICE OF YOU TO MAKE *TIME* FOR IT IN THE FACE OF *TOTAL ANNIHILATION.*
IT'S A LEGION THING. SO YOU WANT TO TELL *THEM?*
I DON'T ABANDON MY FRIENDS NO MATTER *WHAT* TEAM THEY'RE ON.
I'M TAKING US *ALL* BACK TO THE TWENTY-FIRST CENTURY, WHERE WE'LL *ALL* BE SAFE.
ONCE THAT HAPPENS, *THEN* WE'LL FIGURE OUT A WAY TO RETURN THE LEGION TO THEIR HOMETIME.
EVERYBODY GET SET. I'M LOWERING MY TACTILE TELEKINETIC FIELD AND WE'RE ALL GOING--
IT'S MINE!
MINE!!

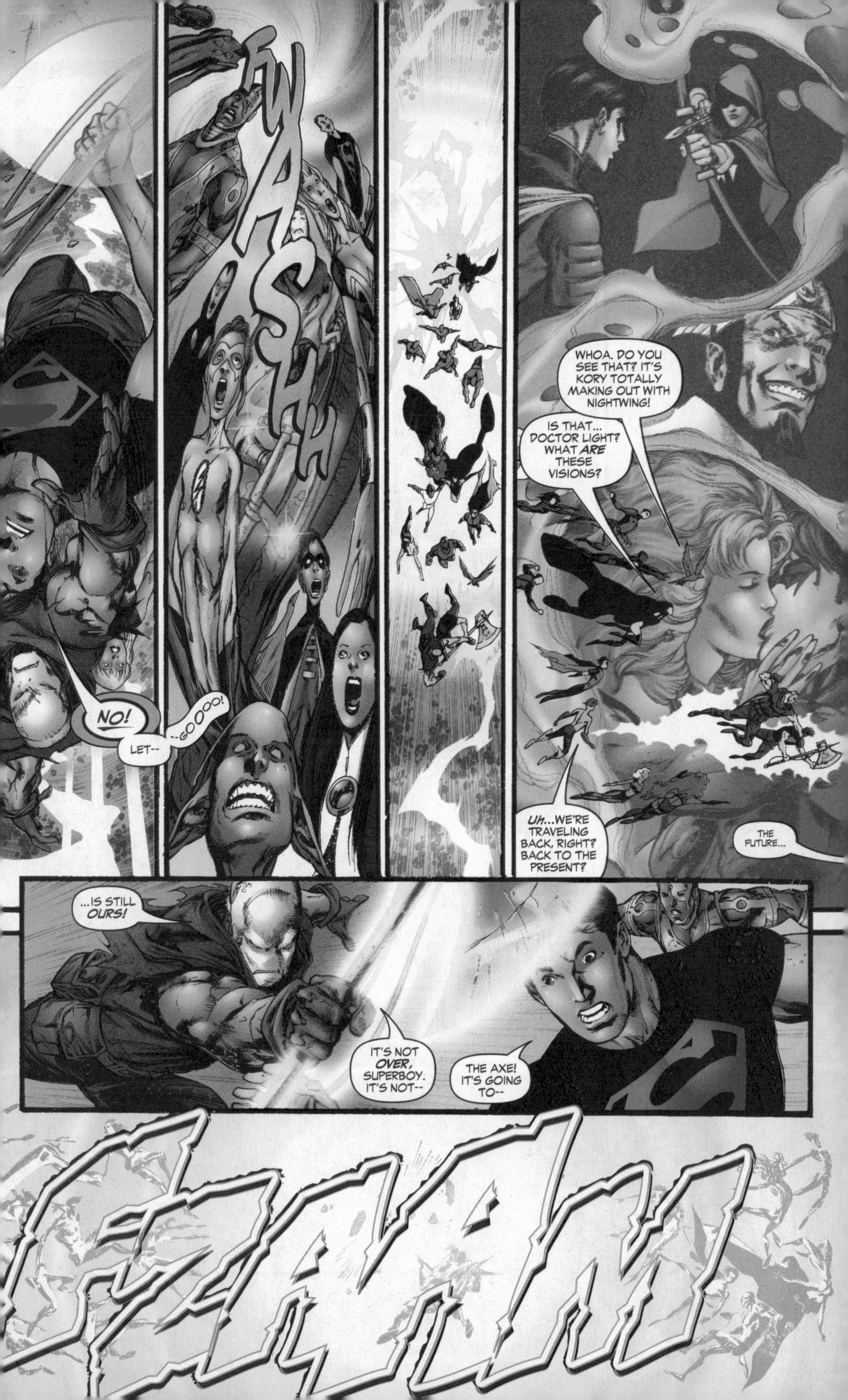
NO!
LET--
--GOOOO!
WHOA. DO YOU SEE THAT? IT'S KORY TOTALLY MAKING OUT WITH NIGHTWING!
IS THAT... DOCTOR LIGHT? WHAT *ARE* THESE VISIONS?
Uh...WE'RE TRAVELING BACK, RIGHT? BACK TO THE PRESENT?
THE FUTURE...
...IS STILL *OURS!*
IT'S NOT *OVER*, SUPERBOY. IT'S NOT--
THE AXE! IT'S GOING TO--

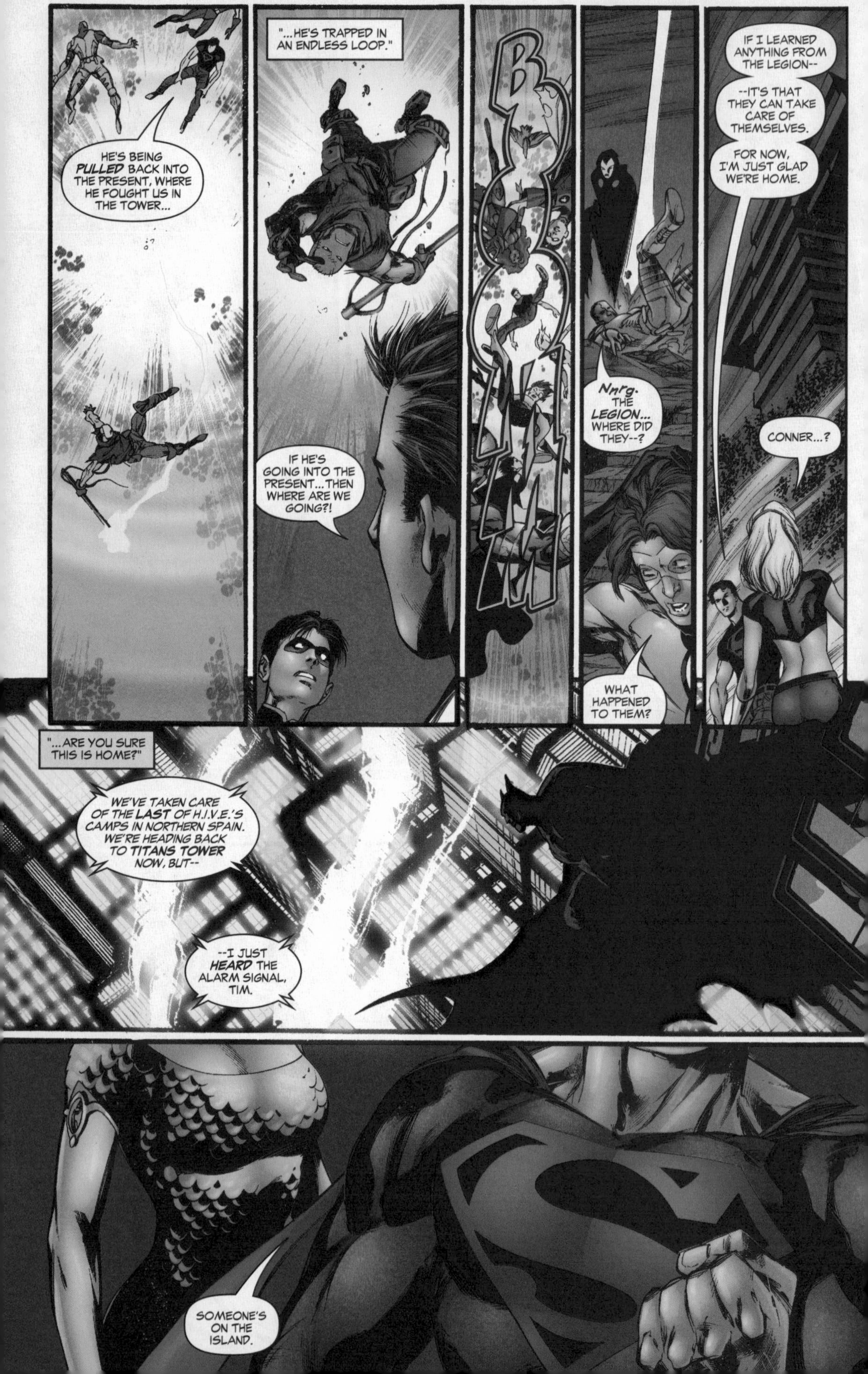
HE'S BEING PULLED BACK INTO THE PRESENT, WHERE HE FOUGHT US IN THE TOWER...
"...HE'S TRAPPED IN AN ENDLESS LOOP."
IF HE'S GOING INTO THE PRESENT...THEN WHERE ARE WE GOING?!
B
Nnrg. THE LEGION... WHERE DID THEY--?
WHAT HAPPENED TO THEM?
IF I LEARNED ANYTHING FROM THE LEGION--
--IT'S THAT THEY CAN TAKE CARE OF THEMSELVES.
FOR NOW, I'M JUST GLAD WE'RE HOME.
CONNER...?
"...ARE YOU SURE THIS IS HOME?"
WE'VE TAKEN CARE OF THE LAST OF H.I.V.E.'S CAMPS IN NORTHERN SPAIN. WE'RE HEADING BACK TO TITANS TOWER NOW, BUT--
--I JUST HEARD THE ALARM SIGNAL, TIM.
SOMEONE'S ON THE ISLAND.

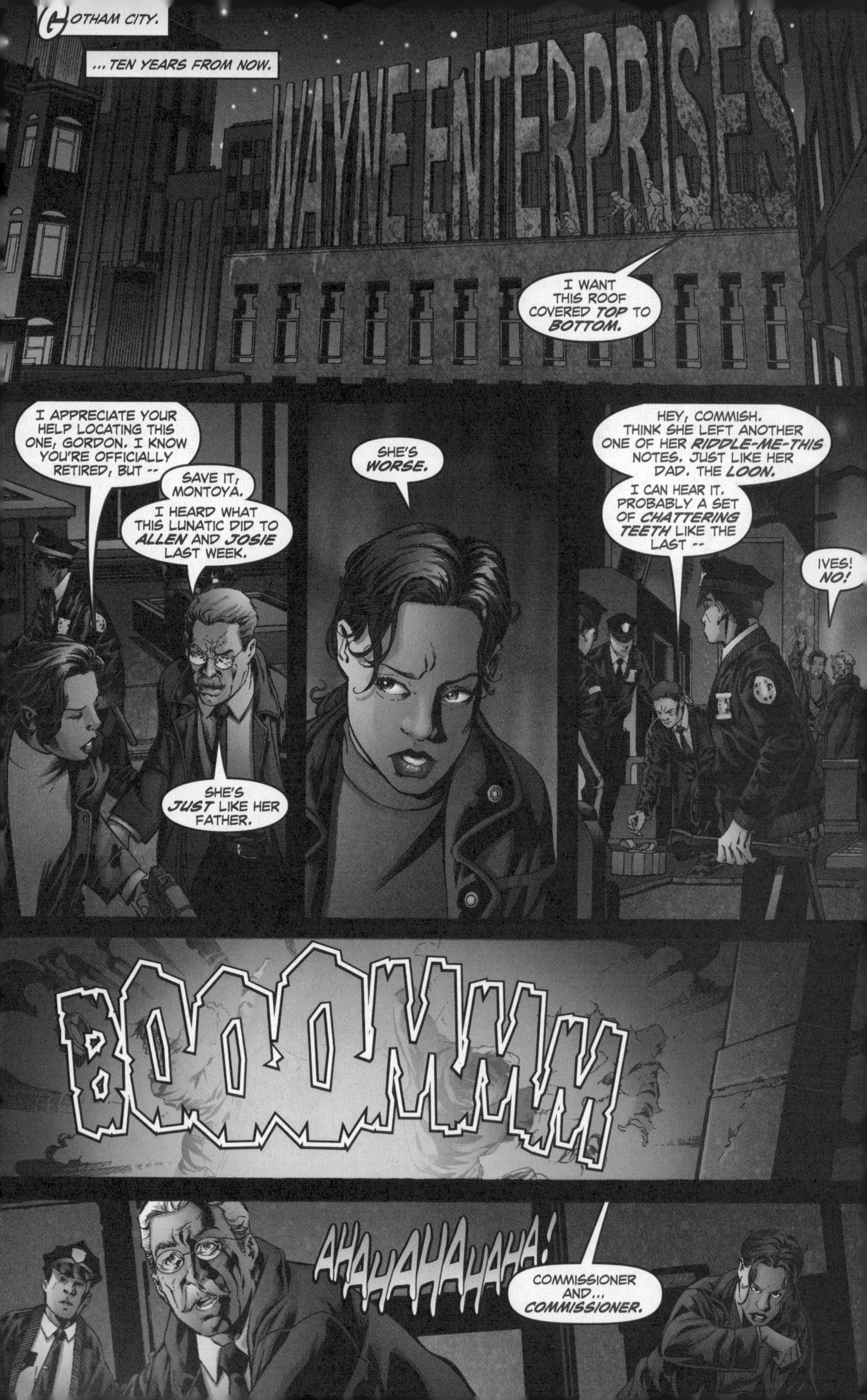
GOTHAM CITY.
...TEN YEARS FROM NOW.
WAYNE ENTERPRISES
I WANT THIS ROOF COVERED TOP TO BOTTOM.
I APPRECIATE YOUR HELP LOCATING THIS ONE, GORDON. I KNOW YOU'RE OFFICIALLY RETIRED, BUT --
SAVE IT, MONTOYA.
I HEARD WHAT THIS LUNATIC DID TO ALLEN AND JOSIE LAST WEEK.
SHE'S JUST LIKE HER FATHER.
SHE'S WORSE.
HEY, COMMISH. THINK SHE LEFT ANOTHER ONE OF HER RIDDLE-ME-THIS NOTES. JUST LIKE HER DAD. THE LOON.
I CAN HEAR IT. PROBABLY A SET OF CHATTERING TEETH LIKE THE LAST --
IVES! NO!
BOOOMMMM
AHAHAHAHAHAHA!
COMMISSIONER AND... COMMISSIONER.

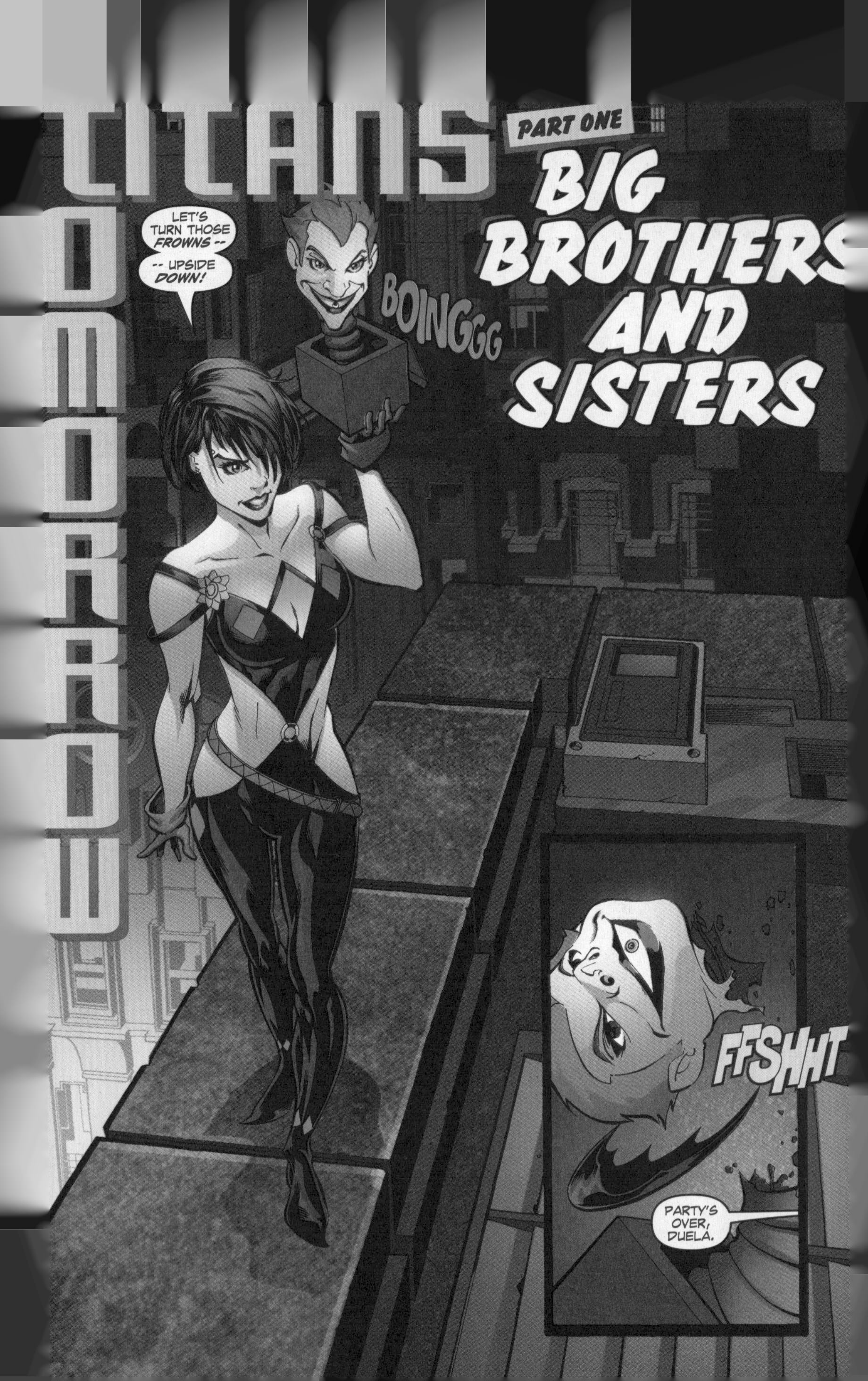
TITANS TOMORROW
PART ONE
BIG BROTHERS AND SISTERS
LET'S TURN THOSE FROWNS --
-- UPSIDE DOWN!
BOINGGG
FFSHHT
PARTY'S OVER, DUELA.

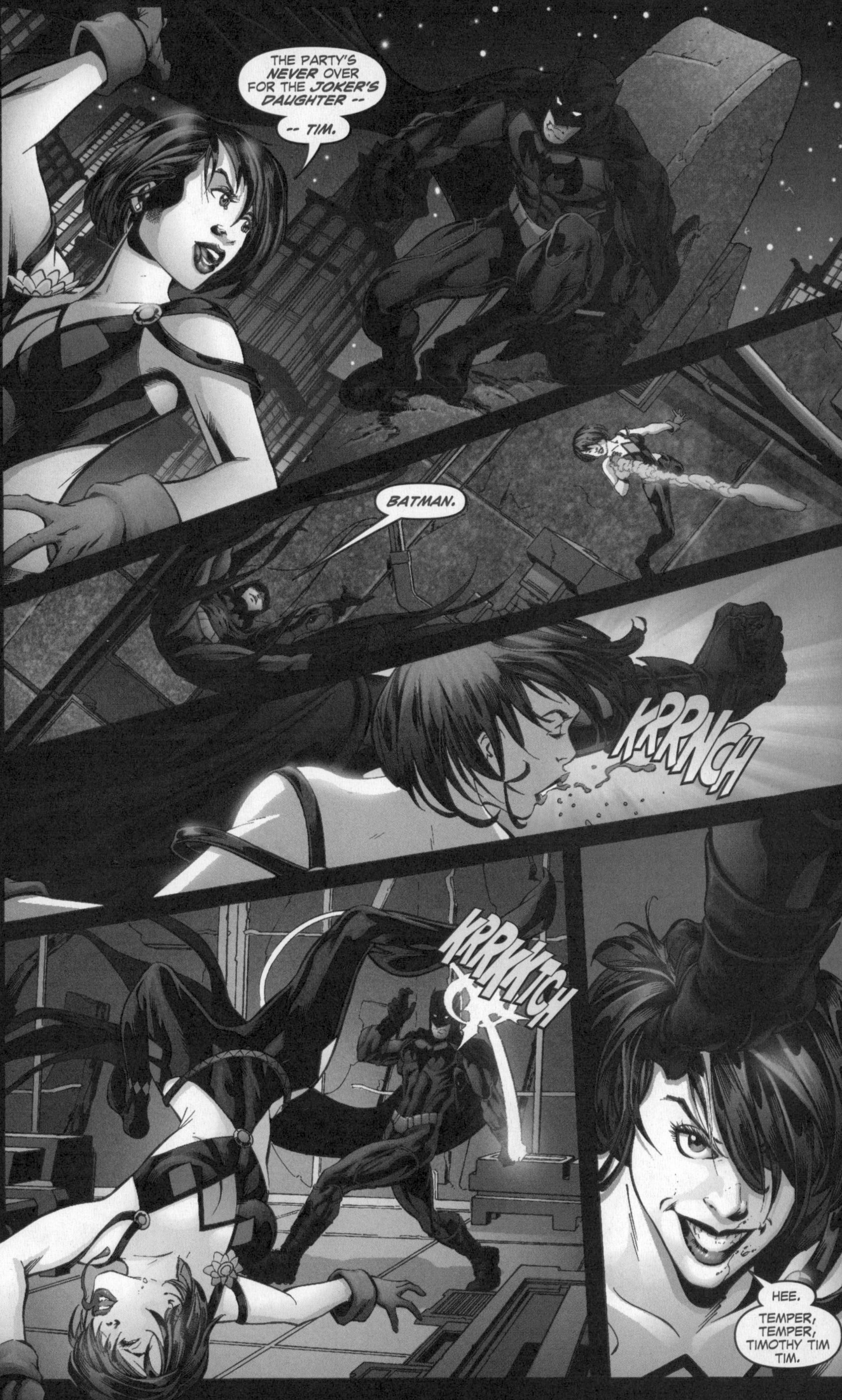
THE PARTY'S *NEVER* OVER FOR THE *JOKER'S DAUGHTER* --
-- *TIM.*
BATMAN.
KRRNCH
KRRKTCH
HEE.
TEMPER, TEMPER, TIMOTHY TIM TIM.

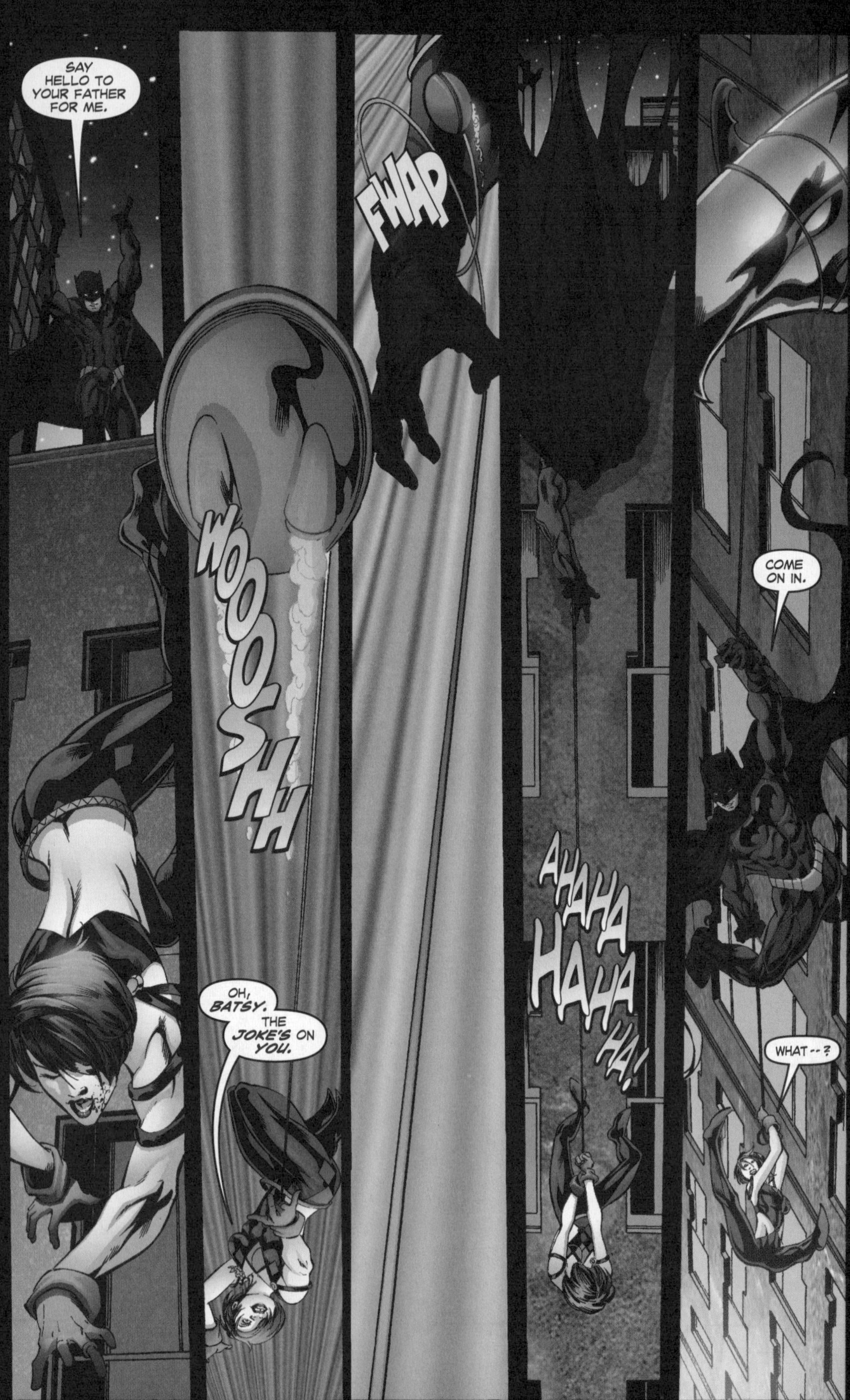
SAY HELLO TO YOUR FATHER FOR ME.
WOOOOSHHH
OH, BATSY. THE JOKE'S ON YOU.
FWAP
AHAHA HAHAHA!
COME ON IN.
WHAT--?

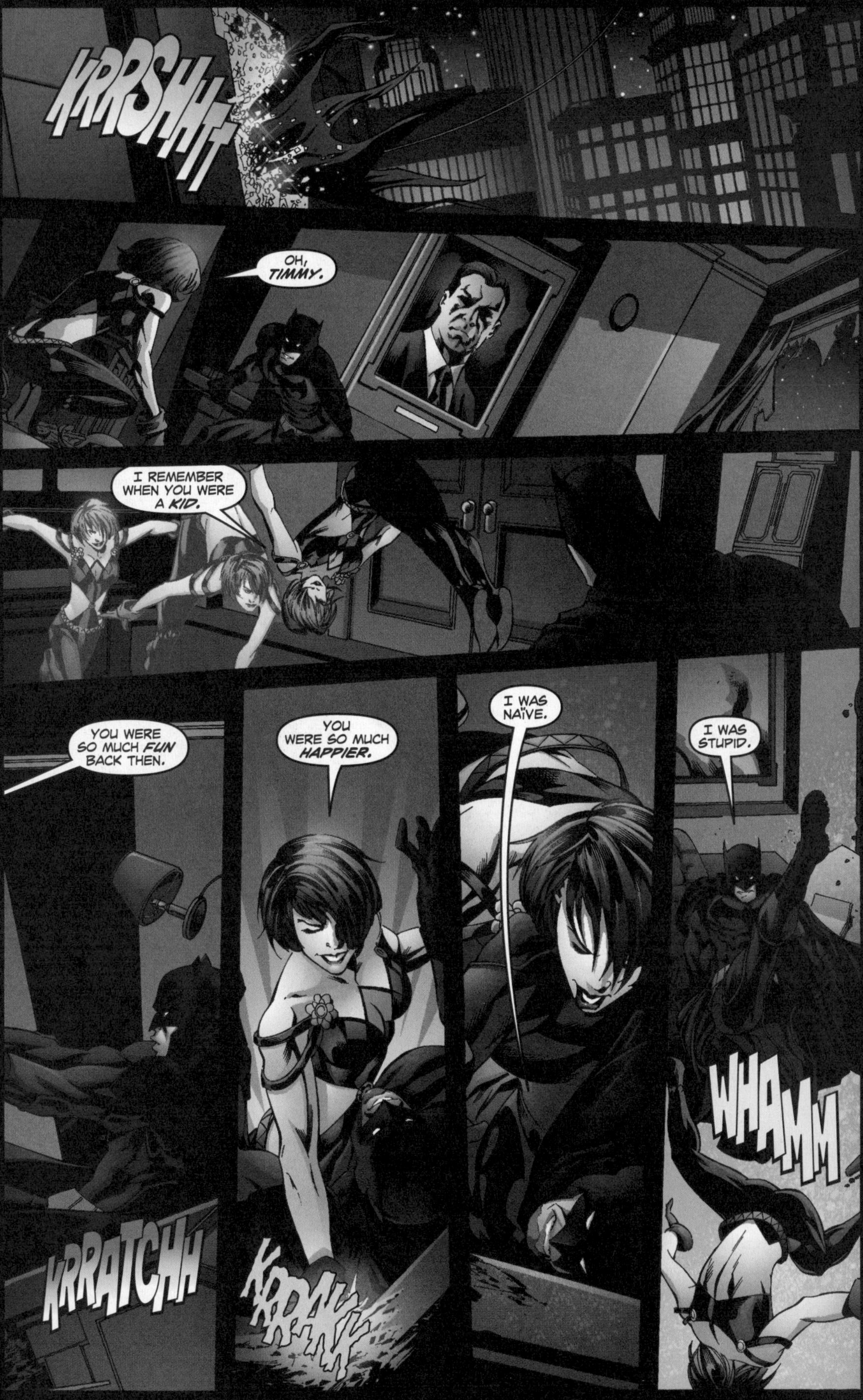
KRRSHHT
OH, TIMMY.
I REMEMBER WHEN YOU WERE A KID.
YOU WERE SO MUCH FUN BACK THEN.
YOU WERE SO MUCH HAPPIER.
I WAS NAÏVE.
I WAS STUPID.
KRRATCHH
KRRAKK
WHAMM

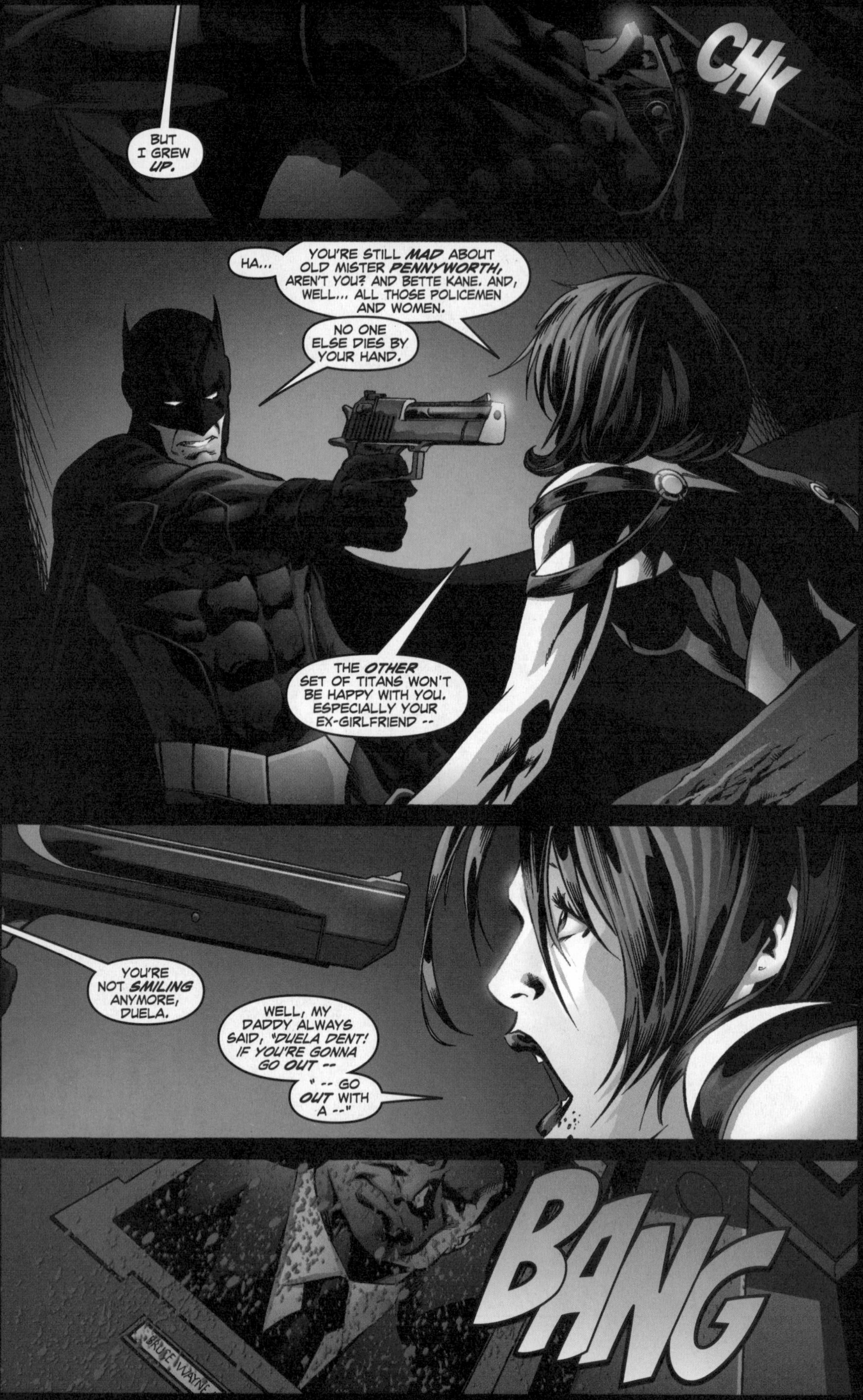
BUT I GREW *UP*.
CHK
HA...
YOU'RE STILL *MAD* ABOUT OLD MISTER *PENNYWORTH,* AREN'T YOU? AND BETTE KANE. AND, WELL... ALL THOSE POLICEMEN AND WOMEN.
NO ONE ELSE DIES BY YOUR HAND.
THE *OTHER* SET OF TITANS WON'T BE HAPPY WITH YOU. ESPECIALLY YOUR EX-GIRLFRIEND --
YOU'RE NOT *SMILING* ANYMORE, DUELA.
WELL, MY DADDY ALWAYS SAID, "*DUELA DENT! IF YOU'RE GONNA GO OUT* --
" -- GO *OUT* WITH A --"
BANG

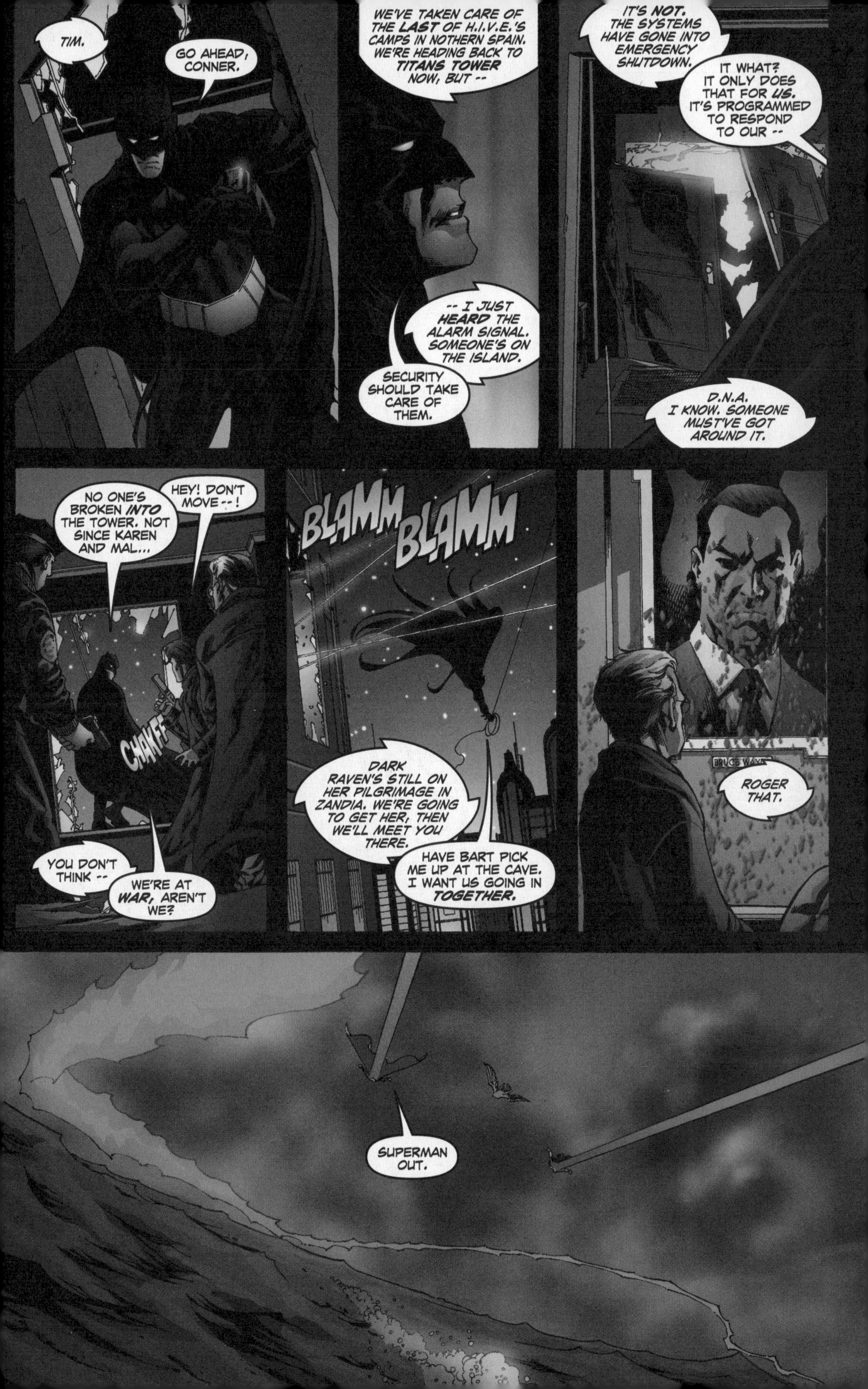
TIM.
GO AHEAD, CONNER.
WE'VE TAKEN CARE OF THE LAST OF H.I.V.E.'S CAMPS IN NOTHERN SPAIN. WE'RE HEADING BACK TO TITANS TOWER NOW, BUT --
-- I JUST HEARD THE ALARM SIGNAL. SOMEONE'S ON THE ISLAND.
SECURITY SHOULD TAKE CARE OF THEM.
IT'S NOT. THE SYSTEMS HAVE GONE INTO EMERGENCY SHUTDOWN.
IT WHAT? IT ONLY DOES THAT FOR US. IT'S PROGRAMMED TO RESPOND TO OUR --
D.N.A. I KNOW. SOMEONE MUST'VE GOT AROUND IT.
NO ONE'S BROKEN INTO THE TOWER. NOT SINCE KAREN AND MAL...
HEY! DON'T MOVE --!
CHAKFF
YOU DON'T THINK --
WE'RE AT WAR, AREN'T WE?
BLAMM BLAMM
DARK RAVEN'S STILL ON HER PILGRIMAGE IN ZANDIA. WE'RE GOING TO GET HER, THEN WE'LL MEET YOU THERE.
HAVE BART PICK ME UP AT THE CAVE. I WANT US GOING IN TOGETHER.
ROGER THAT.
SUPERMAN OUT.

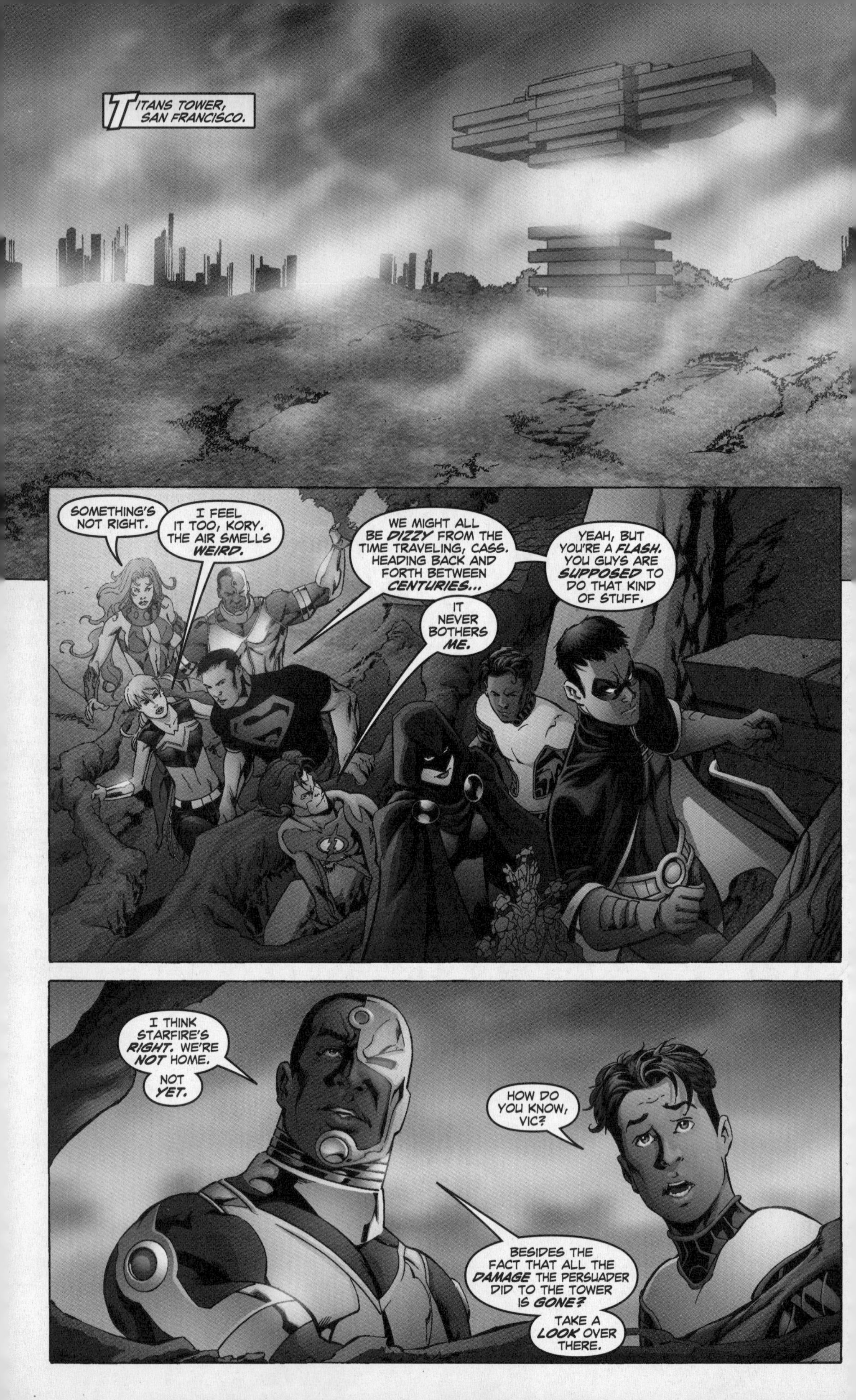
TITANS TOWER, SAN FRANCISCO.
SOMETHING'S NOT RIGHT.
I FEEL IT TOO, KORY. THE AIR SMELLS WEIRD.
WE MIGHT ALL BE DIZZY FROM THE TIME TRAVELING, CASS. HEADING BACK AND FORTH BETWEEN CENTURIES...
YEAH, BUT YOU'RE A FLASH. YOU GUYS ARE SUPPOSED TO DO THAT KIND OF STUFF.
IT NEVER BOTHERS ME.
I THINK STARFIRE'S RIGHT. WE'RE NOT HOME.
NOT YET.
HOW DO YOU KNOW, VIC?
BESIDES THE FACT THAT ALL THE DAMAGE THE PERSUADER DID TO THE TOWER IS GONE?
TAKE A LOOK OVER THERE.

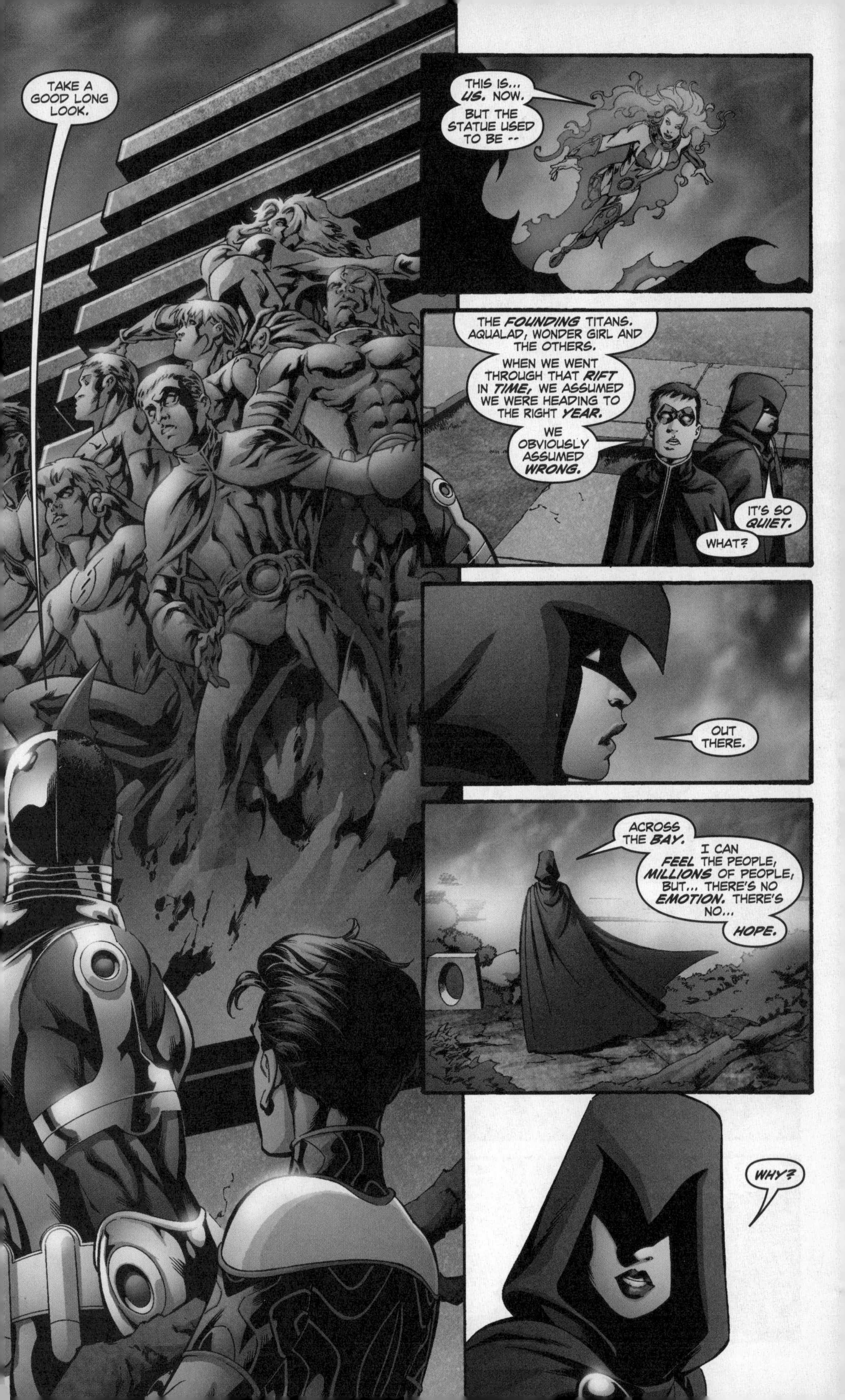

TAKE A GOOD LONG LOOK.
THIS IS... *US.* NOW.
BUT THE STATUE USED TO BE --
THE *FOUNDING* TITANS. AQUALAD, WONDER GIRL AND THE OTHERS.
WHEN WE WENT THROUGH THAT *RIFT* IN *TIME,* WE ASSUMED WE WERE HEADING TO THE RIGHT *YEAR.*
WE OBVIOUSLY ASSUMED *WRONG.*
IT'S SO *QUIET.*
WHAT?
OUT THERE.
ACROSS THE *BAY.*
I CAN *FEEL* THE PEOPLE, *MILLIONS* OF PEOPLE, BUT... THERE'S NO *EMOTION.* THERE'S NO...
HOPE.
WHY?

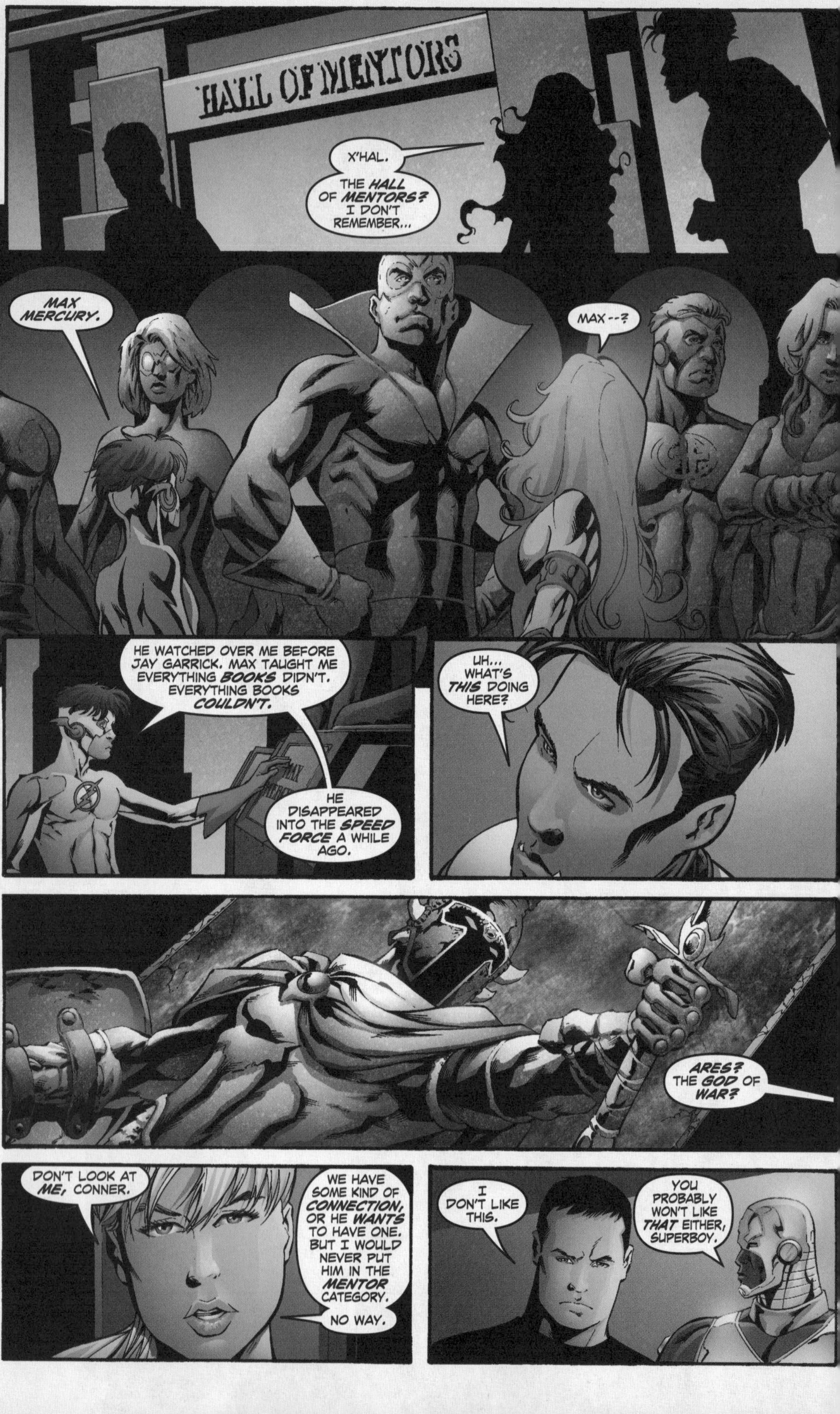
HALL OF MENTORS
X'HAL.
THE HALL OF MENTORS? I DON'T REMEMBER...
MAX MERCURY.
MAX--?
HE WATCHED OVER ME BEFORE JAY GARRICK. MAX TAUGHT ME EVERYTHING BOOKS DIDN'T. EVERYTHING BOOKS COULDN'T.
HE DISAPPEARED INTO THE SPEED FORCE A WHILE AGO.
UH... WHAT'S THIS DOING HERE?
ARES? THE GOD OF WAR?
DON'T LOOK AT ME, CONNER.
WE HAVE SOME KIND OF CONNECTION, OR HE WANTS TO HAVE ONE. BUT I WOULD NEVER PUT HIM IN THE MENTOR CATEGORY.
NO WAY.
I DON'T LIKE THIS.
YOU PROBABLY WON'T LIKE THAT EITHER, SUPERBOY.

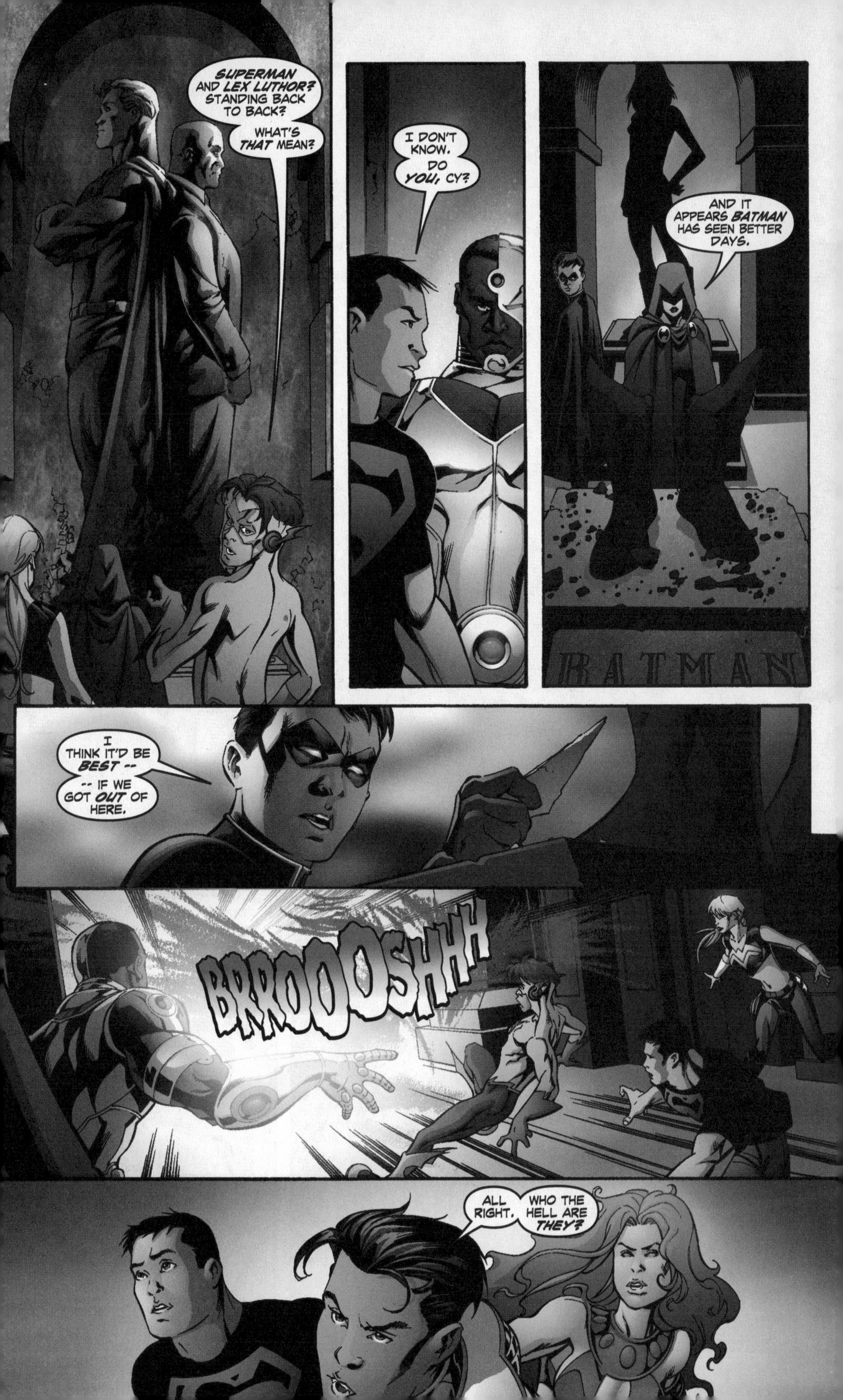
SUPERMAN AND LEX LUTHOR? STANDING BACK TO BACK?
WHAT'S THAT MEAN?
I DON'T KNOW.
DO YOU, CY?
AND IT APPEARS BATMAN HAS SEEN BETTER DAYS.
BATMAN
I THINK IT'D BE BEST --
-- IF WE GOT OUT OF HERE.
BRROOOSHHH
ALL RIGHT.
WHO THE HELL ARE THEY?

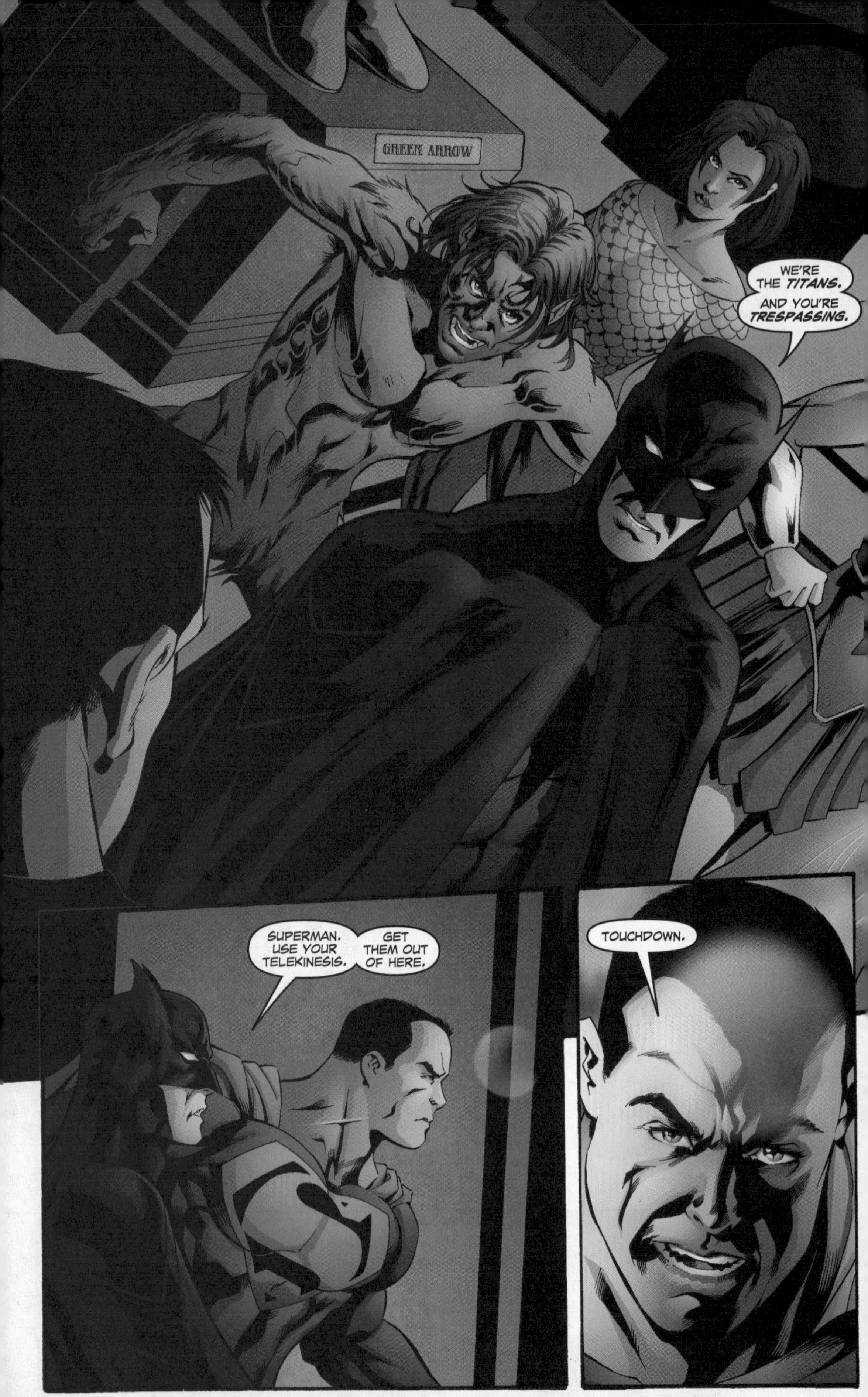
GREEN ARROW
WE'RE THE *TITANS.*
AND YOU'RE *TRESPASSING.*
SUPERMAN. USE YOUR TELEKINESIS.
GET THEM OUT OF HERE.
TOUCHDOWN.

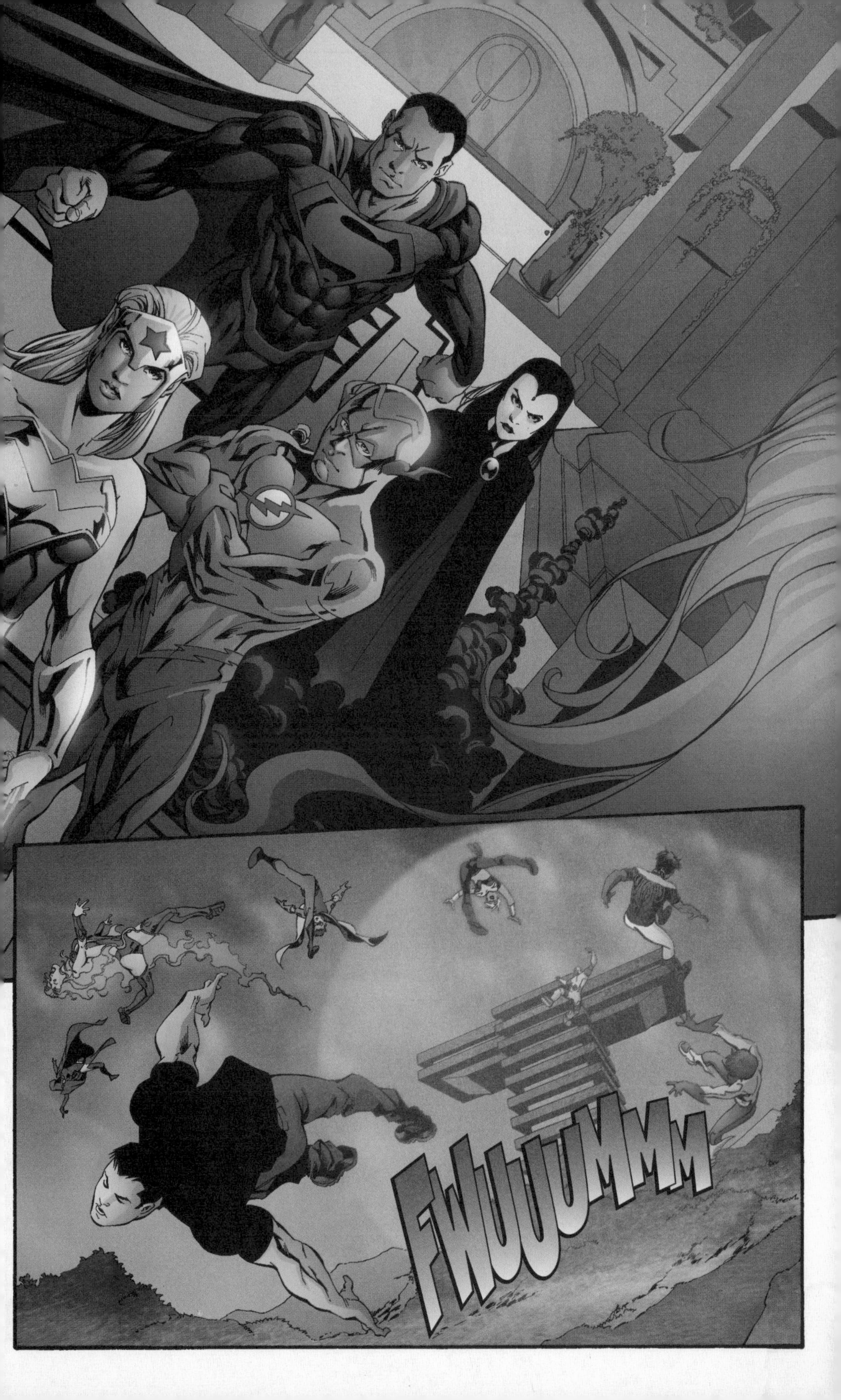
FWUUUMMM

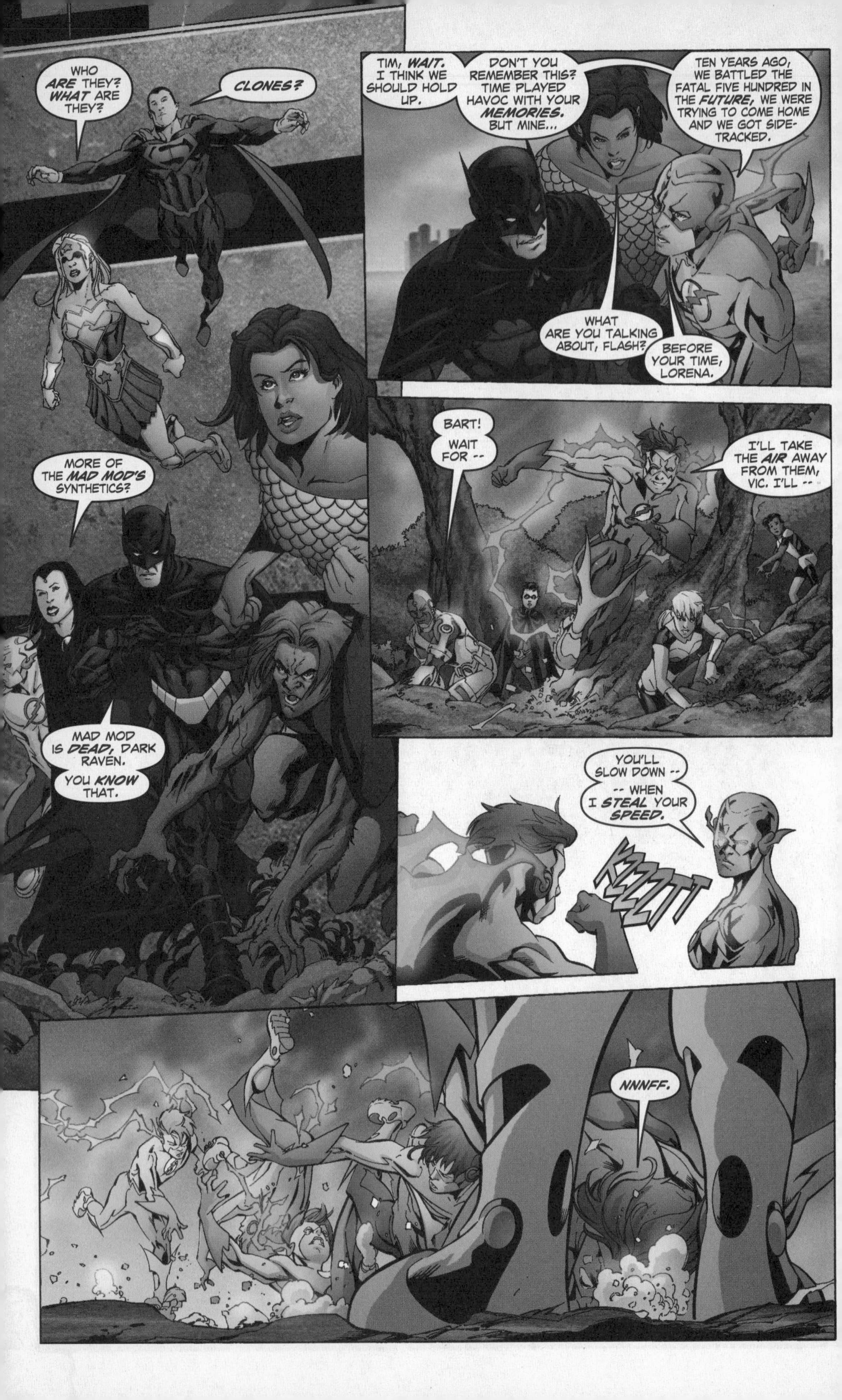
WHO ARE THEY? WHAT ARE THEY?
CLONES?
MORE OF THE MAD MOD'S SYNTHETICS?
MAD MOD IS DEAD, DARK RAVEN.
YOU KNOW THAT.
TIM, WAIT. I THINK WE SHOULD HOLD UP.
DON'T YOU REMEMBER THIS? TIME PLAYED HAVOC WITH YOUR MEMORIES. BUT MINE...
TEN YEARS AGO, WE BATTLED THE FATAL FIVE HUNDRED IN THE FUTURE, WE WERE TRYING TO COME HOME AND WE GOT SIDE-TRACKED.
WHAT ARE YOU TALKING ABOUT, FLASH?
BEFORE YOUR TIME, LORENA.
BART! WAIT FOR --
I'LL TAKE THE AIR AWAY FROM THEM, VIC. I'LL --
YOU'LL SLOW DOWN --
-- WHEN I STEAL YOUR SPEED.
KZZZTT
NNNFF.

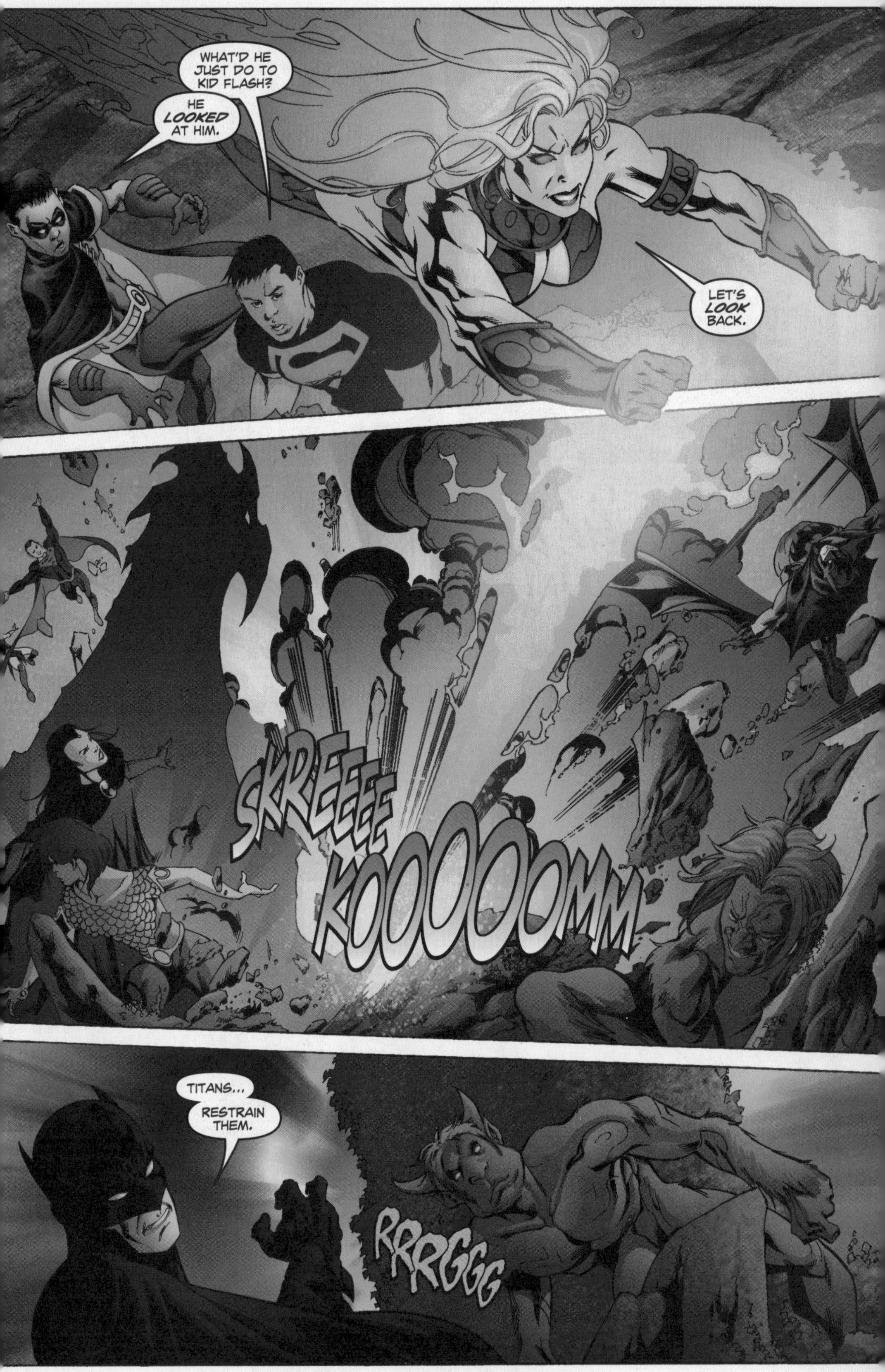
WHAT'D HE JUST DO TO KID FLASH?
HE LOOKED AT HIM.
LET'S LOOK BACK.
SKREEEE
KOOOOOMM
TITANS... RESTRAIN THEM.
RRRGGG

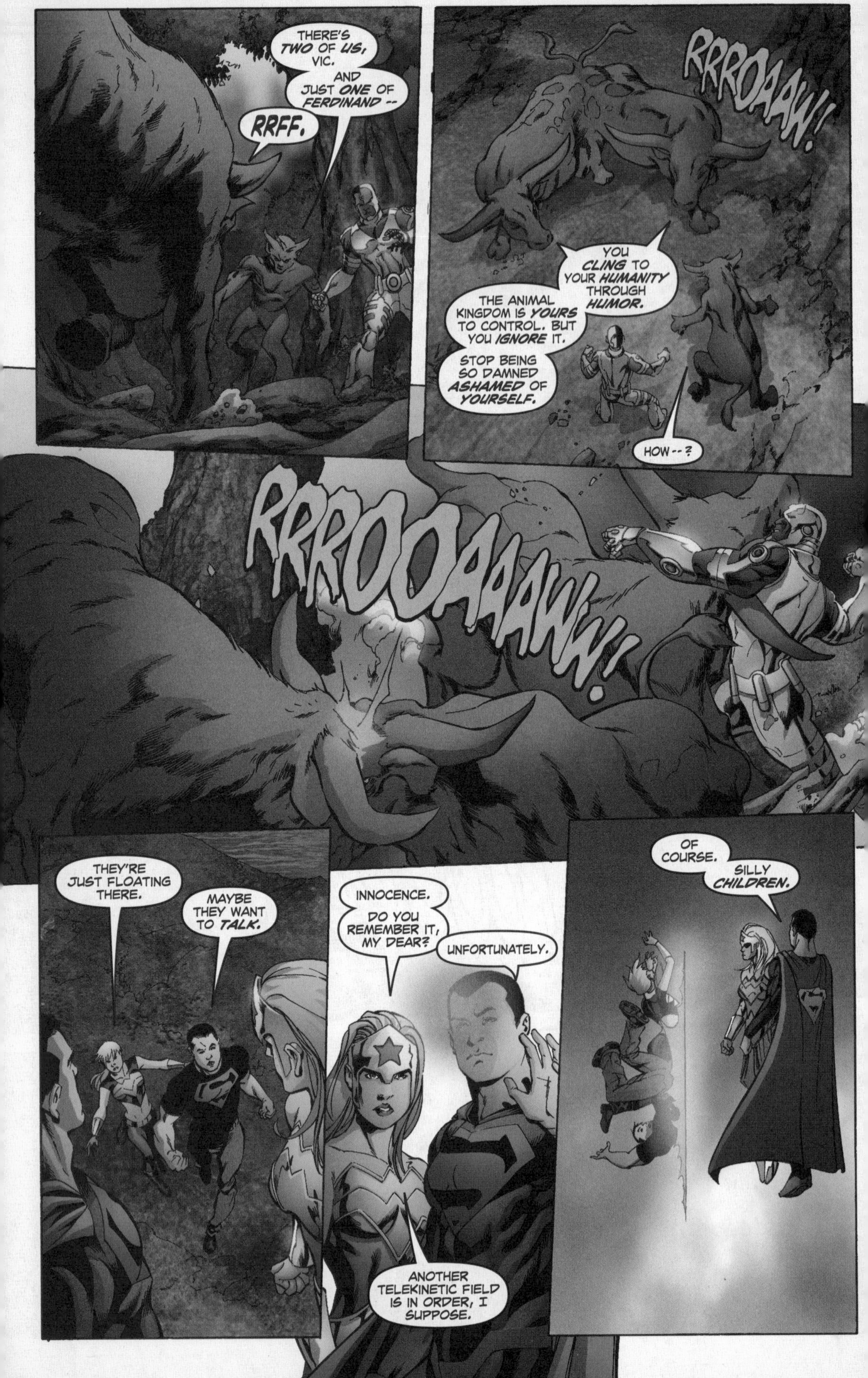
THERE'S TWO OF US, VIC.
AND JUST ONE OF FERDINAND --
RRFF.
RRROAAW!!
YOU CLING TO YOUR HUMANITY THROUGH HUMOR.
THE ANIMAL KINGDOM IS YOURS TO CONTROL. BUT YOU IGNORE IT.
STOP BEING SO DAMNED ASHAMED OF YOURSELF.
HOW -- ?
RRROOAAAWW!!
THEY'RE JUST FLOATING THERE.
MAYBE THEY WANT TO TALK.
INNOCENCE.
DO YOU REMEMBER IT, MY DEAR?
UNFORTUNATELY.
ANOTHER TELEKINETIC FIELD IS IN ORDER, I SUPPOSE.
OF COURSE.
SILLY CHILDREN.

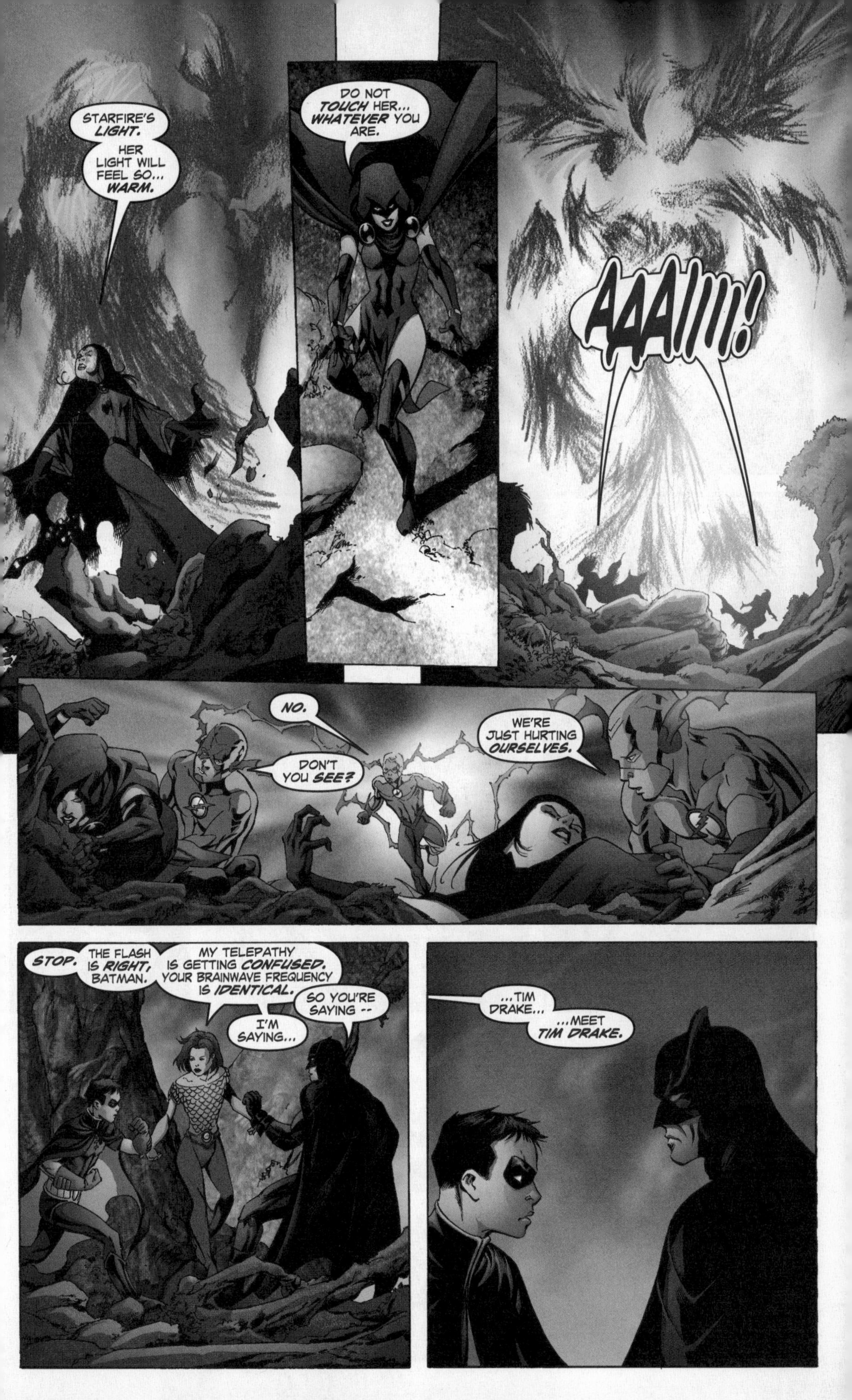

STARFIRE'S LIGHT.
HER LIGHT WILL FEEL SO... WARM.
DO NOT TOUCH HER... WHATEVER YOU ARE.
AAAIIIII!
NO.
DON'T YOU SEE?
WE'RE JUST HURTING OURSELVES.
STOP.
THE FLASH IS RIGHT, BATMAN.
MY TELEPATHY IS GETTING CONFUSED. YOUR BRAINWAVE FREQUENCY IS IDENTICAL.
SO YOU'RE SAYING --
I'M SAYING...
...TIM DRAKE...
...MEET TIM DRAKE.

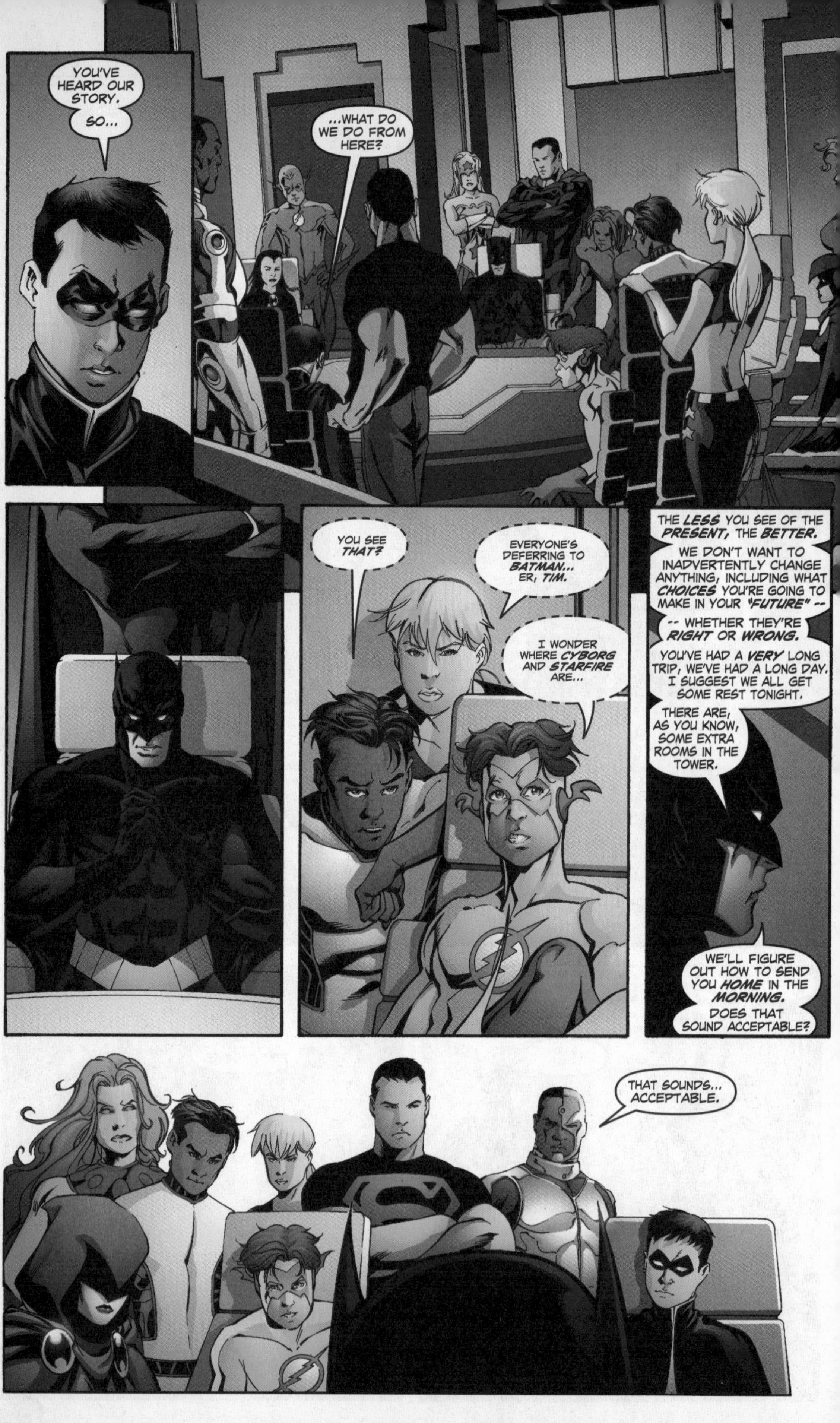
YOU'VE HEARD OUR STORY.
SO...
...WHAT DO WE DO FROM HERE?
YOU SEE THAT?
EVERYONE'S DEFERRING TO BATMAN... ER, TIM.
I WONDER WHERE CYBORG AND STARFIRE ARE...
THE LESS YOU SEE OF THE PRESENT, THE BETTER.
WE DON'T WANT TO INADVERTENTLY CHANGE ANYTHING, INCLUDING WHAT CHOICES YOU'RE GOING TO MAKE IN YOUR "FUTURE" --
-- WHETHER THEY'RE RIGHT OR WRONG.
YOU'VE HAD A VERY LONG TRIP, WE'VE HAD A LONG DAY. I SUGGEST WE ALL GET SOME REST TONIGHT.
THERE ARE, AS YOU KNOW, SOME EXTRA ROOMS IN THE TOWER.
WE'LL FIGURE OUT HOW TO SEND YOU HOME IN THE MORNING.
DOES THAT SOUND ACCEPTABLE?
THAT SOUNDS... ACCEPTABLE.

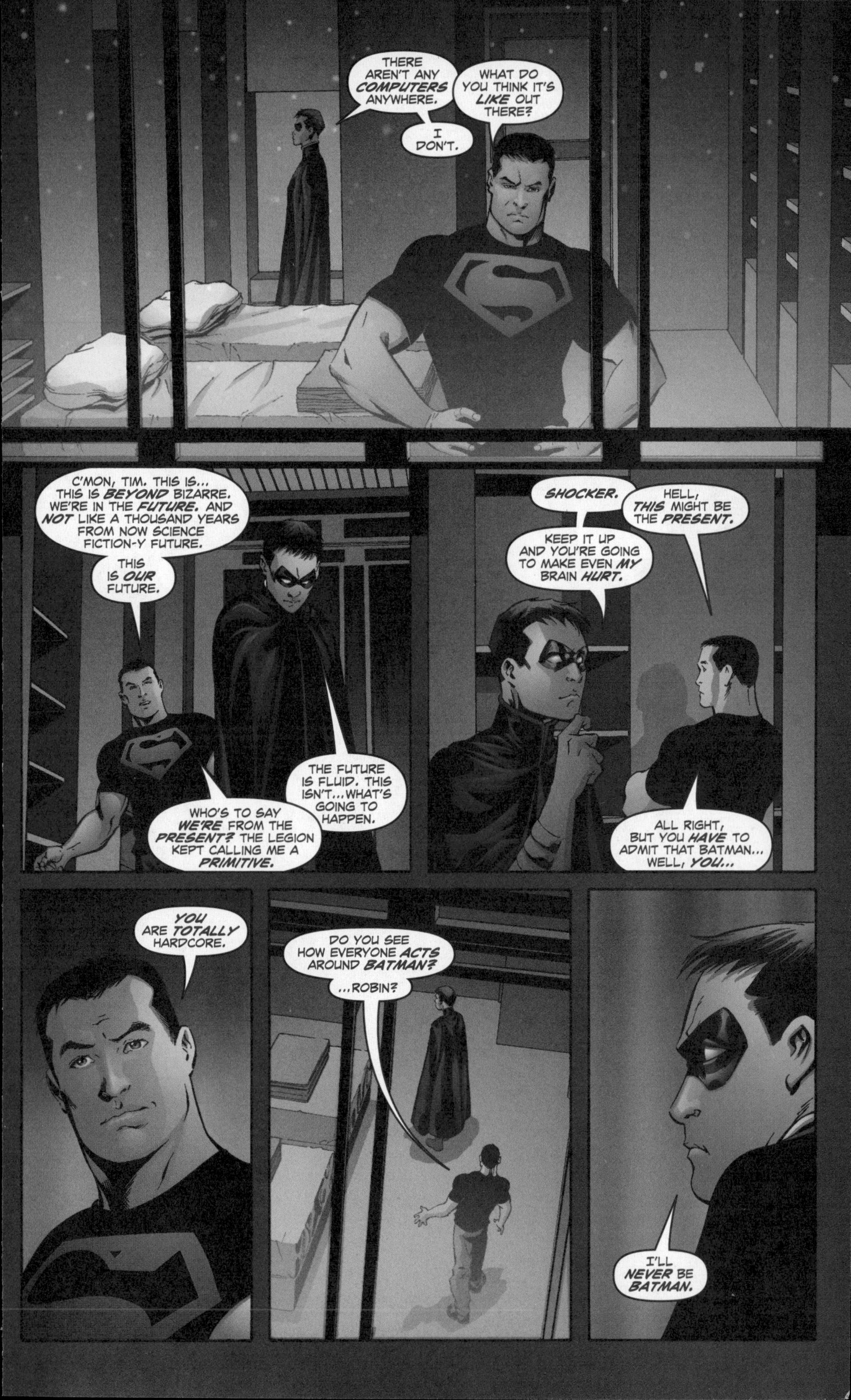
THERE AREN'T ANY COMPUTERS ANYWHERE.
WHAT DO YOU THINK IT'S LIKE OUT THERE?
I DON'T.
C'MON, TIM. THIS IS... THIS IS BEYOND BIZARRE. WE'RE IN THE FUTURE. AND NOT LIKE A THOUSAND YEARS FROM NOW SCIENCE FICTION-Y FUTURE.
THIS IS OUR FUTURE.
THE FUTURE IS FLUID. THIS ISN'T...WHAT'S GOING TO HAPPEN.
WHO'S TO SAY WE'RE FROM THE PRESENT? THE LEGION KEPT CALLING ME A PRIMITIVE.
HELL, THIS MIGHT BE THE PRESENT.
SHOCKER.
KEEP IT UP AND YOU'RE GOING TO MAKE EVEN MY BRAIN HURT.
ALL RIGHT, BUT YOU HAVE TO ADMIT THAT BATMAN... WELL, YOU...
YOU ARE TOTALLY HARDCORE.
DO YOU SEE HOW EVERYONE ACTS AROUND BATMAN?
...ROBIN?
I'LL NEVER BE BATMAN.

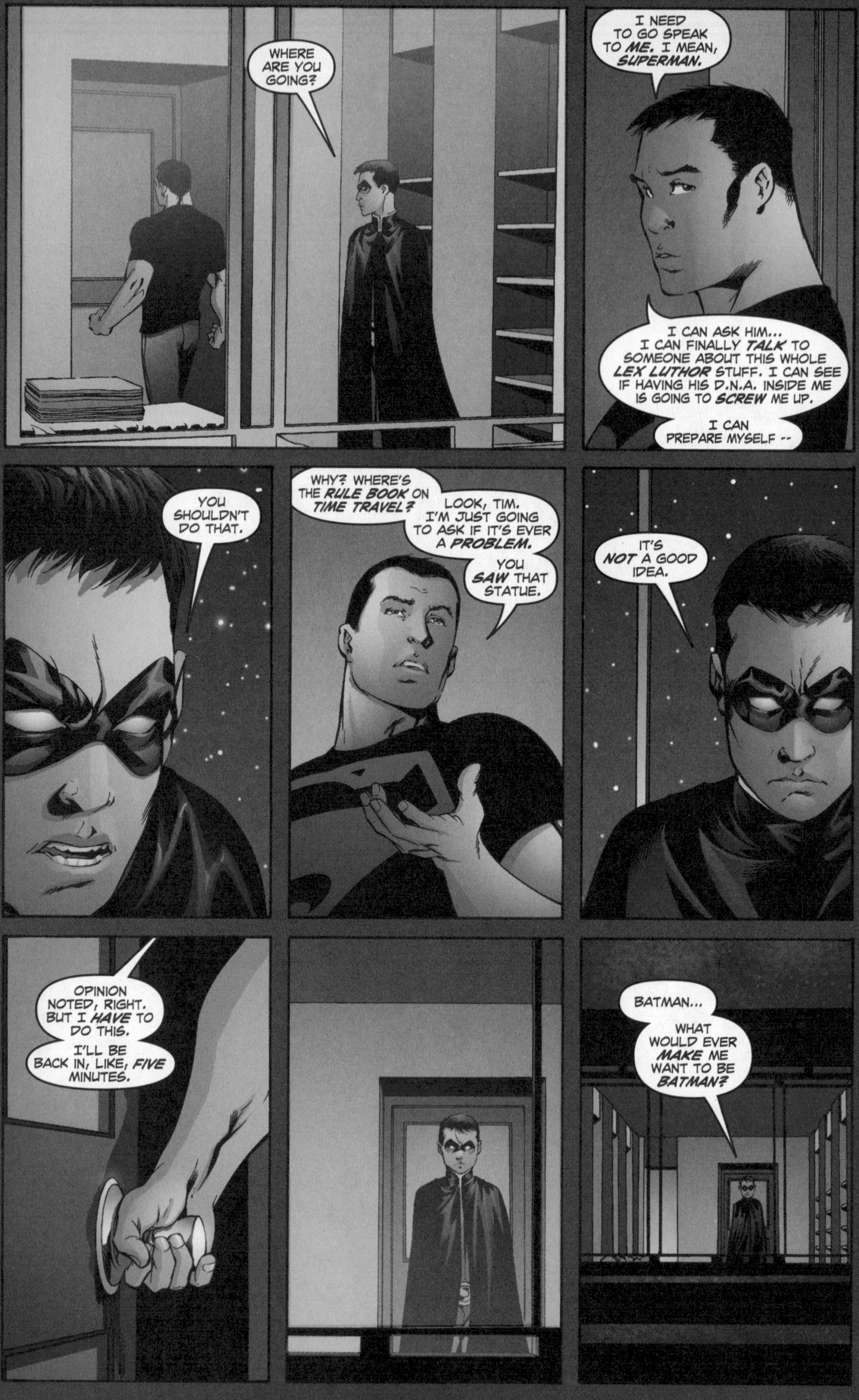
WHERE ARE YOU GOING?
I NEED TO GO SPEAK TO ME. I MEAN, SUPERMAN.
I CAN ASK HIM... I CAN FINALLY TALK TO SOMEONE ABOUT THIS WHOLE LEX LUTHOR STUFF. I CAN SEE IF HAVING HIS D.N.A. INSIDE ME IS GOING TO SCREW ME UP.
I CAN PREPARE MYSELF --
YOU SHOULDN'T DO THAT.
WHY? WHERE'S THE RULE BOOK ON TIME TRAVEL?
LOOK, TIM. I'M JUST GOING TO ASK IF IT'S EVER A PROBLEM.
YOU SAW THAT STATUE.
IT'S NOT A GOOD IDEA.
OPINION NOTED, RIGHT. BUT I HAVE TO DO THIS.
I'LL BE BACK IN, LIKE, FIVE MINUTES.
BATMAN...
WHAT WOULD EVER MAKE ME WANT TO BE BATMAN?

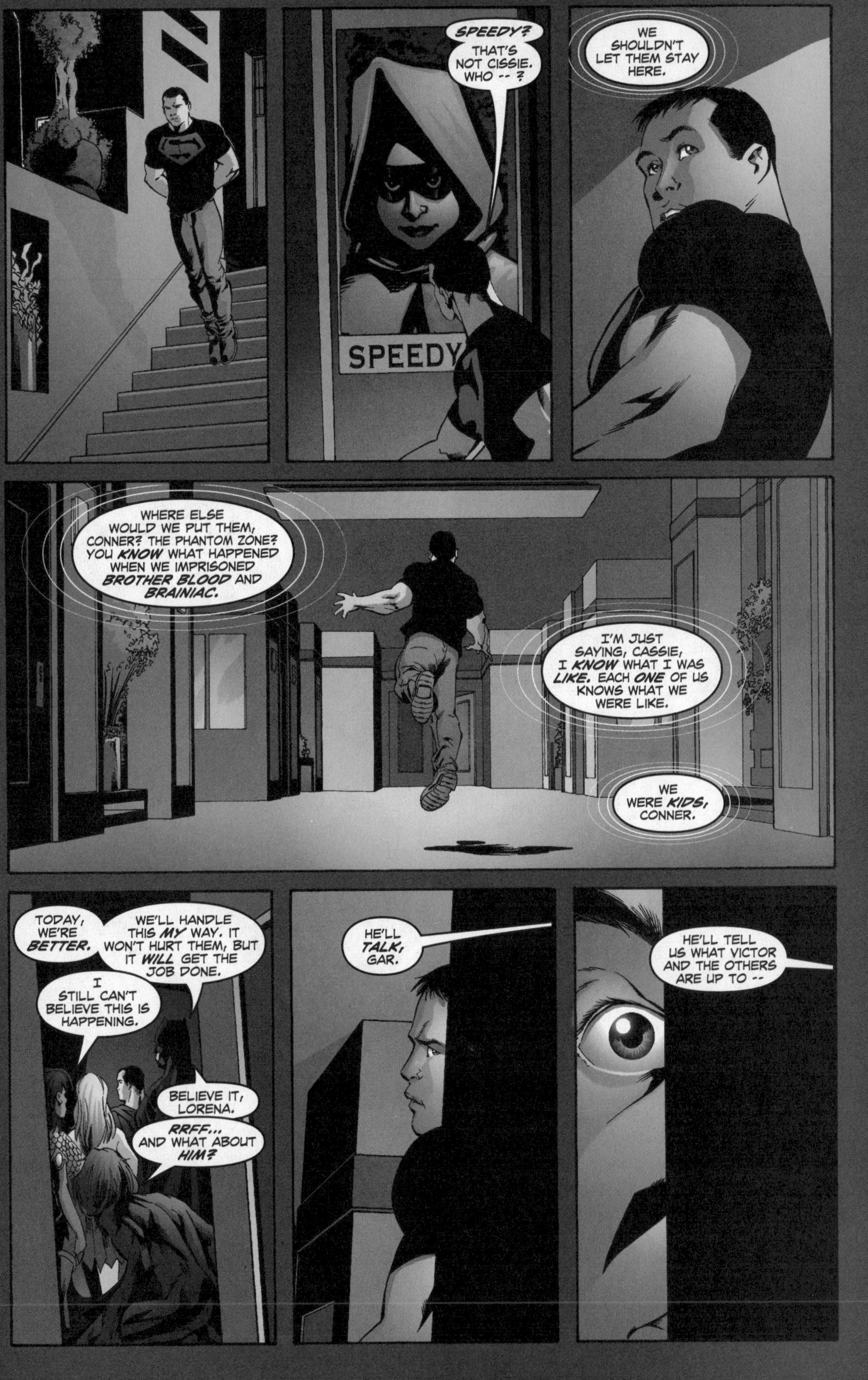

SPEEDY? THAT'S NOT CISSIE. WHO -- ?
SPEEDY
WE SHOULDN'T LET THEM STAY HERE.
WHERE ELSE WOULD WE PUT THEM, CONNER? THE PHANTOM ZONE? YOU KNOW WHAT HAPPENED WHEN WE IMPRISONED BROTHER BLOOD AND BRAINIAC.
I'M JUST SAYING, CASSIE, I KNOW WHAT I WAS LIKE. EACH ONE OF US KNOWS WHAT WE WERE LIKE.
WE WERE KIDS, CONNER.
TODAY, WE'RE BETTER.
WE'LL HANDLE THIS MY WAY. IT WON'T HURT THEM, BUT IT WILL GET THE JOB DONE.
I STILL CAN'T BELIEVE THIS IS HAPPENING.
BELIEVE IT, LORENA.
RRFF... AND WHAT ABOUT HIM?
HE'LL TALK, GAR.
HE'LL TELL US WHAT VICTOR AND THE OTHERS ARE UP TO --

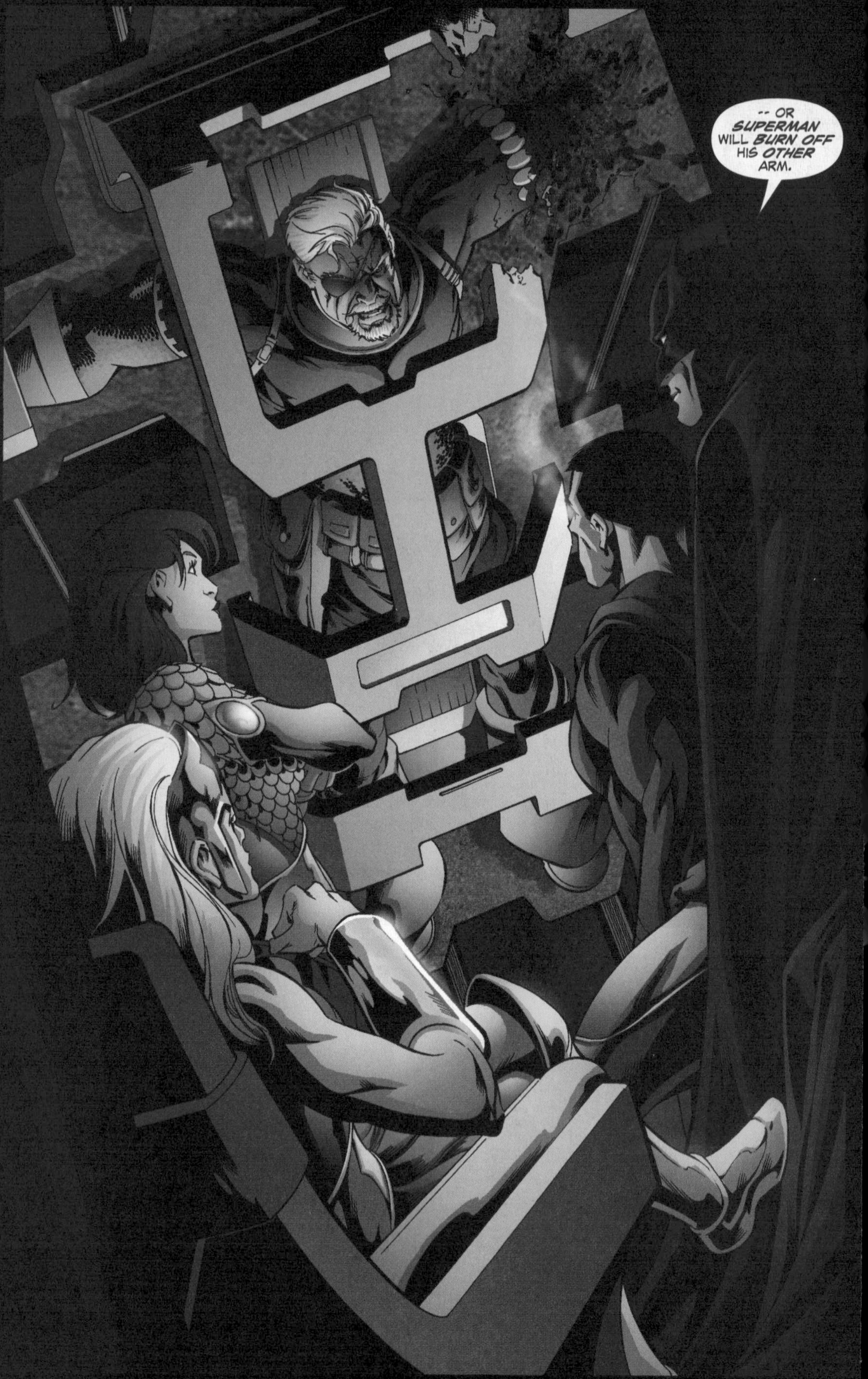
-- OR SUPERMAN WILL BURN OFF HIS OTHER ARM.

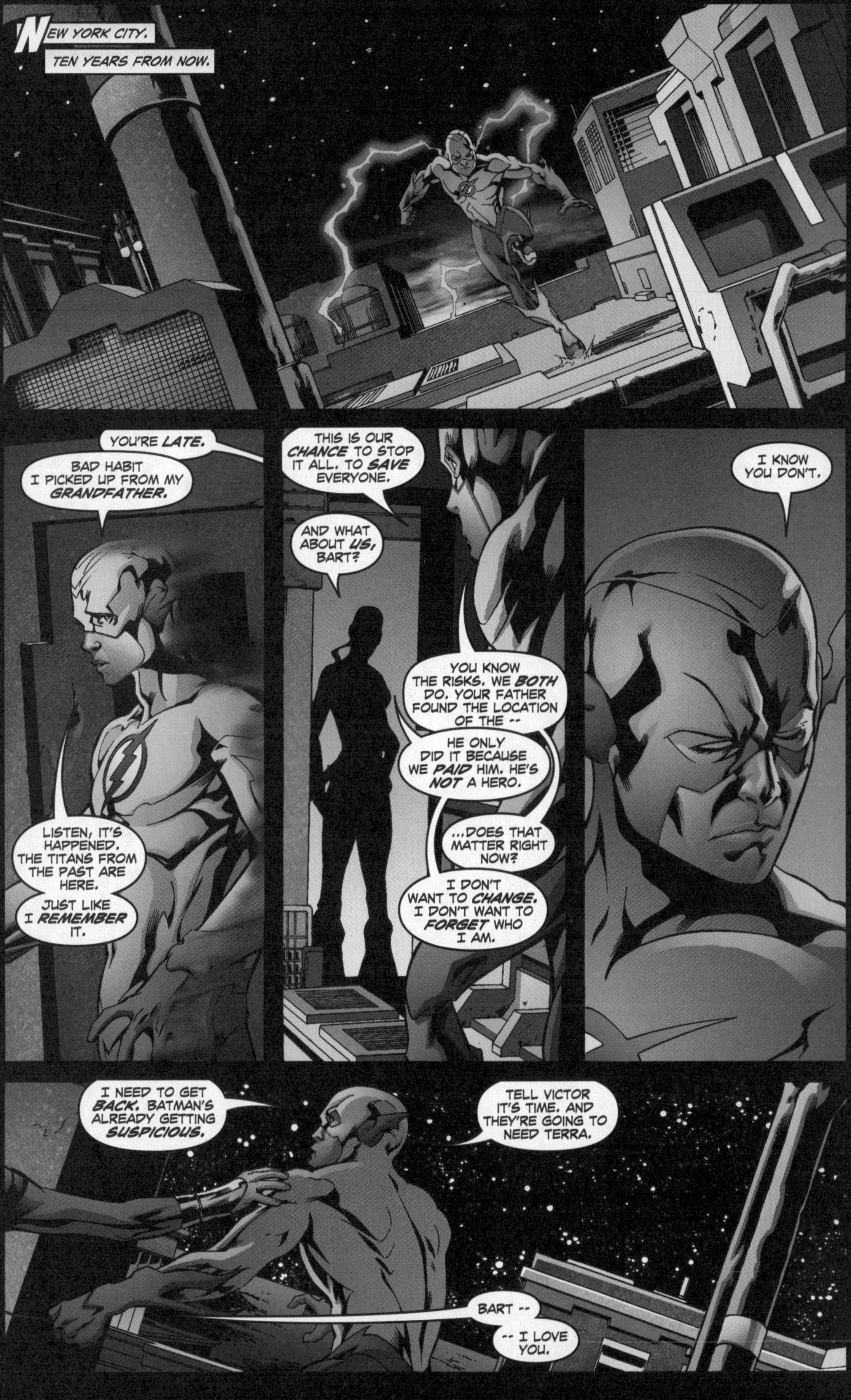
NEW YORK CITY.
TEN YEARS FROM NOW.
YOU'RE LATE.
BAD HABIT I PICKED UP FROM MY GRANDFATHER.
LISTEN, IT'S HAPPENED. THE TITANS FROM THE PAST ARE HERE.
JUST LIKE I REMEMBER IT.
THIS IS OUR CHANCE TO STOP IT ALL. TO SAVE EVERYONE.
AND WHAT ABOUT US, BART?
YOU KNOW THE RISKS. WE BOTH DO. YOUR FATHER FOUND THE LOCATION OF THE --
HE ONLY DID IT BECAUSE WE PAID HIM. HE'S NOT A HERO.
...DOES THAT MATTER RIGHT NOW?
I DON'T WANT TO CHANGE. I DON'T WANT TO FORGET WHO I AM.
I KNOW YOU DON'T.
I NEED TO GET BACK. BATMAN'S ALREADY GETTING SUSPICIOUS.
TELL VICTOR IT'S TIME. AND THEY'RE GOING TO NEED TERRA.
BART --
-- I LOVE YOU.

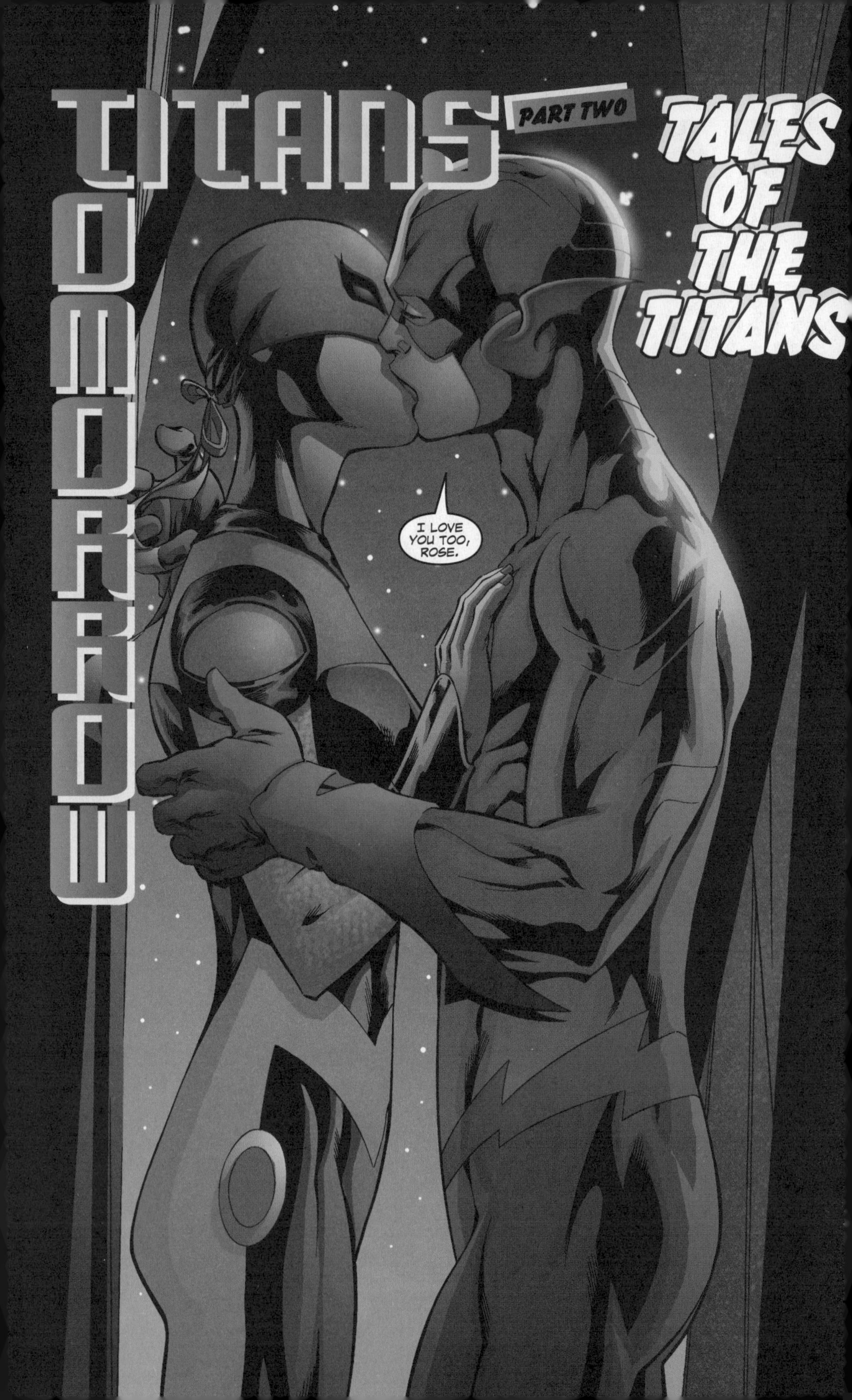

TITANS TOMORROW
PART TWO
TALES OF THE TITANS
I LOVE YOU TOO, ROSE.

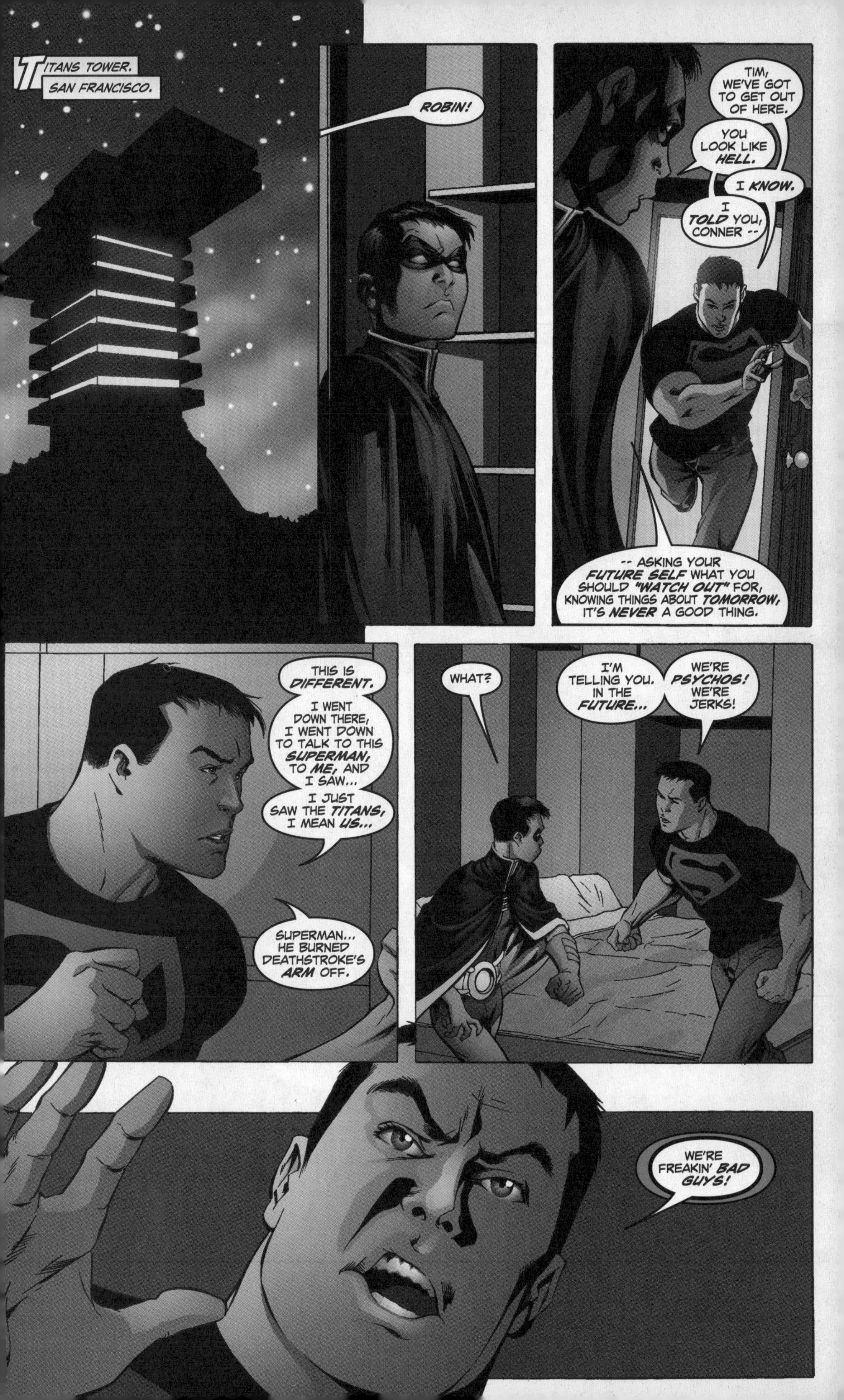
TITANS TOWER.
SAN FRANCISCO.
ROBIN!
TIM, WE'VE GOT TO GET OUT OF HERE.
YOU LOOK LIKE HELL.
I KNOW.
I TOLD YOU, CONNER --
-- ASKING YOUR FUTURE SELF WHAT YOU SHOULD "WATCH OUT" FOR, KNOWING THINGS ABOUT TOMORROW, IT'S NEVER A GOOD THING.
THIS IS DIFFERENT.
I WENT DOWN THERE, I WENT DOWN TO TALK TO THIS SUPERMAN, TO ME, AND I SAW... I JUST SAW THE TITANS, I MEAN US...
SUPERMAN... HE BURNED DEATHSTROKE'S ARM OFF.
WHAT?
I'M TELLING YOU. IN THE FUTURE...
WE'RE PSYCHOS! WE'RE JERKS!
WE'RE FREAKIN' BAD GUYS!

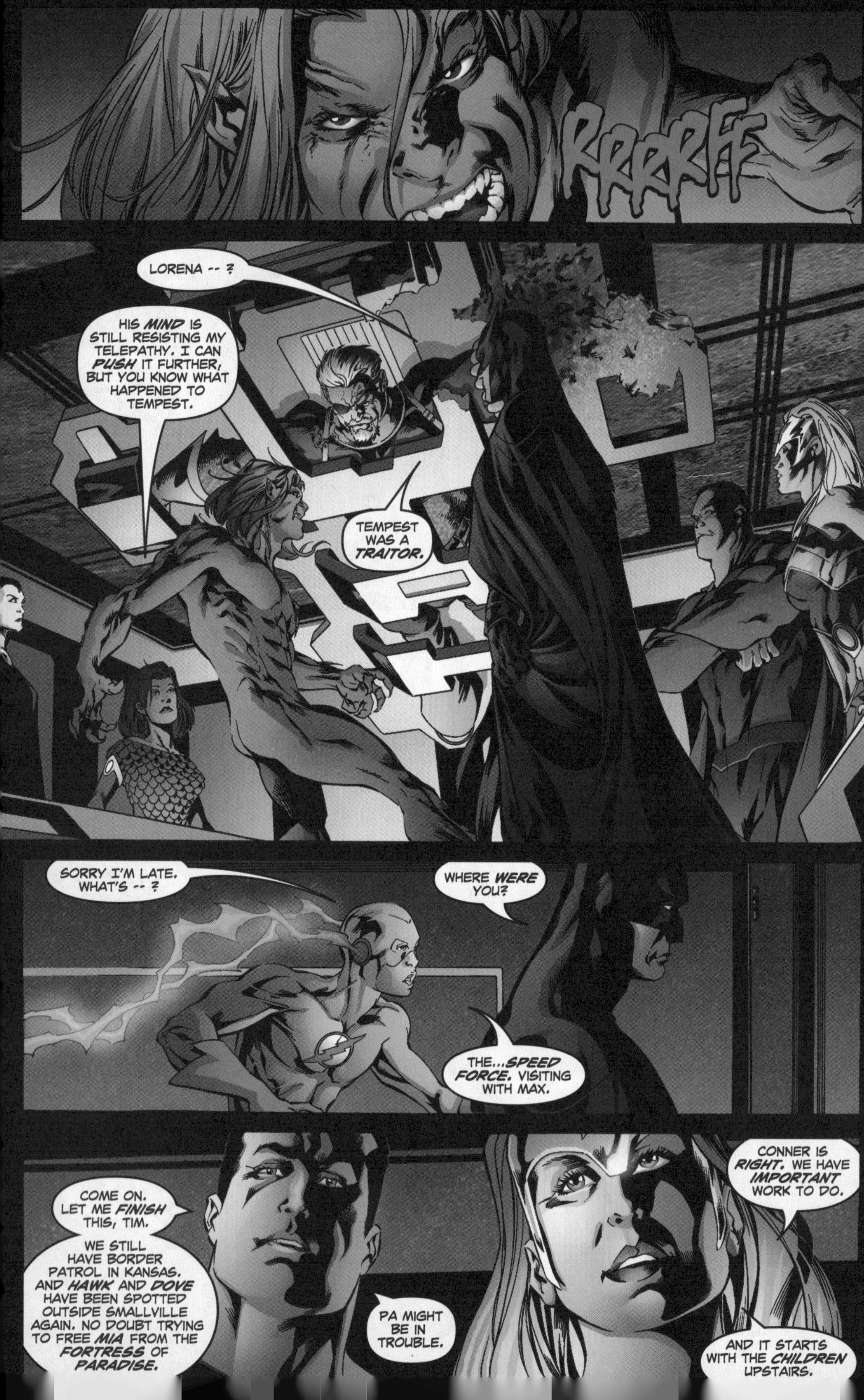
RRRRFF
LORENA -- ?
HIS MIND IS STILL RESISTING MY TELEPATHY. I CAN PUSH IT FURTHER, BUT YOU KNOW WHAT HAPPENED TO TEMPEST.
TEMPEST WAS A TRAITOR.
SORRY I'M LATE. WHAT'S -- ?
WHERE WERE YOU?
THE...SPEED FORCE. VISITING WITH MAX.
COME ON. LET ME FINISH THIS, TIM.
WE STILL HAVE BORDER PATROL IN KANSAS. AND HAWK AND DOVE HAVE BEEN SPOTTED OUTSIDE SMALLVILLE AGAIN. NO DOUBT TRYING TO FREE MIA FROM THE FORTRESS OF PARADISE.
PA MIGHT BE IN TROUBLE.
CONNER IS RIGHT. WE HAVE IMPORTANT WORK TO DO.
AND IT STARTS WITH THE CHILDREN UPSTAIRS.

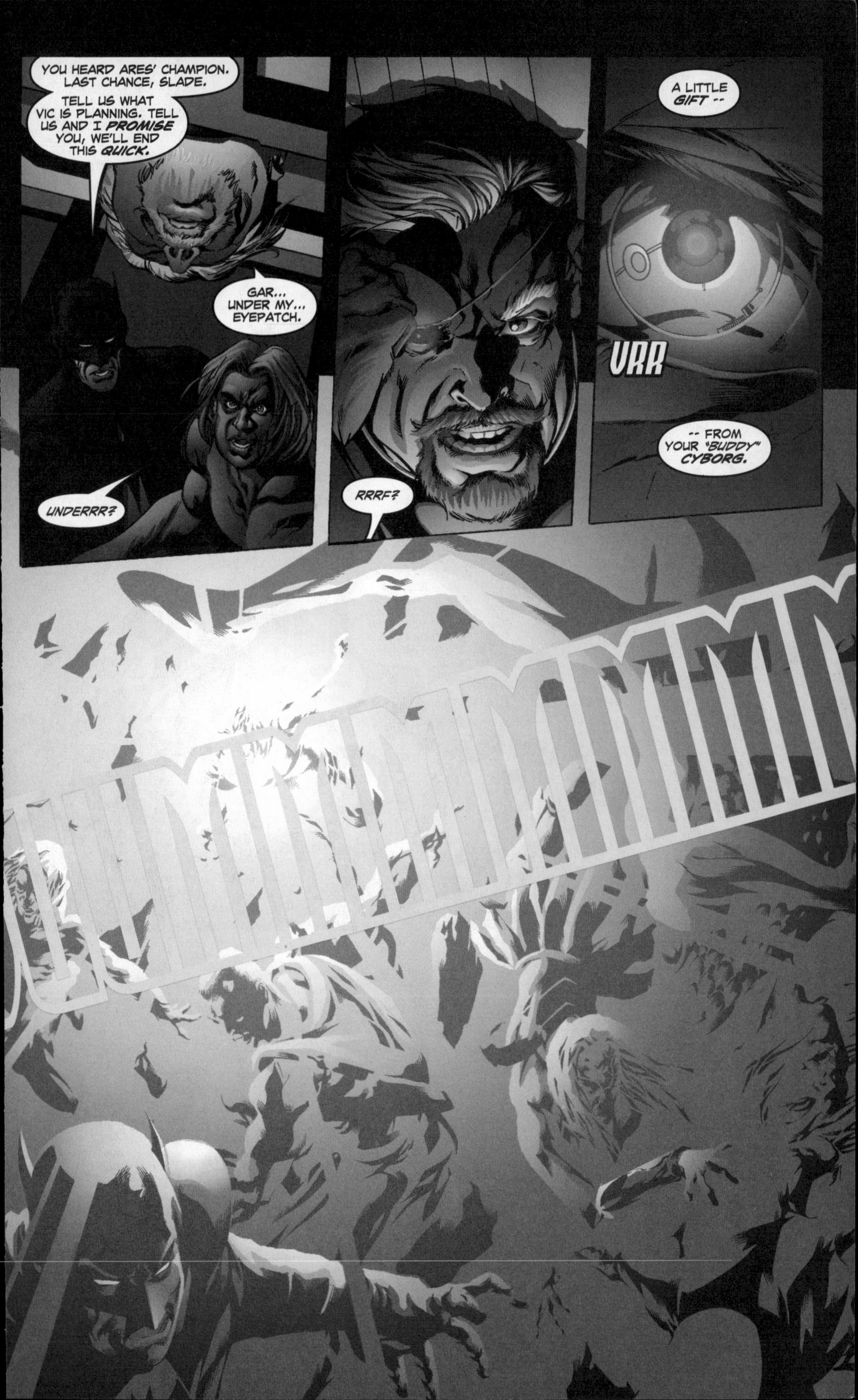
YOU HEARD ARES' CHAMPION. LAST CHANCE, SLADE.
TELL US WHAT VIC IS PLANNING. TELL US AND I PROMISE YOU, WE'LL END THIS QUICK.
GAR... UNDER MY... EYEPATCH.
UNDERRR?
RRRF?
A LITTLE GIFT --
VRR
-- FROM YOUR "BUDDY" CYBORG.

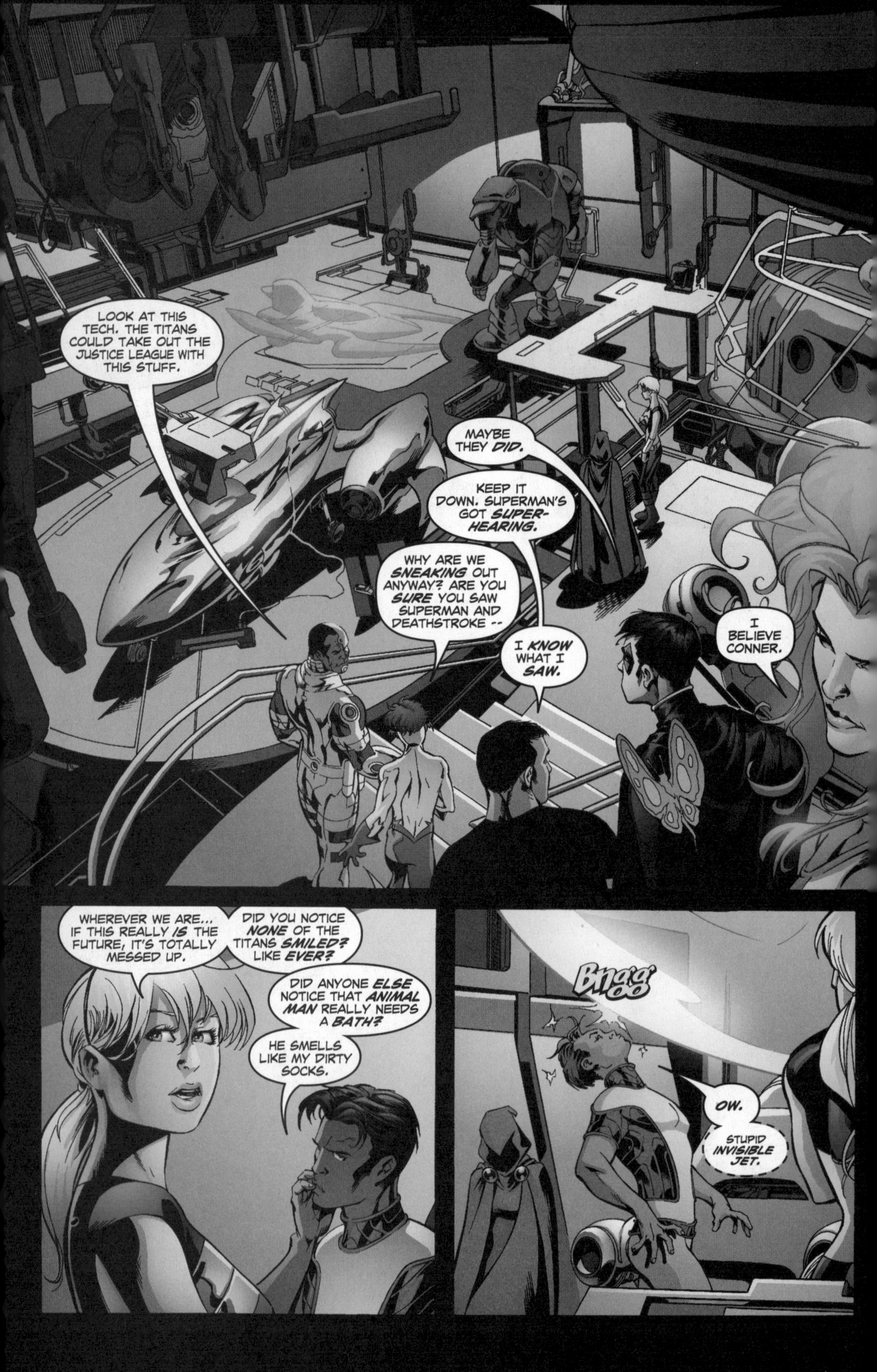
LOOK AT THIS TECH. THE TITANS COULD TAKE OUT THE JUSTICE LEAGUE WITH THIS STUFF.
MAYBE THEY DID.
KEEP IT DOWN. SUPERMAN'S GOT SUPER-HEARING.
WHY ARE WE SNEAKING OUT ANYWAY? ARE YOU SURE YOU SAW SUPERMAN AND DEATHSTROKE --
I KNOW WHAT I SAW.
I BELIEVE CONNER.
WHEREVER WE ARE... IF THIS REALLY IS THE FUTURE, IT'S TOTALLY MESSED UP.
DID YOU NOTICE NONE OF THE TITANS SMILED? LIKE EVER?
DID ANYONE ELSE NOTICE THAT ANIMAL MAN REALLY NEEDS A BATH?
HE SMELLS LIKE MY DIRTY SOCKS.
Bngg
OW.
STUPID INVISIBLE JET.

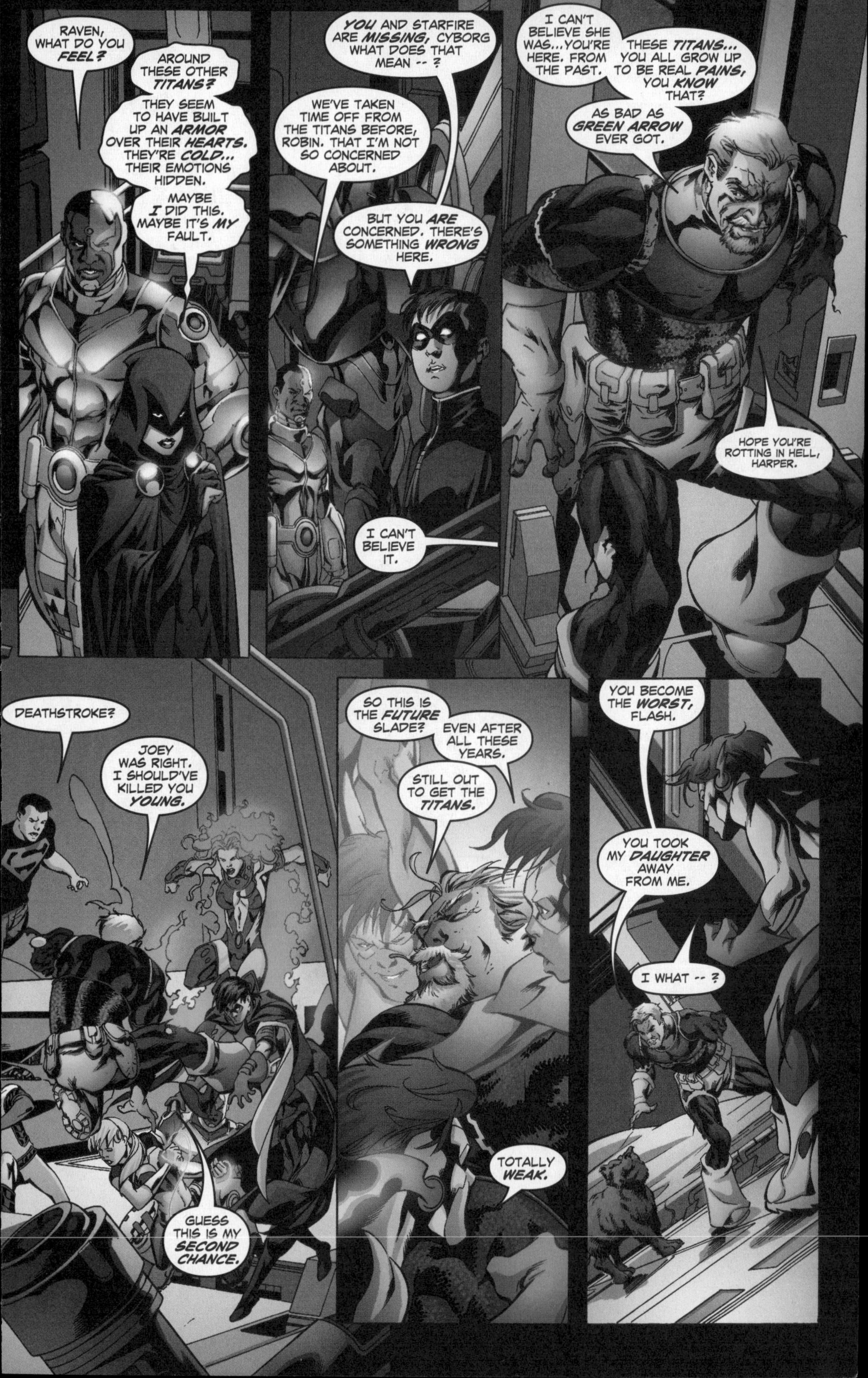
RAVEN, WHAT DO YOU FEEL?
AROUND THESE OTHER TITANS?
THEY SEEM TO HAVE BUILT UP AN ARMOR OVER THEIR HEARTS. THEY'RE COLD... THEIR EMOTIONS HIDDEN.
MAYBE I DID THIS. MAYBE IT'S MY FAULT.
YOU AND STARFIRE ARE MISSING, CYBORG WHAT DOES THAT MEAN -- ?
WE'VE TAKEN TIME OFF FROM THE TITANS BEFORE, ROBIN. THAT I'M NOT SO CONCERNED ABOUT.
BUT YOU ARE CONCERNED. THERE'S SOMETHING WRONG HERE.
I CAN'T BELIEVE IT.
I CAN'T BELIEVE SHE WAS...YOU'RE HERE. FROM THE PAST.
THESE TITANS... YOU ALL GROW UP TO BE REAL PAINS, YOU KNOW THAT?
AS BAD AS GREEN ARROW EVER GOT.
HOPE YOU'RE ROTTING IN HELL, HARPER.
DEATHSTROKE?
JOEY WAS RIGHT. I SHOULD'VE KILLED YOU YOUNG.
GUESS THIS IS MY SECOND CHANCE.
SO THIS IS THE FUTURE SLADE?
EVEN AFTER ALL THESE YEARS.
STILL OUT TO GET THE TITANS.
TOTALLY WEAK.
YOU BECOME THE WORST, FLASH.
YOU TOOK MY DAUGHTER AWAY FROM ME.
I WHAT -- ?

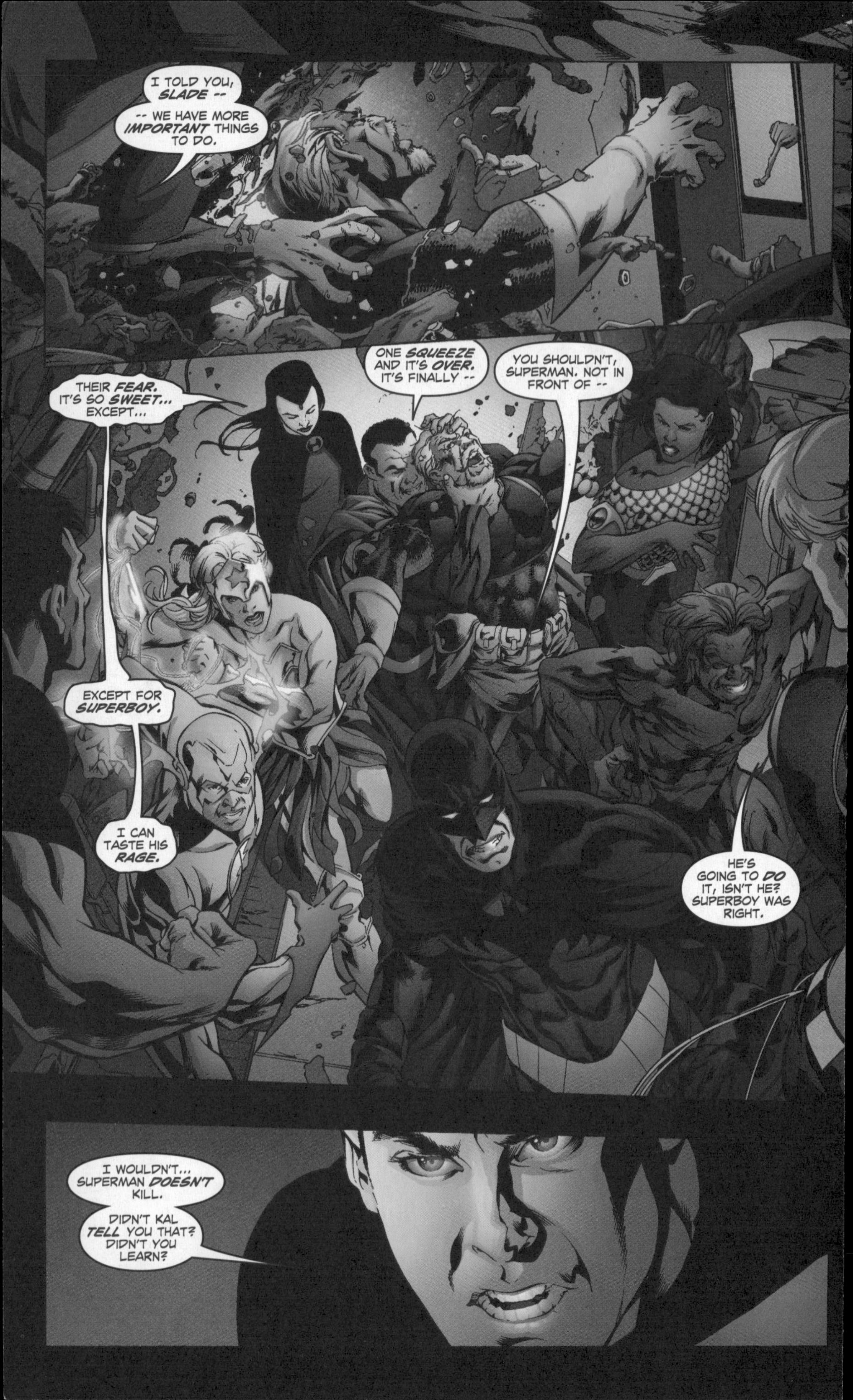
I TOLD YOU, SLADE --
-- WE HAVE MORE IMPORTANT THINGS TO DO.
THEIR FEAR. IT'S SO SWEET... EXCEPT...
ONE SQUEEZE AND IT'S OVER. IT'S FINALLY --
YOU SHOULDN'T, SUPERMAN. NOT IN FRONT OF --
EXCEPT FOR SUPERBOY.
I CAN TASTE HIS RAGE.
HE'S GOING TO DO IT, ISN'T HE? SUPERBOY WAS RIGHT.
I WOULDN'T... SUPERMAN DOESN'T KILL.
DIDN'T KAL TELL YOU THAT? DIDN'T YOU LEARN?

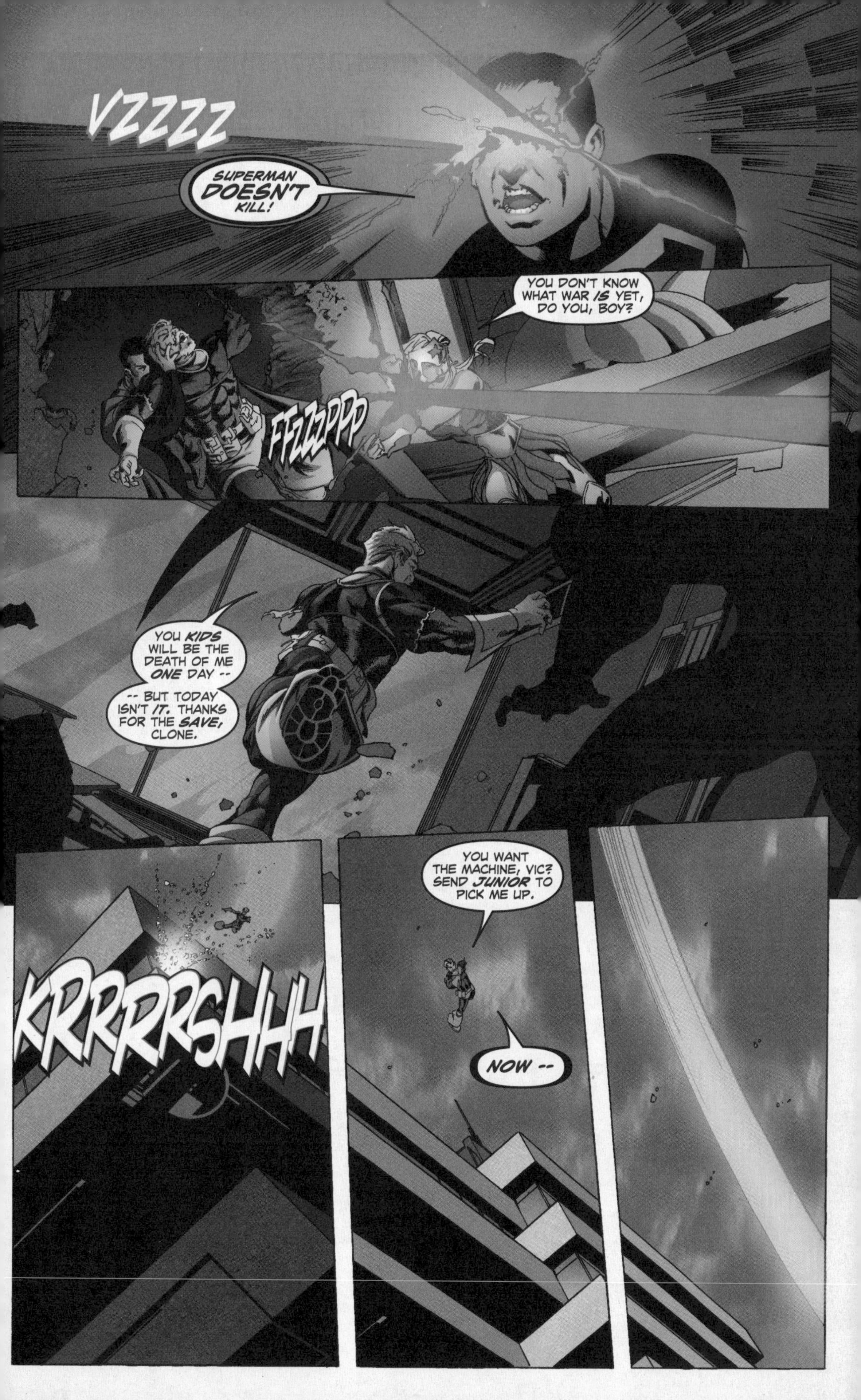
VZZZZ
SUPERMAN DOESN'T KILL!
YOU DON'T KNOW WHAT WAR IS YET, DO YOU, BOY?
FFZZZPPP
YOU KIDS WILL BE THE DEATH OF ME ONE DAY --
-- BUT TODAY ISN'T IT. THANKS FOR THE SAVE, CLONE.
KRRRRSHHH
YOU WANT THE MACHINE, VIC? SEND JUNIOR TO PICK ME UP.
NOW --

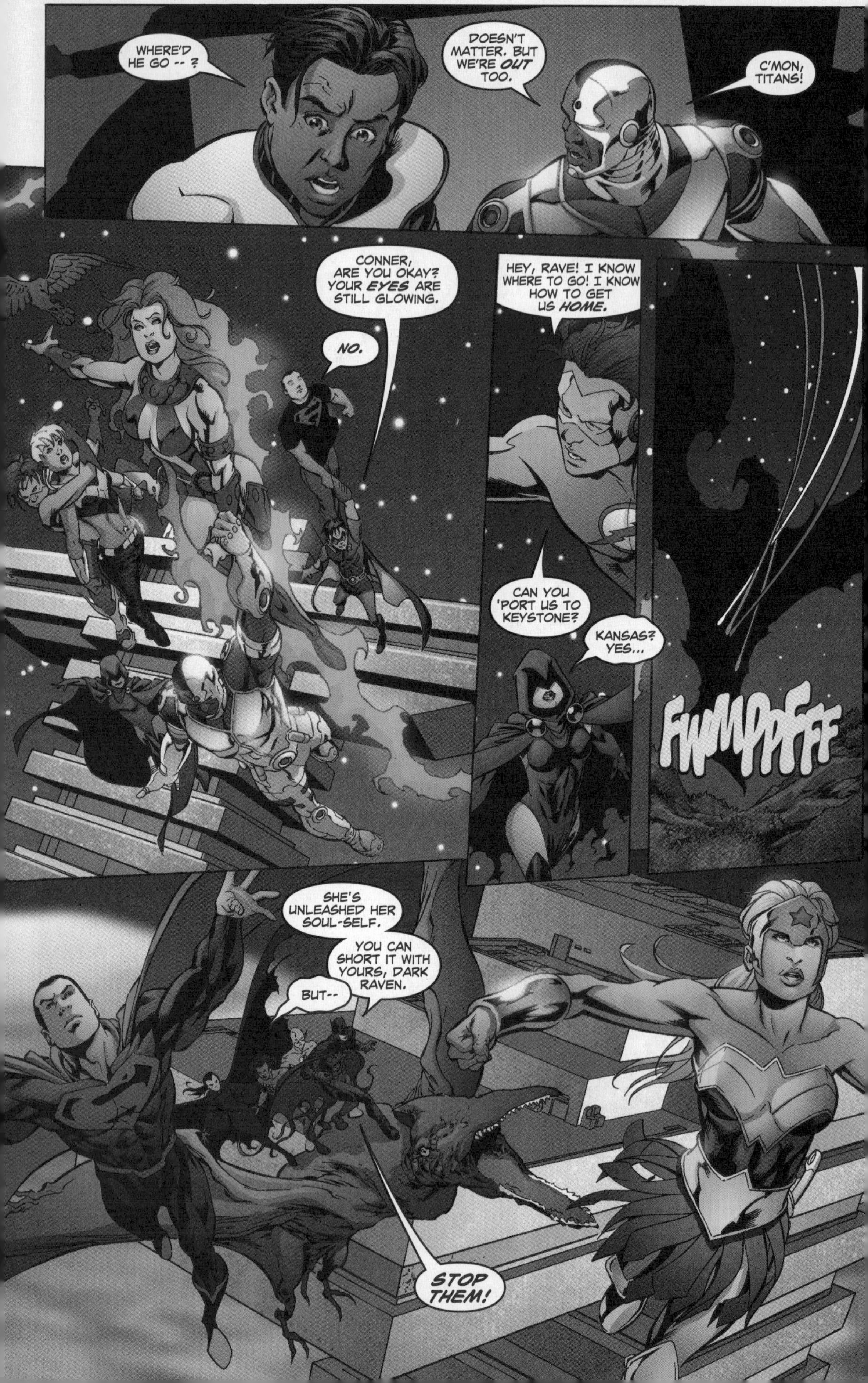
WHERE'D HE GO -- ?
DOESN'T MATTER. BUT WE'RE *OUT* TOO.
C'MON, TITANS!
CONNER, ARE YOU OKAY? YOUR *EYES* ARE STILL GLOWING.
NO.
HEY, RAVE! I KNOW WHERE TO GO! I KNOW HOW TO GET US *HOME.*
CAN YOU 'PORT US TO KEYSTONE?
KANSAS? YES...
FWMDPFFF
SHE'S UNLEASHED HER SOUL-SELF.
YOU CAN SHORT IT WITH YOURS, DARK RAVEN.
BUT--
STOP THEM!

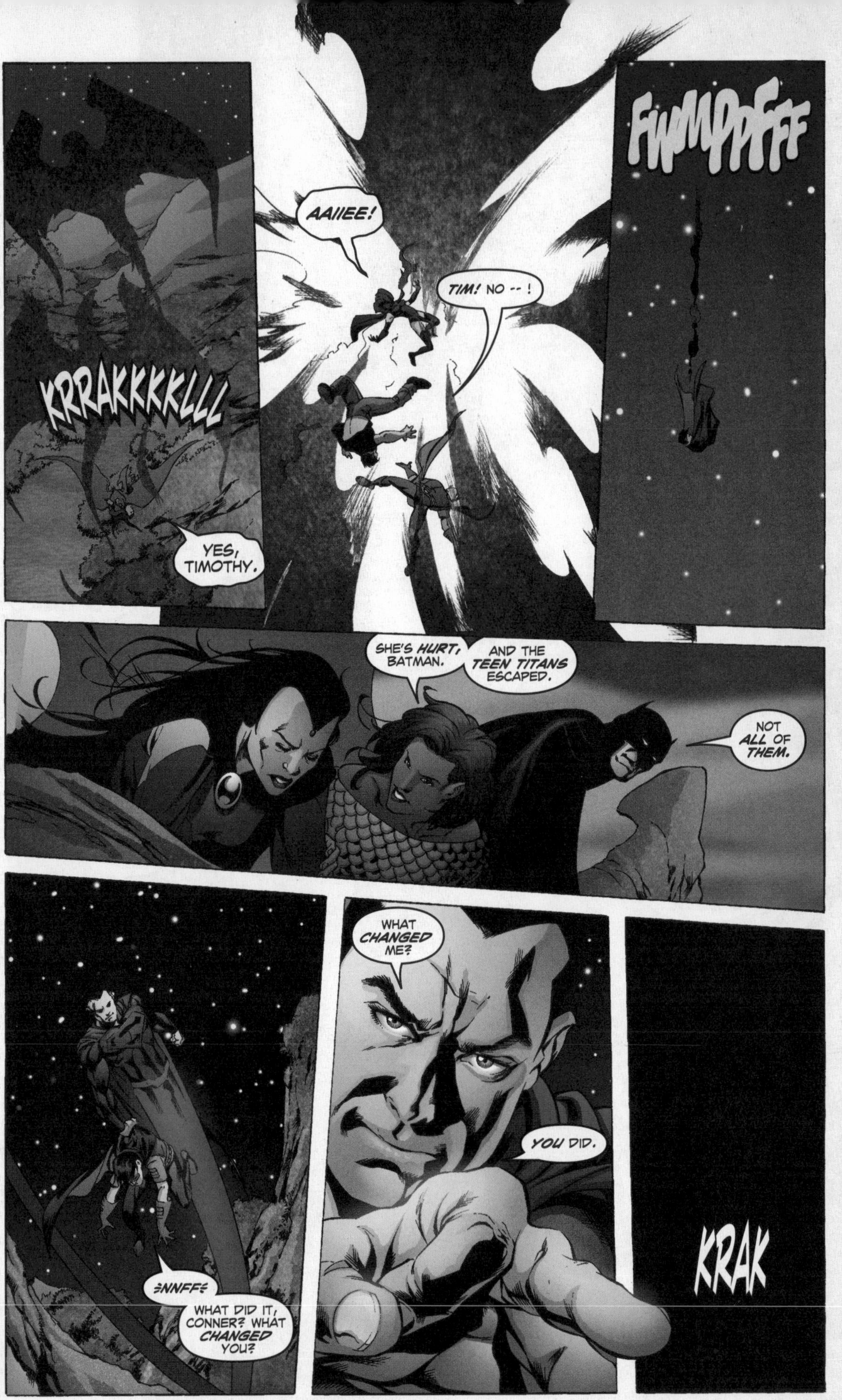

KRRAKKKKLLL
YES, TIMOTHY.
AAIIEE!
TIM! NO -- !
FWMPPFFF
SHE'S HURT, BATMAN.
AND THE TEEN TITANS ESCAPED.
NOT ALL OF THEM.
≠NNFF≠
WHAT DID IT, CONNER? WHAT CHANGED YOU?
WHAT CHANGED ME?
YOU DID.
KRAK

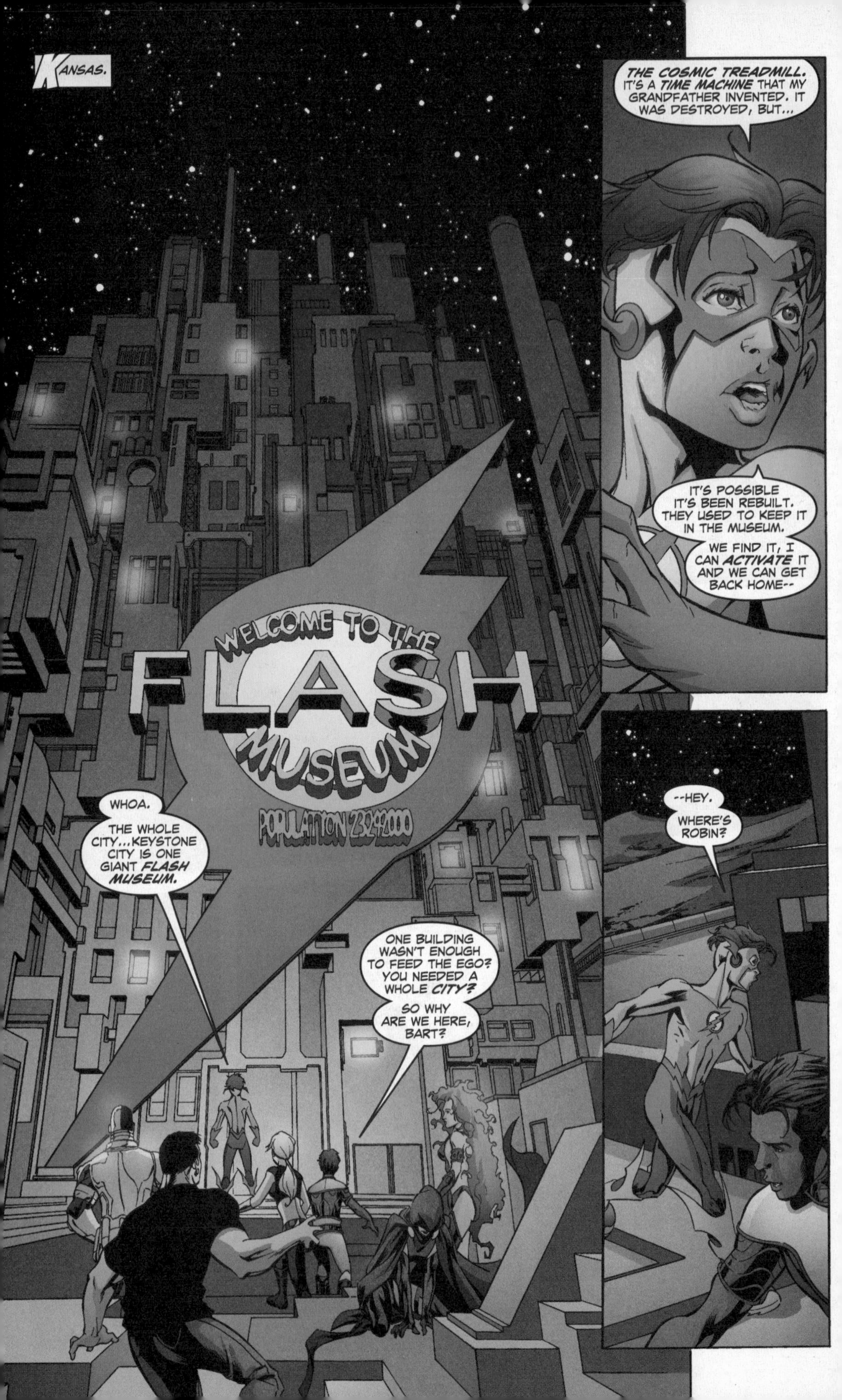
KANSAS.
WELCOME TO THE FLASH MUSEUM
POPULATION 23292000
WHOA.
THE WHOLE CITY...KEYSTONE CITY IS ONE GIANT FLASH MUSEUM.
ONE BUILDING WASN'T ENOUGH TO FEED THE EGO? YOU NEEDED A WHOLE CITY?
SO WHY ARE WE HERE, BART?
THE COSMIC TREADMILL. IT'S A TIME MACHINE THAT MY GRANDFATHER INVENTED. IT WAS DESTROYED, BUT...
IT'S POSSIBLE IT'S BEEN REBUILT. THEY USED TO KEEP IT IN THE MUSEUM.
WE FIND IT, I CAN ACTIVATE IT AND WE CAN GET BACK HOME--
--HEY.
WHERE'S ROBIN?

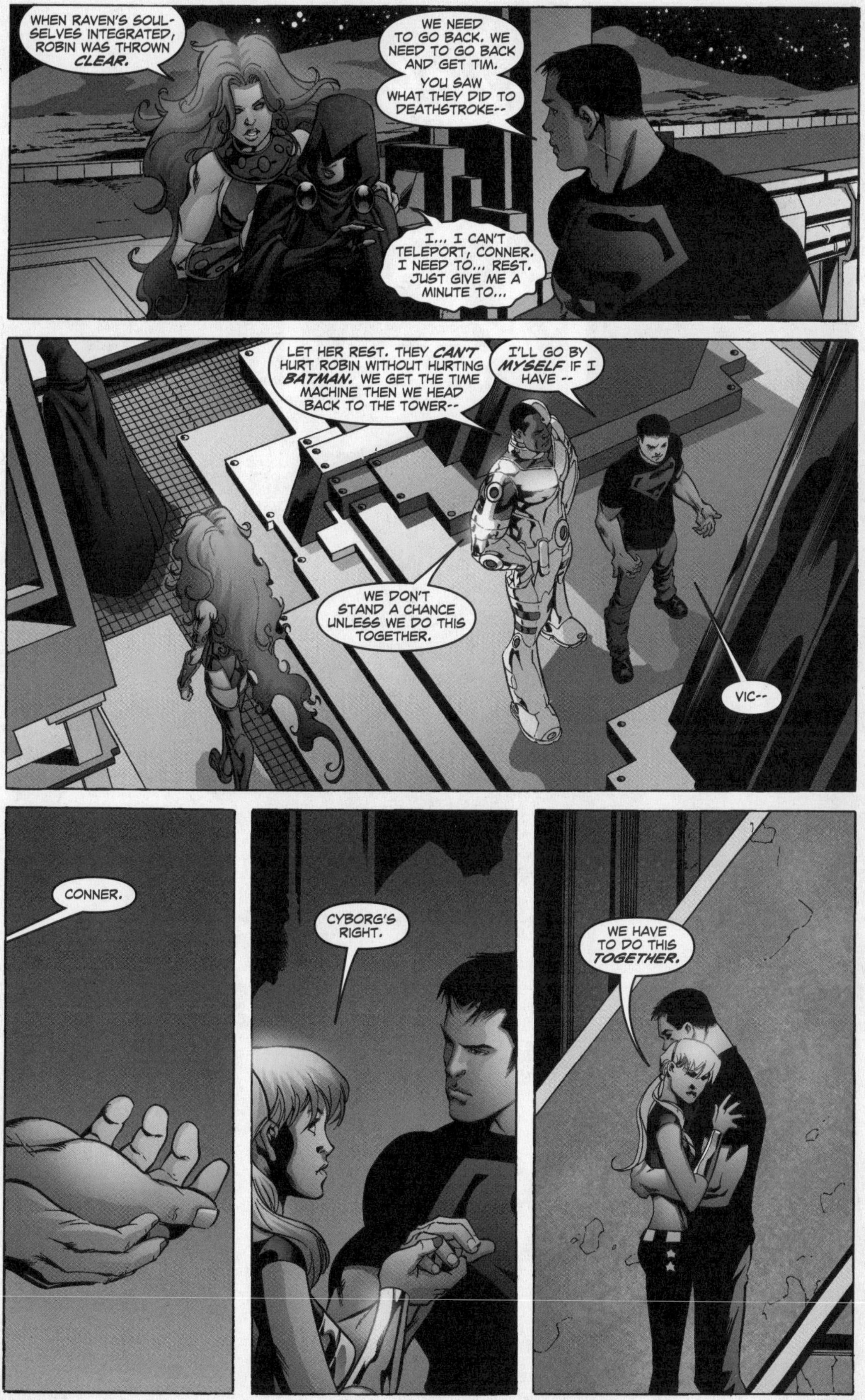
WHEN RAVEN'S SOUL-SELVES INTEGRATED, ROBIN WAS THROWN CLEAR.
WE NEED TO GO BACK. WE NEED TO GO BACK AND GET TIM.
YOU SAW WHAT THEY DID TO DEATHSTROKE--
I... I CAN'T TELEPORT, CONNER. I NEED TO... REST. JUST GIVE ME A MINUTE TO...
LET HER REST. THEY CAN'T HURT ROBIN WITHOUT HURTING BATMAN. WE GET THE TIME MACHINE THEN WE HEAD BACK TO THE TOWER--
I'LL GO BY MYSELF IF I HAVE --
WE DON'T STAND A CHANCE UNLESS WE DO THIS TOGETHER.
VIC--
CONNER.
CYBORG'S RIGHT.
WE HAVE TO DO THIS TOGETHER.

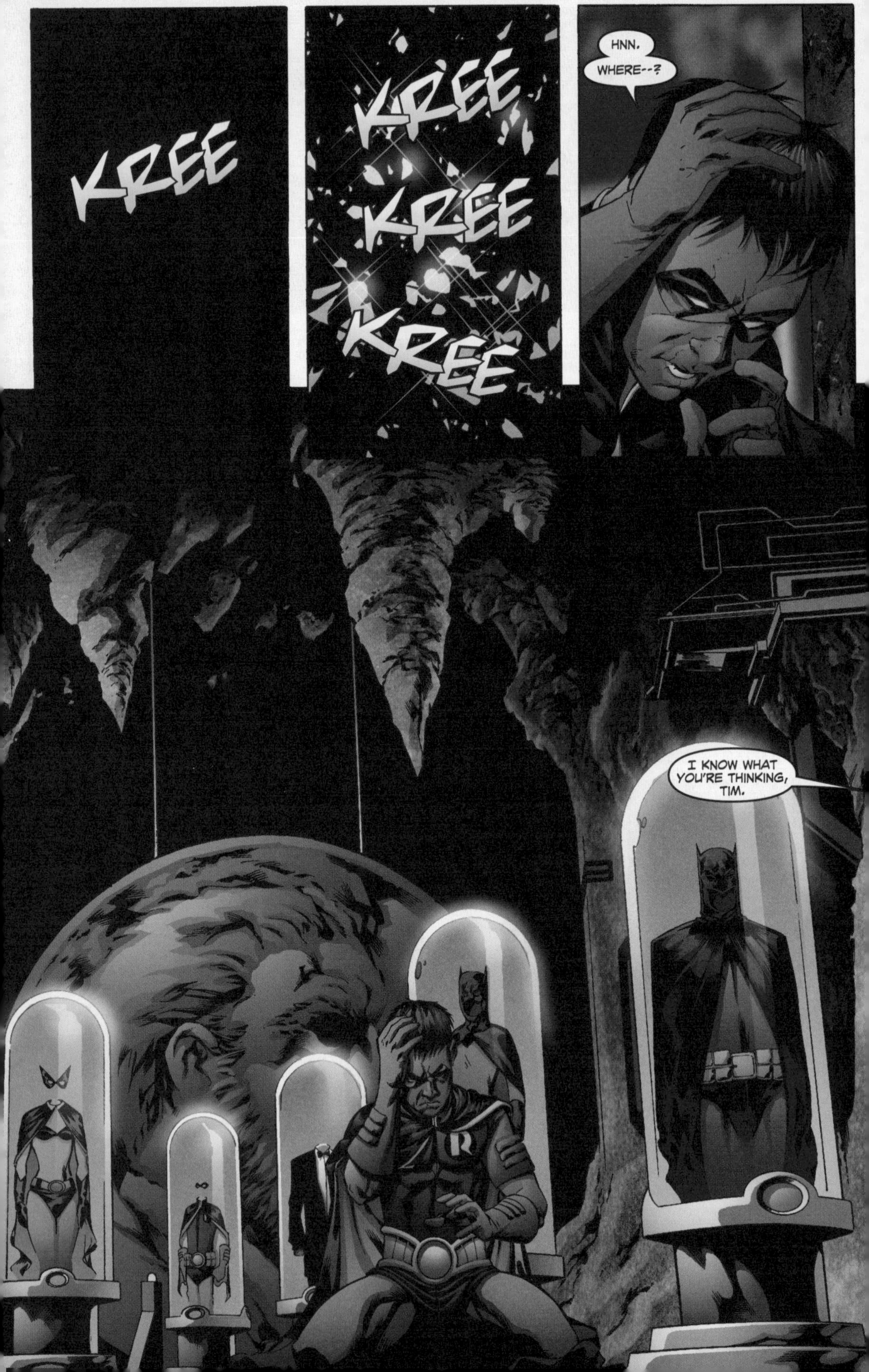
KREE
KREE
KREE
KREE
HNN. WHERE--?
I KNOW WHAT YOU'RE THINKING, TIM.

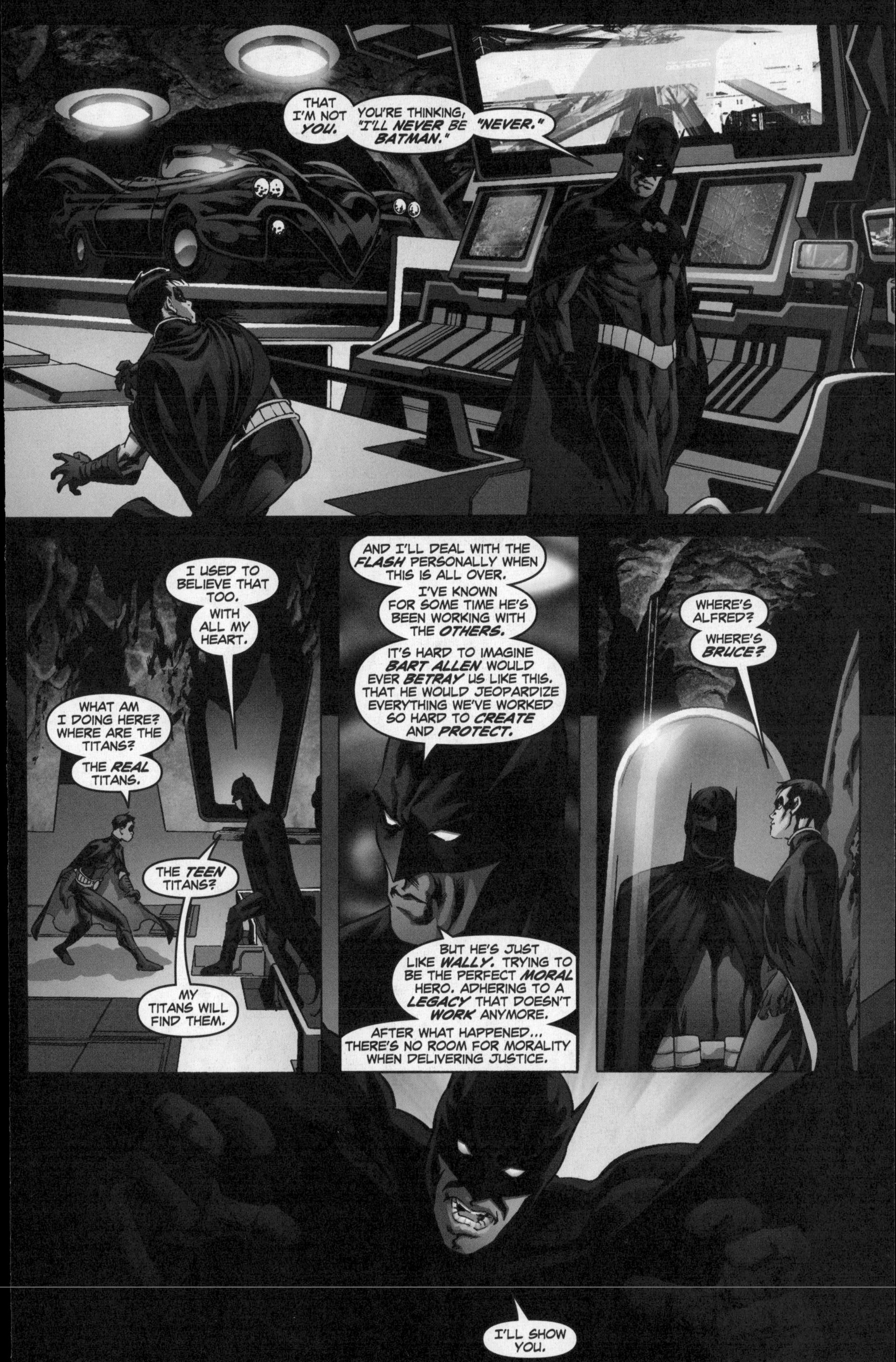

YOU'RE THINKING, "I'LL NEVER BE BATMAN."
"NEVER."
THAT I'M NOT YOU.
I USED TO BELIEVE THAT TOO.
WITH ALL MY HEART.
WHAT AM I DOING HERE? WHERE ARE THE TITANS?
THE REAL TITANS.
THE TEEN TITANS?
MY TITANS WILL FIND THEM.
AND I'LL DEAL WITH THE FLASH PERSONALLY WHEN THIS IS ALL OVER.
I'VE KNOWN FOR SOME TIME HE'S BEEN WORKING WITH THE OTHERS.
IT'S HARD TO IMAGINE BART ALLEN WOULD EVER BETRAY US LIKE THIS. THAT HE WOULD JEOPARDIZE EVERYTHING WE'VE WORKED SO HARD TO CREATE AND PROTECT.
BUT HE'S JUST LIKE WALLY. TRYING TO BE THE PERFECT MORAL HERO. ADHERING TO A LEGACY THAT DOESN'T WORK ANYMORE.
AFTER WHAT HAPPENED... THERE'S NO ROOM FOR MORALITY WHEN DELIVERING JUSTICE.
WHERE'S ALFRED?
WHERE'S BRUCE?
I'LL SHOW YOU.

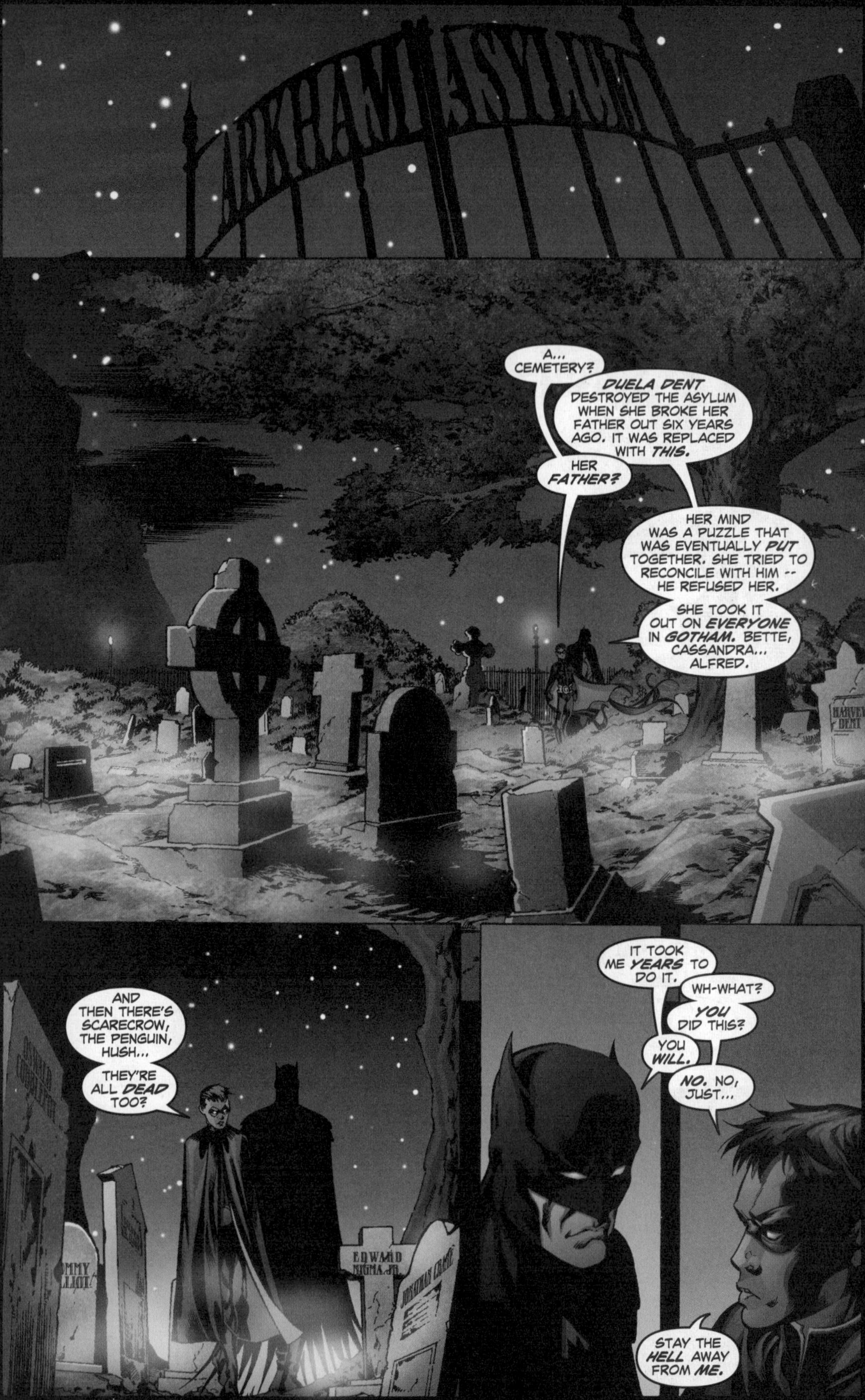
ARKHAM ASYLUM
A... CEMETERY?
DUELA DENT DESTROYED THE ASYLUM WHEN SHE BROKE HER FATHER OUT SIX YEARS AGO. IT WAS REPLACED WITH THIS.
HER FATHER?
HER MIND WAS A PUZZLE THAT WAS EVENTUALLY PUT TOGETHER. SHE TRIED TO RECONCILE WITH HIM -- HE REFUSED HER.
SHE TOOK IT OUT ON EVERYONE IN GOTHAM. BETTE, CASSANDRA... ALFRED.
HARVEY DENT
AND THEN THERE'S SCARECROW, THE PENGUIN, HUSH...
THEY'RE ALL DEAD TOO?
EDWARD NIGMA, JR.
IT TOOK ME YEARS TO DO IT.
WH-WHAT?
YOU DID THIS?
YOU WILL.
NO. NO, JUST...
STAY THE HELL AWAY FROM ME.

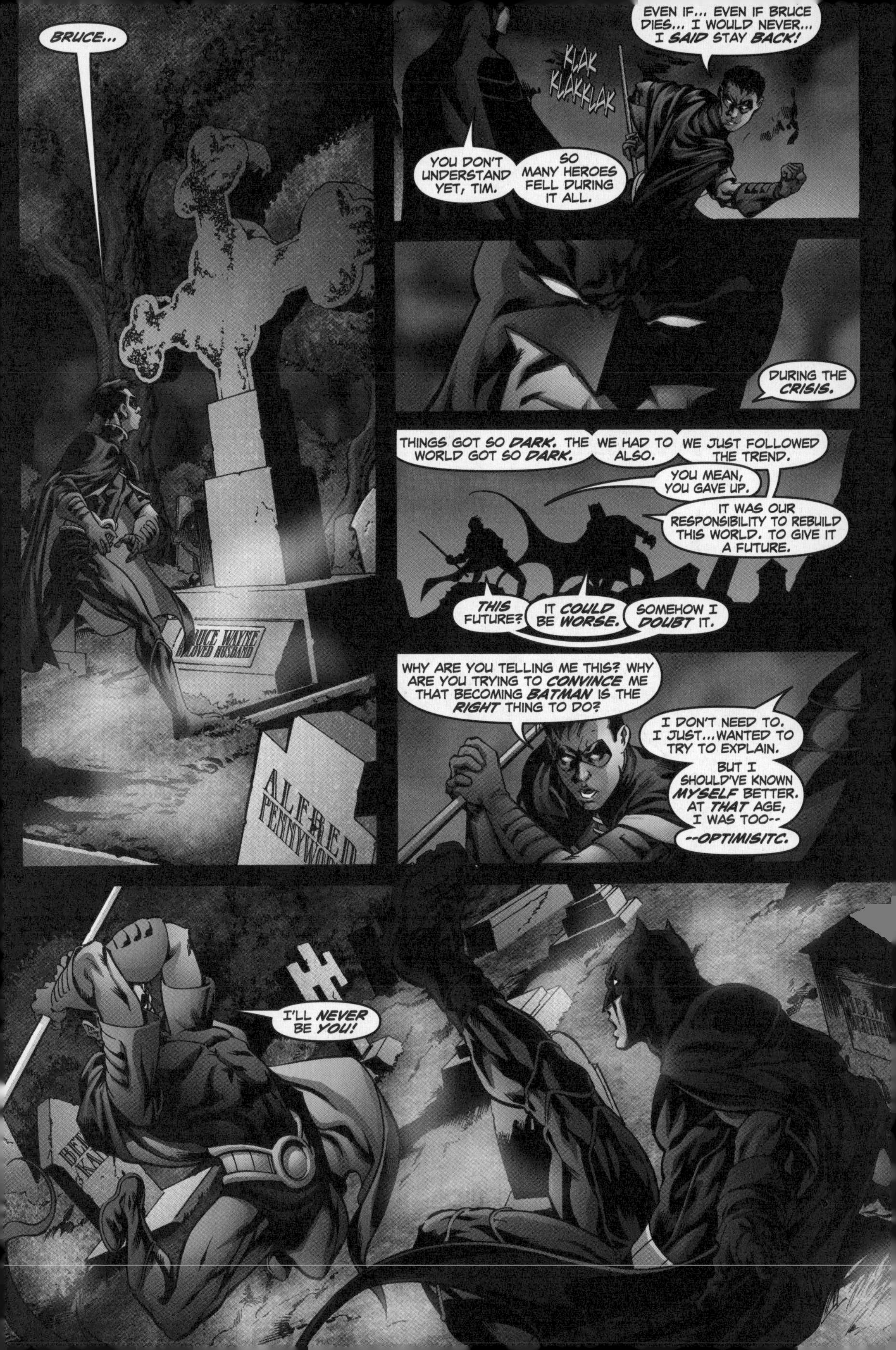
BRUCE...
EVEN IF... EVEN IF BRUCE DIES... I WOULD NEVER... I SAID STAY BACK!
KLAK KLAKKLAK
YOU DON'T UNDERSTAND YET, TIM.
SO MANY HEROES FELL DURING IT ALL.
DURING THE CRISIS.
THINGS GOT SO DARK. THE WORLD GOT SO DARK.
WE HAD TO ALSO.
WE JUST FOLLOWED THE TREND.
YOU MEAN, YOU GAVE UP.
IT WAS OUR RESPONSIBILITY TO REBUILD THIS WORLD. TO GIVE IT A FUTURE.
THIS FUTURE?
IT COULD BE WORSE.
SOMEHOW I DOUBT IT.
WHY ARE YOU TELLING ME THIS? WHY ARE YOU TRYING TO CONVINCE ME THAT BECOMING BATMAN IS THE RIGHT THING TO DO?
I DON'T NEED TO. I JUST...WANTED TO TRY TO EXPLAIN.
BUT I SHOULD'VE KNOWN MYSELF BETTER. AT THAT AGE, I WAS TOO--
--OPTIMISITC.
I'LL NEVER BE YOU!
BRUCE WAYNE BELOVED HUSBAND
ALFRED PENNYWORTH

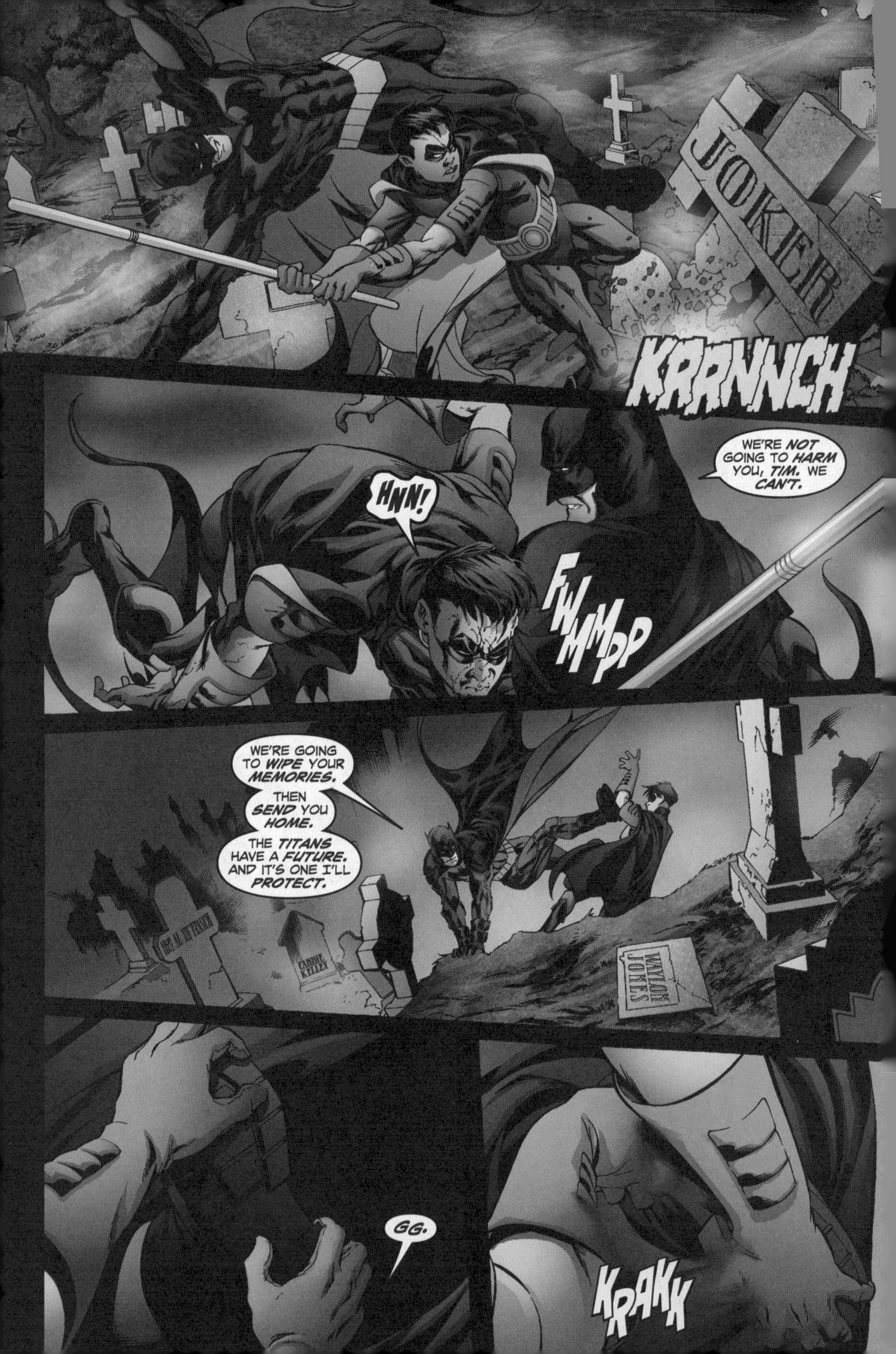
JOKER
KRRNNCH
HNN!
WE'RE NOT GOING TO HARM YOU, TIM. WE CAN'T.
FWMMPP
WE'RE GOING TO WIPE YOUR MEMORIES.
THEN SEND YOU HOME.
THE TITANS HAVE A FUTURE. AND IT'S ONE I'LL PROTECT.
CARRIE KELLEY
WAYLON JONES
GG.
KRAKK

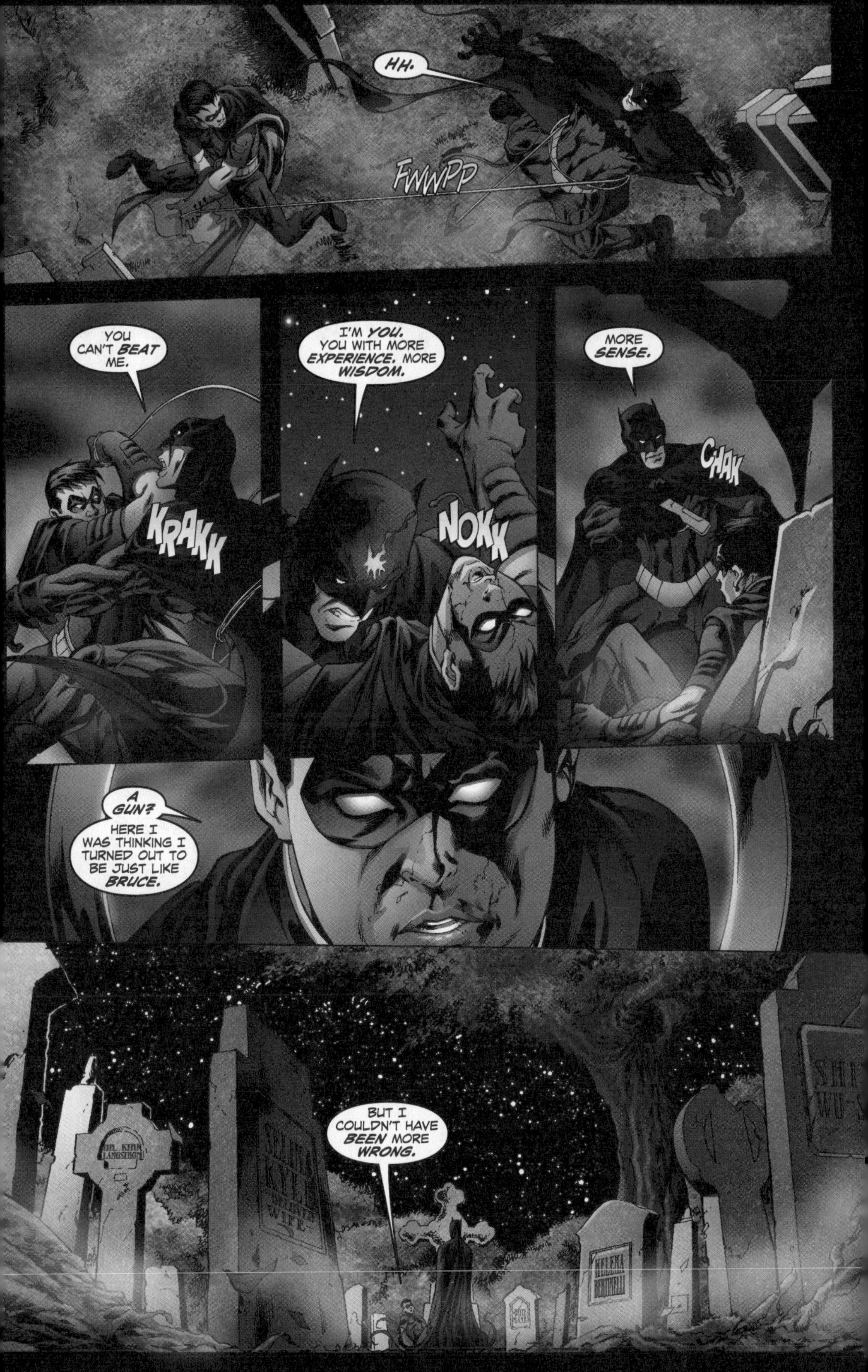
HH.
FWWPP
YOU CAN'T BEAT ME.
KRAKK
I'M YOU. YOU WITH MORE EXPERIENCE. MORE WISDOM.
NOKK
MORE SENSE.
CHAK
A GUN?
HERE I WAS THINKING I TURNED OUT TO BE JUST LIKE BRUCE.
BUT I COULDN'T HAVE BEEN MORE WRONG.

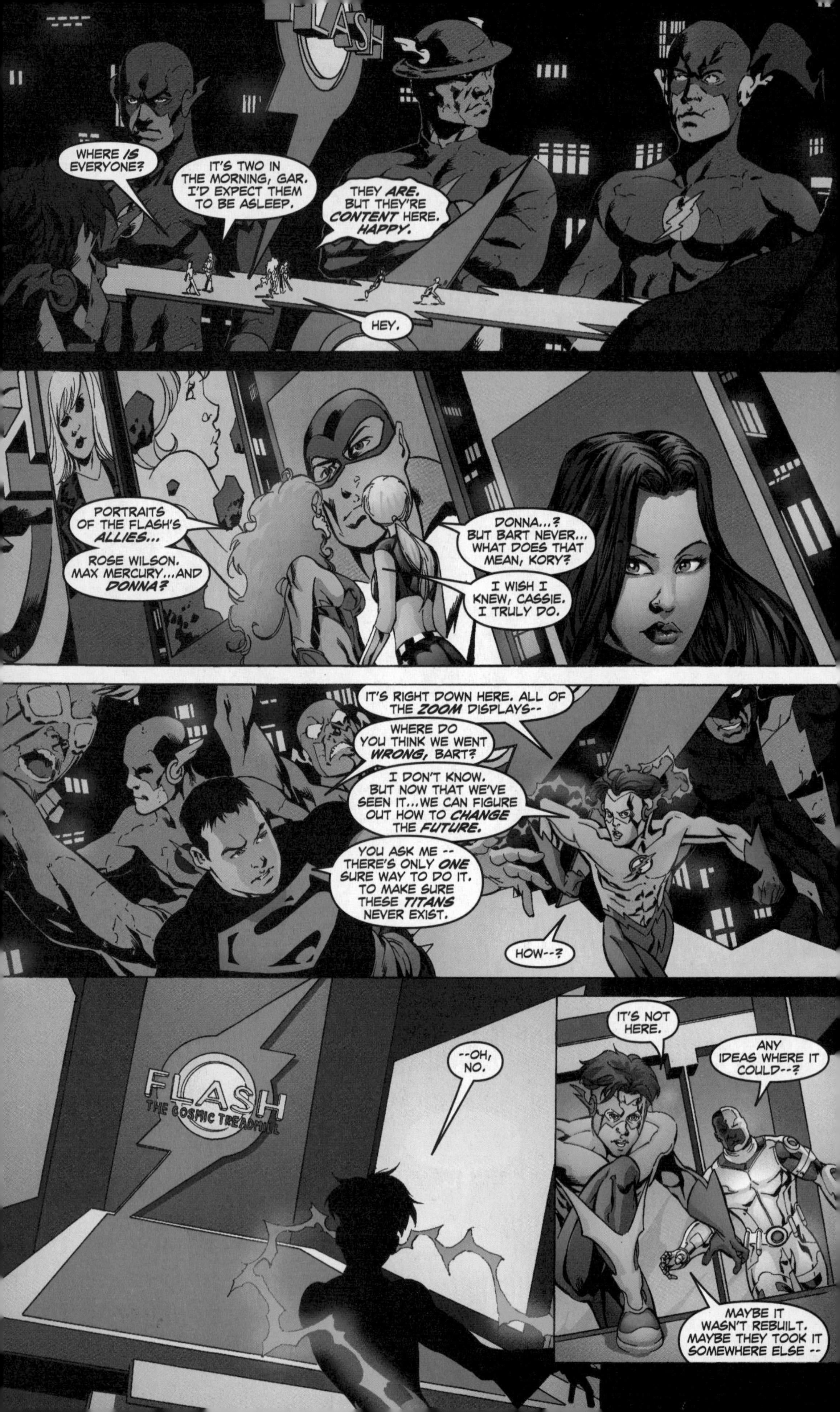

FLASH
WHERE IS EVERYONE?
IT'S TWO IN THE MORNING, GAR. I'D EXPECT THEM TO BE ASLEEP.
THEY ARE. BUT THEY'RE CONTENT HERE. HAPPY.
HEY.
PORTRAITS OF THE FLASH'S ALLIES...
ROSE WILSON. MAX MERCURY...AND DONNA?
DONNA...? BUT BART NEVER... WHAT DOES THAT MEAN, KORY?
I WISH I KNEW, CASSIE. I TRULY DO.
IT'S RIGHT DOWN HERE. ALL OF THE ZOOM DISPLAYS--
WHERE DO YOU THINK WE WENT WRONG, BART?
I DON'T KNOW. BUT NOW THAT WE'VE SEEN IT...WE CAN FIGURE OUT HOW TO CHANGE THE FUTURE.
YOU ASK ME -- THERE'S ONLY ONE SURE WAY TO DO IT. TO MAKE SURE THESE TITANS NEVER EXIST.
HOW--?
FLASH THE COSMIC TREADMILL
--OH, NO.
IT'S NOT HERE.
ANY IDEAS WHERE IT COULD--?
MAYBE IT WASN'T REBUILT. MAYBE THEY TOOK IT SOMEWHERE ELSE --

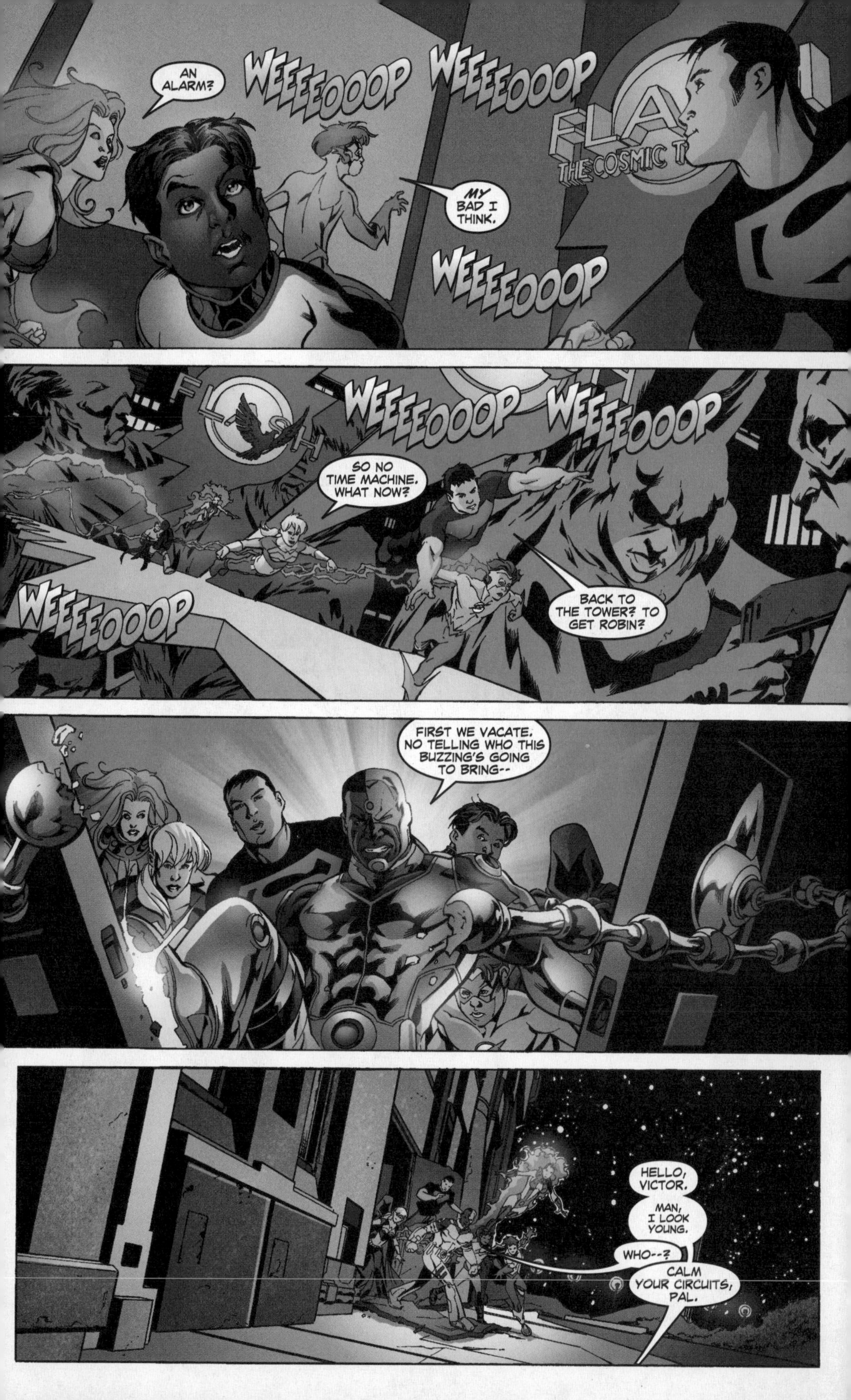
AN ALARM?
WEEEEOOOP WEEEEOOOP
MY BAD I THINK.
WEEEEOOOP
WEEEEOOOP WEEEEOOOP
SO NO TIME MACHINE. WHAT NOW?
BACK TO THE TOWER? TO GET ROBIN?
WEEEEOOOP
FIRST WE VACATE. NO TELLING WHO THIS BUZZING'S GOING TO BRING--
HELLO, VICTOR.
MAN, I LOOK YOUNG.
WHO--?
CALM YOUR CIRCUITS, PAL.

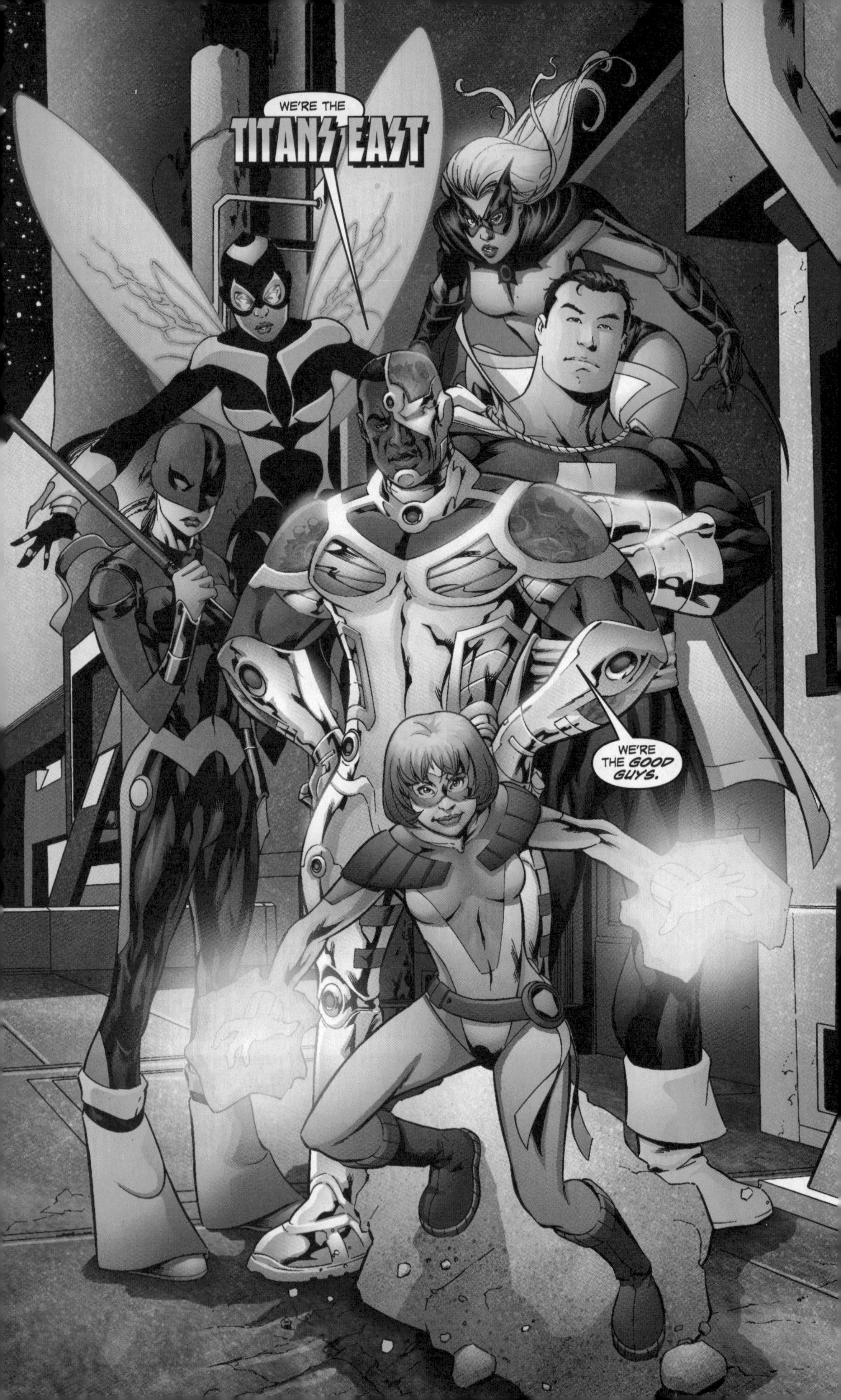
WE'RE THE
TITANS EAST
WE'RE THE GOOD GUYS.

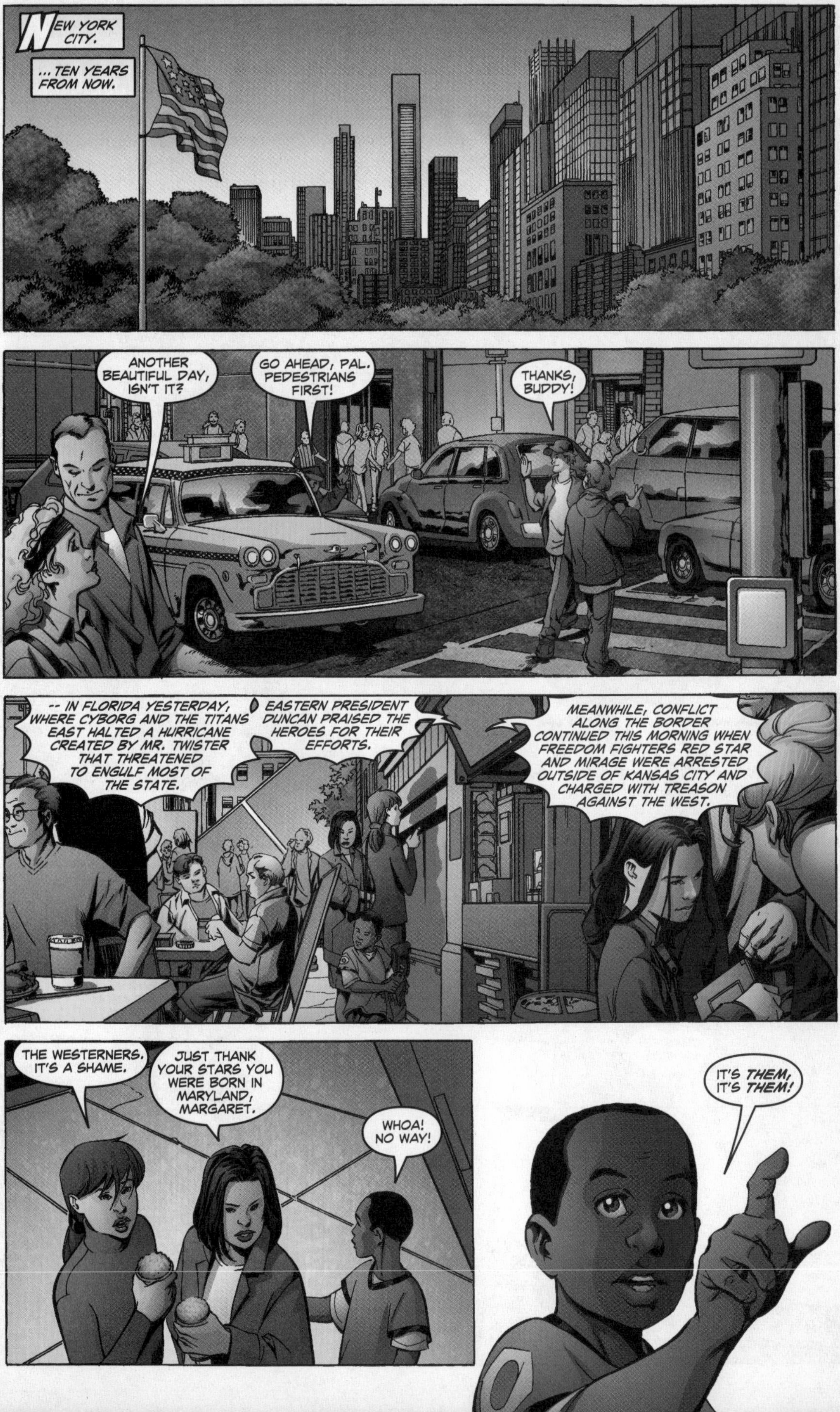
NEW YORK CITY.
...TEN YEARS FROM NOW.
ANOTHER BEAUTIFUL DAY, ISN'T IT?
GO AHEAD, PAL. PEDESTRIANS FIRST!
THANKS, BUDDY!
-- IN FLORIDA YESTERDAY, WHERE CYBORG AND THE TITANS EAST HALTED A HURRICANE CREATED BY MR. TWISTER THAT THREATENED TO ENGULF MOST OF THE STATE.
EASTERN PRESIDENT DUNCAN PRAISED THE HEROES FOR THEIR EFFORTS.
MEANWHILE, CONFLICT ALONG THE BORDER CONTINUED THIS MORNING WHEN FREEDOM FIGHTERS RED STAR AND MIRAGE WERE ARRESTED OUTSIDE OF KANSAS CITY AND CHARGED WITH TREASON AGAINST THE WEST.
THE WESTERNERS. IT'S A SHAME.
JUST THANK YOUR STARS YOU WERE BORN IN MARYLAND, MARGARET.
WHOA! NO WAY!
IT'S *THEM*, IT'S *THEM*!

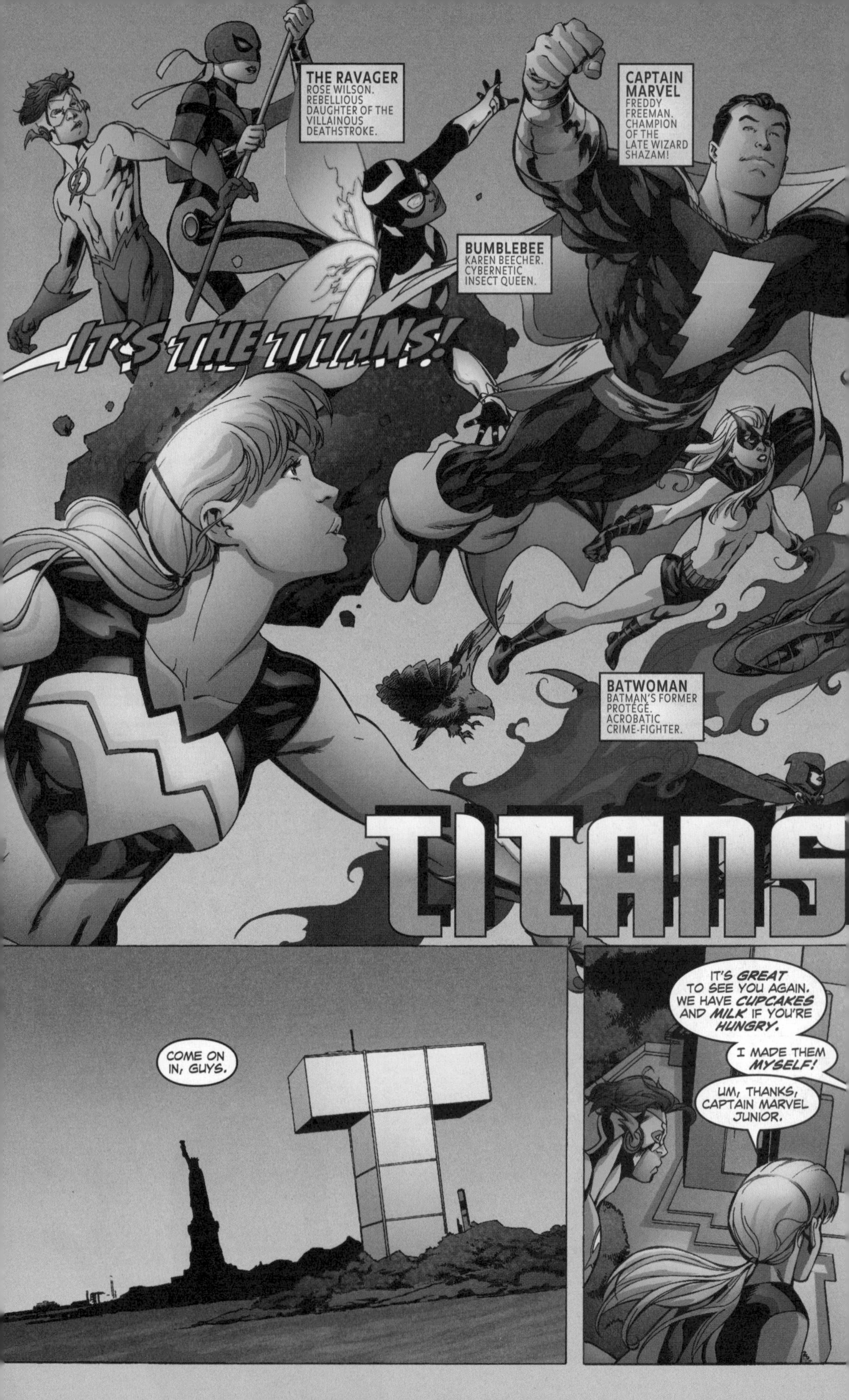
THE RAVAGER ROSE WILSON. REBELLIOUS DAUGHTER OF THE VILLAINOUS DEATHSTROKE.
CAPTAIN MARVEL FREDDY FREEMAN. CHAMPION OF THE LATE WIZARD SHAZAM!
BUMBLEBEE KAREN BEECHER. CYBERNETIC INSECT QUEEN.
IT'S THE TITANS!
BATWOMAN BATMAN'S FORMER PROTÉGÉ. ACROBATIC CRIME-FIGHTER.
TITANS
COME ON IN, GUYS.
IT'S GREAT TO SEE YOU AGAIN. WE HAVE CUPCAKES AND MILK IF YOU'RE HUNGRY.
I MADE THEM MYSELF!
UM, THANKS, CAPTAIN MARVEL JUNIOR.

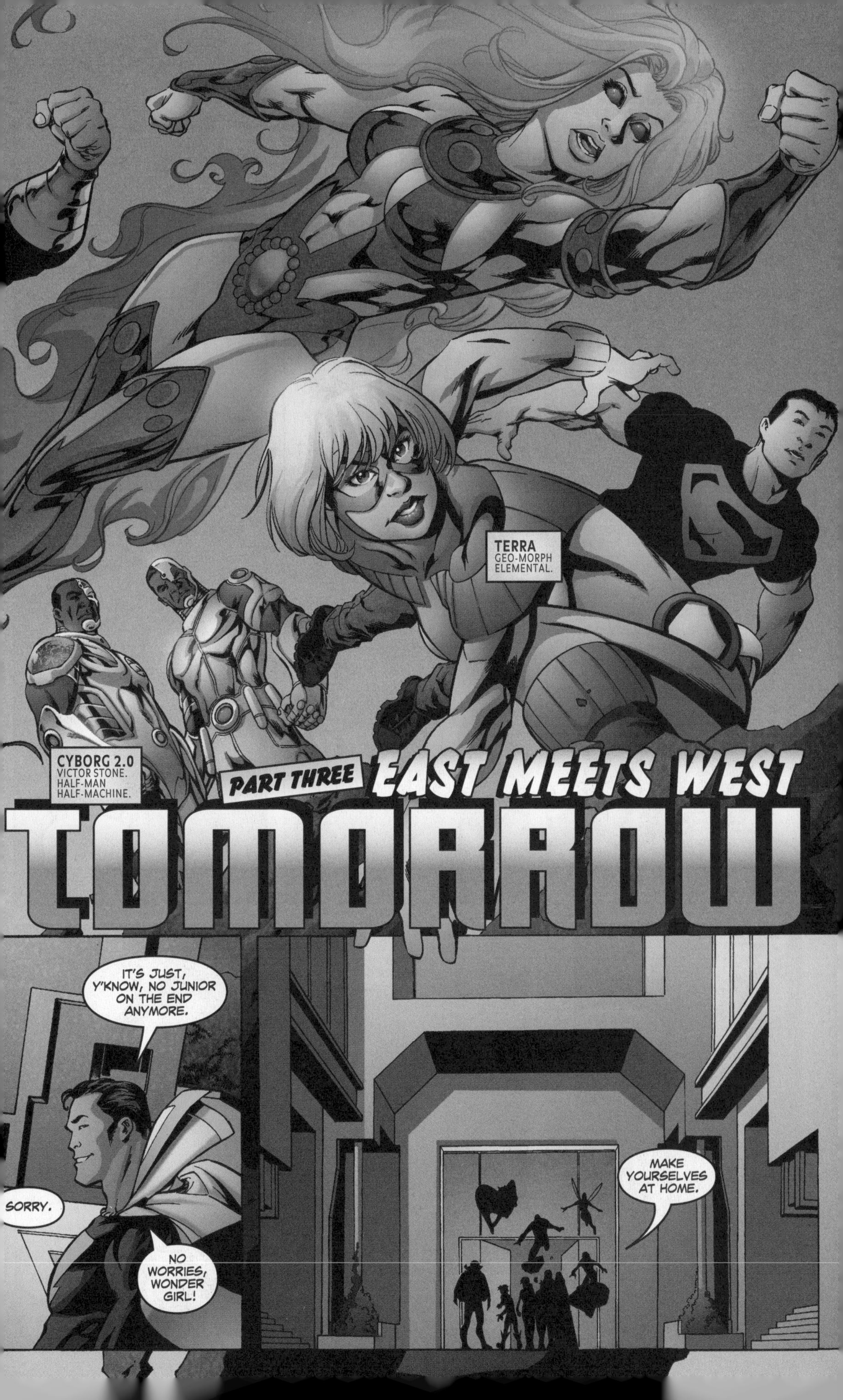
TERRA
GEO-MORPH ELEMENTAL.
CYBORG 2.0
VICTOR STONE. HALF-MAN HALF-MACHINE.
PART THREE EAST MEETS WEST
TOMORROW
IT'S JUST, Y'KNOW, NO JUNIOR ON THE END ANYMORE.
SORRY.
NO WORRIES, WONDER GIRL!
MAKE YOURSELVES AT HOME.

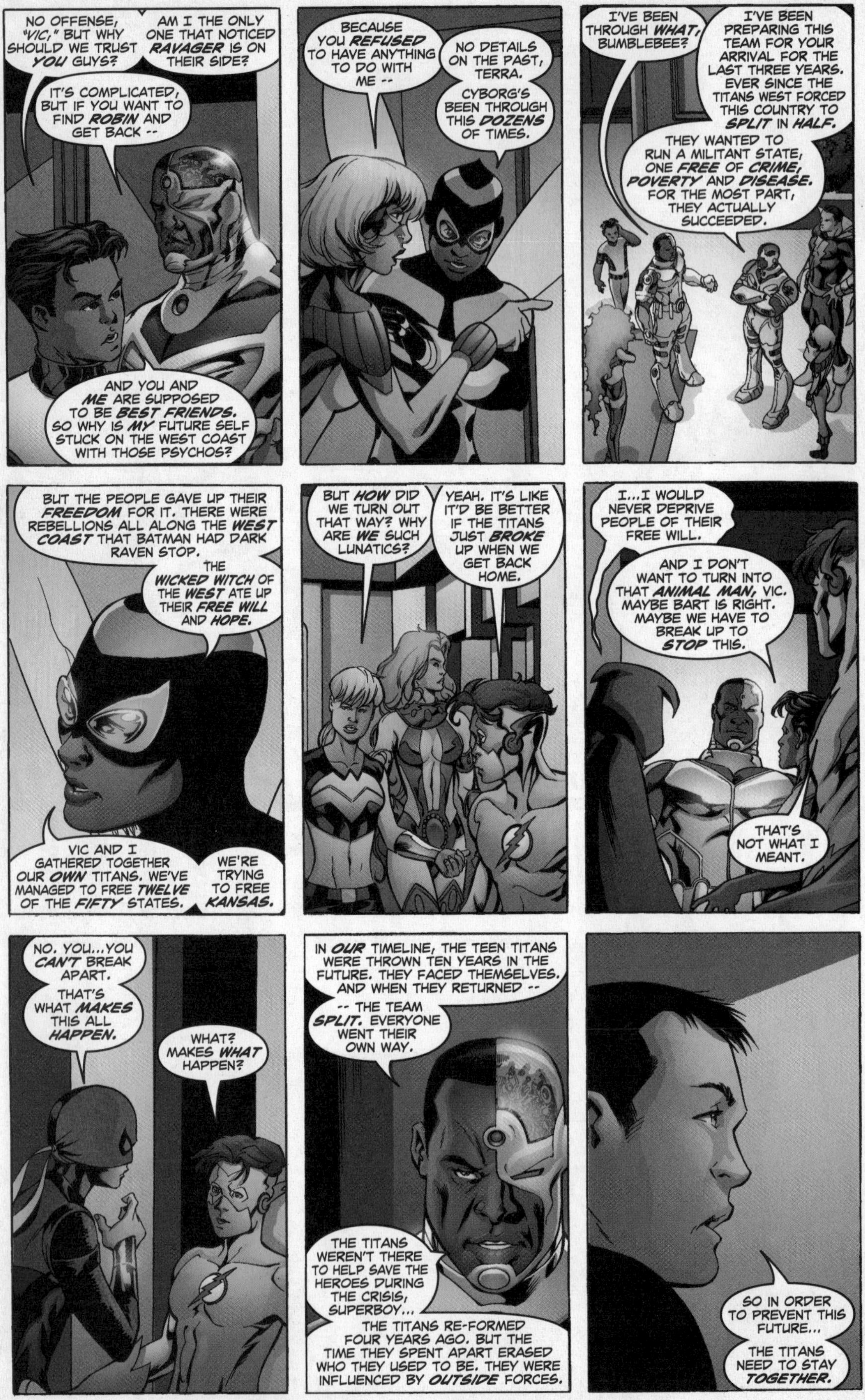
NO OFFENSE, "VIC," BUT WHY SHOULD WE TRUST YOU GUYS?
AM I THE ONLY ONE THAT NOTICED RAVAGER IS ON THEIR SIDE?
IT'S COMPLICATED, BUT IF YOU WANT TO FIND ROBIN AND GET BACK --
AND YOU AND ME ARE SUPPOSED TO BE BEST FRIENDS. SO WHY IS MY FUTURE SELF STUCK ON THE WEST COAST WITH THOSE PSYCHOS?
BECAUSE YOU REFUSED TO HAVE ANYTHING TO DO WITH ME --
NO DETAILS ON THE PAST, TERRA.
CYBORG'S BEEN THROUGH THIS DOZENS OF TIMES.
I'VE BEEN THROUGH WHAT, BUMBLEBEE?
I'VE BEEN PREPARING THIS TEAM FOR YOUR ARRIVAL FOR THE LAST THREE YEARS. EVER SINCE THE TITANS WEST FORCED THIS COUNTRY TO SPLIT IN HALF.
THEY WANTED TO RUN A MILITANT STATE, ONE FREE OF CRIME, POVERTY AND DISEASE. FOR THE MOST PART, THEY ACTUALLY SUCCEEDED.
BUT THE PEOPLE GAVE UP THEIR FREEDOM FOR IT. THERE WERE REBELLIONS ALL ALONG THE WEST COAST THAT BATMAN HAD DARK RAVEN STOP.
THE WICKED WITCH OF THE WEST ATE UP THEIR FREE WILL AND HOPE.
VIC AND I GATHERED TOGETHER OUR OWN TITANS. WE'VE MANAGED TO FREE TWELVE OF THE FIFTY STATES.
WE'RE TRYING TO FREE KANSAS.
BUT HOW DID WE TURN OUT THAT WAY? WHY ARE WE SUCH LUNATICS?
YEAH. IT'S LIKE IT'D BE BETTER IF THE TITANS JUST BROKE UP WHEN WE GET BACK HOME.
I...I WOULD NEVER DEPRIVE PEOPLE OF THEIR FREE WILL.
AND I DON'T WANT TO TURN INTO THAT ANIMAL MAN, VIC. MAYBE BART IS RIGHT. MAYBE WE HAVE TO BREAK UP TO STOP THIS.
THAT'S NOT WHAT I MEANT.
NO. YOU...YOU CAN'T BREAK APART.
THAT'S WHAT MAKES THIS ALL HAPPEN.
WHAT? MAKES WHAT HAPPEN?
IN OUR TIMELINE, THE TEEN TITANS WERE THROWN TEN YEARS IN THE FUTURE. THEY FACED THEMSELVES. AND WHEN THEY RETURNED --
-- THE TEAM SPLIT. EVERYONE WENT THEIR OWN WAY.
THE TITANS WEREN'T THERE TO HELP SAVE THE HEROES DURING THE CRISIS, SUPERBOY...
THE TITANS RE-FORMED FOUR YEARS AGO. BUT THE TIME THEY SPENT APART ERASED WHO THEY USED TO BE. THEY WERE INFLUENCED BY OUTSIDE FORCES.
SO IN ORDER TO PREVENT THIS FUTURE...
THE TITANS NEED TO STAY TOGETHER.

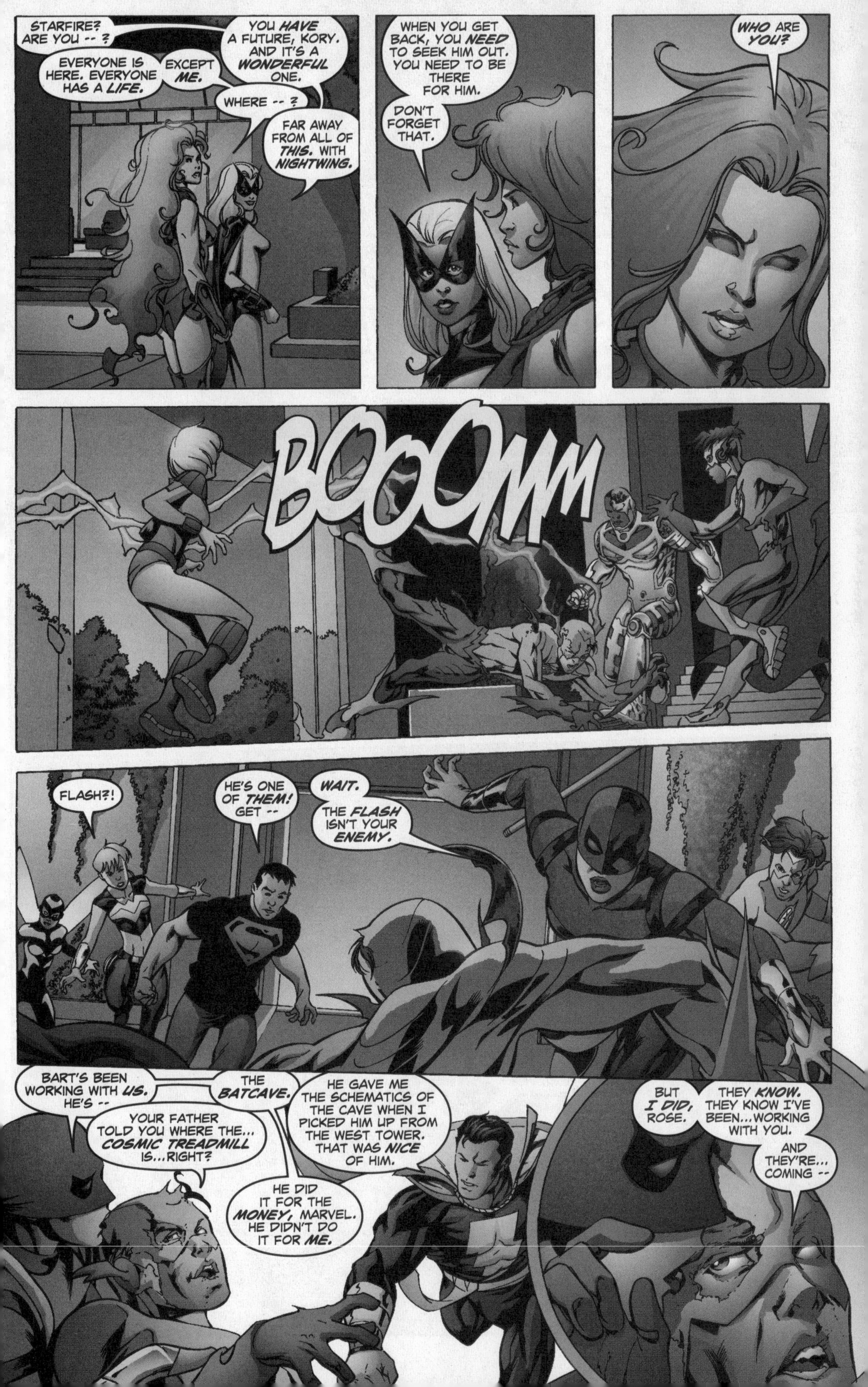
STARFIRE? ARE YOU -- ?
EVERYONE IS HERE. EVERYONE HAS A LIFE.
EXCEPT ME.
YOU HAVE A FUTURE, KORY. AND IT'S A WONDERFUL ONE.
WHERE -- ?
FAR AWAY FROM ALL OF THIS. WITH NIGHTWING.
WHEN YOU GET BACK, YOU NEED TO SEEK HIM OUT. YOU NEED TO BE THERE FOR HIM.
DON'T FORGET THAT.
WHO ARE YOU?
BOOOMM
FLASH?!
HE'S ONE OF THEM! GET --
WAIT.
THE FLASH ISN'T YOUR ENEMY.
BART'S BEEN WORKING WITH US. HE'S --
YOUR FATHER TOLD YOU WHERE THE... COSMIC TREADMILL IS...RIGHT?
THE BATCAVE.
HE GAVE ME THE SCHEMATICS OF THE CAVE WHEN I PICKED HIM UP FROM THE WEST TOWER. THAT WAS NICE OF HIM.
HE DID IT FOR THE MONEY, MARVEL. HE DIDN'T DO IT FOR ME.
BUT I DID, ROSE.
THEY KNOW. THEY KNOW I'VE BEEN...WORKING WITH YOU.
AND THEY'RE... COMING --

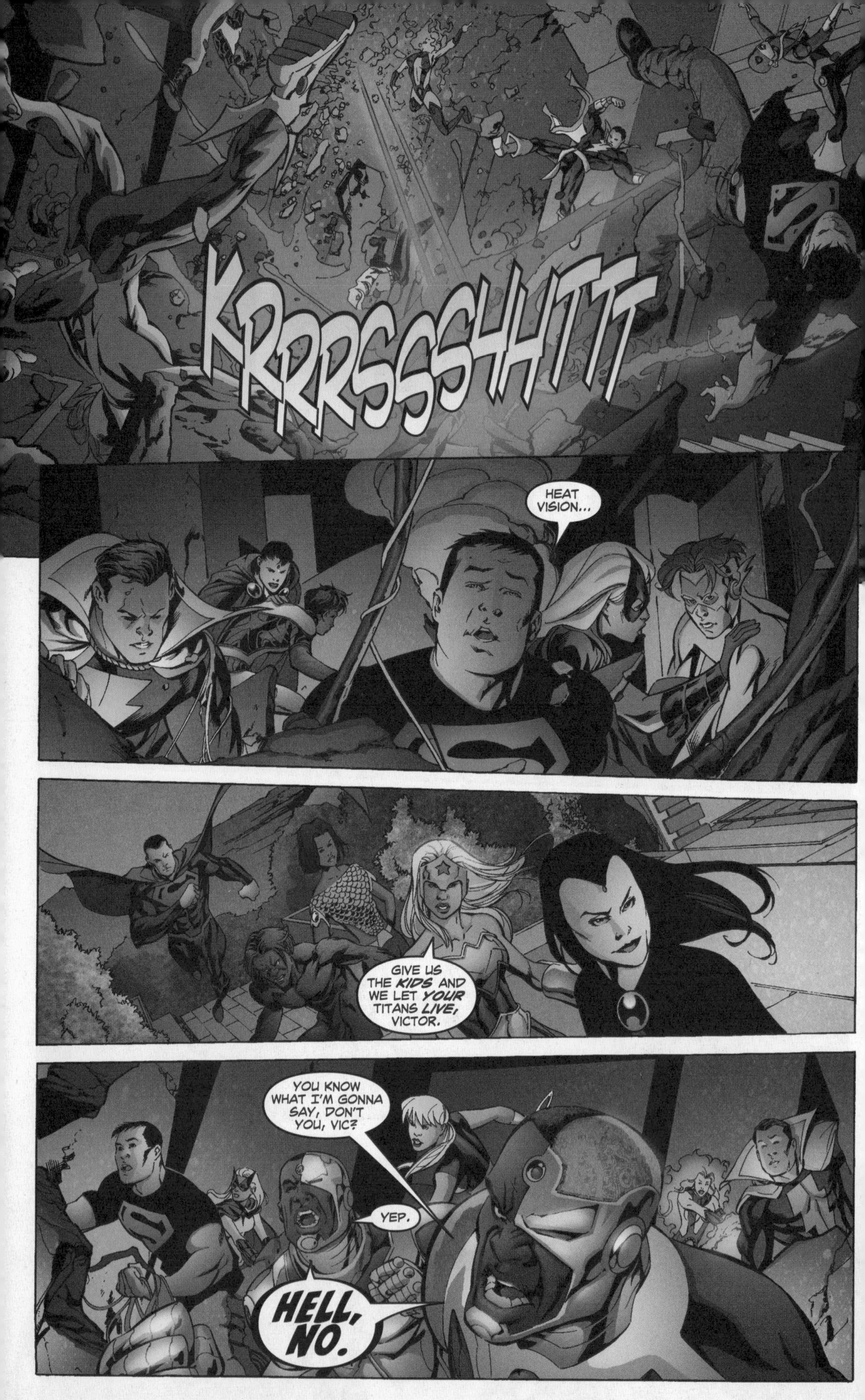
KRRRSSSHTTT
HEAT VISION...
GIVE US THE *KIDS* AND WE LET *YOUR* TITANS *LIVE,* VICTOR.
YOU KNOW WHAT I'M GONNA SAY, DON'T YOU, VIC?
YEP.
HELL, NO.

Teen Titans

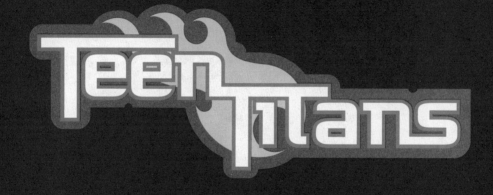

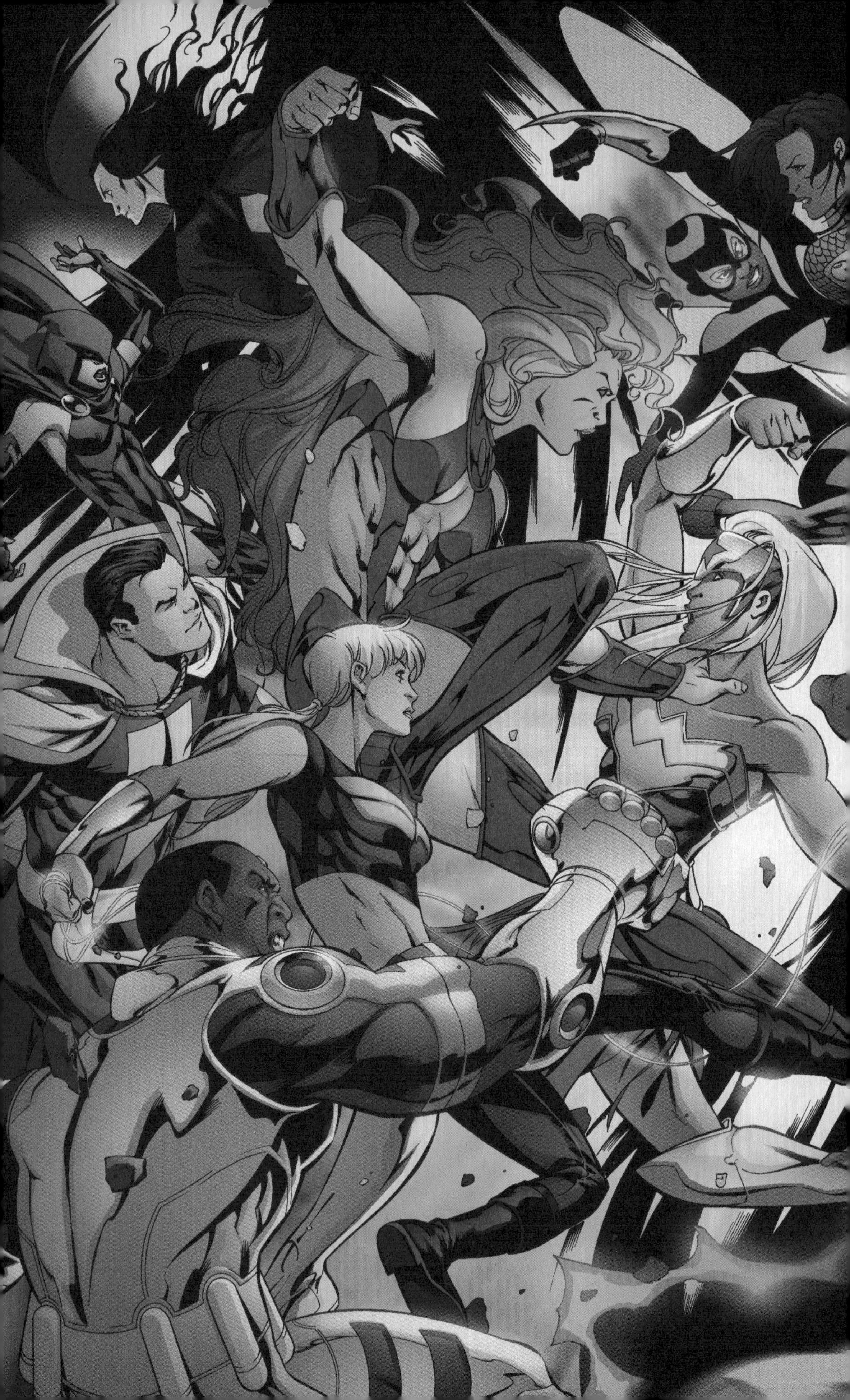

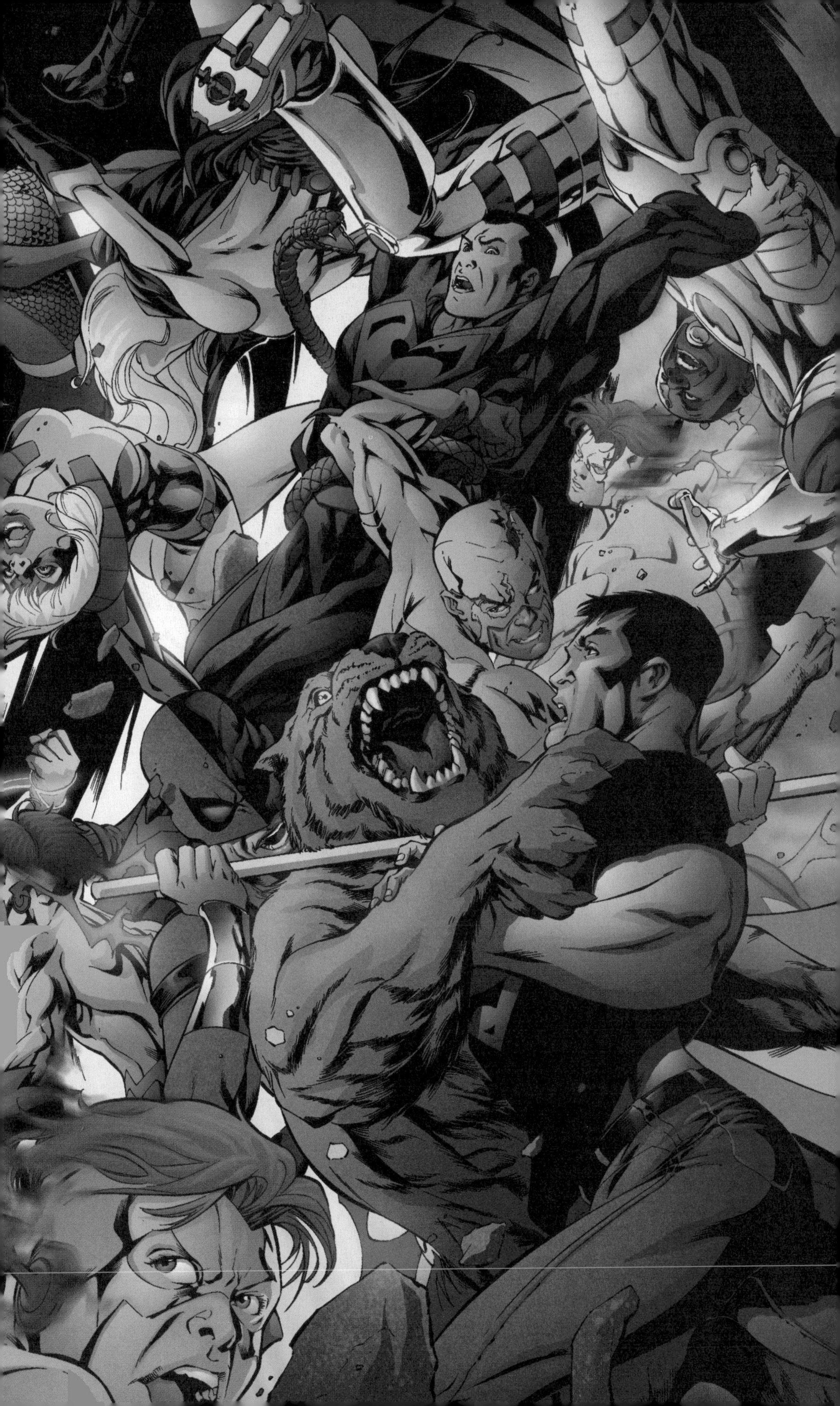

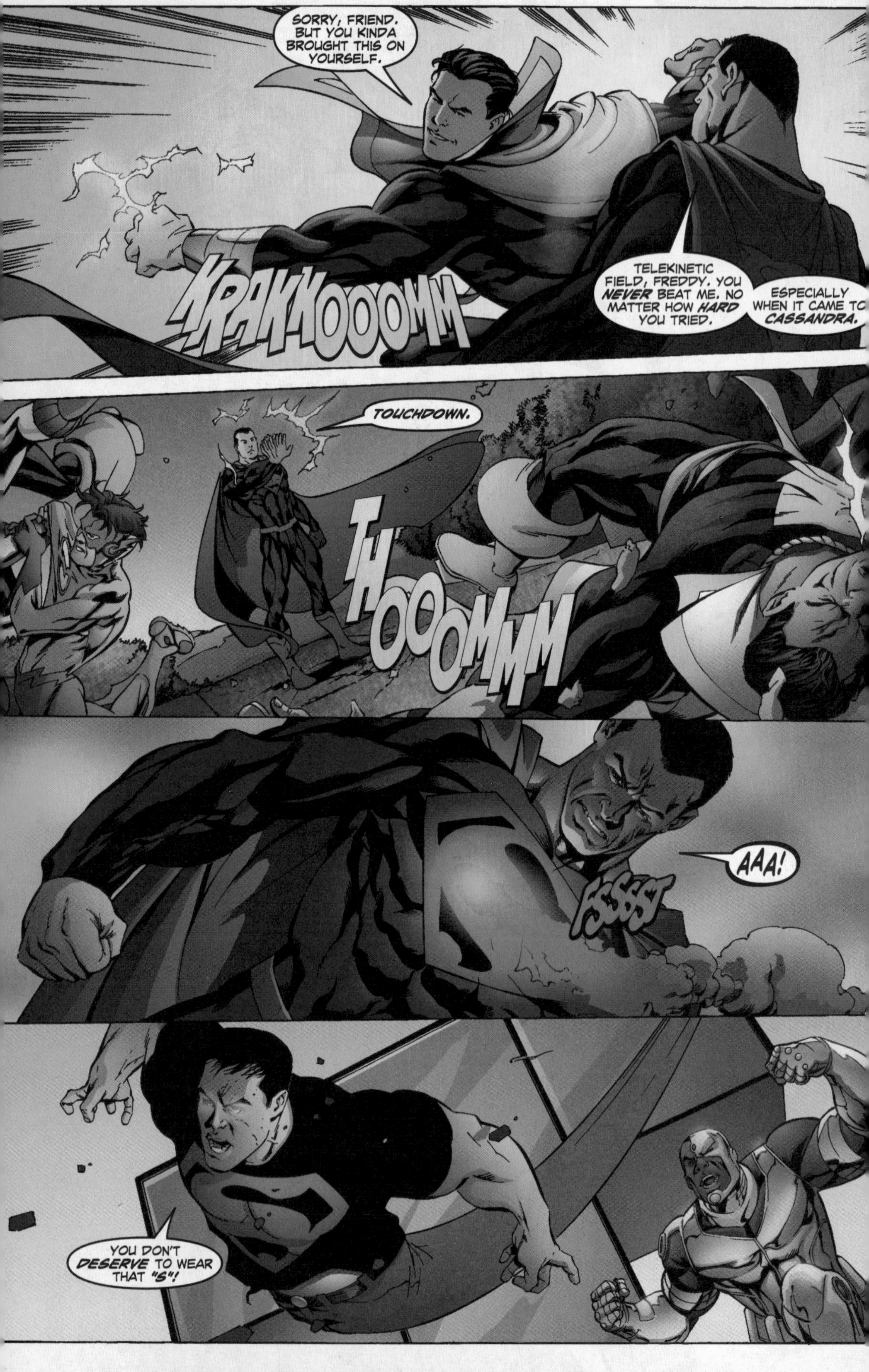
SORRY, FRIEND. BUT YOU KINDA BROUGHT THIS ON YOURSELF.
KRAKKOOOOMM
TELEKINETIC FIELD, FREDDY. YOU NEVER BEAT ME. NO MATTER HOW HARD YOU TRIED.
ESPECIALLY WHEN IT CAME TO CASSANDRA.
TOUCHDOWN.
THOOOMMM
AAA!
FSSSST
YOU DON'T DESERVE TO WEAR THAT "S"!

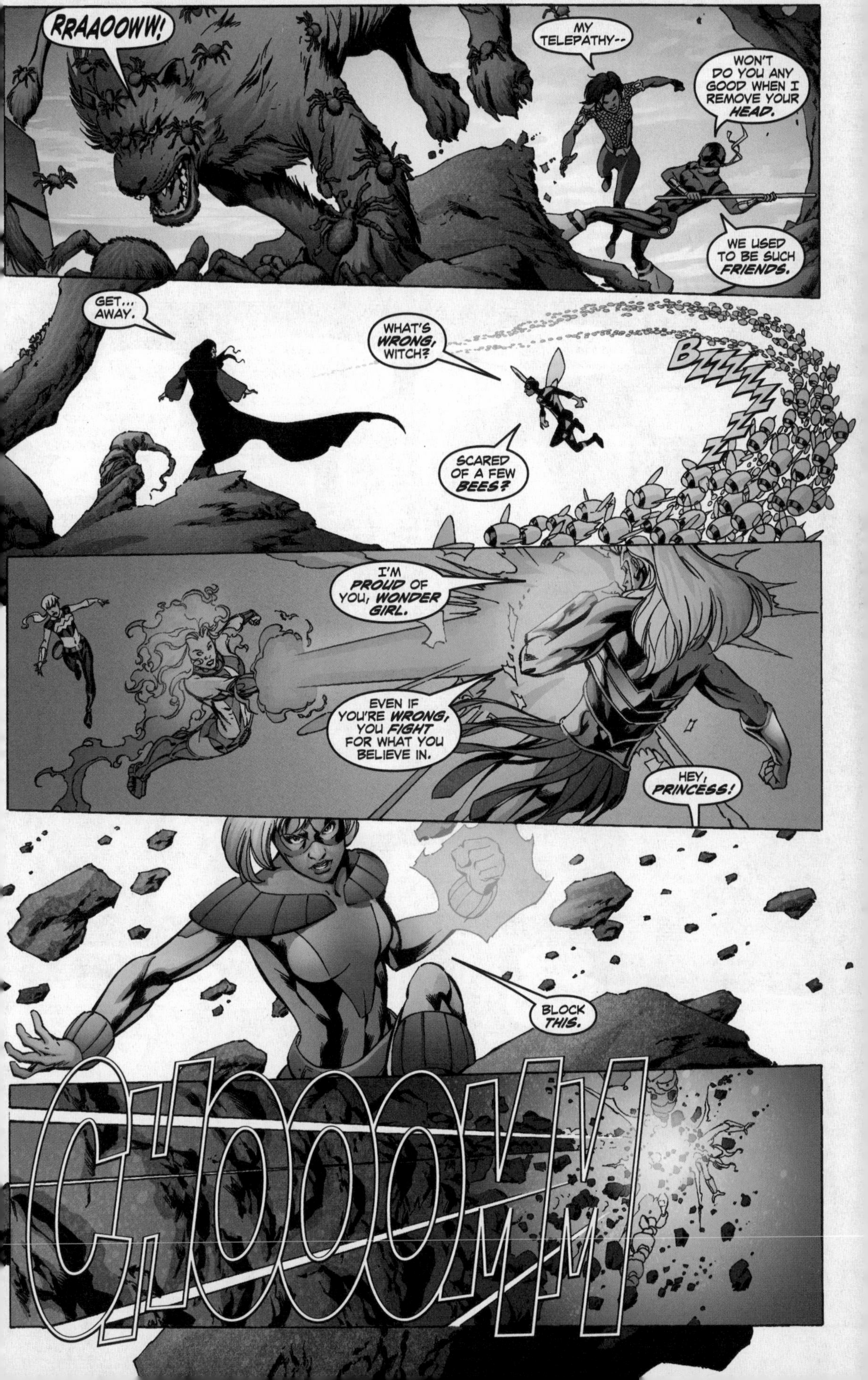
RRAAOOWW!
MY TELEPATHY--
WON'T DO YOU ANY GOOD WHEN I REMOVE YOUR HEAD.
WE USED TO BE SUCH FRIENDS.
GET... AWAY.
WHAT'S WRONG, WITCH?
SCARED OF A FEW BEES?
BZZZZZ
I'M PROUD OF YOU, WONDER GIRL.
EVEN IF YOU'RE WRONG, YOU FIGHT FOR WHAT YOU BELIEVE IN.
HEY, PRINCESS!
BLOCK THIS.
CHOOOOMMM

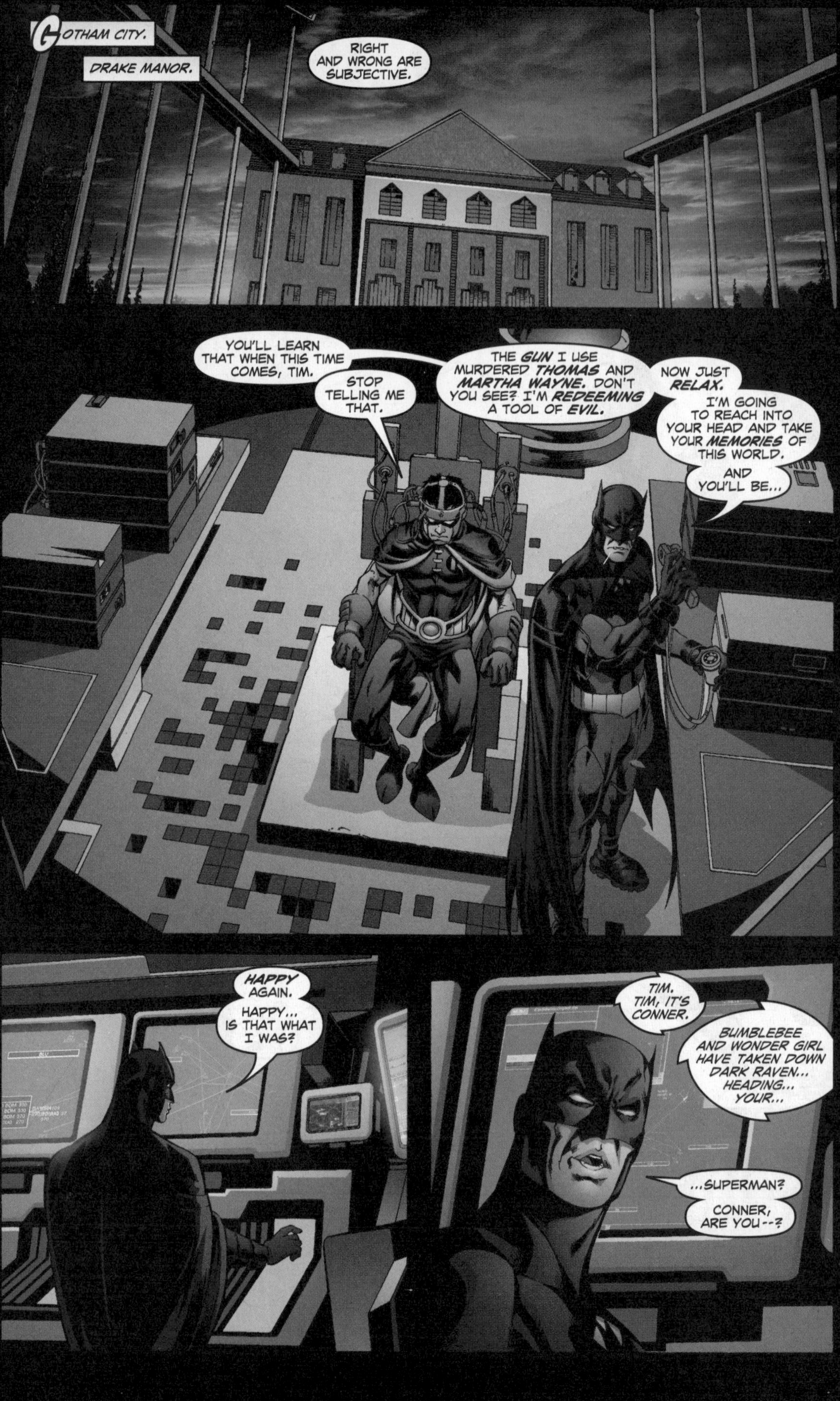
GOTHAM CITY.
DRAKE MANOR.
RIGHT AND WRONG ARE SUBJECTIVE.
YOU'LL LEARN THAT WHEN THIS TIME COMES, TIM.
STOP TELLING ME THAT.
THE GUN I USE MURDERED THOMAS AND MARTHA WAYNE. DON'T YOU SEE? I'M REDEEMING A TOOL OF EVIL.
NOW JUST RELAX.
I'M GOING TO REACH INTO YOUR HEAD AND TAKE YOUR MEMORIES OF THIS WORLD.
AND YOU'LL BE...
HAPPY AGAIN.
HAPPY... IS THAT WHAT I WAS?
TIM. TIM, IT'S CONNER.
BUMBLEBEE AND WONDER GIRL HAVE TAKEN DOWN DARK RAVEN... HEADING... YOUR...
...SUPERMAN?
CONNER, ARE YOU--?

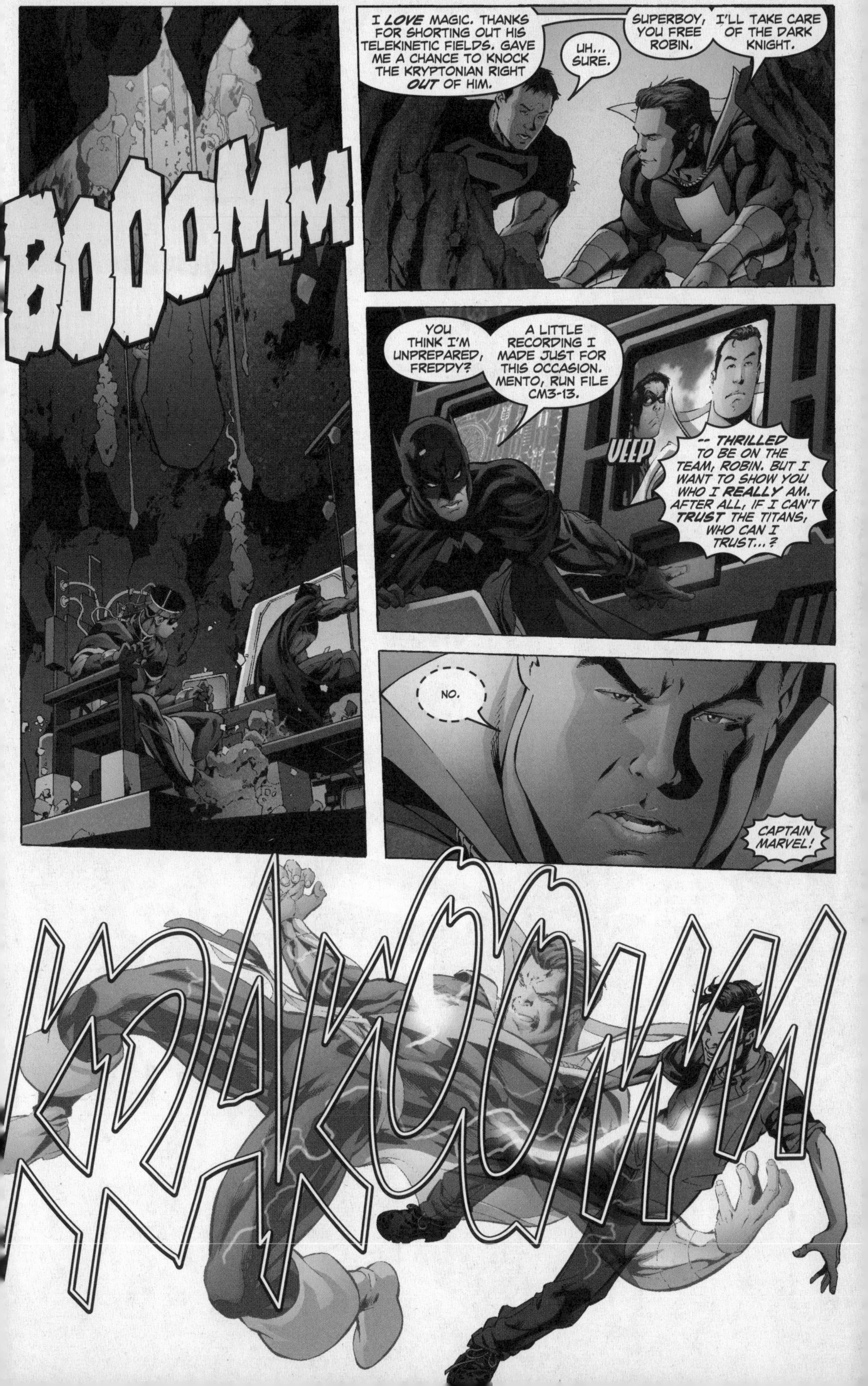
BOOOMM
I LOVE MAGIC. THANKS FOR SHORTING OUT HIS TELEKINETIC FIELDS. GAVE ME A CHANCE TO KNOCK THE KRYPTONIAN RIGHT OUT OF HIM.
UH... SURE.
SUPERBOY, YOU FREE ROBIN.
I'LL TAKE CARE OF THE DARK KNIGHT.
YOU THINK I'M UNPREPARED, FREDDY?
A LITTLE RECORDING I MADE JUST FOR THIS OCCASION. MENTO, RUN FILE CM3-13.
VEEP
-- THRILLED TO BE ON THE TEAM, ROBIN. BUT I WANT TO SHOW YOU WHO I REALLY AM. AFTER ALL, IF I CAN'T TRUST THE TITANS, WHO CAN I TRUST...?
NO.
CAPTAIN MARVEL!
KRAKOOMM

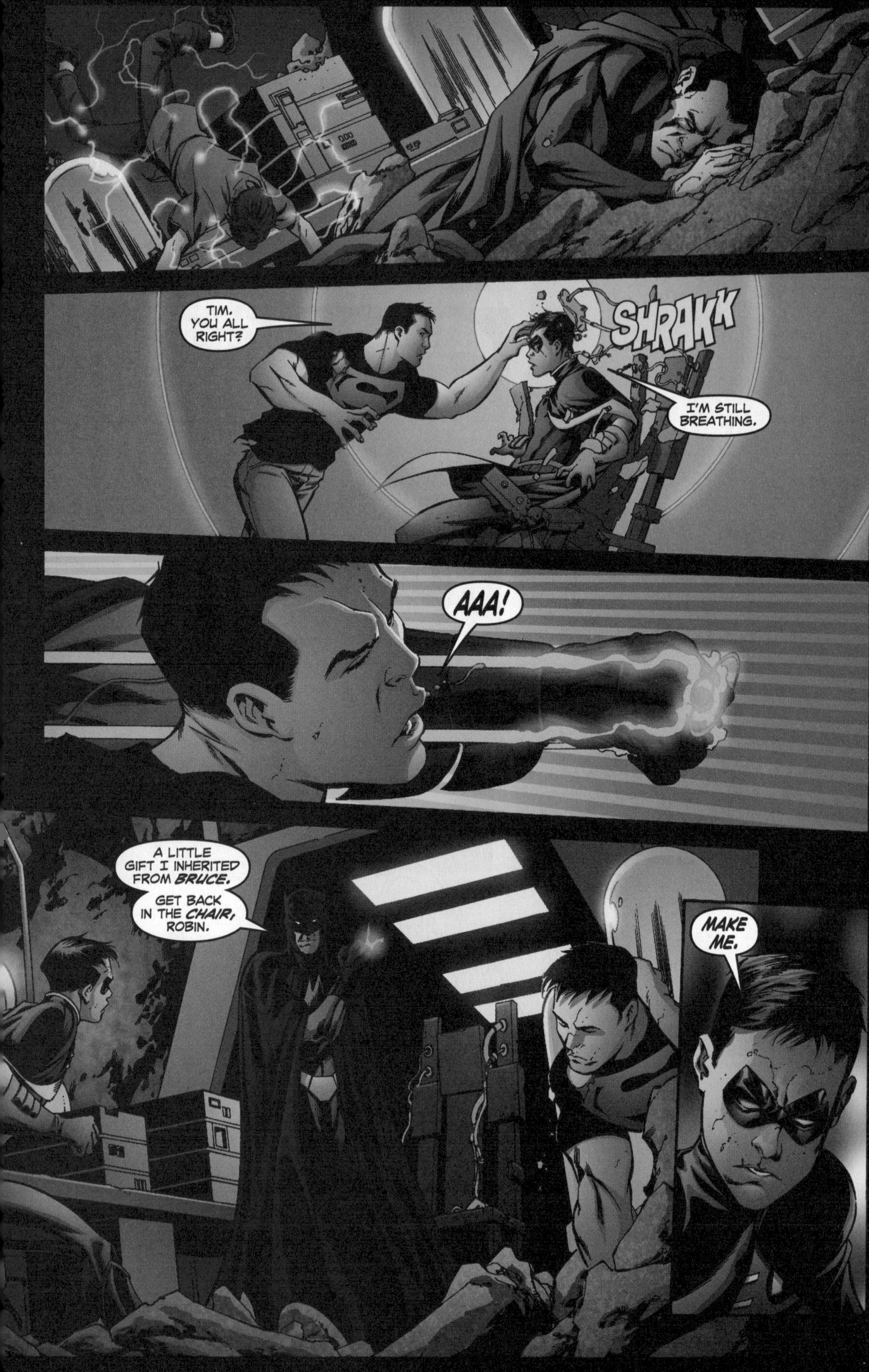

TIM. YOU ALL RIGHT?
SHRAKK
I'M STILL BREATHING.
AAA!
A LITTLE GIFT I INHERITED FROM BRUCE.
GET BACK IN THE CHAIR, ROBIN.
MAKE ME.

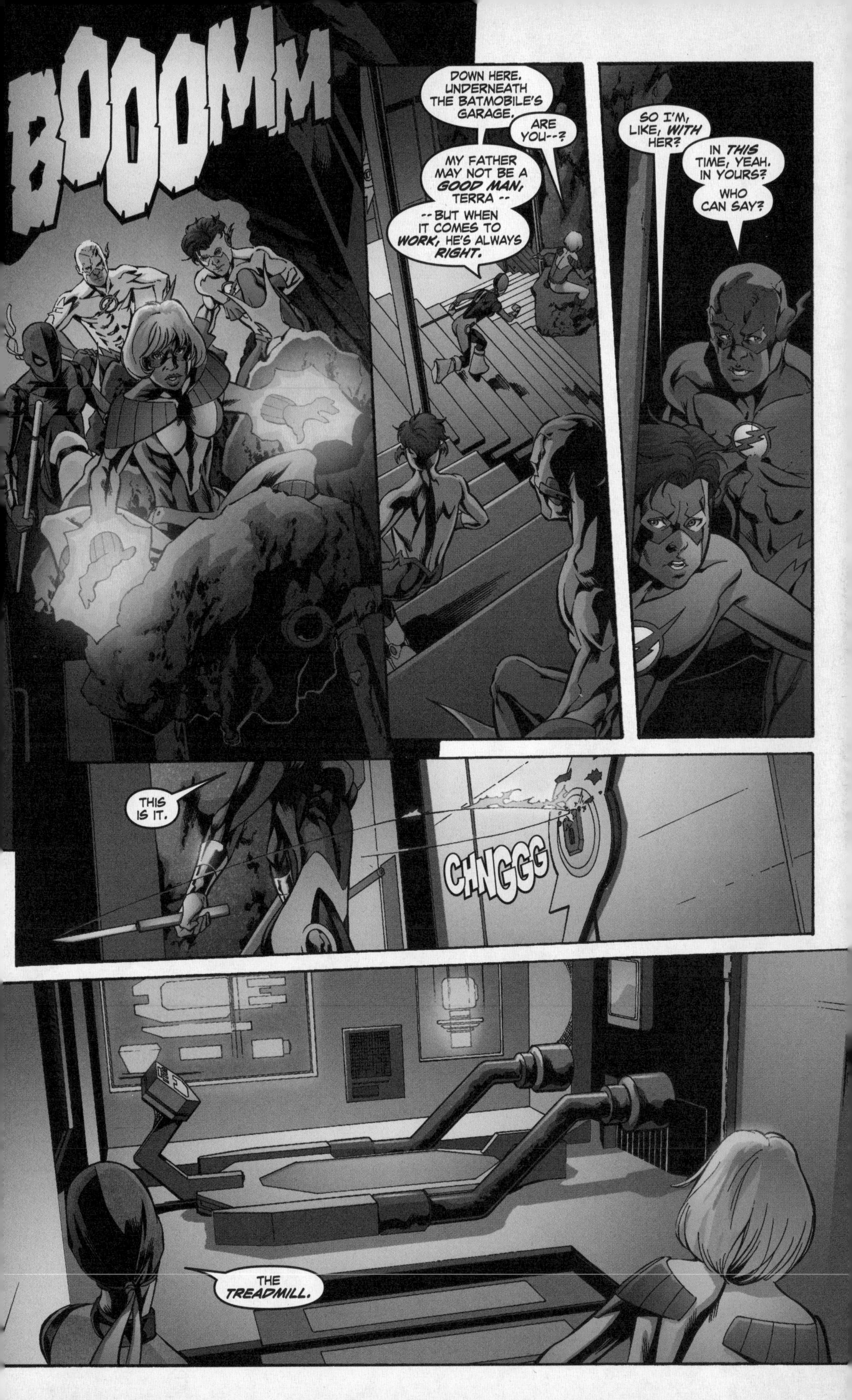
BOOOMM
DOWN HERE. UNDERNEATH THE BATMOBILE'S GARAGE.
ARE YOU--?
MY FATHER MAY NOT BE A GOOD MAN, TERRA --
-- BUT WHEN IT COMES TO WORK, HE'S ALWAYS RIGHT.
SO I'M, LIKE, WITH HER?
IN THIS TIME, YEAH. IN YOURS?
WHO CAN SAY?
THIS IS IT.
CHNGGG
THE TREADMILL.

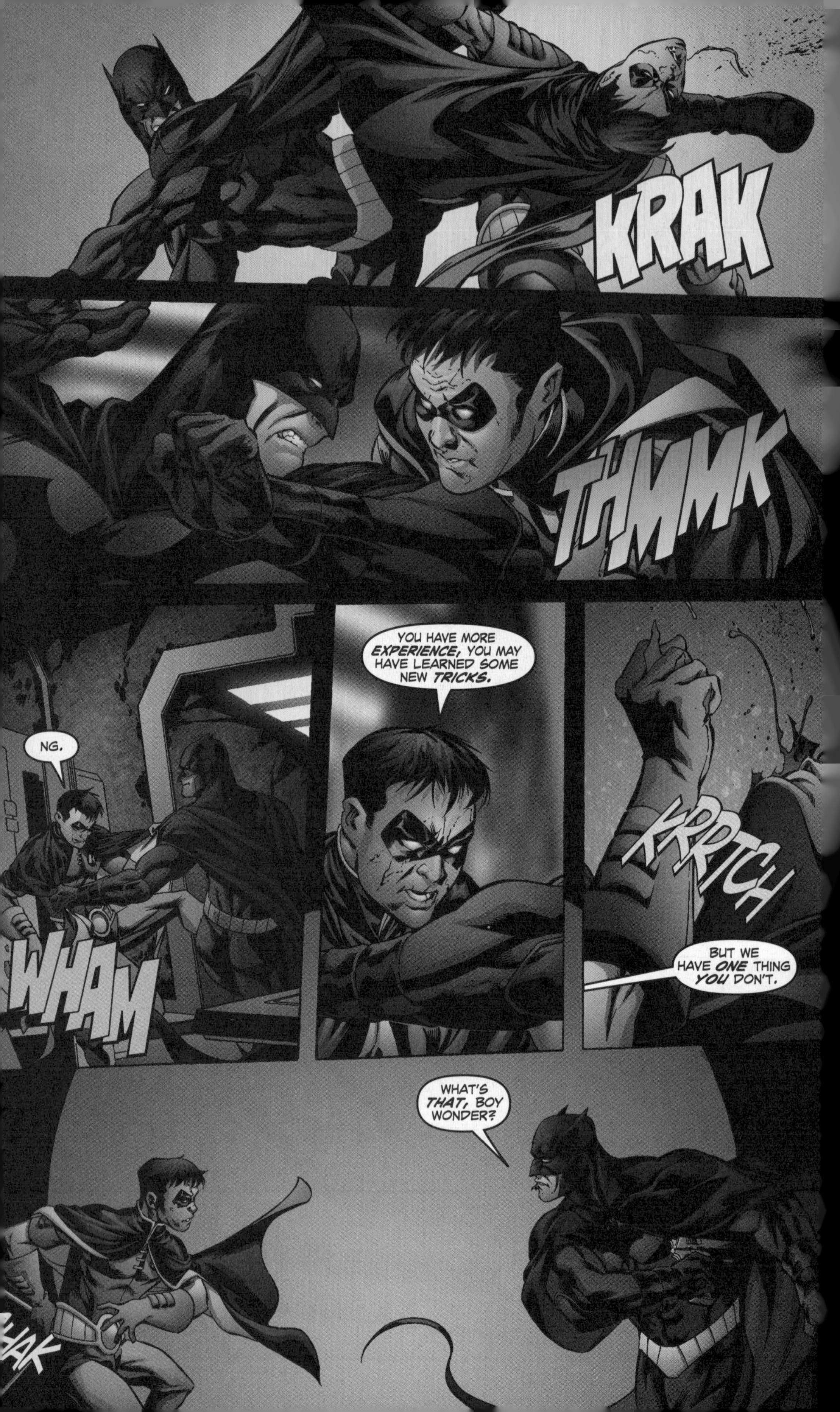
KRAK
THMMK
NG.
WHAM
YOU HAVE MORE EXPERIENCE, YOU MAY HAVE LEARNED SOME NEW TRICKS.
KRRTCH
BUT WE HAVE ONE THING YOU DON'T.
WHAT'S THAT, BOY WONDER?

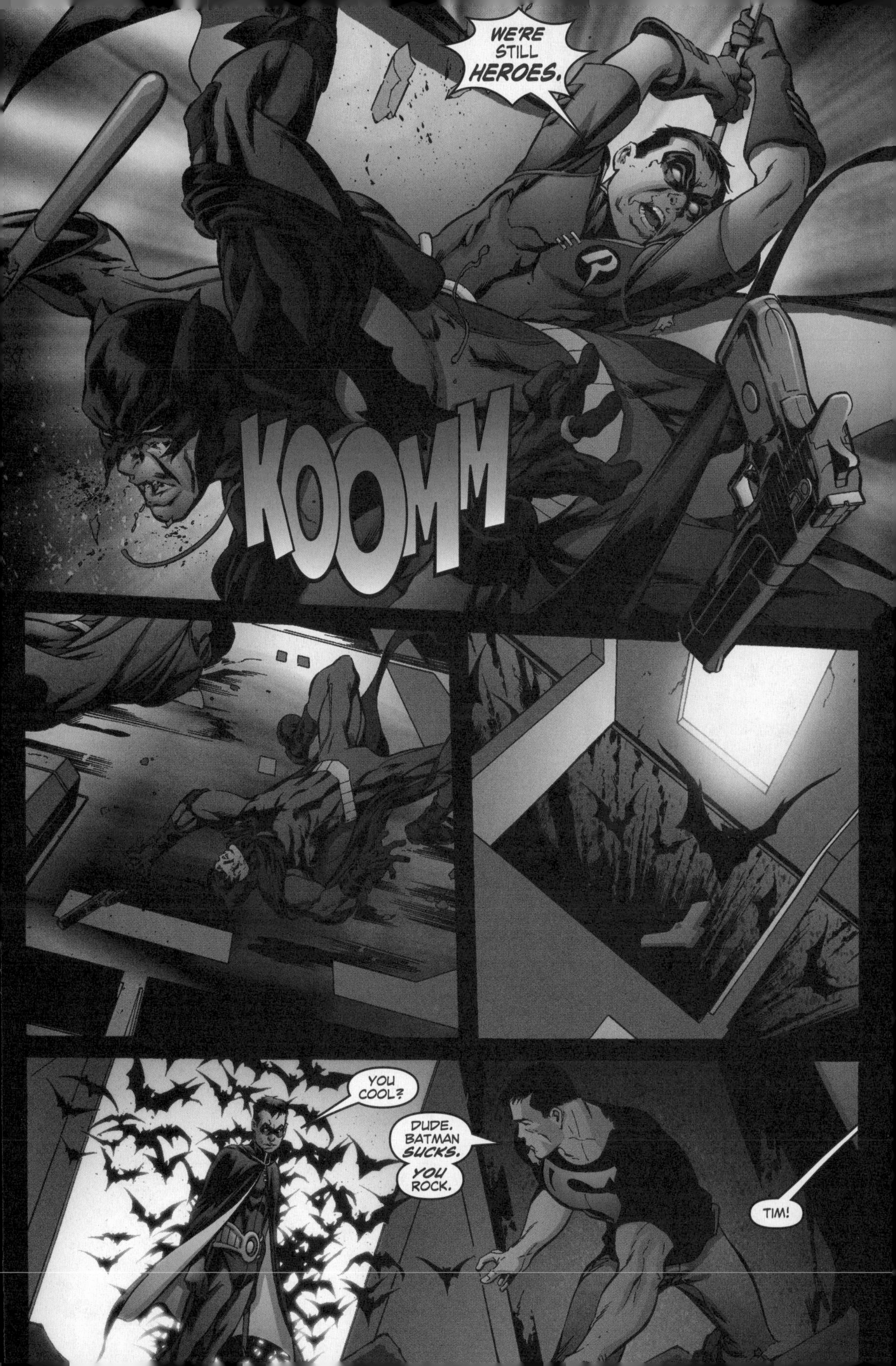
WE'RE STILL HEROES.
KOOMM
YOU COOL?
DUDE. BATMAN SUCKS.
YOU ROCK.
TIM!

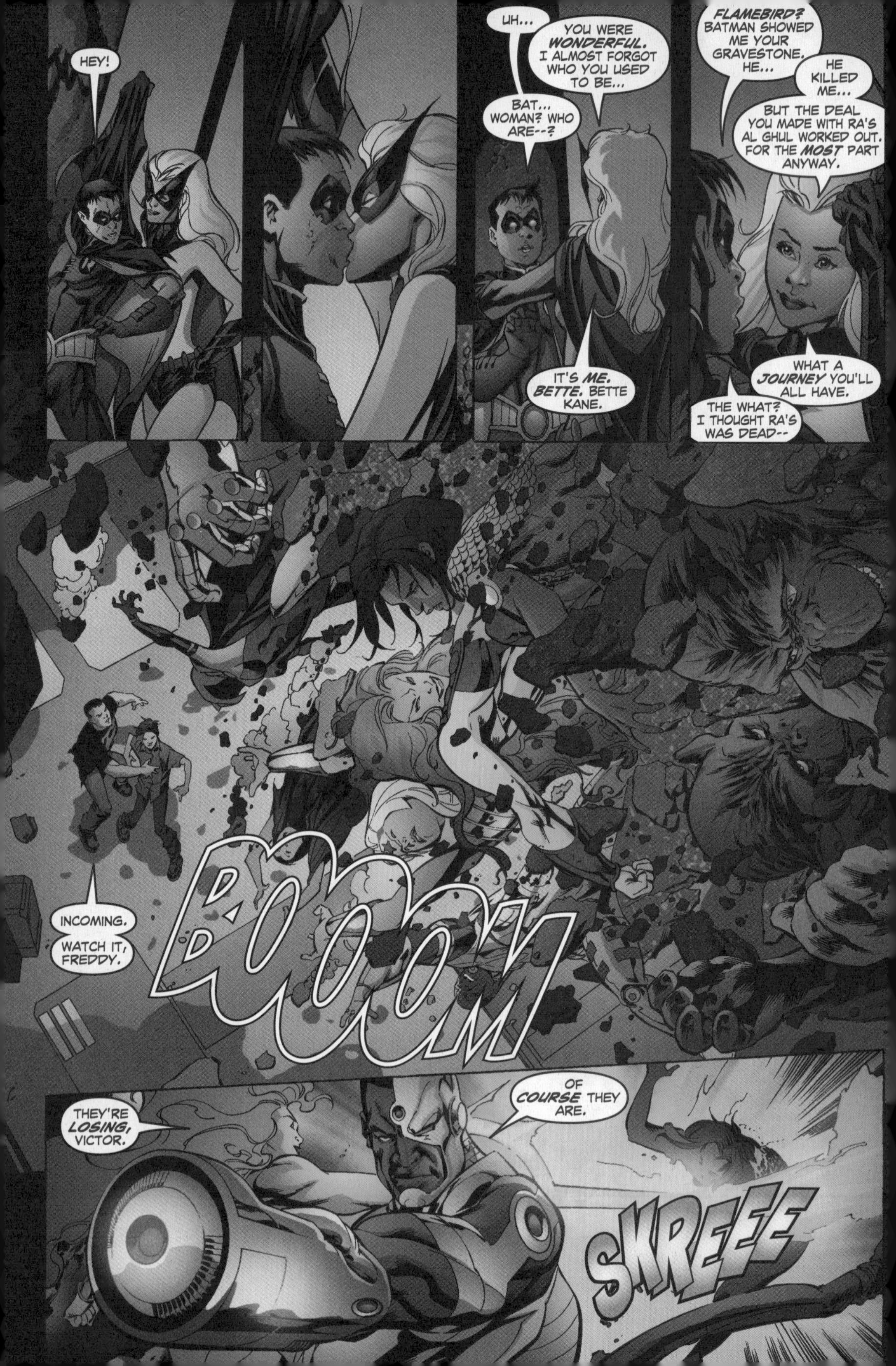
HEY!
UH...
YOU WERE WONDERFUL. I ALMOST FORGOT WHO YOU USED TO BE...
BAT... WOMAN? WHO ARE--?
IT'S ME. BETTE. BETTE KANE.
FLAMEBIRD? BATMAN SHOWED ME YOUR GRAVESTONE. HE...
HE KILLED ME...
BUT THE DEAL YOU MADE WITH RA'S AL GHUL WORKED OUT. FOR THE MOST PART ANYWAY.
WHAT A JOURNEY YOU'LL ALL HAVE.
THE WHAT? I THOUGHT RA'S WAS DEAD--
INCOMING. WATCH IT, FREDDY.
BOOOM
THEY'RE LOSING, VICTOR.
OF COURSE THEY ARE.
SKREEE

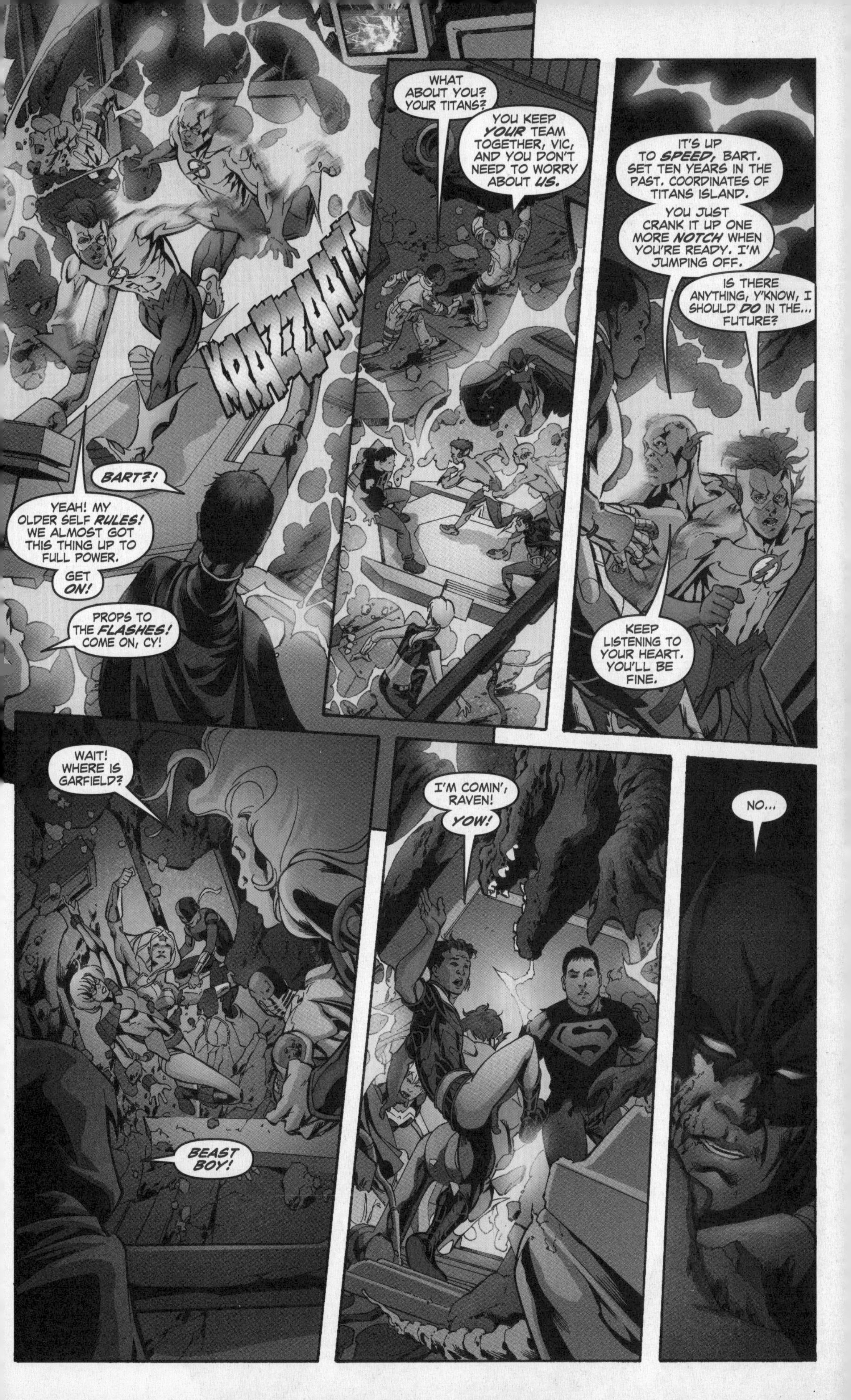

KRAZZAAT!
BART?!
YEAH! MY OLDER SELF RULES! WE ALMOST GOT THIS THING UP TO FULL POWER.
GET ON!
PROPS TO THE FLASHES! COME ON, CY!
WHAT ABOUT YOU? YOUR TITANS?
YOU KEEP YOUR TEAM TOGETHER, VIC, AND YOU DON'T NEED TO WORRY ABOUT US.
IT'S UP TO SPEED, BART. SET TEN YEARS IN THE PAST. COORDINATES OF TITANS ISLAND.
YOU JUST CRANK IT UP ONE MORE NOTCH WHEN YOU'RE READY. I'M JUMPING OFF.
IS THERE ANYTHING, Y'KNOW, I SHOULD DO IN THE... FUTURE?
KEEP LISTENING TO YOUR HEART. YOU'LL BE FINE.
WAIT! WHERE IS GARFIELD?
BEAST BOY!
I'M COMIN', RAVEN!
YOW!
NO...

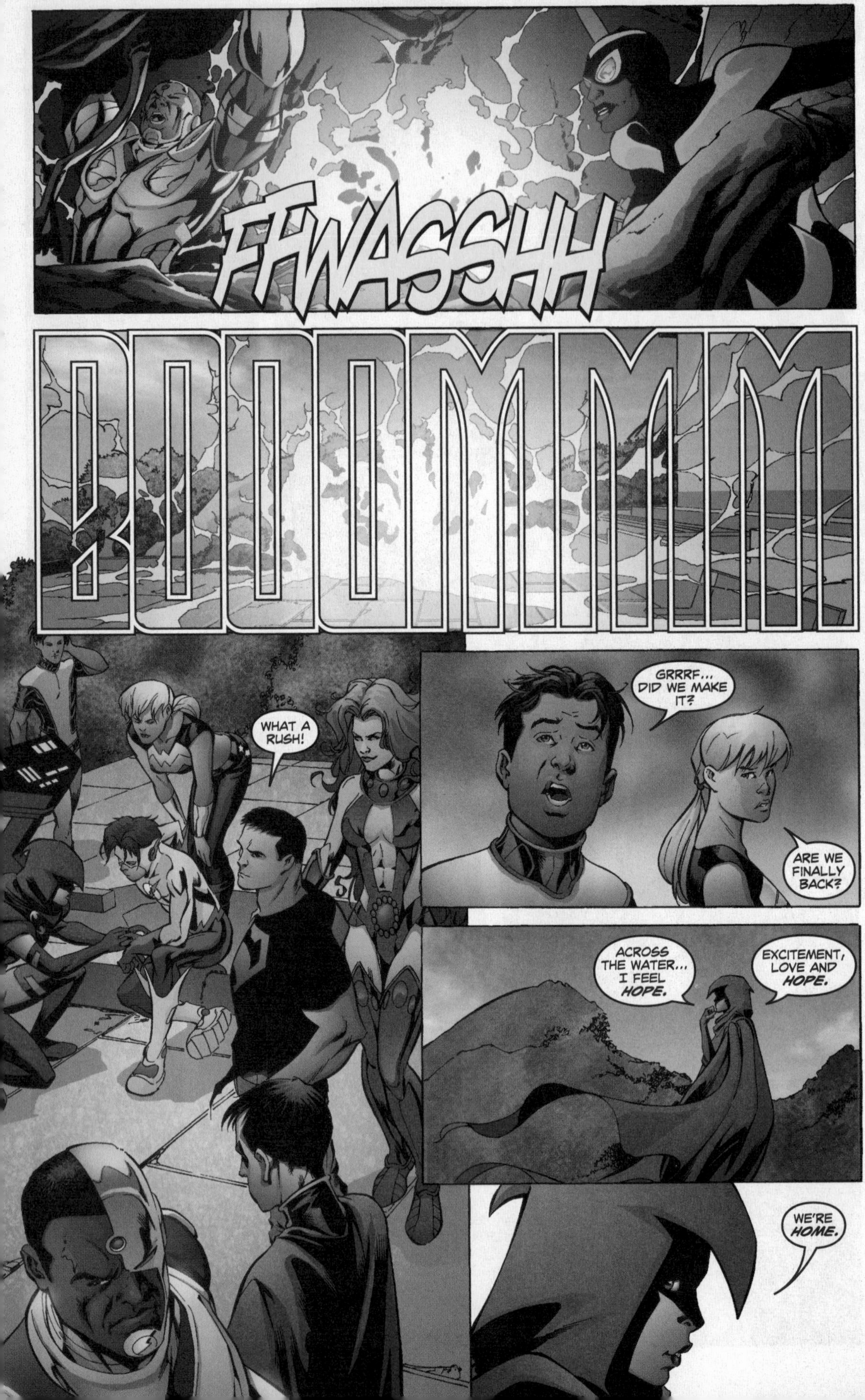
FFWASSHH
BOOOMMMM
WHAT A RUSH!
GRRRF... DID WE MAKE IT?
ARE WE FINALLY BACK?
ACROSS THE WATER... I FEEL HOPE.
EXCITEMENT, LOVE AND HOPE.
WE'RE HOME.

TITANS TOWER.

SAN FRANCISCO.

SATURDAY, 4:45 P.M.

HEY, MAN.

HEY.

CAN I BORROW A SHIRT? I DON'T HAVE ANYTHING HERE WITHOUT AN "S" ON IT.

BART IS MAKING US GO TO DAVE AND BUSTERS. PLAY SOME GAMES. HAVE SOME FUN.

SOMETIMES I THINK WE *FORGOT* HOW TO DO THAT.

IF WHAT WE JUST SAW TAUGHT US *ANYTHING*, TIM--

-- IT'S THAT WE NEED TO *LIGHTEN* UP.

AND WE NEED TO STICK *TOGETHER*.

NO MATTER *WHAT*.

NO MATTER *WHAT*, CONNER.

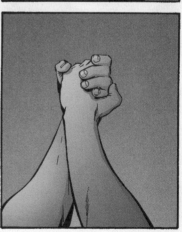

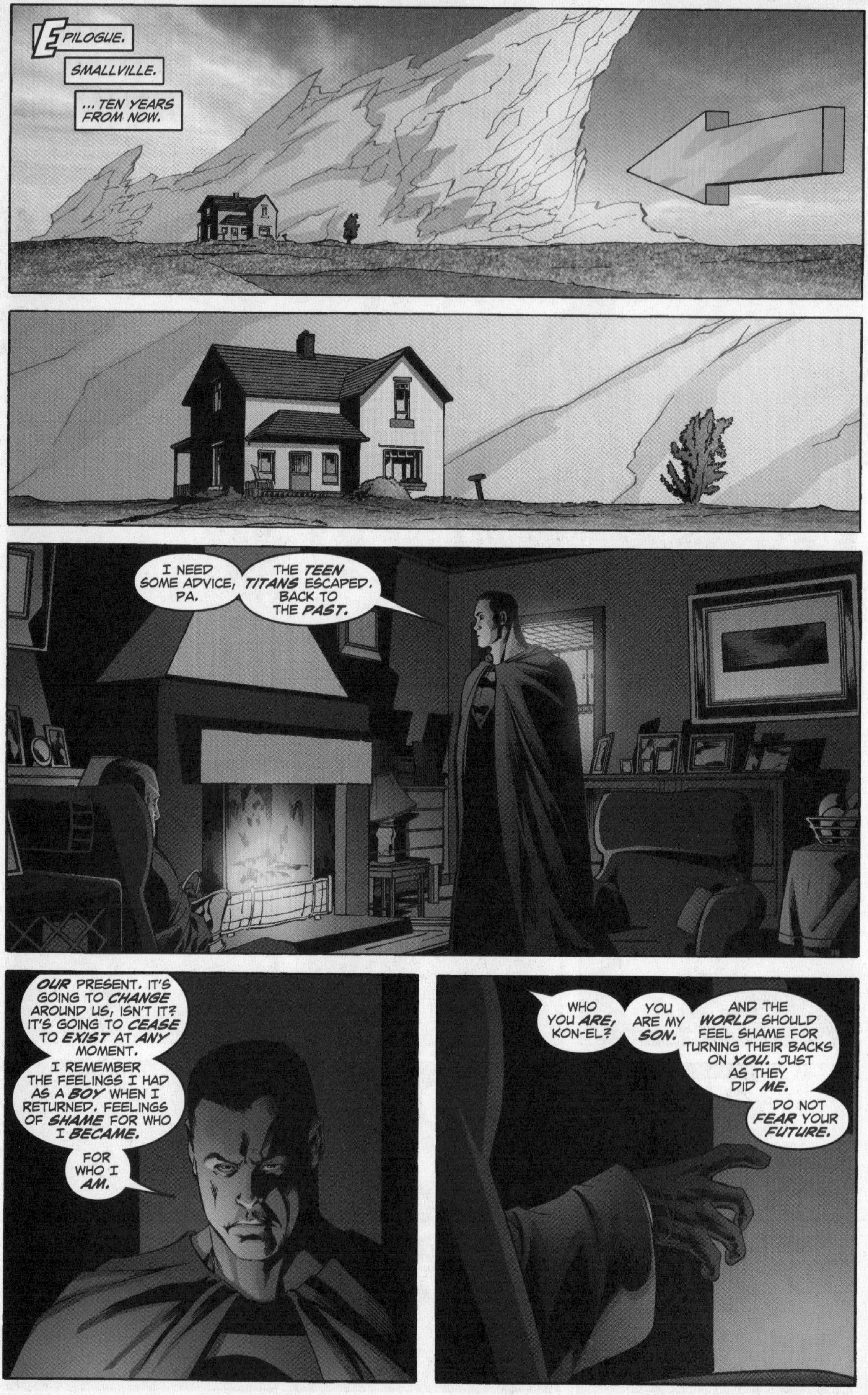
EPILOGUE.
SMALLVILLE.
...TEN YEARS FROM NOW.
I NEED SOME ADVICE, PA.
THE TEEN TITANS ESCAPED. BACK TO THE PAST.
OUR PRESENT. IT'S GOING TO CHANGE AROUND US, ISN'T IT? IT'S GOING TO CEASE TO EXIST AT ANY MOMENT.
I REMEMBER THE FEELINGS I HAD AS A BOY WHEN I RETURNED. FEELINGS OF SHAME FOR WHO I BECAME.
FOR WHO I AM.
WHO YOU ARE, KON-EL?
YOU ARE MY SON.
AND THE WORLD SHOULD FEEL SHAME FOR TURNING THEIR BACKS ON YOU. JUST AS THEY DID ME.
DO NOT FEAR YOUR FUTURE.

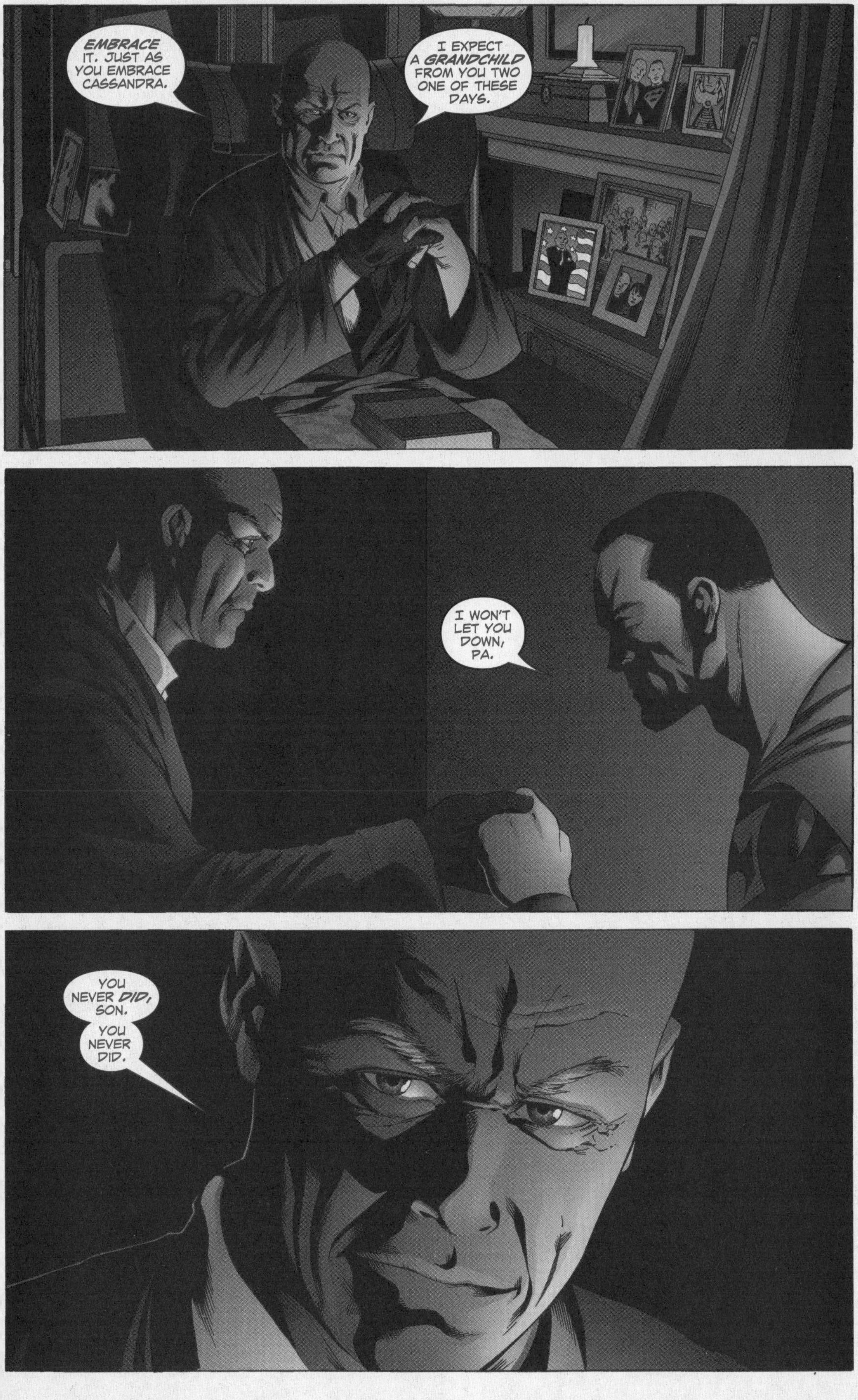
EMBRACE IT. JUST AS YOU EMBRACE CASSANDRA.
I EXPECT A GRANDCHILD FROM YOU TWO ONE OF THESE DAYS.
I WON'T LET YOU DOWN, PA.
YOU NEVER DID, SON.
YOU NEVER DID.

Teen Titans

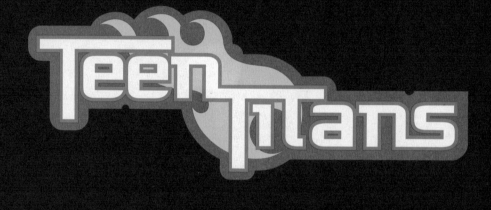

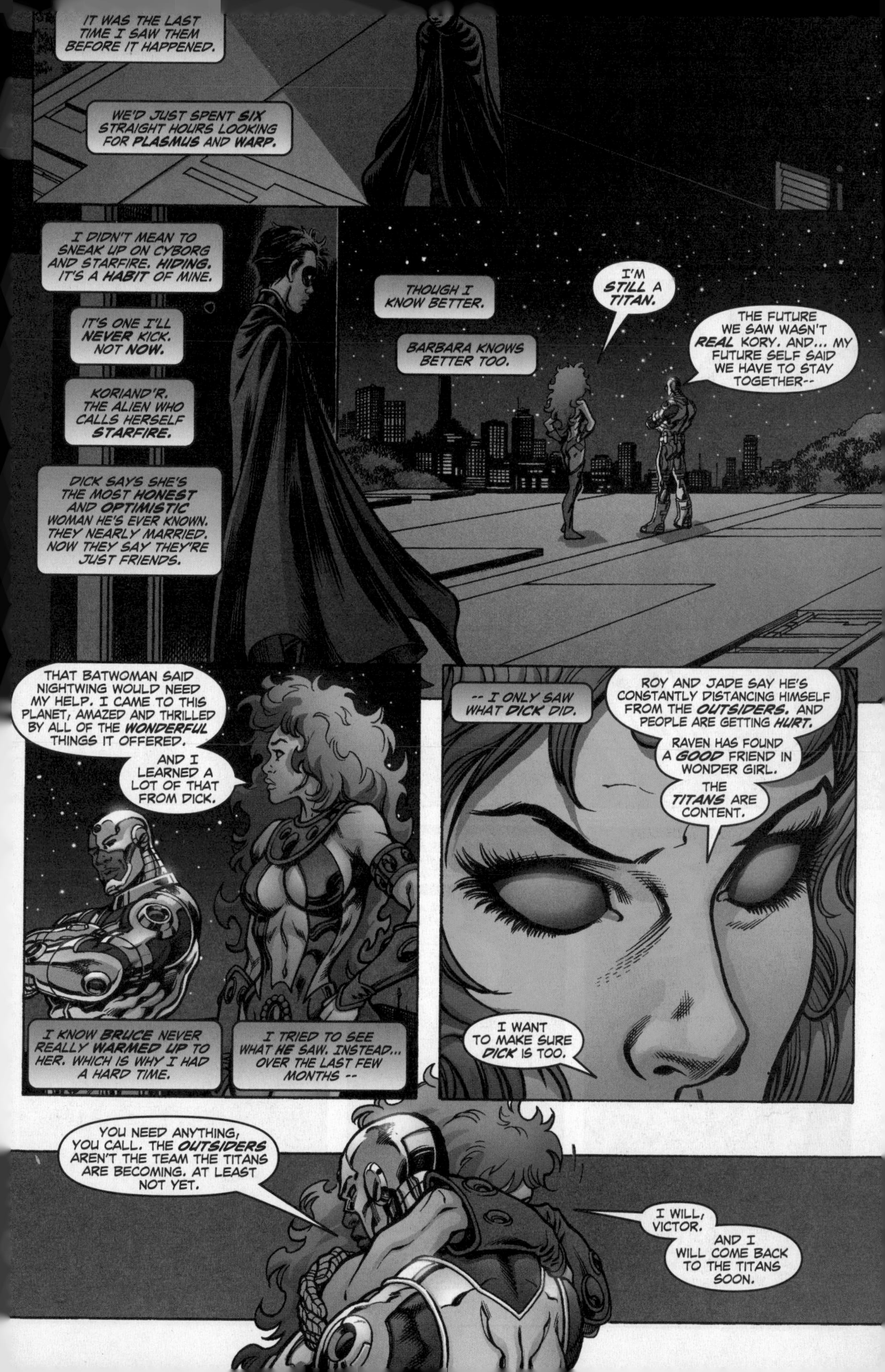
IT WAS THE LAST TIME I SAW THEM BEFORE IT HAPPENED.
WE'D JUST SPENT SIX STRAIGHT HOURS LOOKING FOR PLASMUS AND WARP.
I DIDN'T MEAN TO SNEAK UP ON CYBORG AND STARFIRE. HIDING. IT'S A HABIT OF MINE.
IT'S ONE I'LL NEVER KICK. NOT NOW.
KORIAND'R. THE ALIEN WHO CALLS HERSELF STARFIRE.
DICK SAYS SHE'S THE MOST HONEST AND OPTIMISTIC WOMAN HE'S EVER KNOWN. THEY NEARLY MARRIED. NOW THEY SAY THEY'RE JUST FRIENDS.
THOUGH I KNOW BETTER.
BARBARA KNOWS BETTER TOO.
I'M STILL A TITAN.
THE FUTURE WE SAW WASN'T REAL KORY. AND... MY FUTURE SELF SAID WE HAVE TO STAY TOGETHER--
THAT BATWOMAN SAID NIGHTWING WOULD NEED MY HELP. I CAME TO THIS PLANET, AMAZED AND THRILLED BY ALL OF THE WONDERFUL THINGS IT OFFERED.
AND I LEARNED A LOT OF THAT FROM DICK.
I KNOW BRUCE NEVER REALLY WARMED UP TO HER. WHICH IS WHY I HAD A HARD TIME.
I TRIED TO SEE WHAT HE SAW. INSTEAD... OVER THE LAST FEW MONTHS --
-- I ONLY SAW WHAT DICK DID.
ROY AND JADE SAY HE'S CONSTANTLY DISTANCING HIMSELF FROM THE OUTSIDERS. AND PEOPLE ARE GETTING HURT.
RAVEN HAS FOUND A GOOD FRIEND IN WONDER GIRL.
THE TITANS ARE CONTENT.
I WANT TO MAKE SURE DICK IS TOO.
YOU NEED ANYTHING, YOU CALL. THE OUTSIDERS AREN'T THE TEAM THE TITANS ARE BECOMING. AT LEAST NOT YET.
I WILL, VICTOR.
AND I WILL COME BACK TO THE TITANS SOON.

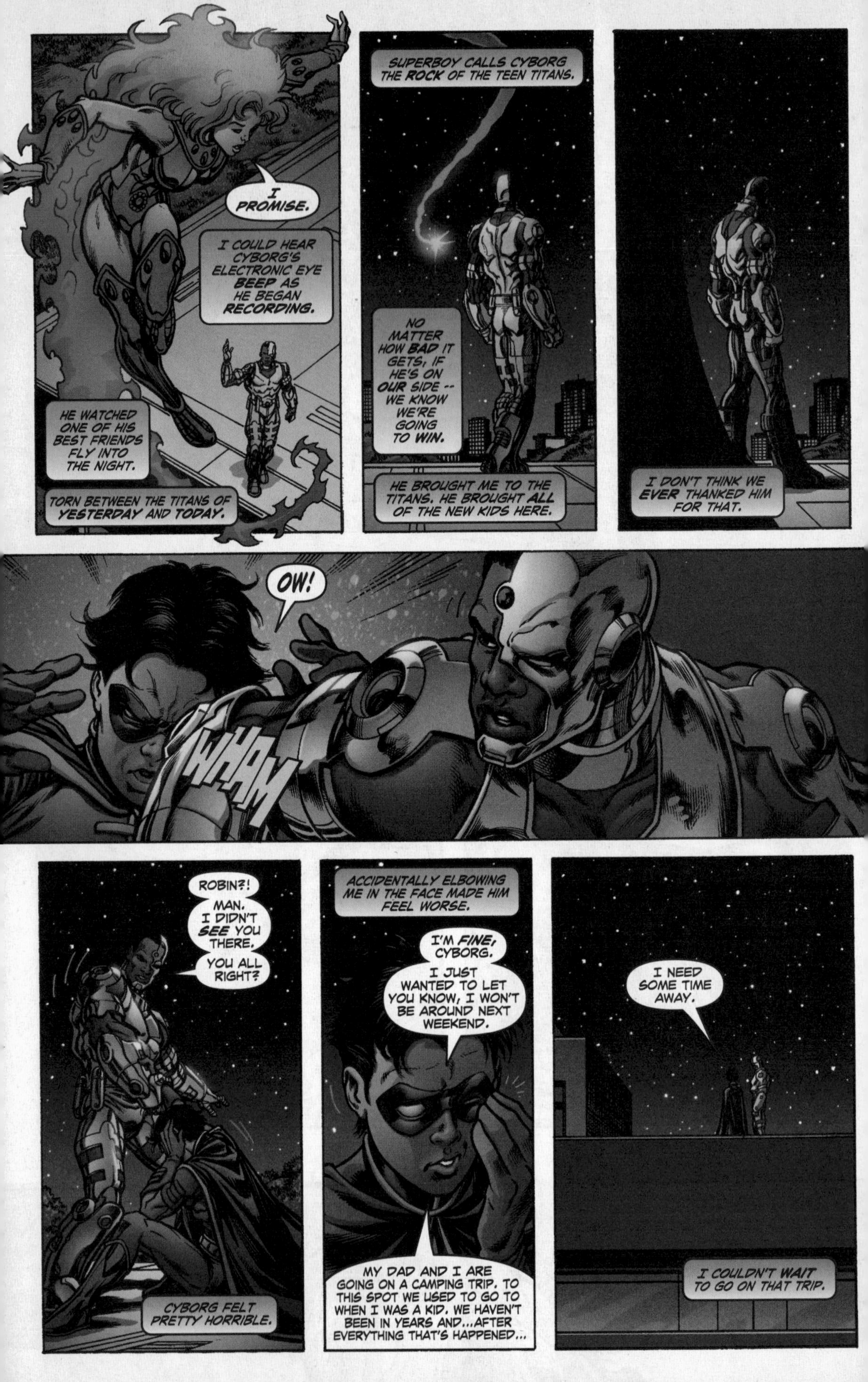
I PROMISE.
I COULD HEAR CYBORG'S ELECTRONIC EYE BEEP AS HE BEGAN RECORDING.
HE WATCHED ONE OF HIS BEST FRIENDS FLY INTO THE NIGHT.
TORN BETWEEN THE TITANS OF YESTERDAY AND TODAY.
SUPERBOY CALLS CYBORG THE ROCK OF THE TEEN TITANS.
NO MATTER HOW BAD IT GETS, IF HE'S ON OUR SIDE -- WE KNOW WE'RE GOING TO WIN.
HE BROUGHT ME TO THE TITANS. HE BROUGHT ALL OF THE NEW KIDS HERE.
I DON'T THINK WE EVER THANKED HIM FOR THAT.
OW!
WHAM
ROBIN?! MAN. I DIDN'T SEE YOU THERE.
YOU ALL RIGHT?
CYBORG FELT PRETTY HORRIBLE.
ACCIDENTALLY ELBOWING ME IN THE FACE MADE HIM FEEL WORSE.
I'M FINE, CYBORG.
I JUST WANTED TO LET YOU KNOW, I WON'T BE AROUND NEXT WEEKEND.
MY DAD AND I ARE GOING ON A CAMPING TRIP. TO THIS SPOT WE USED TO GO TO WHEN I WAS A KID. WE HAVEN'T BEEN IN YEARS AND...AFTER EVERYTHING THAT'S HAPPENED...
I NEED SOME TIME AWAY.
I COULDN'T WAIT TO GO ON THAT TRIP.

HIDING

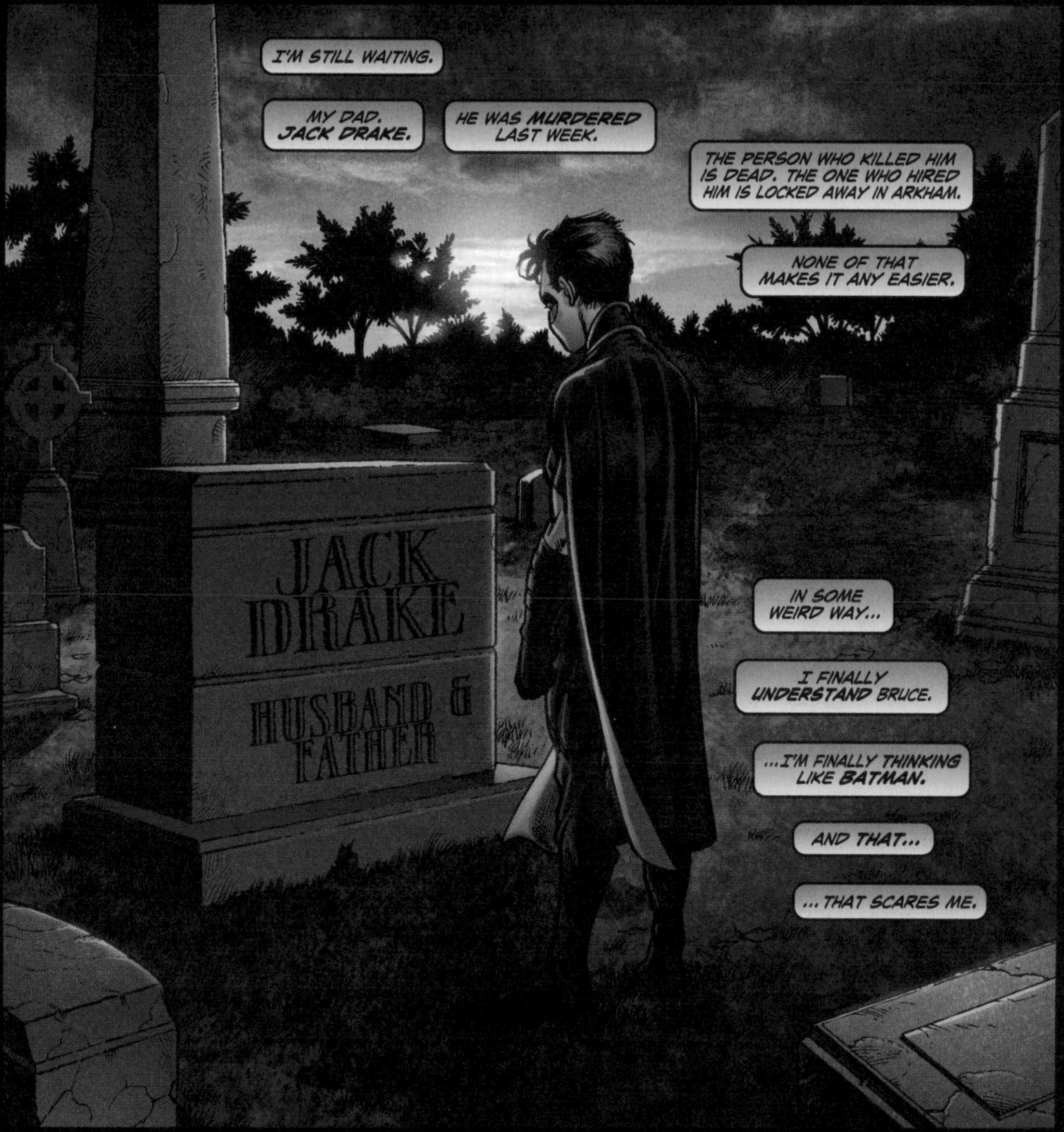
I'M STILL WAITING.
MY DAD. JACK DRAKE.
HE WAS MURDERED LAST WEEK.
THE PERSON WHO KILLED HIM IS DEAD. THE ONE WHO HIRED HIM IS LOCKED AWAY IN ARKHAM.
NONE OF THAT MAKES IT ANY EASIER.
JACK DRAKE
HUSBAND & FATHER
IN SOME WEIRD WAY...
I FINALLY UNDERSTAND BRUCE.
...I'M FINALLY THINKING LIKE BATMAN.
AND THAT...
...THAT SCARES ME.

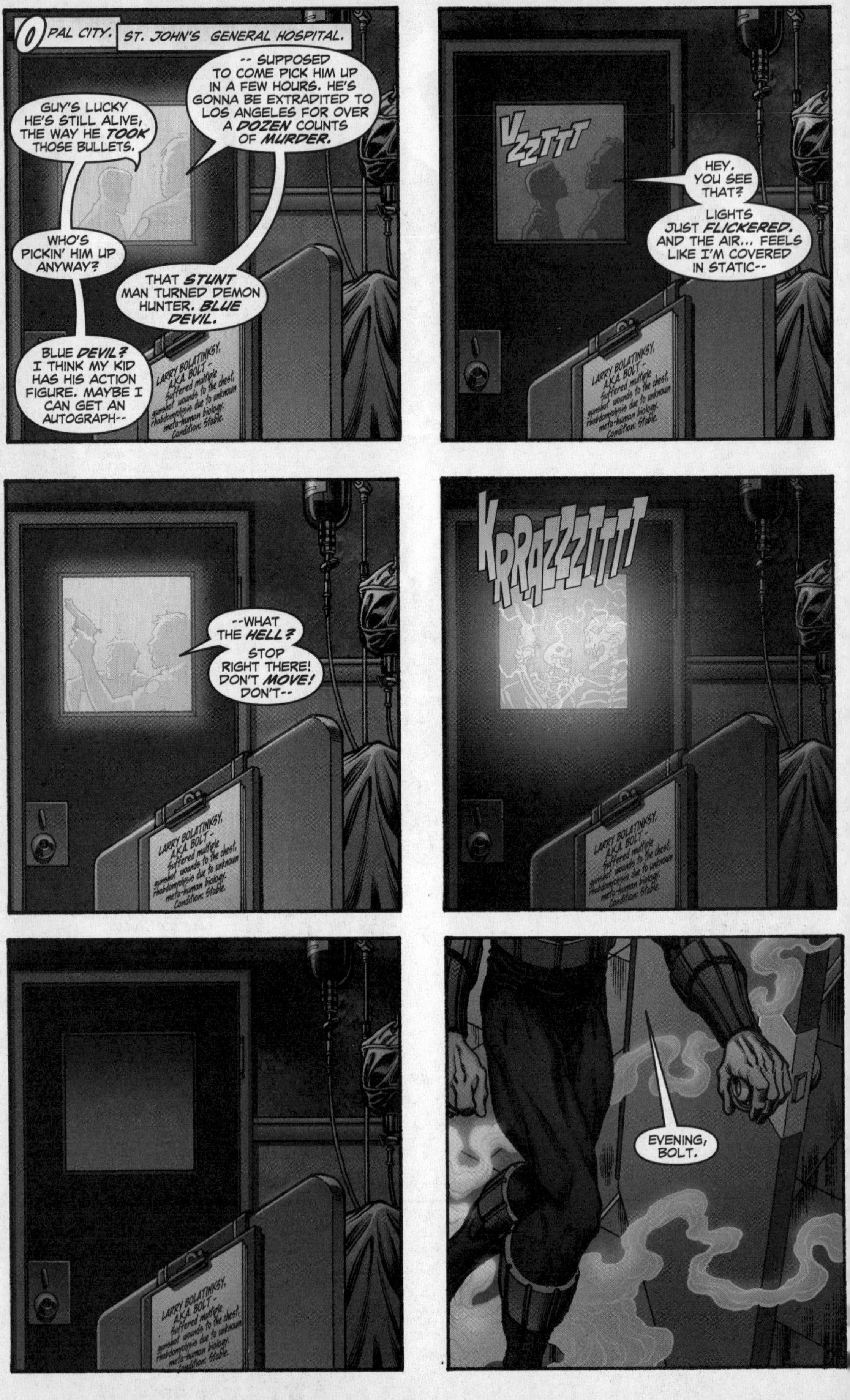
OPAL CITY.
ST. JOHN'S GENERAL HOSPITAL.
GUY'S LUCKY HE'S STILL ALIVE, THE WAY HE TOOK THOSE BULLETS.
-- SUPPOSED TO COME PICK HIM UP IN A FEW HOURS. HE'S GONNA BE EXTRADITED TO LOS ANGELES FOR OVER A DOZEN COUNTS OF MURDER.
WHO'S PICKIN' HIM UP ANYWAY?
THAT STUNT MAN TURNED DEMON HUNTER. BLUE DEVIL.
BLUE DEVIL? I THINK MY KID HAS HIS ACTION FIGURE. MAYBE I CAN GET AN AUTOGRAPH--
LARRY BOLATINKSY, A.K.A. BOLT - Suffered multiple gunshot wounds to the chest, rhabdomyolysis due to unknown meta-human biology. Condition: Stable.
VZZTTT
HEY. YOU SEE THAT?
LIGHTS JUST FLICKERED. AND THE AIR... FEELS LIKE I'M COVERED IN STATIC--
--WHAT THE HELL?
STOP RIGHT THERE! DON'T MOVE! DON'T--
KRRAZZZTTTT
EVENING, BOLT.

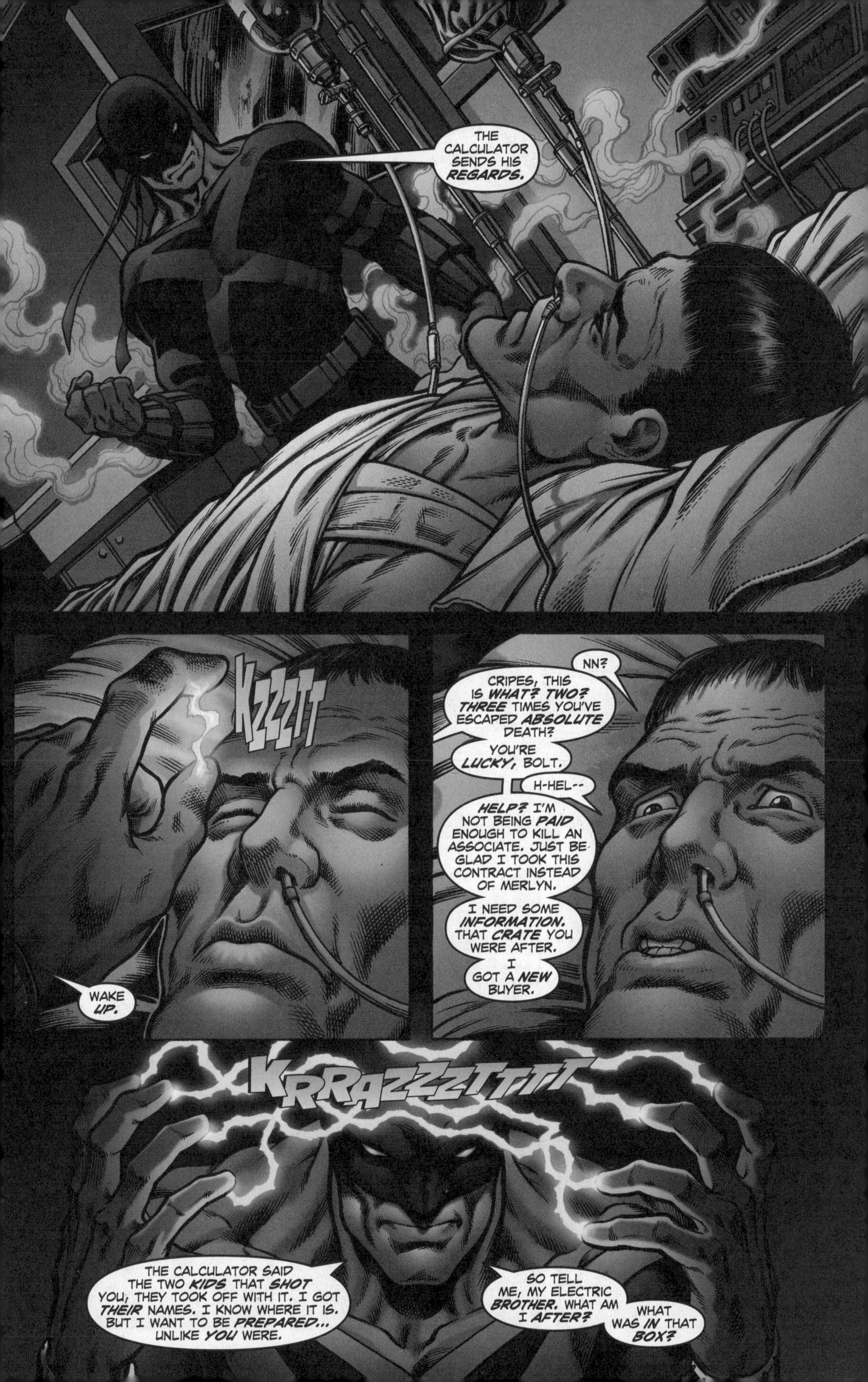

THE CALCULATOR SENDS HIS REGARDS.
KZZZTT
WAKE UP.
NN?
CRIPES, THIS IS WHAT? TWO? THREE TIMES YOU'VE ESCAPED ABSOLUTE DEATH?
YOU'RE LUCKY, BOLT.
H-HEL--
HELP? I'M NOT BEING PAID ENOUGH TO KILL AN ASSOCIATE. JUST BE GLAD I TOOK THIS CONTRACT INSTEAD OF MERLYN.
I NEED SOME INFORMATION. THAT CRATE YOU WERE AFTER.
I GOT A NEW BUYER.
KRRAZZZZTTTTT
THE CALCULATOR SAID THE TWO KIDS THAT SHOT YOU, THEY TOOK OFF WITH IT. I GOT THEIR NAMES. I KNOW WHERE IT IS. BUT I WANT TO BE PREPARED... UNLIKE YOU WERE.
SO TELL ME, MY ELECTRIC BROTHER. WHAT AM I AFTER?
WHAT WAS IN THAT BOX?

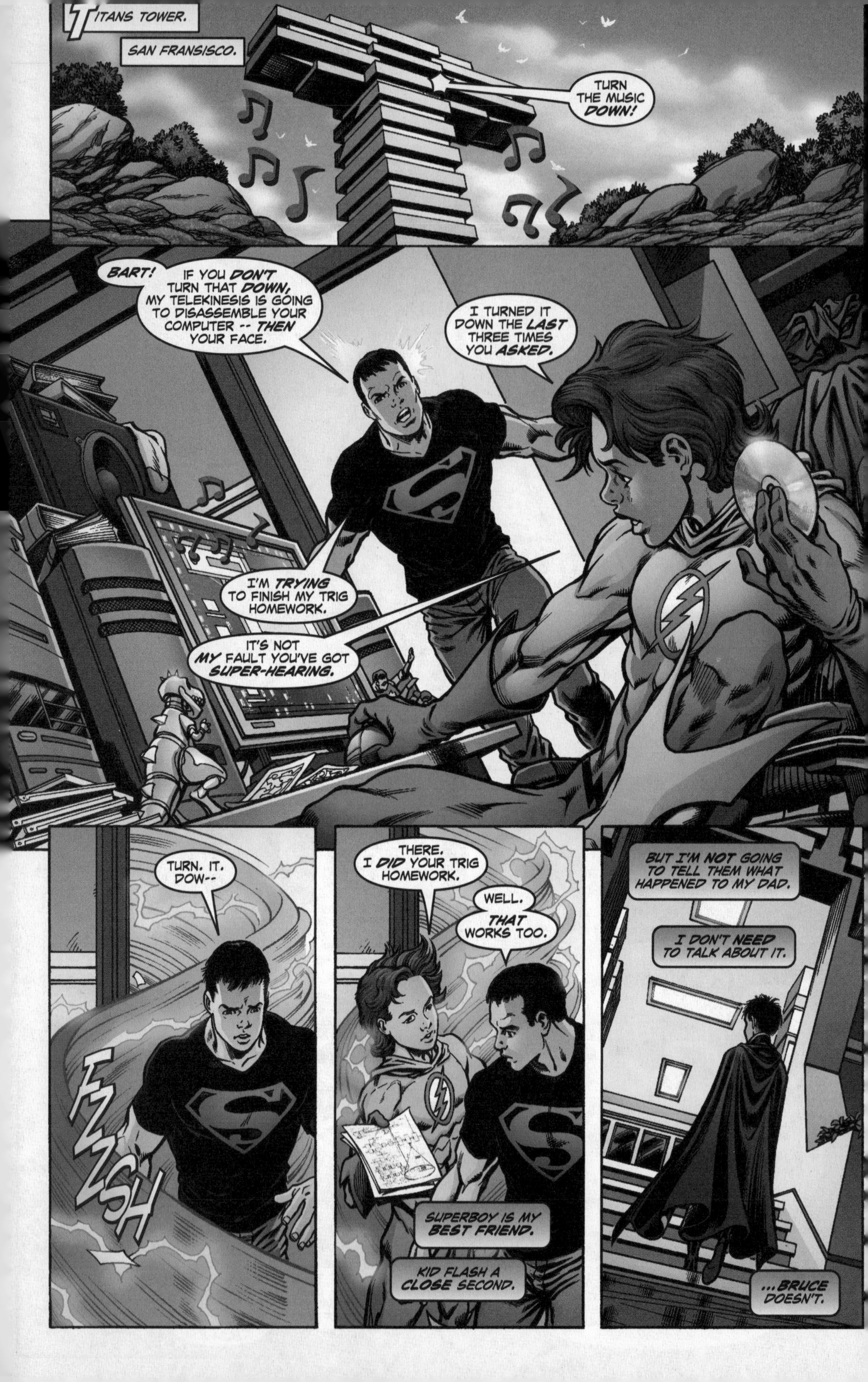
TITANS TOWER.
SAN FRANSISCO.
TURN THE MUSIC DOWN!
BART! IF YOU DON'T TURN THAT DOWN, MY TELEKINESIS IS GOING TO DISASSEMBLE YOUR COMPUTER -- THEN YOUR FACE.
I TURNED IT DOWN THE LAST THREE TIMES YOU ASKED.
I'M TRYING TO FINISH MY TRIG HOMEWORK.
IT'S NOT MY FAULT YOU'VE GOT SUPER-HEARING.
TURN. IT. DOW--
FZZSH
THERE. I DID YOUR TRIG HOMEWORK.
WELL. THAT WORKS TOO.
SUPERBOY IS MY BEST FRIEND.
KID FLASH A CLOSE SECOND.
BUT I'M NOT GOING TO TELL THEM WHAT HAPPENED TO MY DAD.
I DON'T NEED TO TALK ABOUT IT.
...BRUCE DOESN'T.

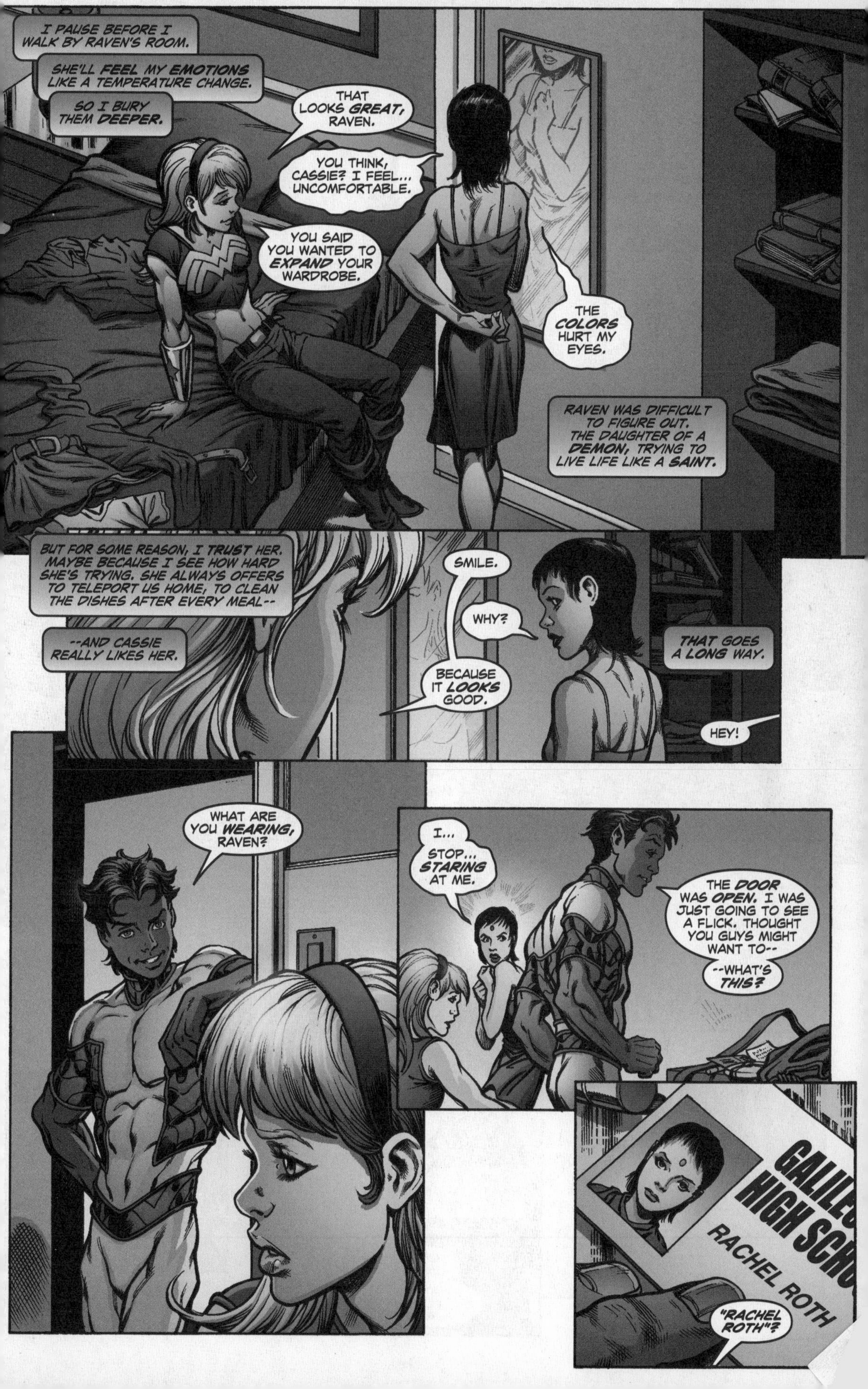

I PAUSE BEFORE I WALK BY RAVEN'S ROOM.
SHE'LL FEEL MY EMOTIONS LIKE A TEMPERATURE CHANGE.
SO I BURY THEM DEEPER.
THAT LOOKS GREAT, RAVEN.
YOU THINK, CASSIE? I FEEL... UNCOMFORTABLE.
YOU SAID YOU WANTED TO EXPAND YOUR WARDROBE.
THE COLORS HURT MY EYES.
RAVEN WAS DIFFICULT TO FIGURE OUT. THE DAUGHTER OF A DEMON, TRYING TO LIVE LIFE LIKE A SAINT.
BUT FOR SOME REASON, I TRUST HER. MAYBE BECAUSE I SEE HOW HARD SHE'S TRYING. SHE ALWAYS OFFERS TO TELEPORT US HOME, TO CLEAN THE DISHES AFTER EVERY MEAL--
--AND CASSIE REALLY LIKES HER.
SMILE.
WHY?
BECAUSE IT LOOKS GOOD.
THAT GOES A LONG WAY.
HEY!
WHAT ARE YOU WEARING, RAVEN?
I... STOP... STARING AT ME.
THE DOOR WAS OPEN. I WAS JUST GOING TO SEE A FLICK. THOUGHT YOU GUYS MIGHT WANT TO--
--WHAT'S THIS?
GALILE
HIGH SCH
RACHEL ROTH
"RACHEL ROTH"?

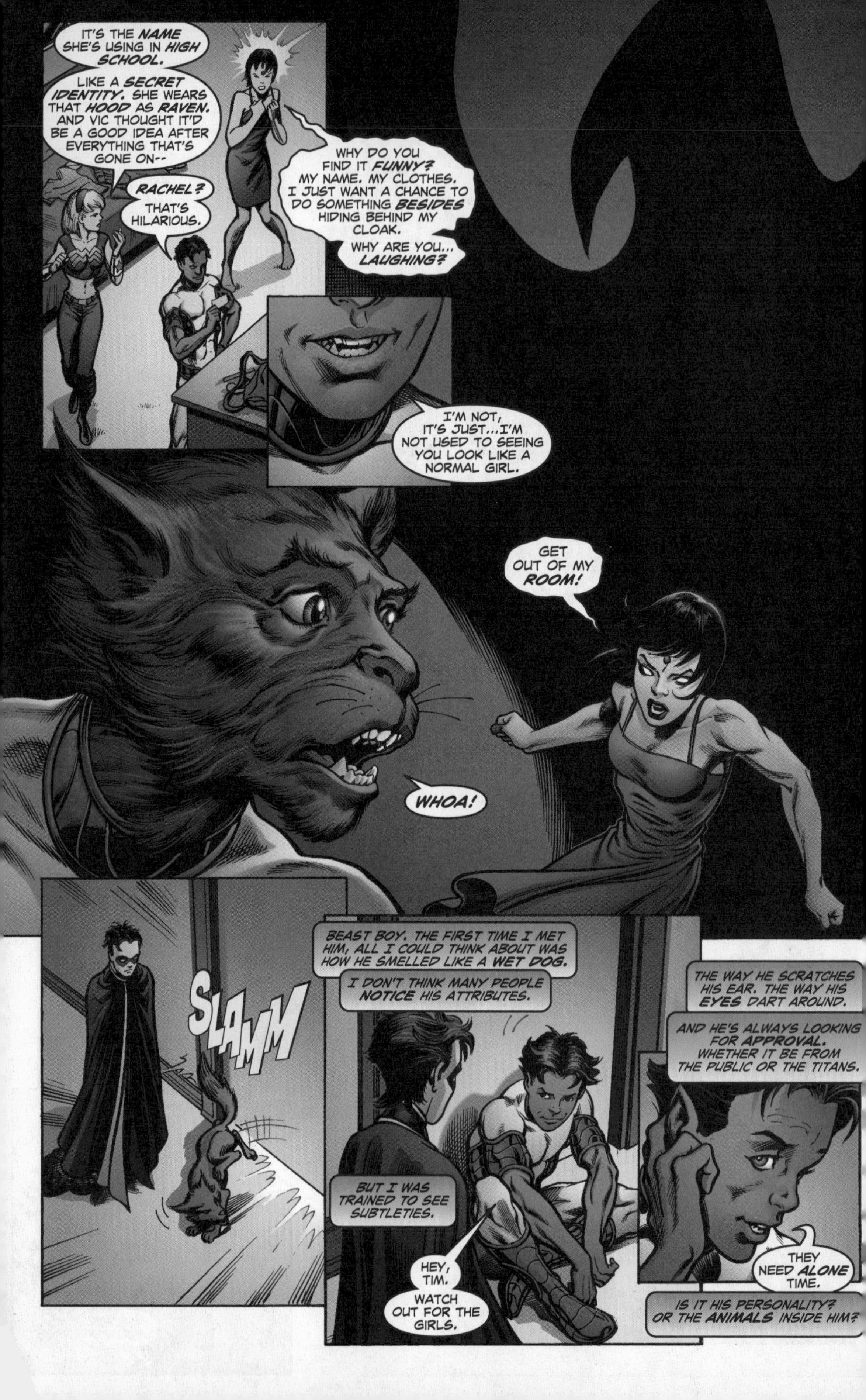
IT'S THE NAME SHE'S USING IN HIGH SCHOOL.
LIKE A SECRET IDENTITY. SHE WEARS THAT HOOD AS RAVEN. AND VIC THOUGHT IT'D BE A GOOD IDEA AFTER EVERYTHING THAT'S GONE ON--
RACHEL?
THAT'S HILARIOUS.
WHY DO YOU FIND IT FUNNY? MY NAME. MY CLOTHES. I JUST WANT A CHANCE TO DO SOMETHING BESIDES HIDING BEHIND MY CLOAK.
WHY ARE YOU... LAUGHING?
I'M NOT, IT'S JUST...I'M NOT USED TO SEEING YOU LOOK LIKE A NORMAL GIRL.
GET OUT OF MY ROOM!
WHOA!
SLAMM
BEAST BOY. THE FIRST TIME I MET HIM, ALL I COULD THINK ABOUT WAS HOW HE SMELLED LIKE A WET DOG.
I DON'T THINK MANY PEOPLE NOTICE HIS ATTRIBUTES.
BUT I WAS TRAINED TO SEE SUBTLETIES.
HEY, TIM.
WATCH OUT FOR THE GIRLS.
THE WAY HE SCRATCHES HIS EAR. THE WAY HIS EYES DART AROUND.
AND HE'S ALWAYS LOOKING FOR APPROVAL. WHETHER IT BE FROM THE PUBLIC OR THE TITANS.
THEY NEED ALONE TIME.
IS IT HIS PERSONALITY? OR THE ANIMALS INSIDE HIM?

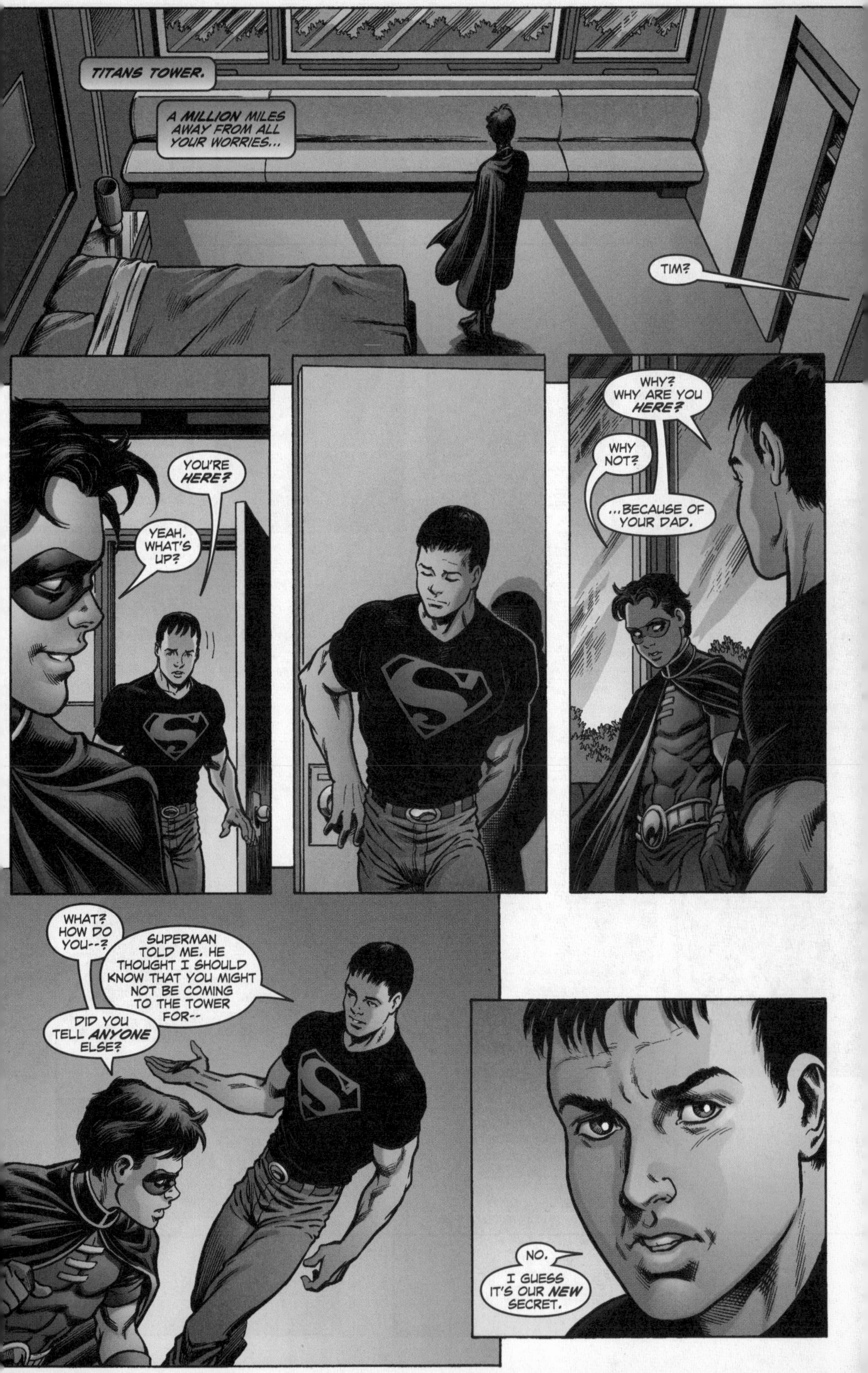
TITANS TOWER.
A MILLION MILES AWAY FROM ALL YOUR WORRIES...
TIM?
YOU'RE HERE?
YEAH. WHAT'S UP?
WHY? WHY ARE YOU HERE?
WHY NOT?
...BECAUSE OF YOUR DAD.
WHAT? HOW DO YOU--?
SUPERMAN TOLD ME. HE THOUGHT I SHOULD KNOW THAT YOU MIGHT NOT BE COMING TO THE TOWER FOR--
DID YOU TELL ANYONE ELSE?
NO.
I GUESS IT'S OUR NEW SECRET.

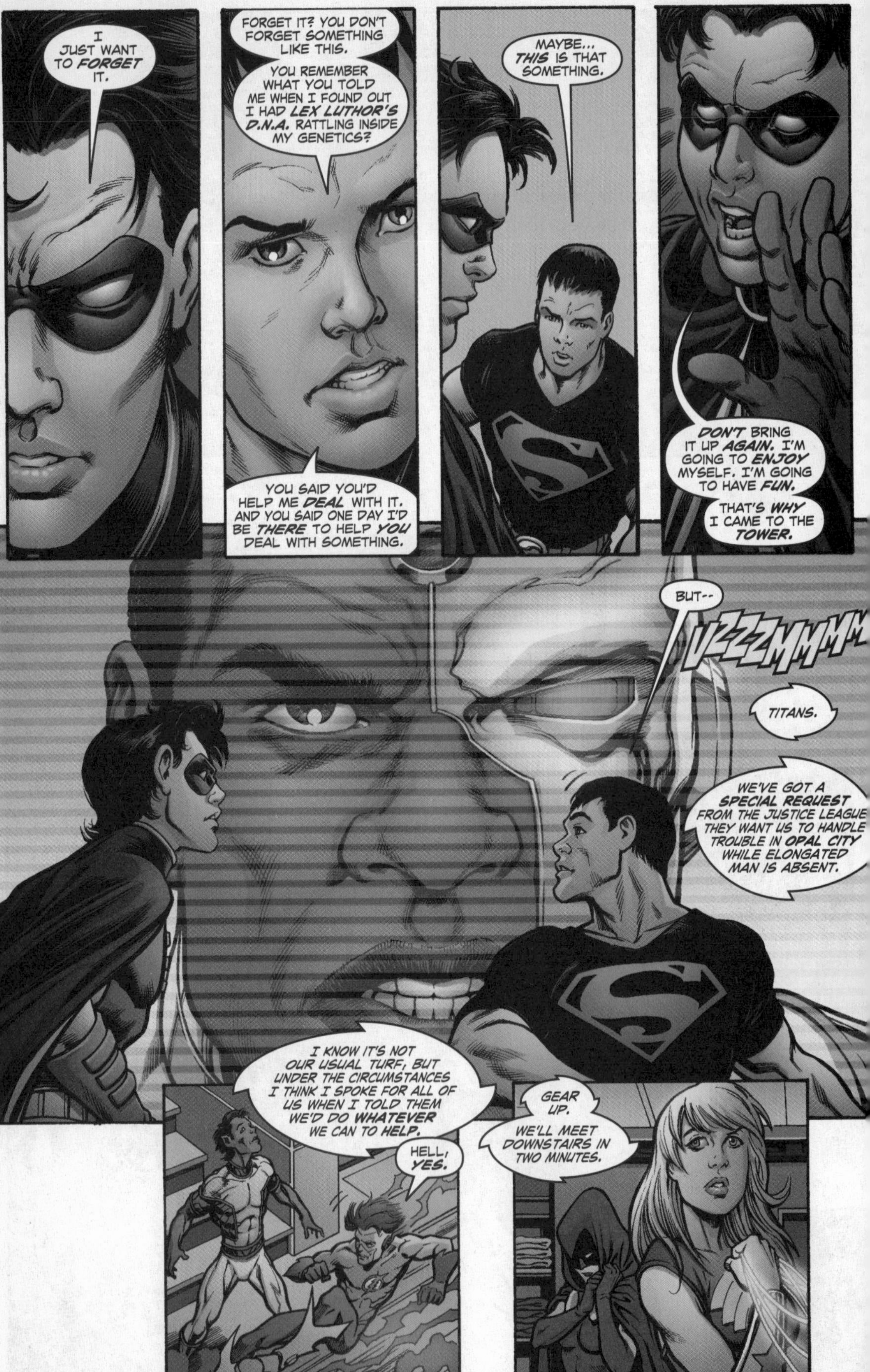
I JUST WANT TO FORGET IT.
FORGET IT? YOU DON'T FORGET SOMETHING LIKE THIS.
YOU REMEMBER WHAT YOU TOLD ME WHEN I FOUND OUT I HAD LEX LUTHOR'S D.N.A. RATTLING INSIDE MY GENETICS?
YOU SAID YOU'D HELP ME DEAL WITH IT. AND YOU SAID ONE DAY I'D BE THERE TO HELP YOU DEAL WITH SOMETHING.
MAYBE... THIS IS THAT SOMETHING.
DON'T BRING IT UP AGAIN. I'M GOING TO ENJOY MYSELF. I'M GOING TO HAVE FUN.
THAT'S WHY I CAME TO THE TOWER.
BUT--
VZZZMMMM
TITANS.
WE'VE GOT A SPECIAL REQUEST FROM THE JUSTICE LEAGUE THEY WANT US TO HANDLE TROUBLE IN OPAL CITY WHILE ELONGATED MAN IS ABSENT.
I KNOW IT'S NOT OUR USUAL TURF, BUT UNDER THE CIRCUMSTANCES I THINK I SPOKE FOR ALL OF US WHEN I TOLD THEM WE'D DO WHATEVER WE CAN TO HELP.
HELL, YES.
GEAR UP.
WE'LL MEET DOWNSTAIRS IN TWO MINUTES.

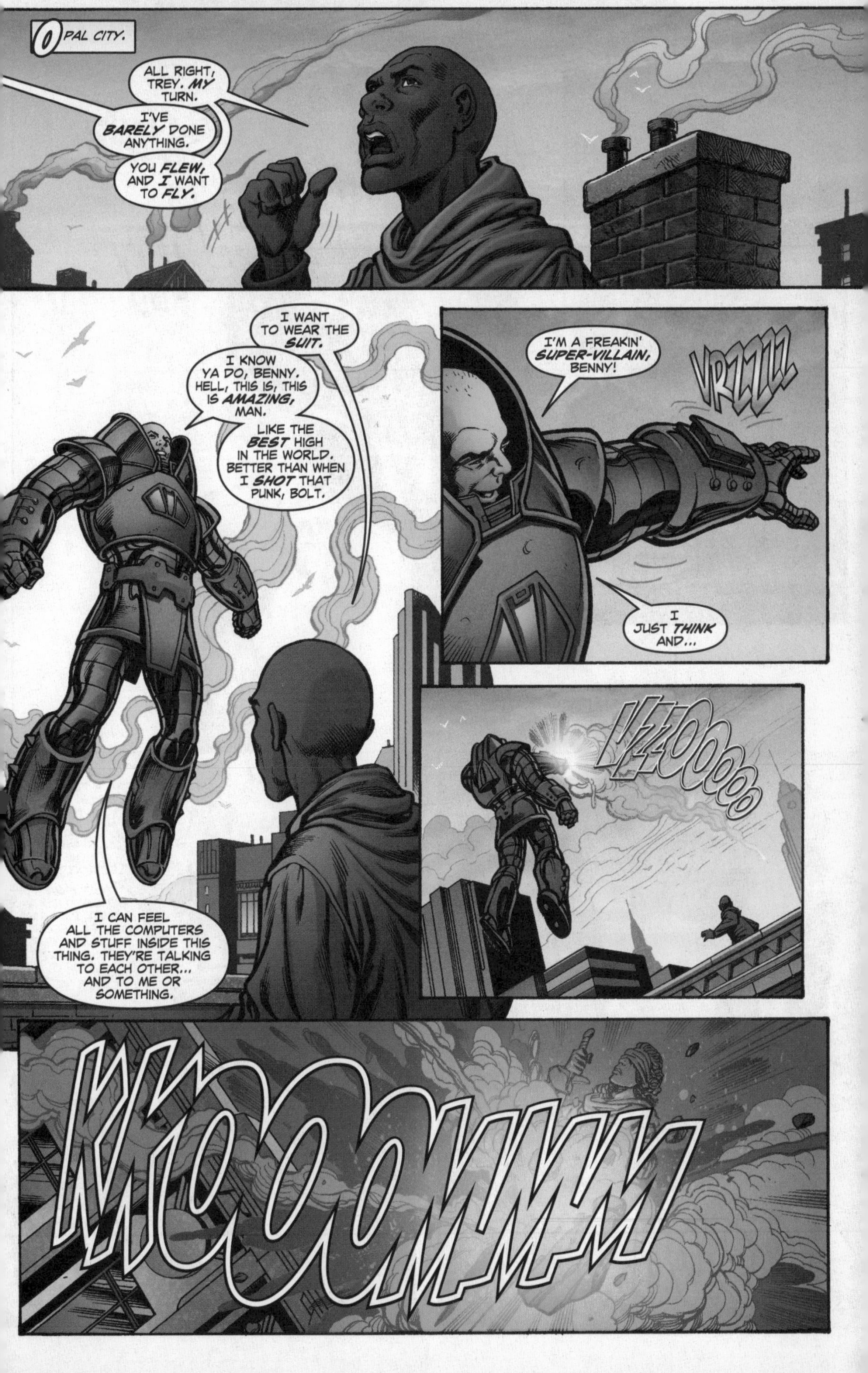
OPAL CITY.
ALL RIGHT, TREY. MY TURN.
I'VE BARELY DONE ANYTHING.
YOU FLEW, AND I WANT TO FLY.
I WANT TO WEAR THE SUIT.
I KNOW YA DO, BENNY. HELL, THIS IS, THIS IS AMAZING, MAN.
LIKE THE BEST HIGH IN THE WORLD. BETTER THAN WHEN I SHOT THAT PUNK, BOLT.
I CAN FEEL ALL THE COMPUTERS AND STUFF INSIDE THIS THING. THEY'RE TALKING TO EACH OTHER... AND TO ME OR SOMETHING.
I'M A FREAKIN' SUPER-VILLAIN, BENNY!
VRZZZZ
I JUST THINK AND...
VZZOOOOOO
KWOOOMMMM

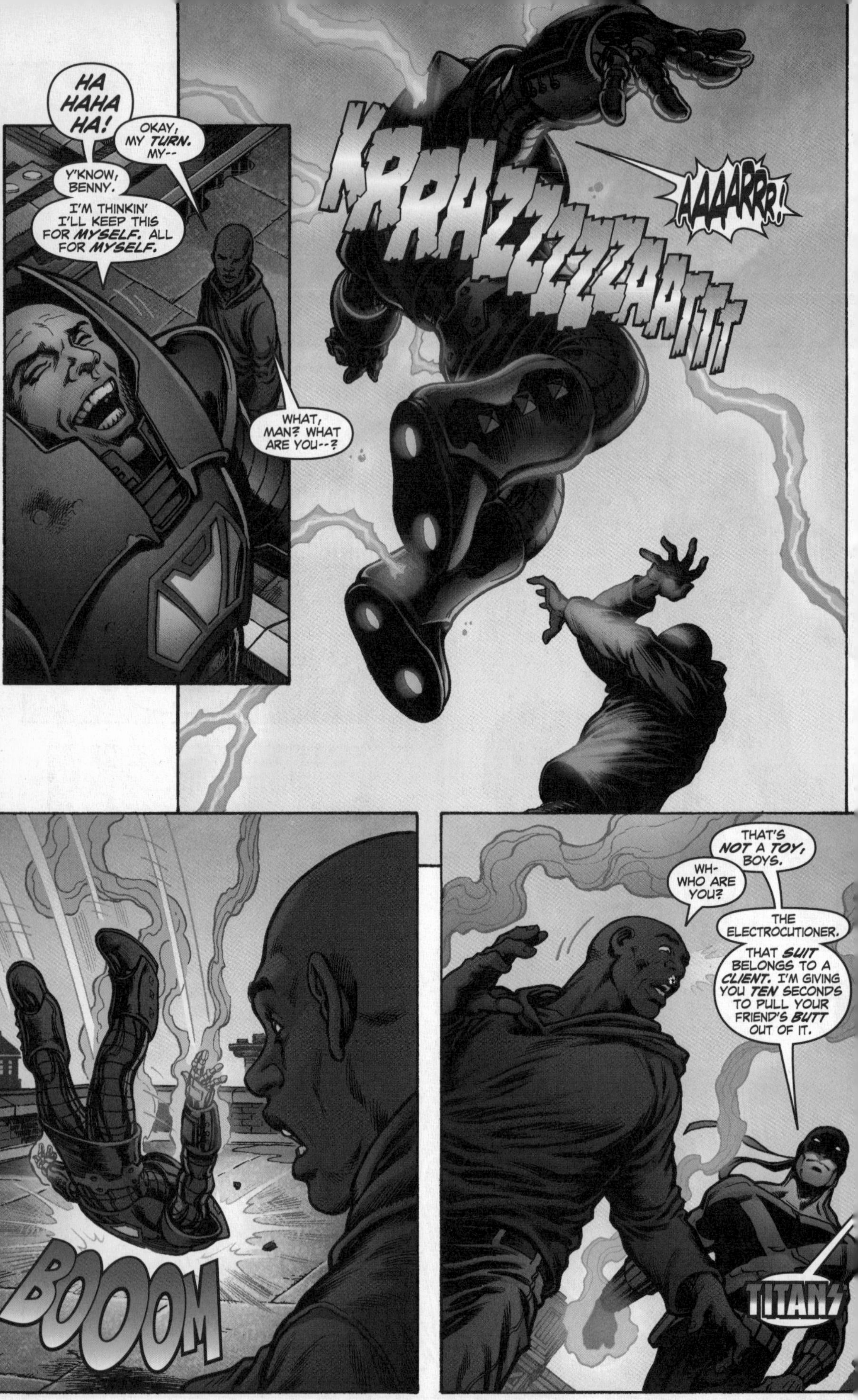
HA HAHA HA!
Y'KNOW, BENNY.
I'M THINKIN' I'LL KEEP THIS FOR *MYSELF*. ALL FOR *MYSELF*.
OKAY, MY *TURN*. MY--
WHAT, MAN? WHAT ARE YOU--?
KRRAZZZZZZAATTT
AAAARRR!
BOOOM
THAT'S *NOT* A *TOY*, BOYS.
WH- WHO ARE YOU?
THE ELECTROCUTIONER.
THAT *SUIT* BELONGS TO A *CLIENT*. I'M GIVING YOU *TEN* SECONDS TO PULL YOUR FRIEND'S *BUTT* OUT OF IT.
TITANS

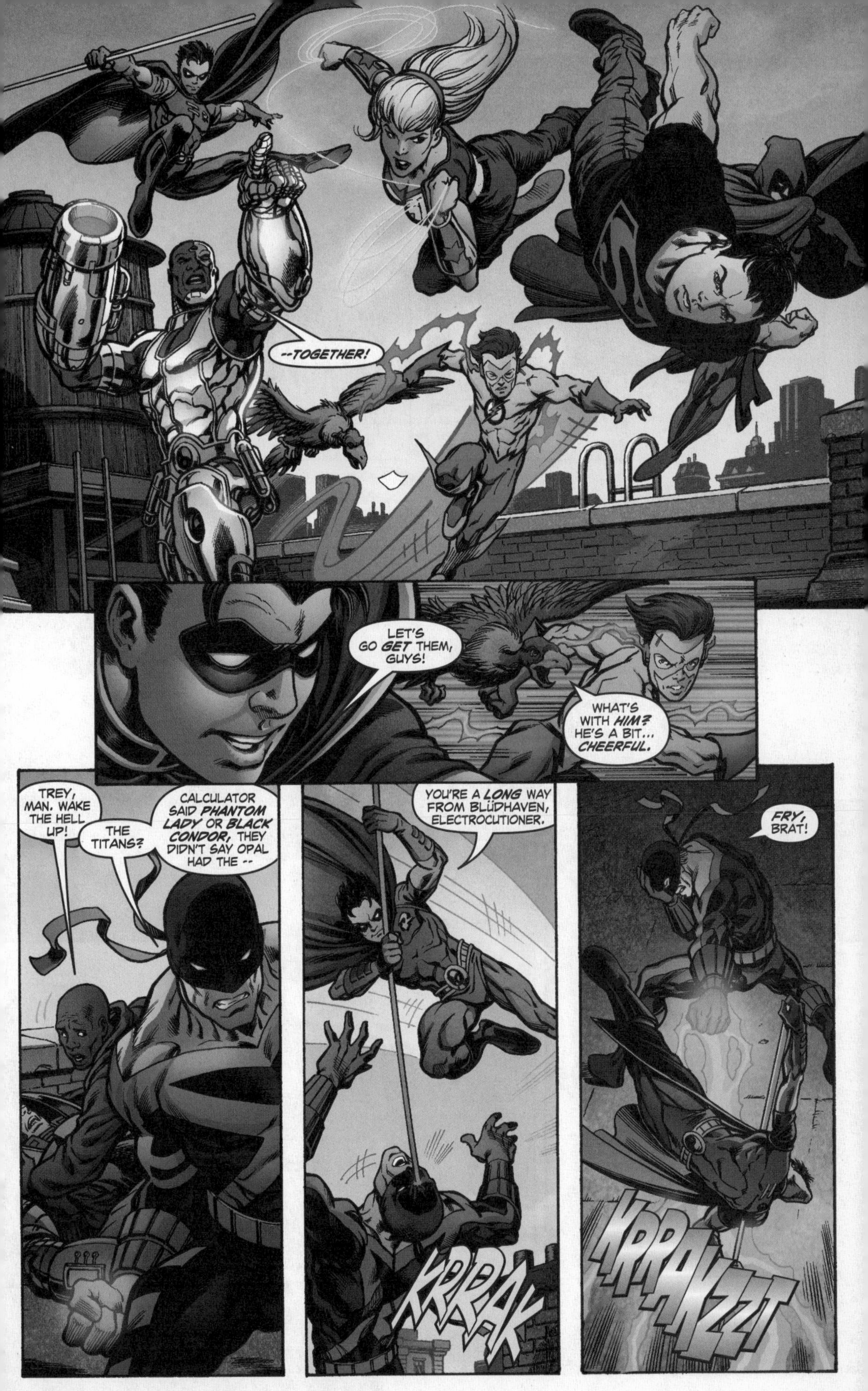
--TOGETHER!
LET'S GO GET THEM, GUYS!
WHAT'S WITH HIM? HE'S A BIT... CHEERFUL.
TREY, MAN. WAKE THE HELL UP!
THE TITANS?
CALCULATOR SAID PHANTOM LADY OR BLACK CONDOR, THEY DIDN'T SAY OPAL HAD THE --
YOU'RE A LONG WAY FROM BLÜDHAVEN, ELECTROCUTIONER.
KRRAK
FRY, BRAT!
KRRAKZZT

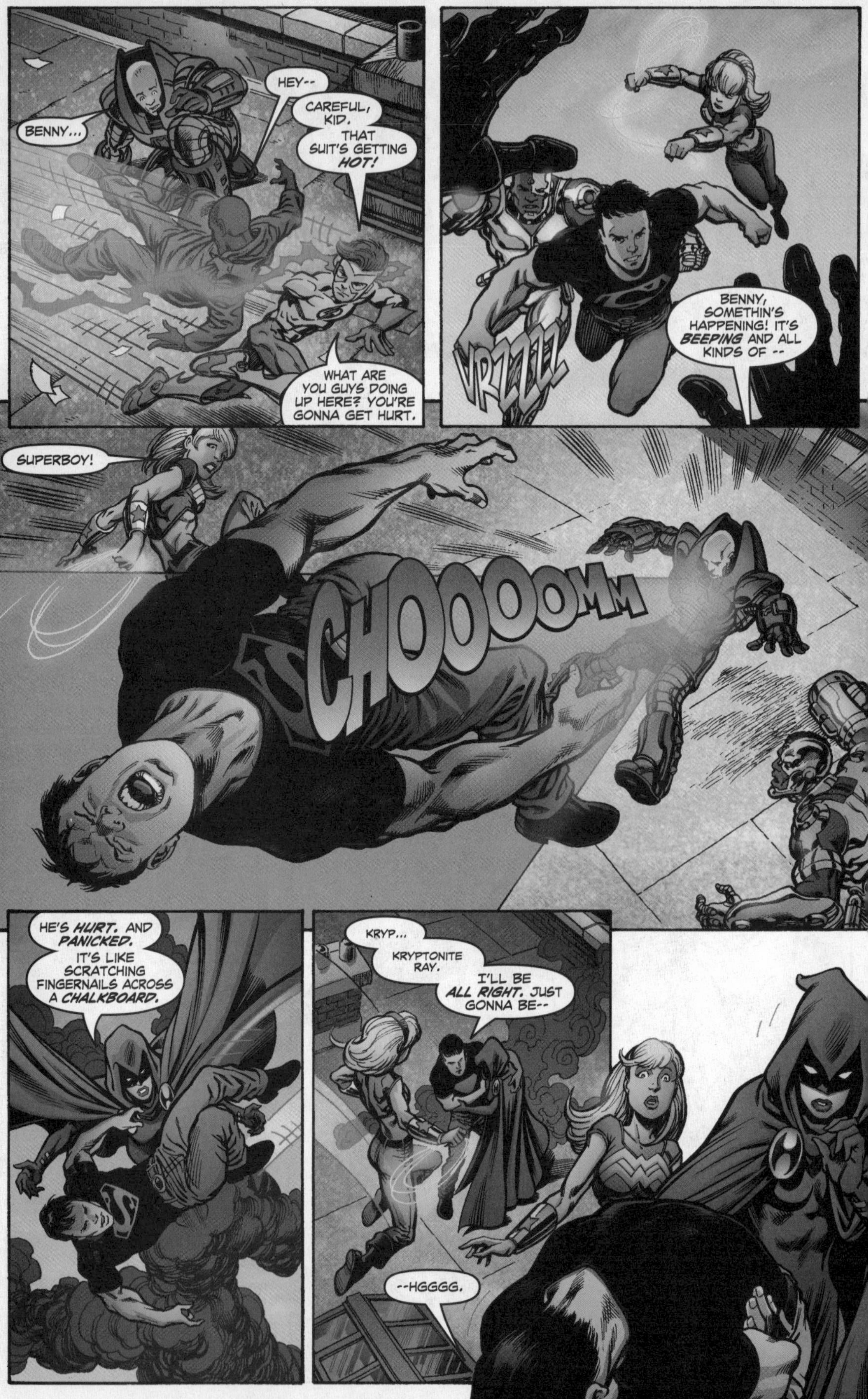
BENNY...
HEY--
CAREFUL, KID.
THAT SUIT'S GETTING HOT!
WHAT ARE YOU GUYS DOING UP HERE? YOU'RE GONNA GET HURT.
VRZZZZ
BENNY, SOMETHIN'S HAPPENING! IT'S BEEPING AND ALL KINDS OF --
SUPERBOY!
CHOOOOMM
HE'S HURT. AND PANICKED.
IT'S LIKE SCRATCHING FINGERNAILS ACROSS A CHALKBOARD.
KRYP...
KRYPTONITE RAY.
I'LL BE ALL RIGHT. JUST GONNA BE--
--HGGGG.

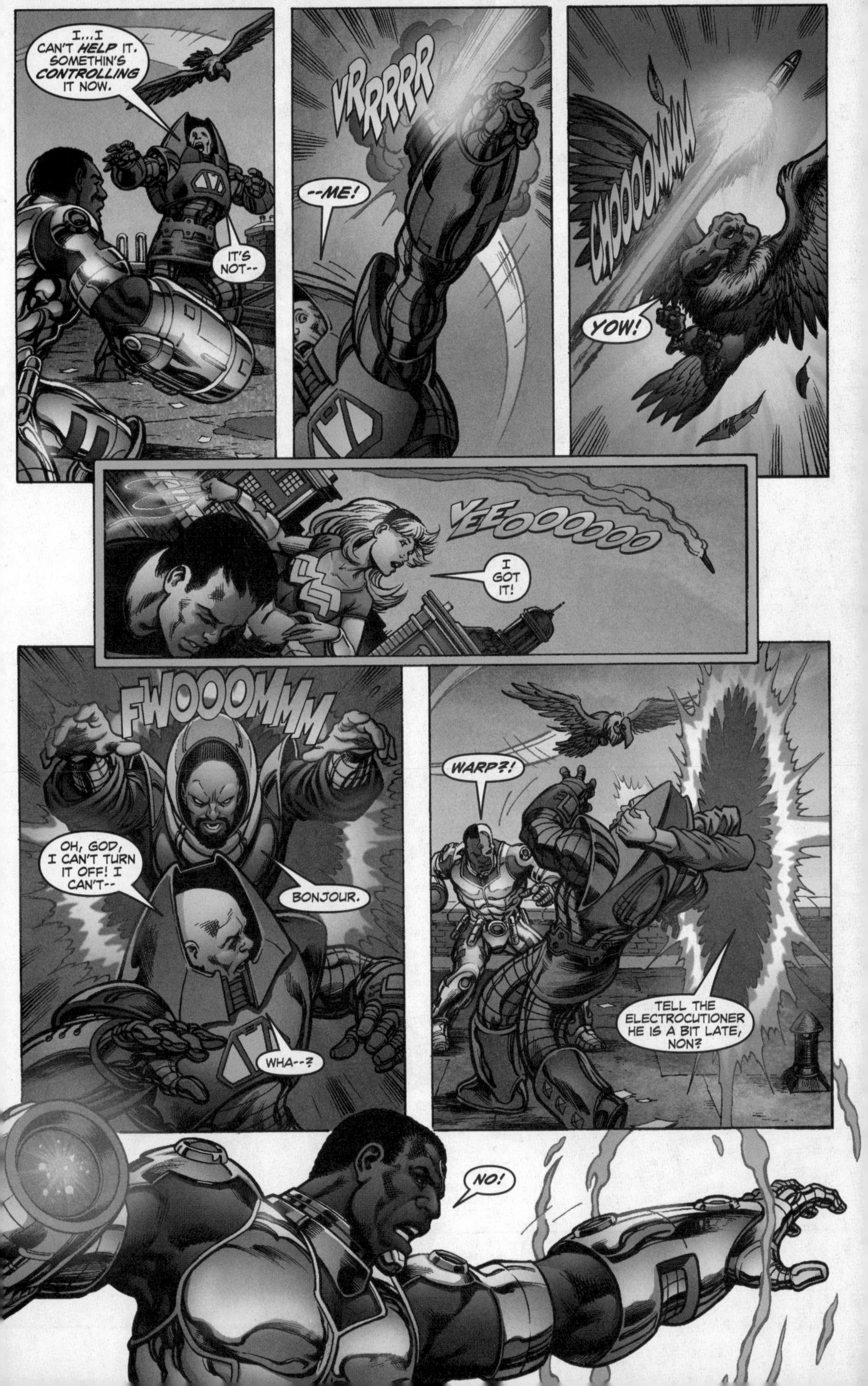
I...I CAN'T HELP IT. SOMETHIN'S CONTROLLING IT NOW.
IT'S NOT--
VRRRRR
--ME!
CHOOOOMMM
YOW!
YEEOOOOOOO
I GOT IT!
FWOOOMMM
OH, GOD, I CAN'T TURN IT OFF! I CAN'T--
BONJOUR.
WHA--?
WARP?!
TELL THE ELECTROCUTIONER HE IS A BIT LATE, NON?
NO!

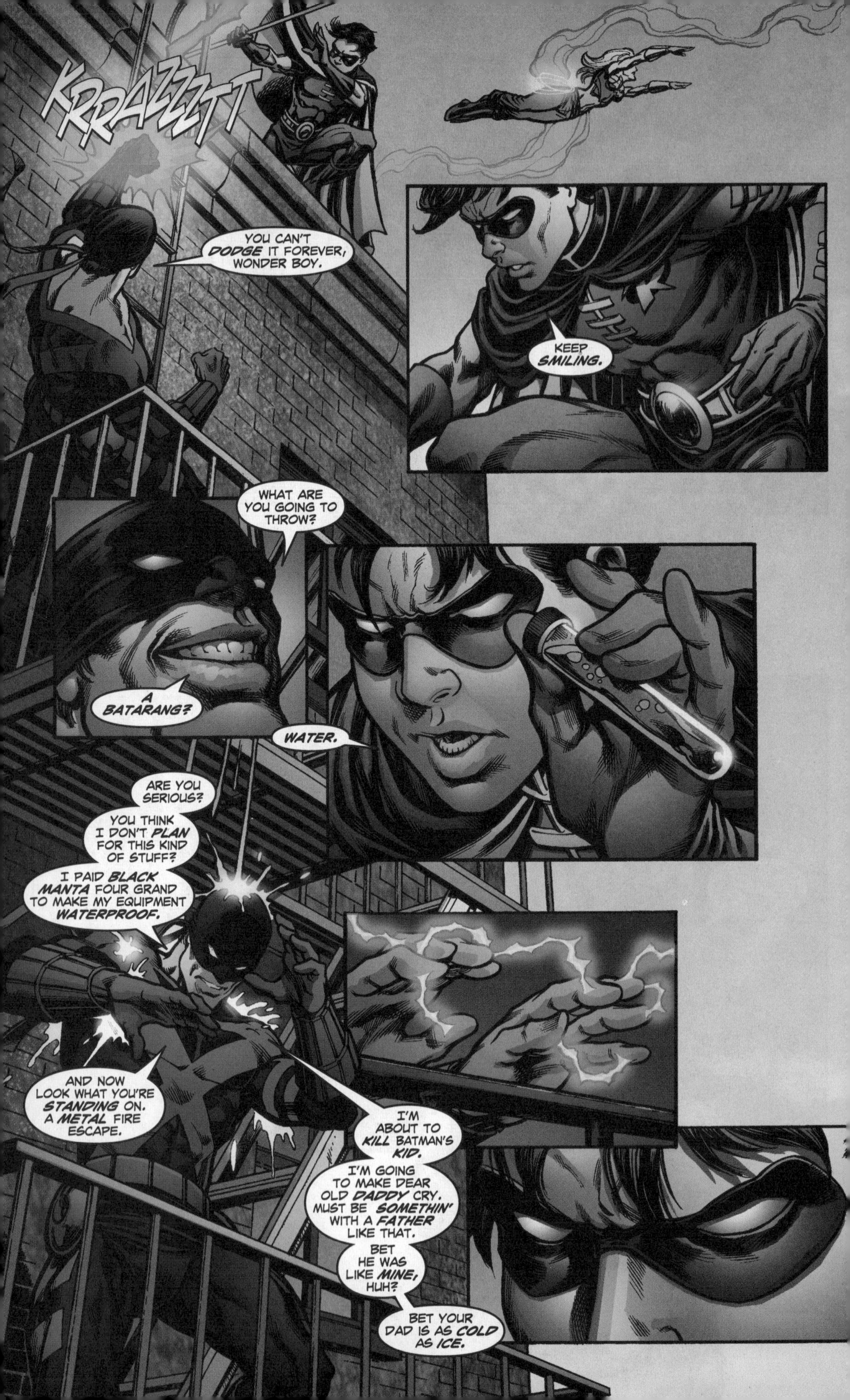
KRRAZZZZTT
YOU CAN'T DODGE IT FOREVER, WONDER BOY.
KEEP SMILING.
WHAT ARE YOU GOING TO THROW?
A BATARANG?
WATER.
ARE YOU SERIOUS?
YOU THINK I DON'T PLAN FOR THIS KIND OF STUFF?
I PAID BLACK MANTA FOUR GRAND TO MAKE MY EQUIPMENT WATERPROOF.
AND NOW LOOK WHAT YOU'RE STANDING ON. A METAL FIRE ESCAPE.
I'M ABOUT TO KILL BATMAN'S KID.
I'M GOING TO MAKE DEAR OLD DADDY CRY. MUST BE SOMETHIN' WITH A FATHER LIKE THAT.
BET HE WAS LIKE MINE, HUH?
BET YOUR DAD IS AS COLD AS ICE.

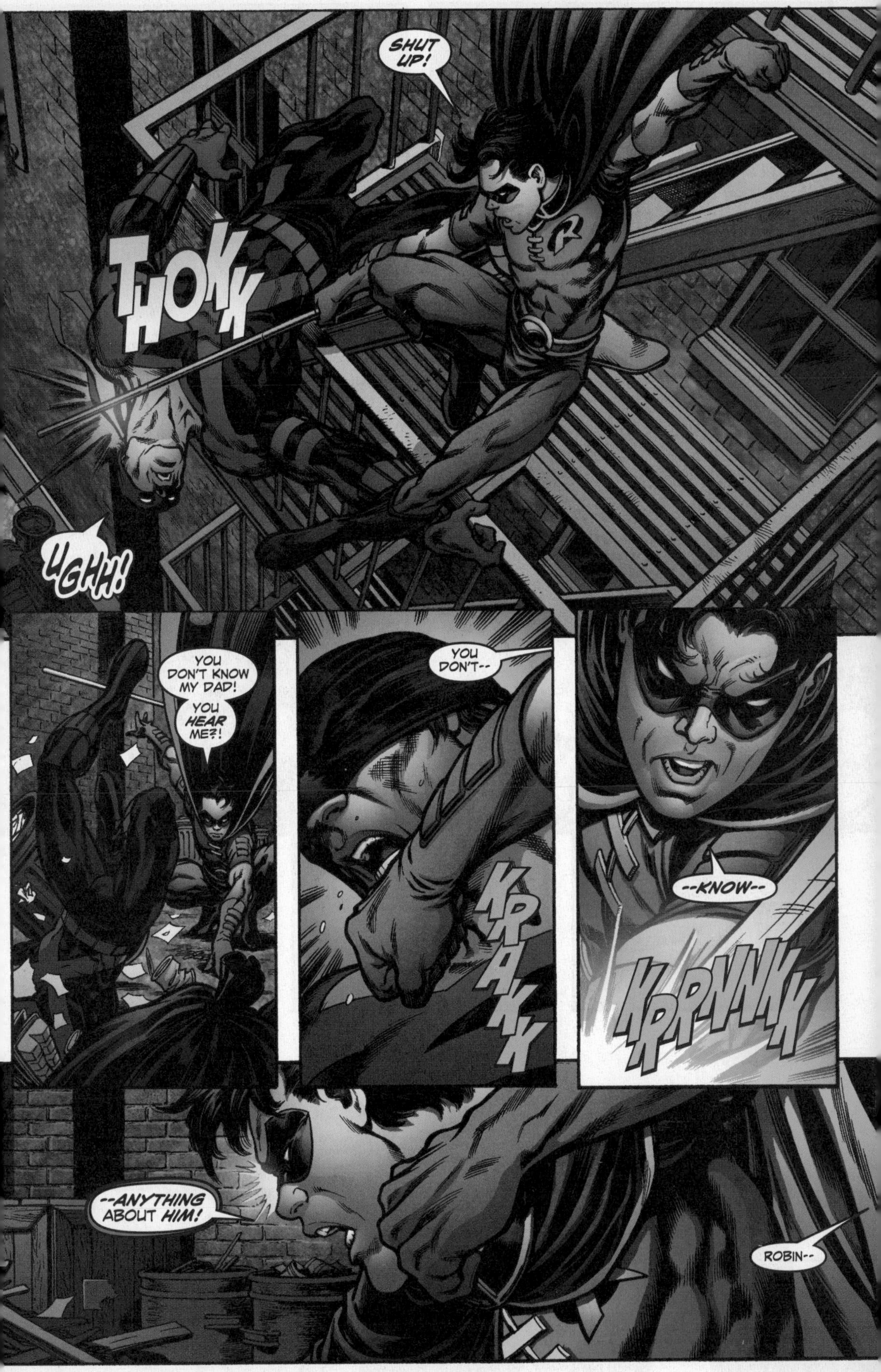

SHUT UP!
THOKK
UGHH!
YOU DON'T KNOW MY DAD!
YOU HEAR ME?!
YOU DON'T--
KRAKK
--KNOW--
KRRNNKK
--ANYTHING ABOUT HIM!
ROBIN--

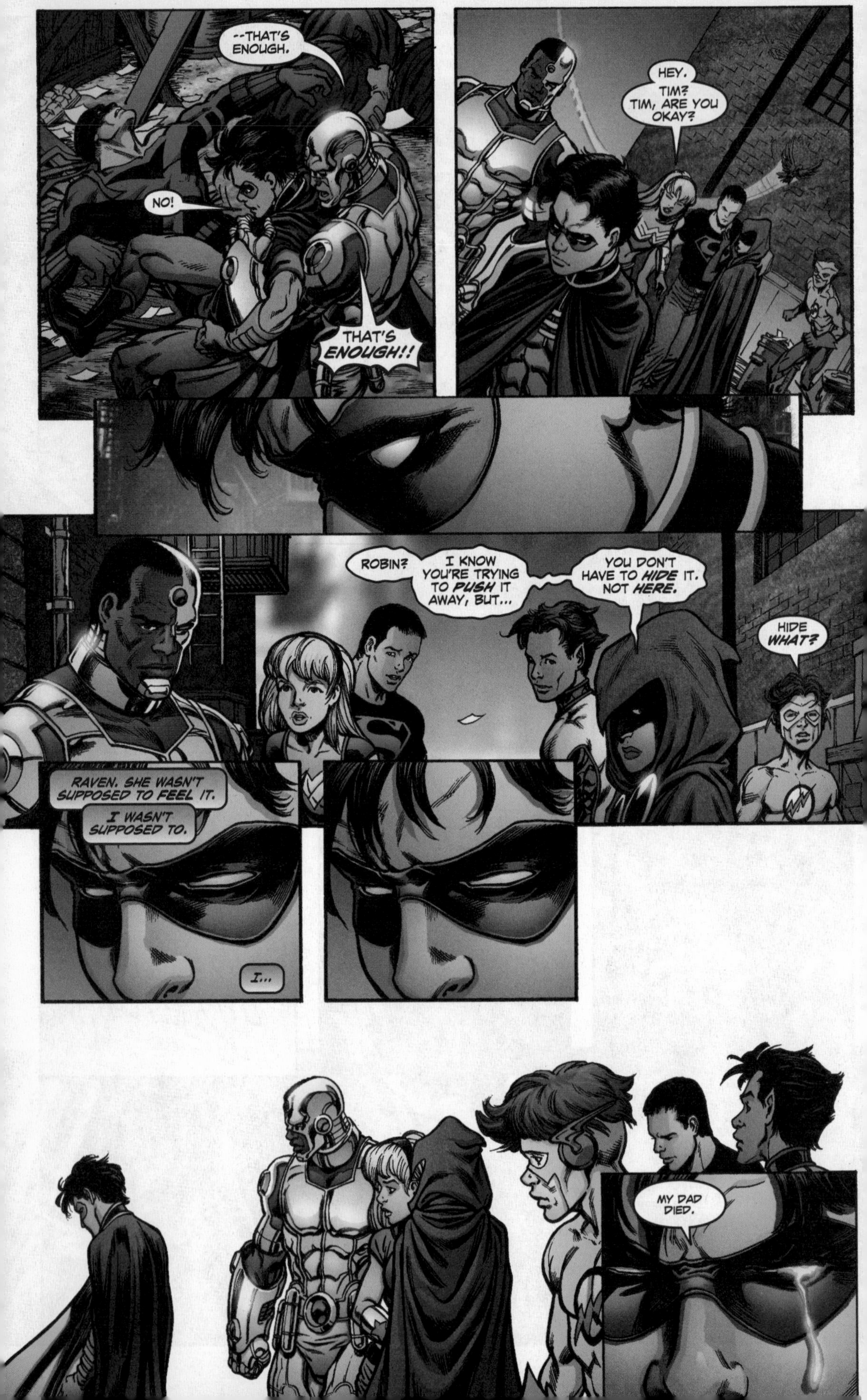
--THAT'S ENOUGH.
NO!
THAT'S ENOUGH!!
HEY.
TIM?
TIM, ARE YOU OKAY?
ROBIN?
I KNOW YOU'RE TRYING TO PUSH IT AWAY, BUT...
YOU DON'T HAVE TO HIDE IT. NOT HERE.
HIDE WHAT?
RAVEN. SHE WASN'T SUPPOSED TO FEEL IT.
I WASN'T SUPPOSED TO.
I...
MY DAD DIED.

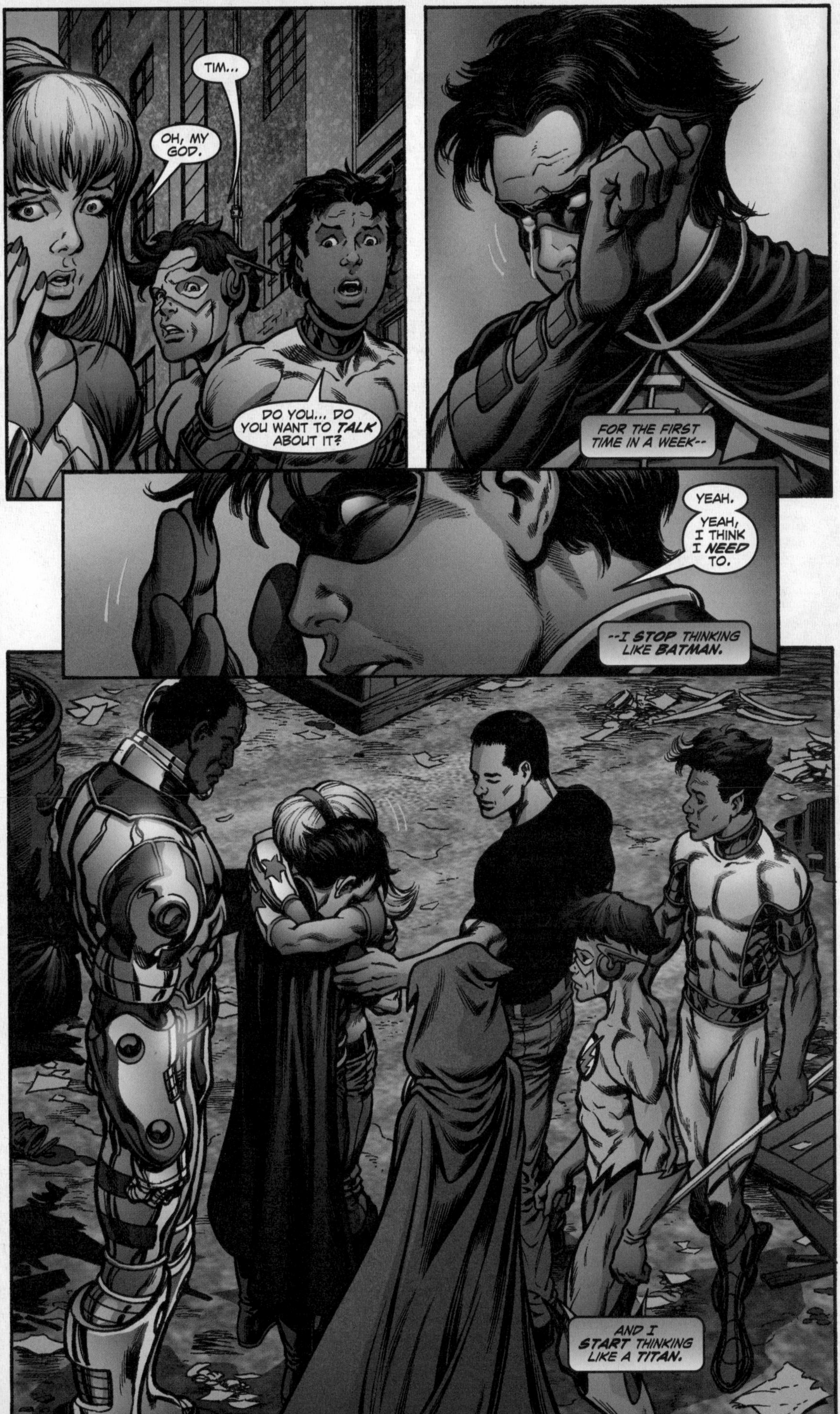
TIM...
OH, MY GOD.
DO YOU... DO YOU WANT TO TALK ABOUT IT?
FOR THE FIRST TIME IN A WEEK--
YEAH.
YEAH, I THINK I NEED TO.
--I STOP THINKING LIKE BATMAN.
AND I START THINKING LIKE A TITAN.

EPILOGUE ONE

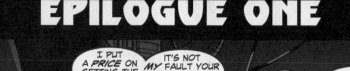

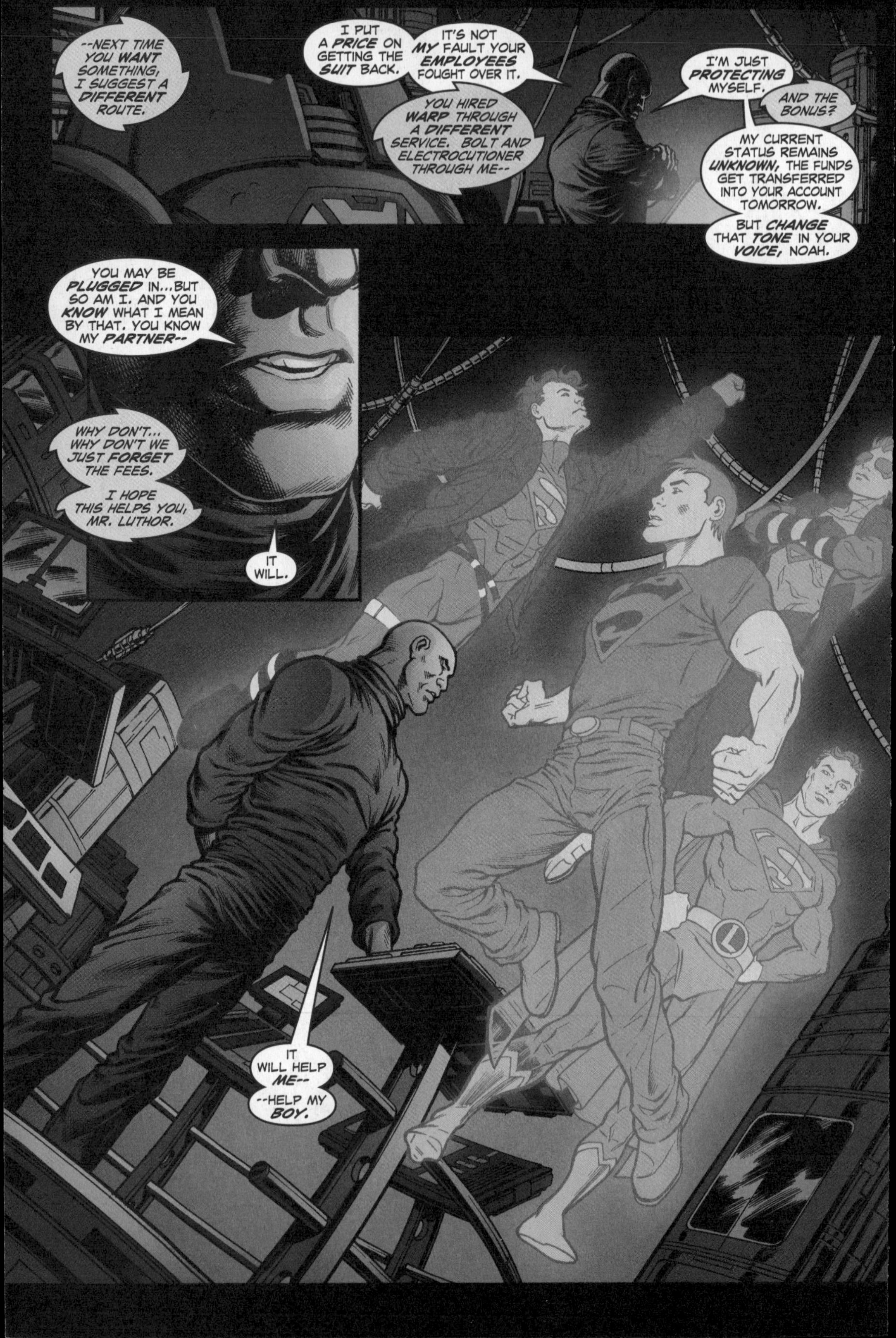
--NEXT TIME YOU WANT SOMETHING, I SUGGEST A DIFFERENT ROUTE.
I PUT A PRICE ON GETTING THE SUIT BACK.
IT'S NOT MY FAULT YOUR EMPLOYEES FOUGHT OVER IT.
YOU HIRED WARP THROUGH A DIFFERENT SERVICE. BOLT AND ELECTROCUTIONER THROUGH ME--
I'M JUST PROTECTING MYSELF.
AND THE BONUS?
MY CURRENT STATUS REMAINS UNKNOWN, THE FUNDS GET TRANSFERRED INTO YOUR ACCOUNT TOMORROW.
BUT CHANGE THAT TONE IN YOUR VOICE, NOAH.
YOU MAY BE PLUGGED IN...BUT SO AM I. AND YOU KNOW WHAT I MEAN BY THAT. YOU KNOW MY PARTNER--
WHY DON'T... WHY DON'T WE JUST FORGET THE FEES.
I HOPE THIS HELPS YOU, MR. LUTHOR.
IT WILL.
IT WILL HELP ME--
--HELP MY BOY.

EPILOGUE TWO

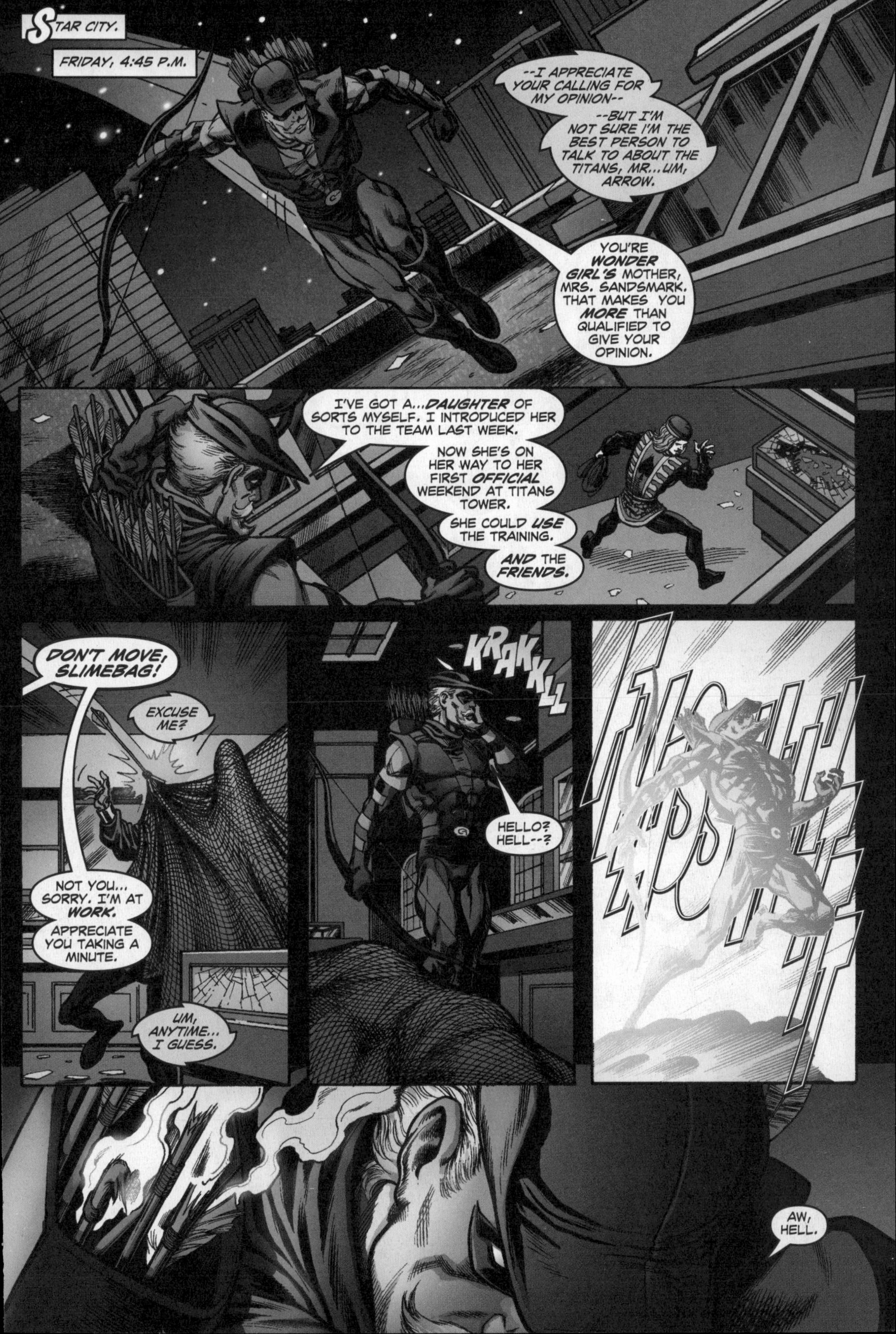

STAR CITY.
FRIDAY, 4:45 P.M.
--I APPRECIATE YOUR CALLING FOR MY OPINION--
--BUT I'M NOT SURE I'M THE BEST PERSON TO TALK TO ABOUT THE TITANS, MR...UM, ARROW.
YOU'RE WONDER GIRL'S MOTHER, MRS. SANDSMARK. THAT MAKES YOU MORE THAN QUALIFIED TO GIVE YOUR OPINION.
I'VE GOT A...DAUGHTER OF SORTS MYSELF. I INTRODUCED HER TO THE TEAM LAST WEEK.
NOW SHE'S ON HER WAY TO HER FIRST OFFICIAL WEEKEND AT TITANS TOWER.
SHE COULD USE THE TRAINING.
AND THE FRIENDS.
DON'T MOVE, SLIMEBAG!
EXCUSE ME?
NOT YOU... SORRY. I'M AT WORK.
APPRECIATE YOU TAKING A MINUTE.
UM, ANYTIME... I GUESS.
KRAKKLL
HELLO? HELL--?
AW, HELL.

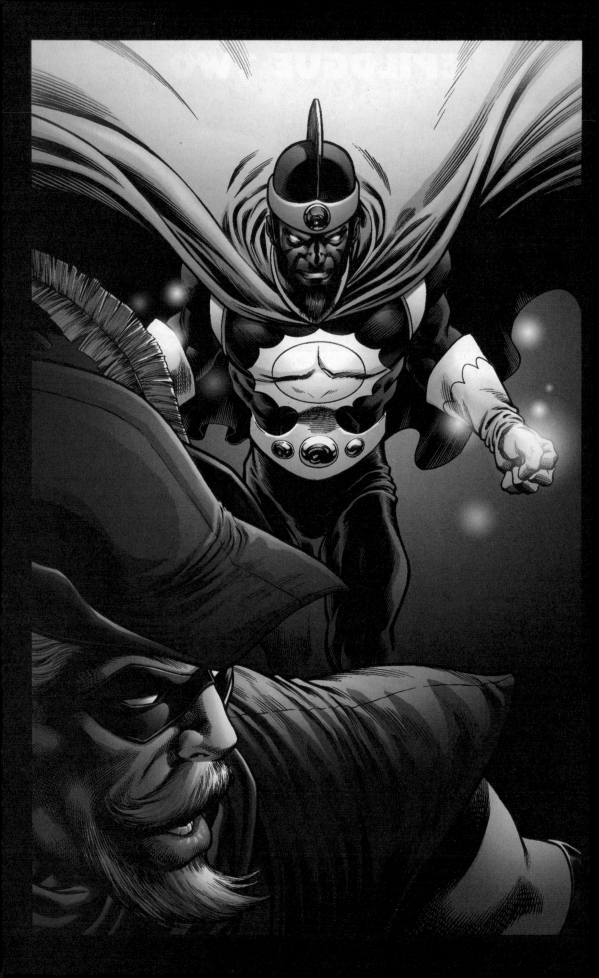

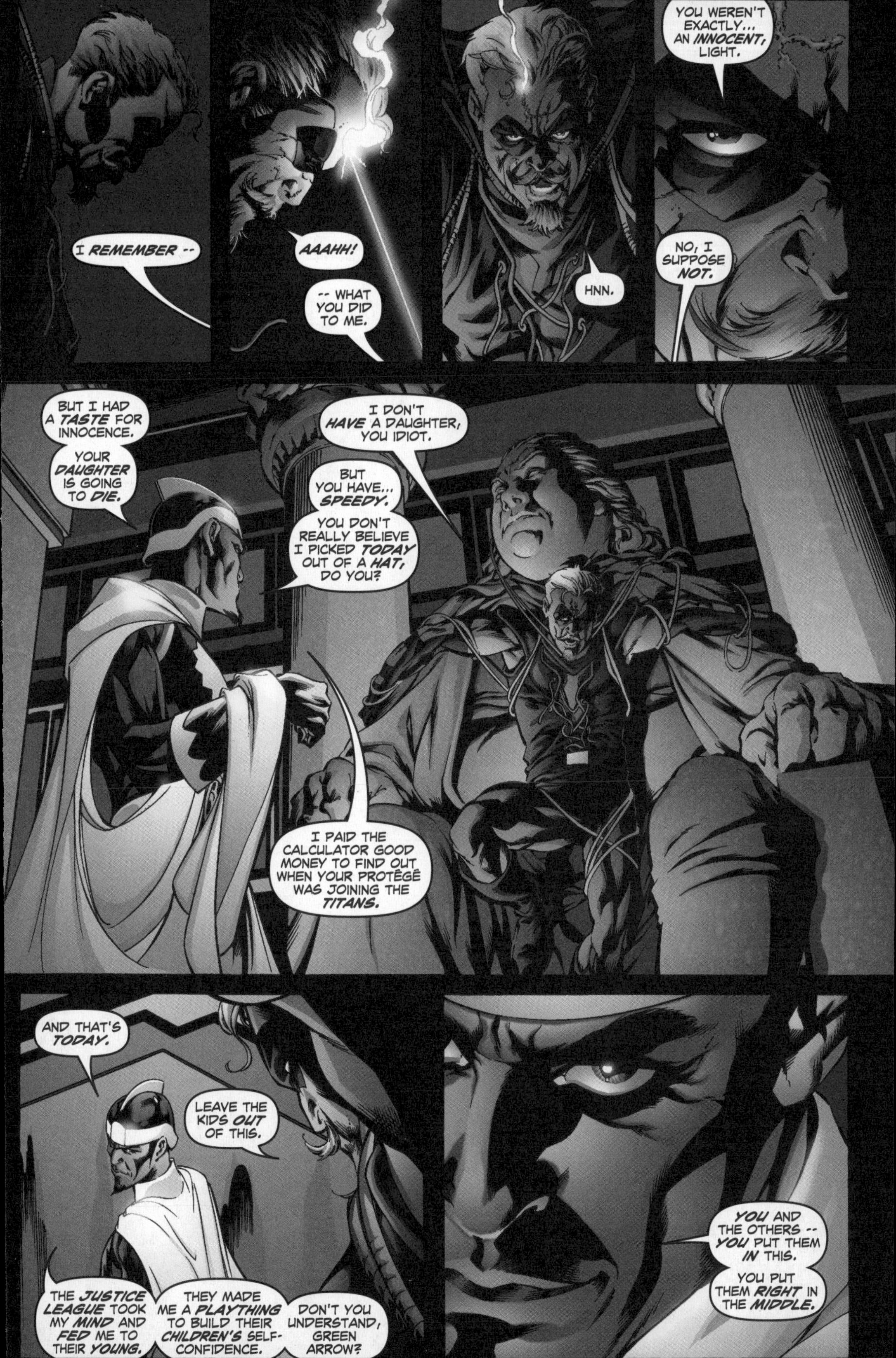
I REMEMBER --
AAAHH!
-- WHAT YOU DID TO ME.
HNN.
YOU WEREN'T EXACTLY... AN INNOCENT, LIGHT.
NO, I SUPPOSE NOT.
BUT I HAD A TASTE FOR INNOCENCE.
YOUR DAUGHTER IS GOING TO DIE.
I DON'T HAVE A DAUGHTER, YOU IDIOT.
BUT YOU HAVE... SPEEDY.
YOU DON'T REALLY BELIEVE I PICKED TODAY OUT OF A HAT, DO YOU?
I PAID THE CALCULATOR GOOD MONEY TO FIND OUT WHEN YOUR PROTÉGÉ WAS JOINING THE TITANS.
AND THAT'S TODAY.
LEAVE THE KIDS OUT OF THIS.
THE JUSTICE LEAGUE TOOK MY MIND AND FED ME TO THEIR YOUNG.
THEY MADE ME A PLAYTHING TO BUILD THEIR CHILDREN'S SELF-CONFIDENCE.
DON'T YOU UNDERSTAND, GREEN ARROW?
YOU AND THE OTHERS -- YOU PUT THEM IN THIS.
YOU PUT THEM RIGHT IN THE MIDDLE.

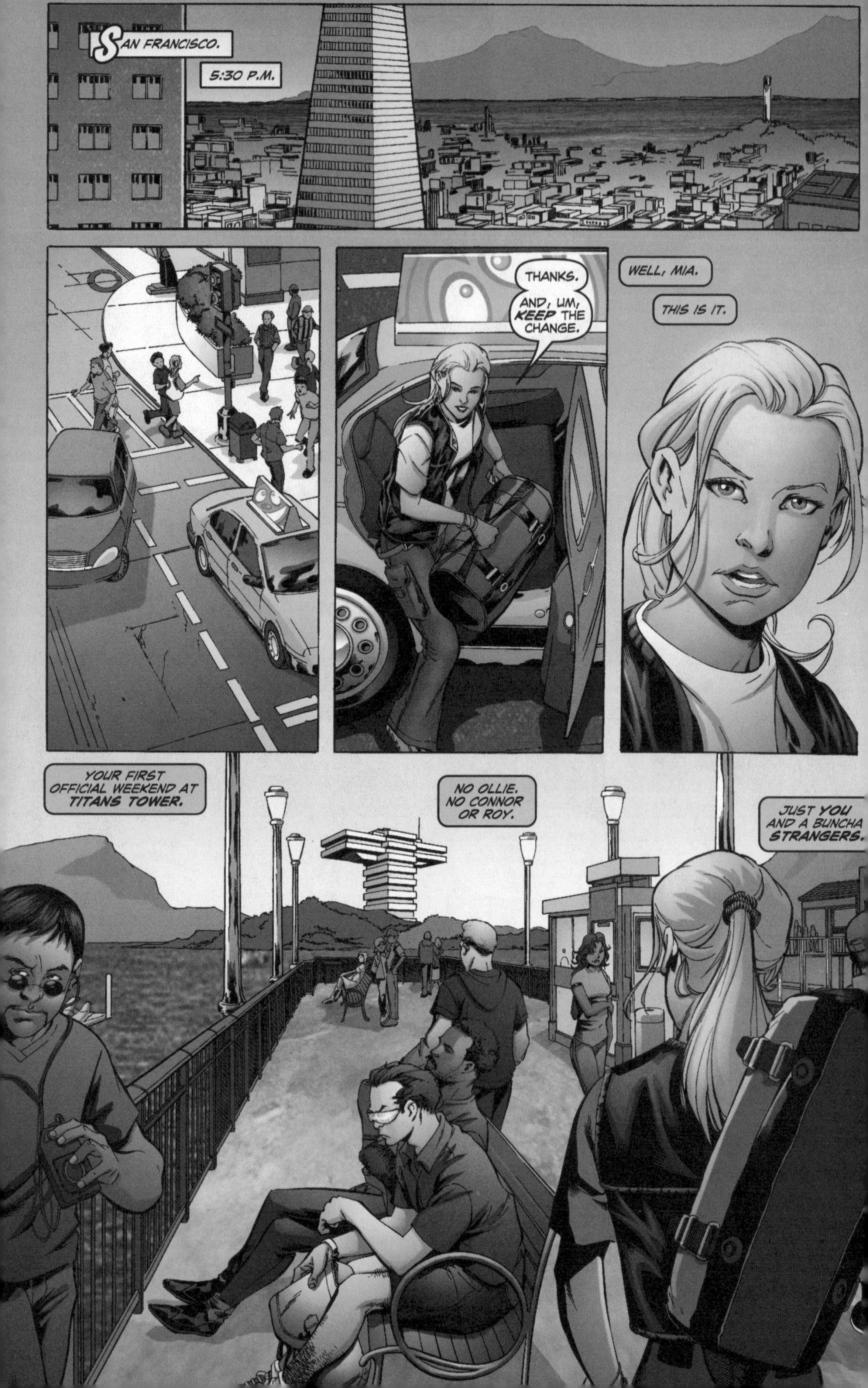
SAN FRANCISCO.
5:30 P.M.
THANKS.
AND, UM, KEEP THE CHANGE.
WELL, MIA.
THIS IS IT.
YOUR FIRST OFFICIAL WEEKEND AT TITANS TOWER.
NO OLLIE. NO CONNOR OR ROY.
JUST YOU AND A BUNCHA STRANGERS.

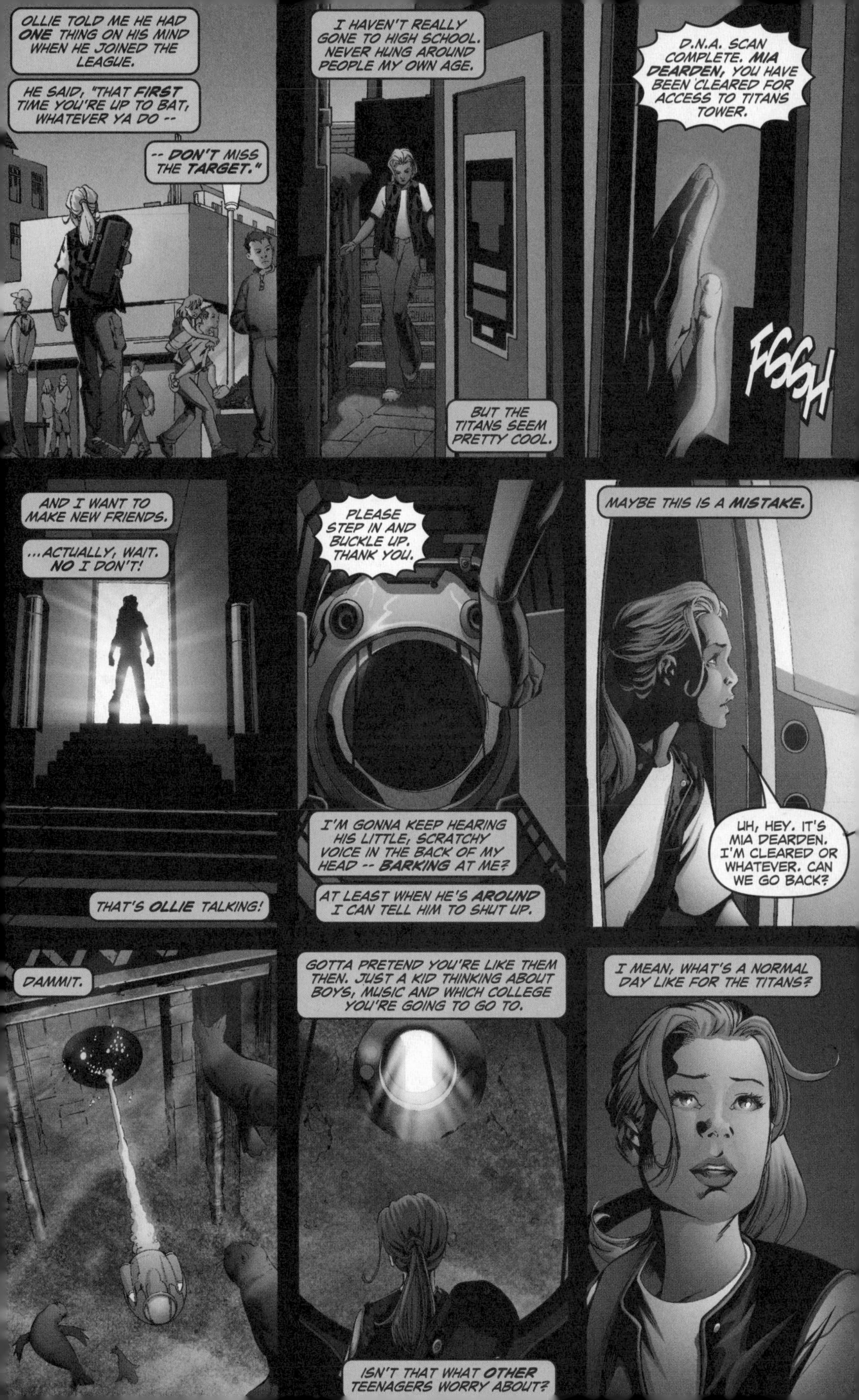
OLLIE TOLD ME HE HAD ONE THING ON HIS MIND WHEN HE JOINED THE LEAGUE.
HE SAID, "THAT FIRST TIME YOU'RE UP TO BAT, WHATEVER YA DO --
-- DON'T MISS THE TARGET."
I HAVEN'T REALLY GONE TO HIGH SCHOOL. NEVER HUNG AROUND PEOPLE MY OWN AGE.
BUT THE TITANS SEEM PRETTY COOL.
D.N.A. SCAN COMPLETE. MIA DEARDEN, YOU HAVE BEEN CLEARED FOR ACCESS TO TITANS TOWER.
FSSH
AND I WANT TO MAKE NEW FRIENDS.
...ACTUALLY, WAIT. NO I DON'T!
THAT'S OLLIE TALKING!
PLEASE STEP IN AND BUCKLE UP. THANK YOU.
I'M GONNA KEEP HEARING HIS LITTLE, SCRATCHY VOICE IN THE BACK OF MY HEAD -- BARKING AT ME?
AT LEAST WHEN HE'S AROUND I CAN TELL HIM TO SHUT UP.
MAYBE THIS IS A MISTAKE.
UH, HEY. IT'S MIA DEARDEN. I'M CLEARED OR WHATEVER. CAN WE GO BACK?
DAMMIT.
GOTTA PRETEND YOU'RE LIKE THEM THEN. JUST A KID THINKING ABOUT BOYS, MUSIC AND WHICH COLLEGE YOU'RE GOING TO GO TO.
ISN'T THAT WHAT OTHER TEENAGERS WORRY ABOUT?
I MEAN, WHAT'S A NORMAL DAY LIKE FOR THE TITANS?

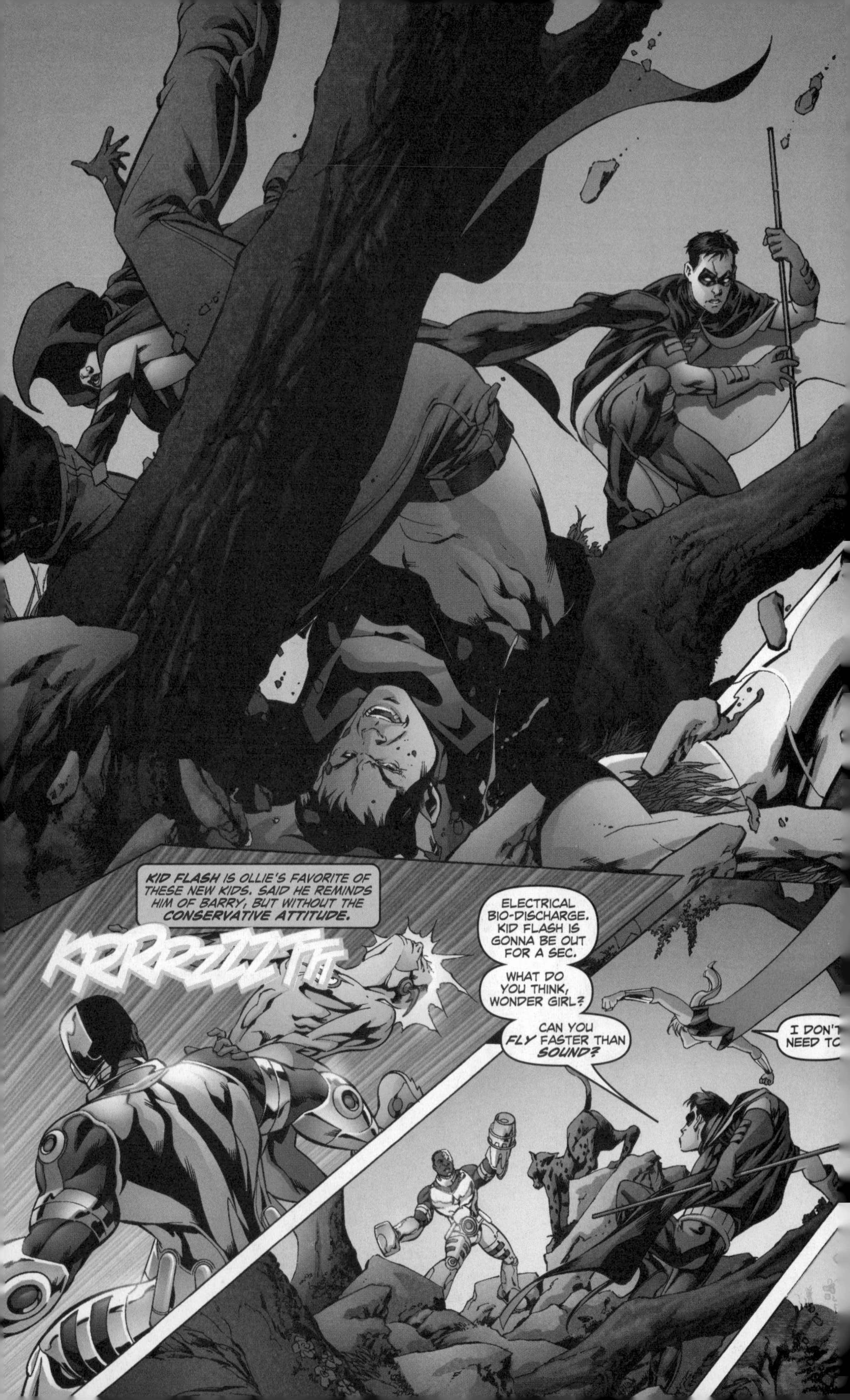
KID FLASH IS OLLIE'S FAVORITE OF THESE NEW KIDS. SAID HE REMINDS HIM OF BARRY, BUT WITHOUT THE CONSERVATIVE ATTITUDE.
KRRRZZZTTT
ELECTRICAL BIO-DISCHARGE. KID FLASH IS GONNA BE OUT FOR A SEC.
WHAT DO YOU THINK, WONDER GIRL?
CAN YOU FLY FASTER THAN SOUND?
I DON'T NEED TO

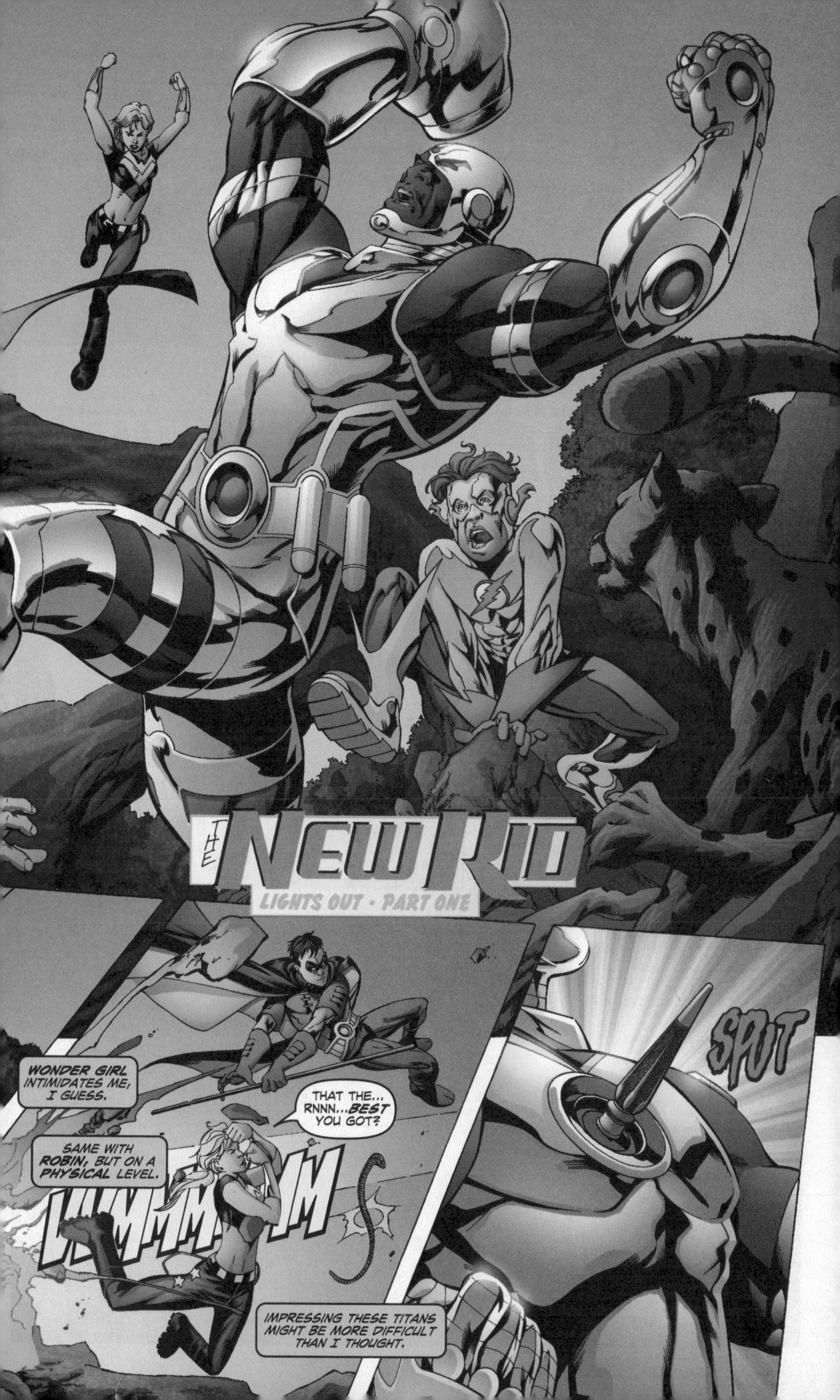
THE NEW KID
LIGHTS OUT • PART ONE
WONDER GIRL INTIMIDATES ME, I GUESS.
THAT THE... RNNN...BEST YOU GOT?
SAME WITH ROBIN, BUT ON A PHYSICAL LEVEL.
SPUT
IMPRESSING THESE TITANS MIGHT BE MORE DIFFICULT THAN I THOUGHT.

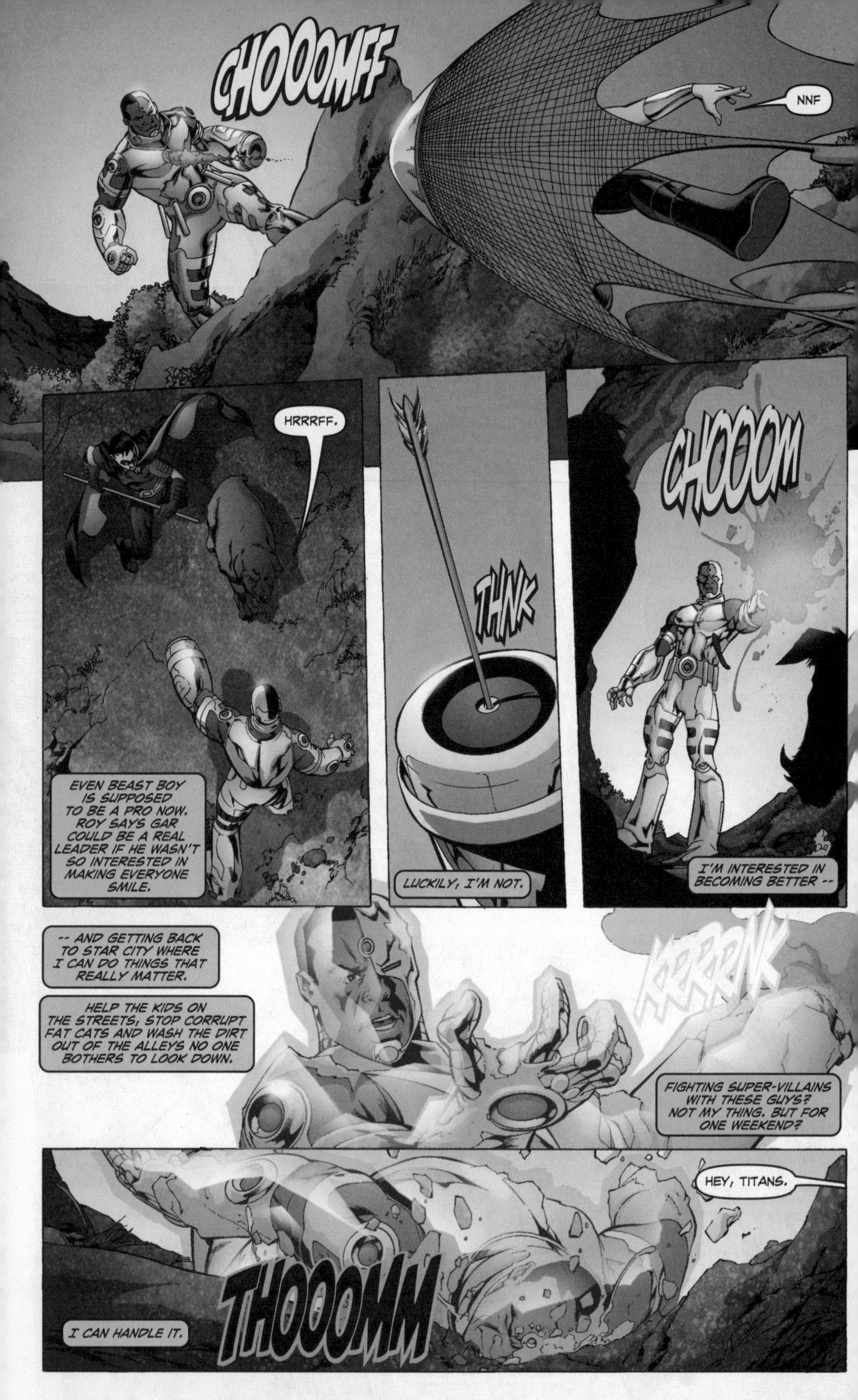
CHOOOMFF
NNF
HRRRFF.
EVEN BEAST BOY IS SUPPOSED TO BE A PRO NOW. ROY SAYS GAR COULD BE A REAL LEADER IF HE WASN'T SO INTERESTED IN MAKING EVERYONE SMILE.
THNK
LUCKILY, I'M NOT.
CHOOOM
I'M INTERESTED IN BECOMING BETTER --
-- AND GETTING BACK TO STAR CITY WHERE I CAN DO THINGS THAT REALLY MATTER.
HELP THE KIDS ON THE STREETS, STOP CORRUPT FAT CATS AND WASH THE DIRT OUT OF THE ALLEYS NO ONE BOTHERS TO LOOK DOWN.
KRRRNK
FIGHTING SUPER-VILLAINS WITH THESE GUYS? NOT MY THING. BUT FOR ONE WEEKEND?
HEY, TITANS.
THOOOMM
I CAN HANDLE IT.

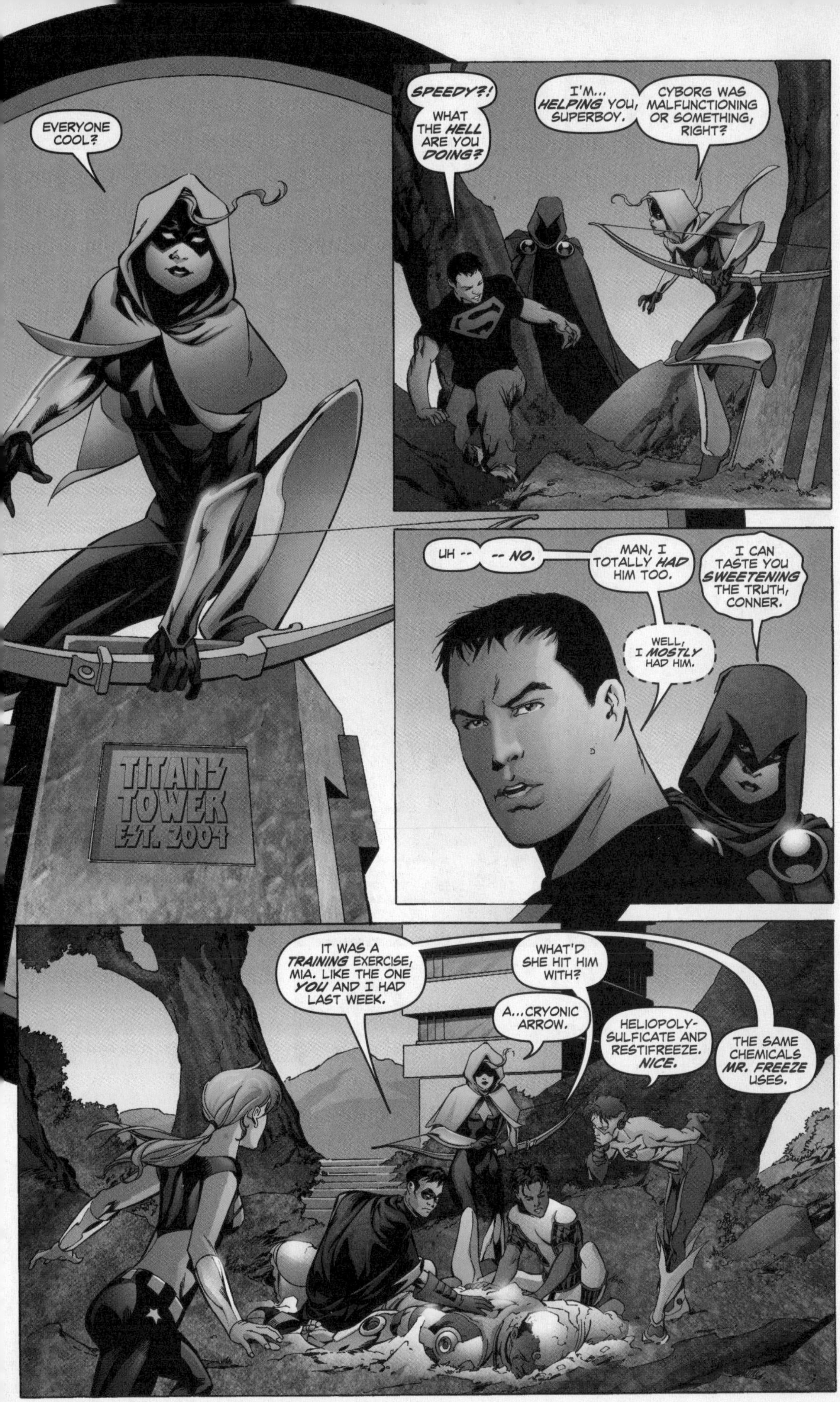
EVERYONE COOL?
SPEEDY?! WHAT THE HELL ARE YOU DOING?
I'M... HELPING YOU, SUPERBOY.
CYBORG WAS MALFUNCTIONING OR SOMETHING, RIGHT?
UH --
-- NO.
MAN, I TOTALLY HAD HIM TOO.
WELL, I MOSTLY HAD HIM.
I CAN TASTE YOU SWEETENING THE TRUTH, CONNER.
TITANS TOWER EST. 2004
IT WAS A TRAINING EXERCISE, MIA. LIKE THE ONE YOU AND I HAD LAST WEEK.
WHAT'D SHE HIT HIM WITH?
A...CRYONIC ARROW.
HELIOPOLY-SULFICATE AND RESTIFREEZE. NICE.
THE SAME CHEMICALS MR. FREEZE USES.

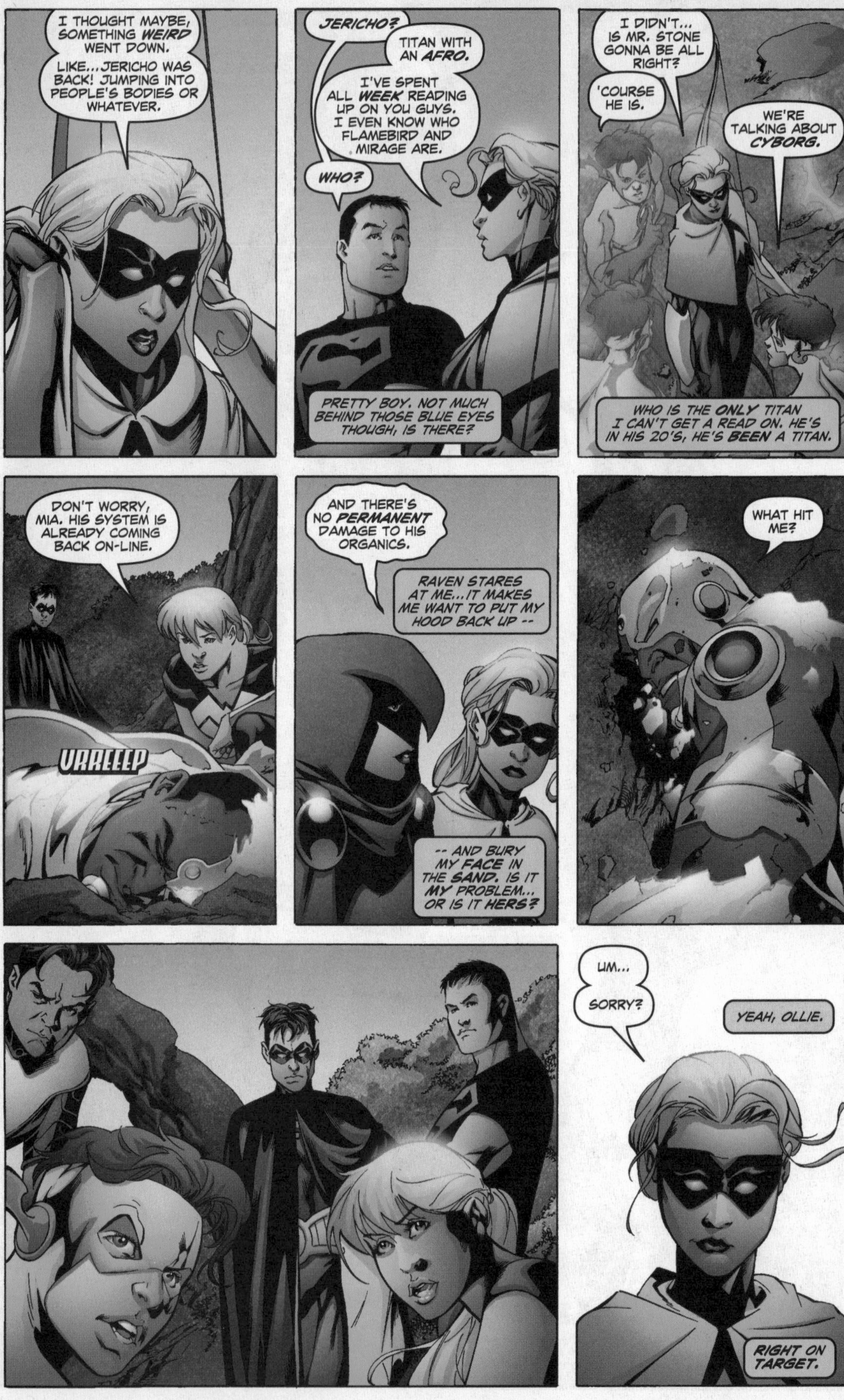
I THOUGHT MAYBE, SOMETHING WEIRD WENT DOWN.
LIKE... JERICHO WAS BACK! JUMPING INTO PEOPLE'S BODIES OR WHATEVER.
JERICHO?
TITAN WITH AN AFRO.
I'VE SPENT ALL WEEK READING UP ON YOU GUYS. I EVEN KNOW WHO FLAMEBIRD AND MIRAGE ARE.
WHO?
PRETTY BOY. NOT MUCH BEHIND THOSE BLUE EYES THOUGH, IS THERE?
I DIDN'T... IS MR. STONE GONNA BE ALL RIGHT?
'COURSE HE IS.
WE'RE TALKING ABOUT CYBORG.
WHO IS THE ONLY TITAN I CAN'T GET A READ ON. HE'S IN HIS 20'S, HE'S BEEN A TITAN.
DON'T WORRY, MIA. HIS SYSTEM IS ALREADY COMING BACK ON-LINE.
VRREEEP
AND THERE'S NO PERMANENT DAMAGE TO HIS ORGANICS.
RAVEN STARES AT ME... IT MAKES ME WANT TO PUT MY HOOD BACK UP --
-- AND BURY MY FACE IN THE SAND. IS IT MY PROBLEM... OR IS IT HERS?
WHAT HIT ME?
UM...
SORRY?
YEAH, OLLIE.
RIGHT ON TARGET.

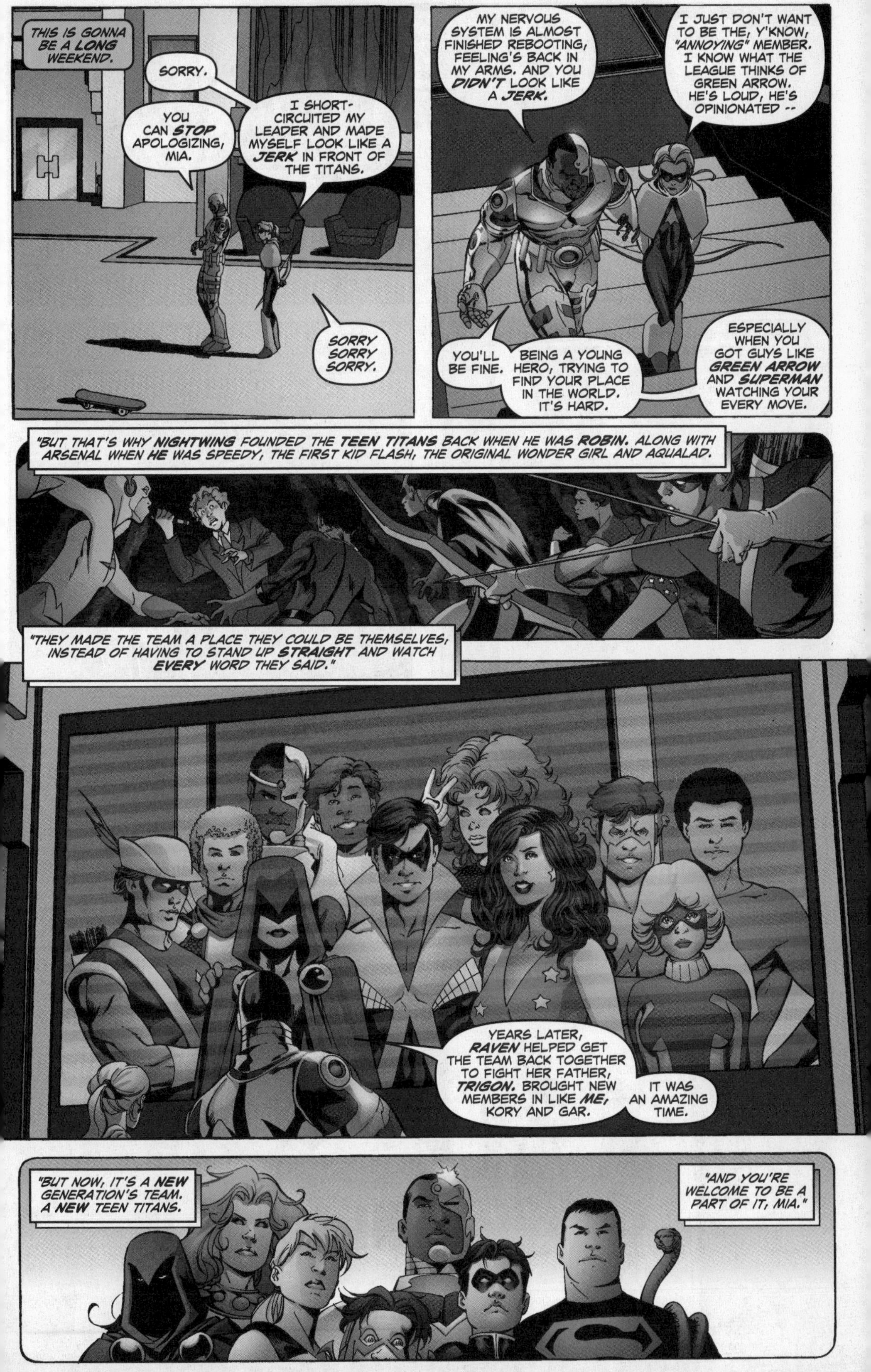
THIS IS GONNA BE A LONG WEEKEND.
SORRY.
YOU CAN STOP APOLOGIZING, MIA.
I SHORT-CIRCUITED MY LEADER AND MADE MYSELF LOOK LIKE A JERK IN FRONT OF THE TITANS.
SORRY SORRY SORRY.
MY NERVOUS SYSTEM IS ALMOST FINISHED REBOOTING, FEELING'S BACK IN MY ARMS. AND YOU DIDN'T LOOK LIKE A JERK.
I JUST DON'T WANT TO BE THE, Y'KNOW, "ANNOYING" MEMBER. I KNOW WHAT THE LEAGUE THINKS OF GREEN ARROW. HE'S LOUD, HE'S OPINIONATED --
YOU'LL BE FINE.
BEING A YOUNG HERO, TRYING TO FIND YOUR PLACE IN THE WORLD. IT'S HARD.
ESPECIALLY WHEN YOU GOT GUYS LIKE GREEN ARROW AND SUPERMAN WATCHING YOUR EVERY MOVE.
"BUT THAT'S WHY NIGHTWING FOUNDED THE TEEN TITANS BACK WHEN HE WAS ROBIN. ALONG WITH ARSENAL WHEN HE WAS SPEEDY, THE FIRST KID FLASH, THE ORIGINAL WONDER GIRL AND AQUALAD.
"THEY MADE THE TEAM A PLACE THEY COULD BE THEMSELVES, INSTEAD OF HAVING TO STAND UP STRAIGHT AND WATCH EVERY WORD THEY SAID."
YEARS LATER, RAVEN HELPED GET THE TEAM BACK TOGETHER TO FIGHT HER FATHER, TRIGON. BROUGHT NEW MEMBERS IN LIKE ME, KORY AND GAR.
IT WAS AN AMAZING TIME.
"BUT NOW, IT'S A NEW GENERATION'S TEAM. A NEW TEEN TITANS.
"AND YOU'RE WELCOME TO BE A PART OF IT, MIA."

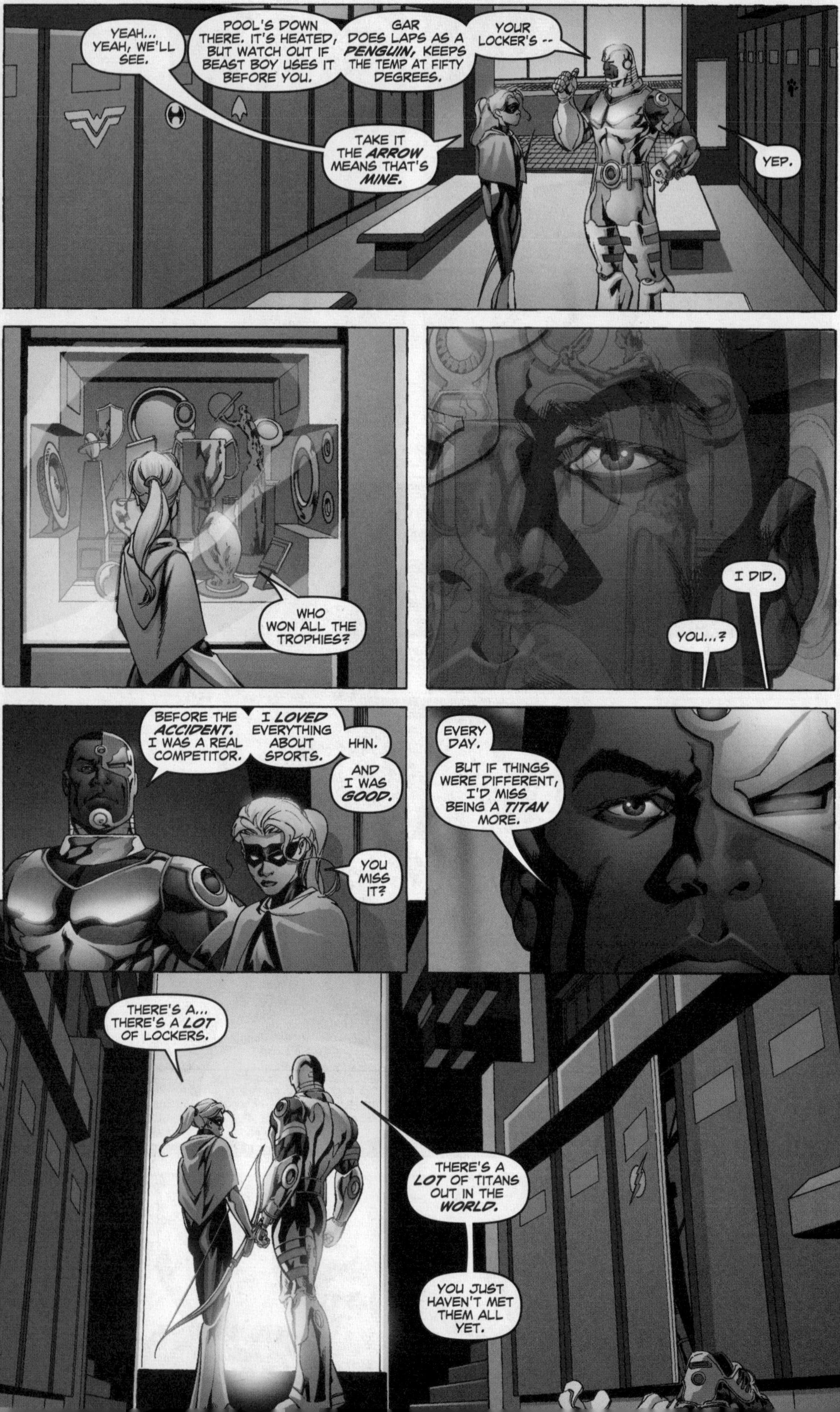

YEAH... YEAH, WE'LL SEE.
POOL'S DOWN THERE. IT'S HEATED, BUT WATCH OUT IF BEAST BOY USES IT BEFORE YOU.
GAR DOES LAPS AS A PENGUIN, KEEPS THE TEMP AT FIFTY DEGREES.
YOUR LOCKER'S --
TAKE IT THE ARROW MEANS THAT'S MINE.
YEP.
WHO WON ALL THE TROPHIES?
I DID.
YOU...?
BEFORE THE ACCIDENT. I WAS A REAL COMPETITOR.
I LOVED EVERYTHING ABOUT SPORTS.
HHN.
AND I WAS GOOD.
YOU MISS IT?
EVERY DAY.
BUT IF THINGS WERE DIFFERENT, I'D MISS BEING A TITAN MORE.
THERE'S A... THERE'S A LOT OF LOCKERS.
THERE'S A LOT OF TITANS OUT IN THE WORLD.
YOU JUST HAVEN'T MET THEM ALL YET.

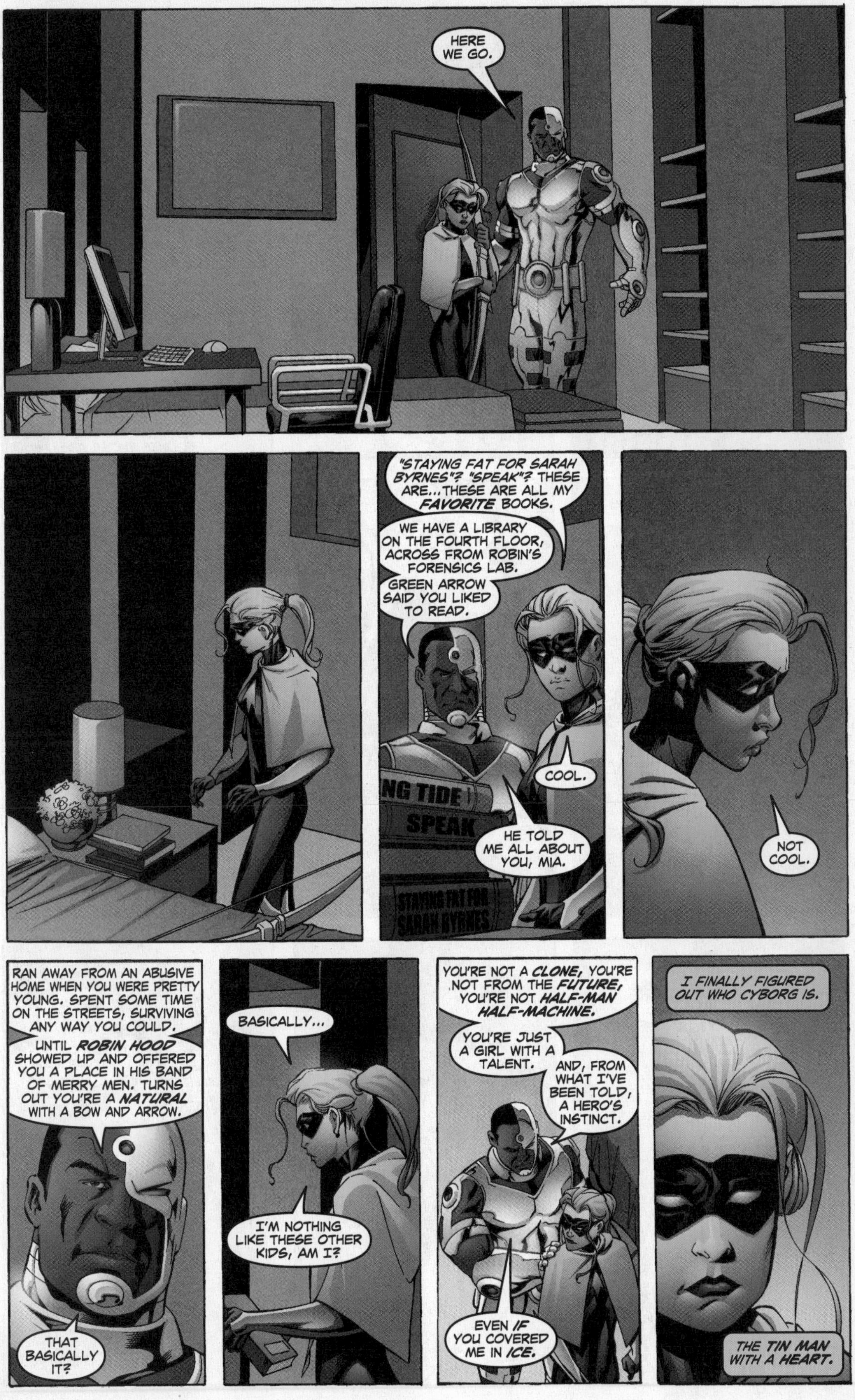
HERE WE GO.
"STAYING FAT FOR SARAH BYRNES"? "SPEAK"? THESE ARE... THESE ARE ALL MY FAVORITE BOOKS.
WE HAVE A LIBRARY ON THE FOURTH FLOOR, ACROSS FROM ROBIN'S FORENSICS LAB.
GREEN ARROW SAID YOU LIKED TO READ.
COOL.
NG TIDE
SPEAK
STAYING FAT FOR SARAH BYRNES
HE TOLD ME ALL ABOUT YOU, MIA.
NOT COOL.
RAN AWAY FROM AN ABUSIVE HOME WHEN YOU WERE PRETTY YOUNG. SPENT SOME TIME ON THE STREETS, SURVIVING ANY WAY YOU COULD.
UNTIL ROBIN HOOD SHOWED UP AND OFFERED YOU A PLACE IN HIS BAND OF MERRY MEN. TURNS OUT YOU'RE A NATURAL WITH A BOW AND ARROW.
THAT BASICALLY IT?
BASICALLY...
I'M NOTHING LIKE THESE OTHER KIDS, AM I?
YOU'RE NOT A CLONE, YOU'RE NOT FROM THE FUTURE; YOU'RE NOT HALF-MAN HALF-MACHINE.
YOU'RE JUST A GIRL WITH A TALENT.
AND, FROM WHAT I'VE BEEN TOLD, A HERO'S INSTINCT.
EVEN IF YOU COVERED ME IN ICE.
I FINALLY FIGURED OUT WHO CYBORG IS.
THE TIN MAN WITH A HEART.

I GOT SOMETHIN' FOR YOU.

WHAT ARE--?

THEY BELONGED TO SPEEDY BEFORE HE TRADED IN THE *TRICK ARROWS* FOR HIS *ARSENAL* IDENTITY.

ROY WANTED YOU TO HAVE THEM. SAID HE MISSED YOUR SEVENTEENTH BIRTHDAY.

IT WAS, UH, LAST WEEK.

HE MENTIONED THE MAGNESIUM FLARES WERE PROBABLY EXPIRED. WHICHEVER ONES THOSE ARE.

THESE, WITH THE GLASS BULBS ON THE END.

HEY.

WHAT'S THE *BLUE* ONE FOR?

DON'T KNOW.

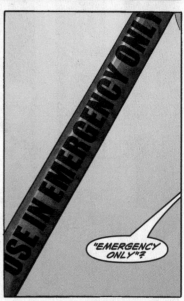

USE IN EMERGENCY ONLY

"EMERGENCY ONLY"?

CYBORG. I ALSO... I NEED TO TELL YOU ALL SOMETHING ELSE--

YO!

AAAA!

SORRY, SPEEDY, BUT... YOU GUYS BETTER *SEE* THIS.

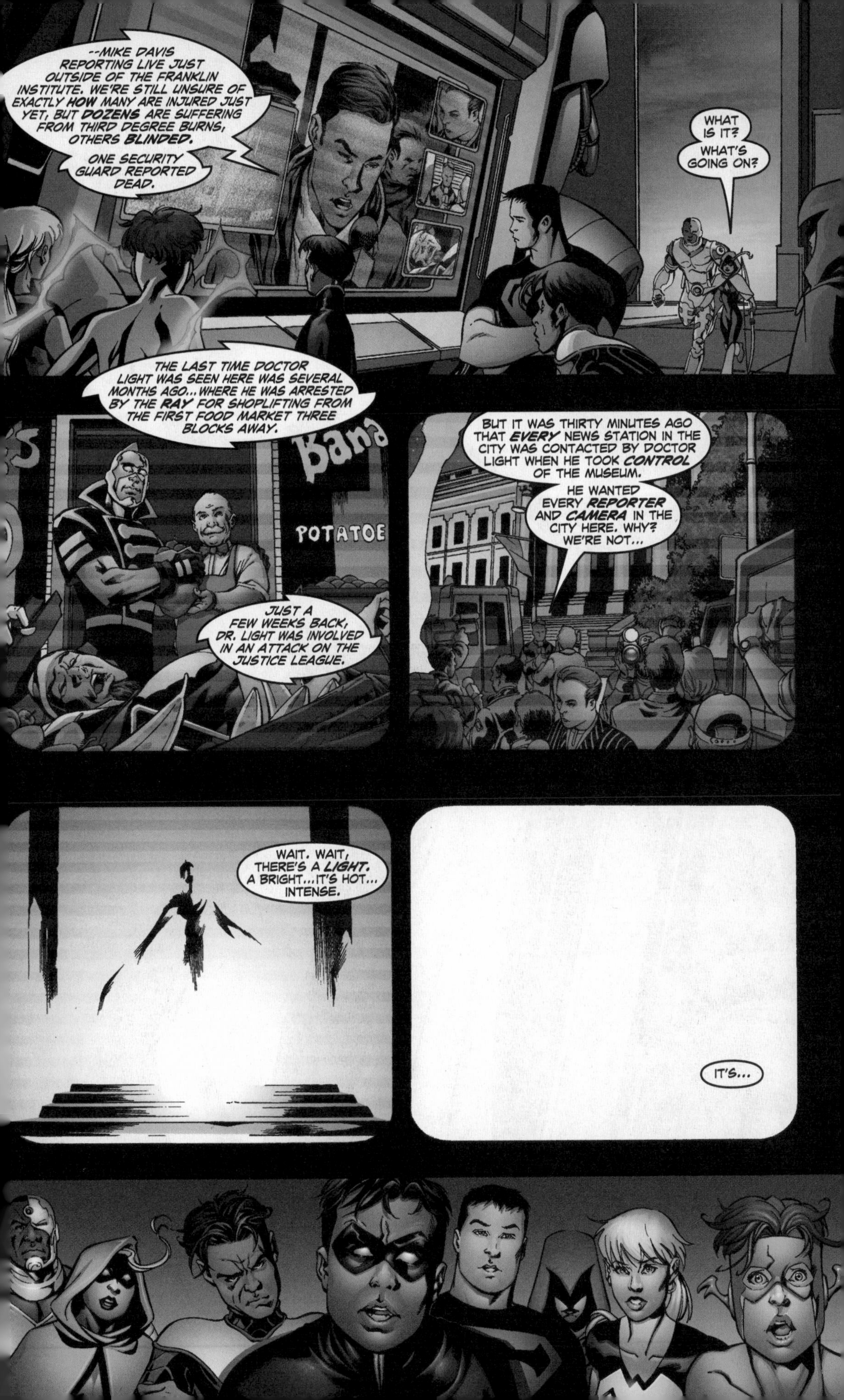
--MIKE DAVIS REPORTING LIVE JUST OUTSIDE OF THE FRANKLIN INSTITUTE. WE'RE STILL UNSURE OF EXACTLY HOW MANY ARE INJURED JUST YET, BUT DOZENS ARE SUFFERING FROM THIRD DEGREE BURNS, OTHERS BLINDED.
ONE SECURITY GUARD REPORTED DEAD.
WHAT IS IT?
WHAT'S GOING ON?
THE LAST TIME DOCTOR LIGHT WAS SEEN HERE WAS SEVERAL MONTHS AGO...WHERE HE WAS ARRESTED BY THE RAY FOR SHOPLIFTING FROM THE FIRST FOOD MARKET THREE BLOCKS AWAY.
POTATOE
JUST A FEW WEEKS BACK, DR. LIGHT WAS INVOLVED IN AN ATTACK ON THE JUSTICE LEAGUE.
BUT IT WAS THIRTY MINUTES AGO THAT EVERY NEWS STATION IN THE CITY WAS CONTACTED BY DOCTOR LIGHT WHEN HE TOOK CONTROL OF THE MUSEUM.
HE WANTED EVERY REPORTER AND CAMERA IN THE CITY HERE. WHY? WE'RE NOT...
WAIT. WAIT, THERE'S A LIGHT. A BRIGHT...IT'S HOT... INTENSE.
IT'S...

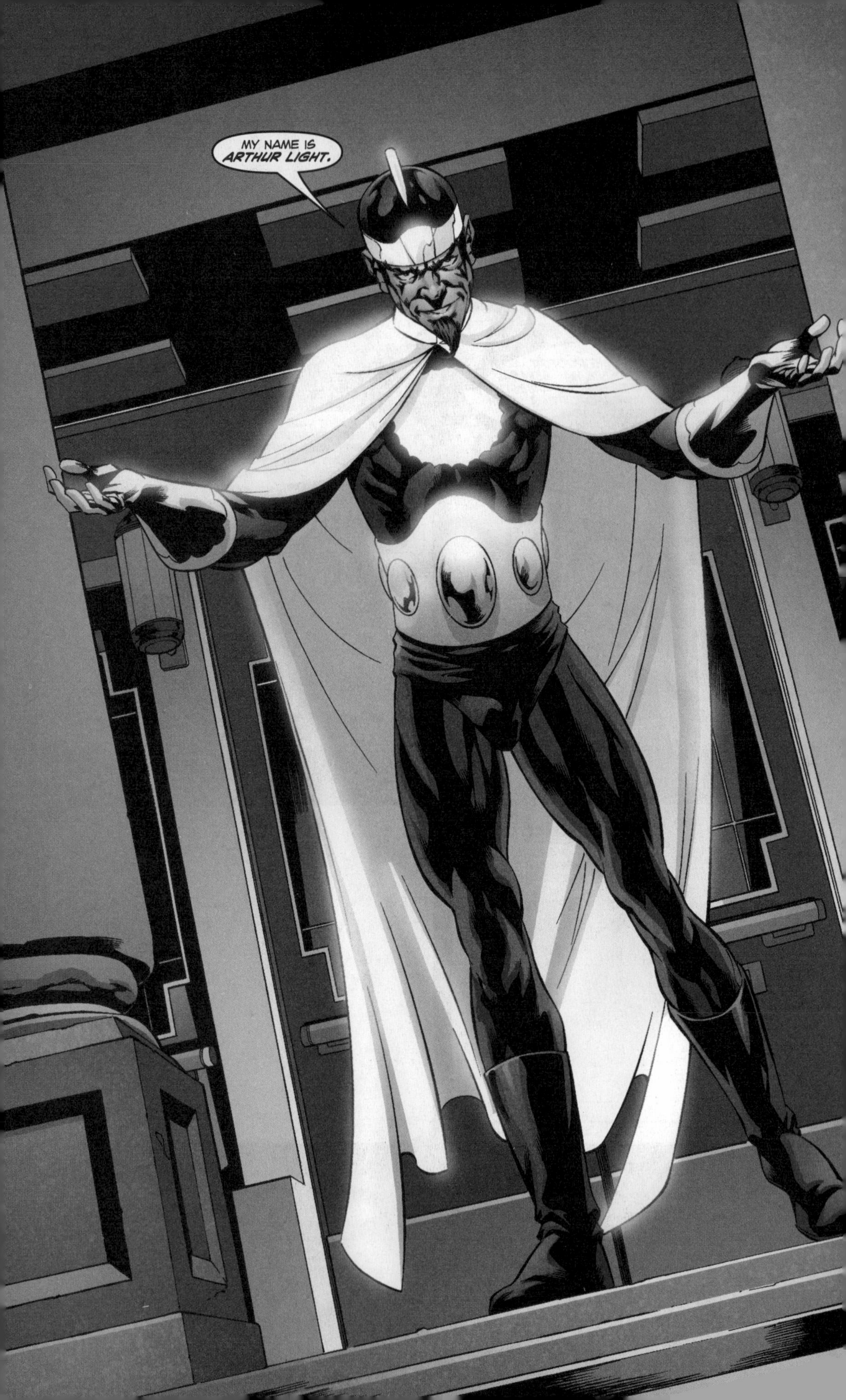
MY NAME IS ARTHUR LIGHT.

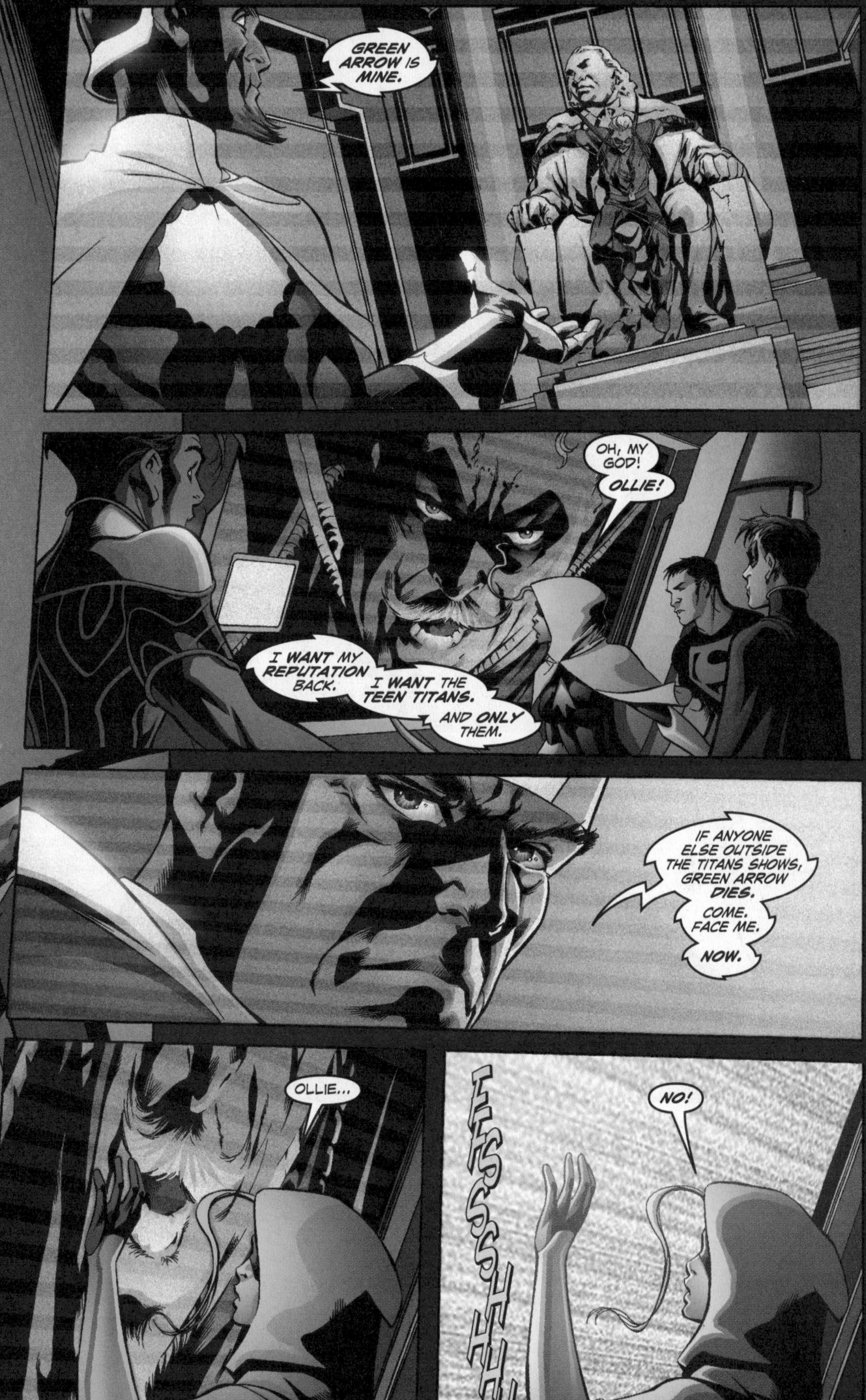
GREEN ARROW IS MINE.
OH, MY GOD! OLLIE!
I WANT MY REPUTATION BACK.
I WANT THE TEEN TITANS.
AND ONLY THEM.
IF ANYONE ELSE OUTSIDE THE TITANS SHOWS, GREEN ARROW DIES.
COME. FACE ME.
NOW.
OLLIE...
FFSSSHHHH
NO!

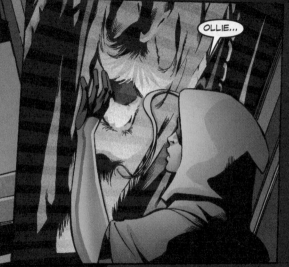

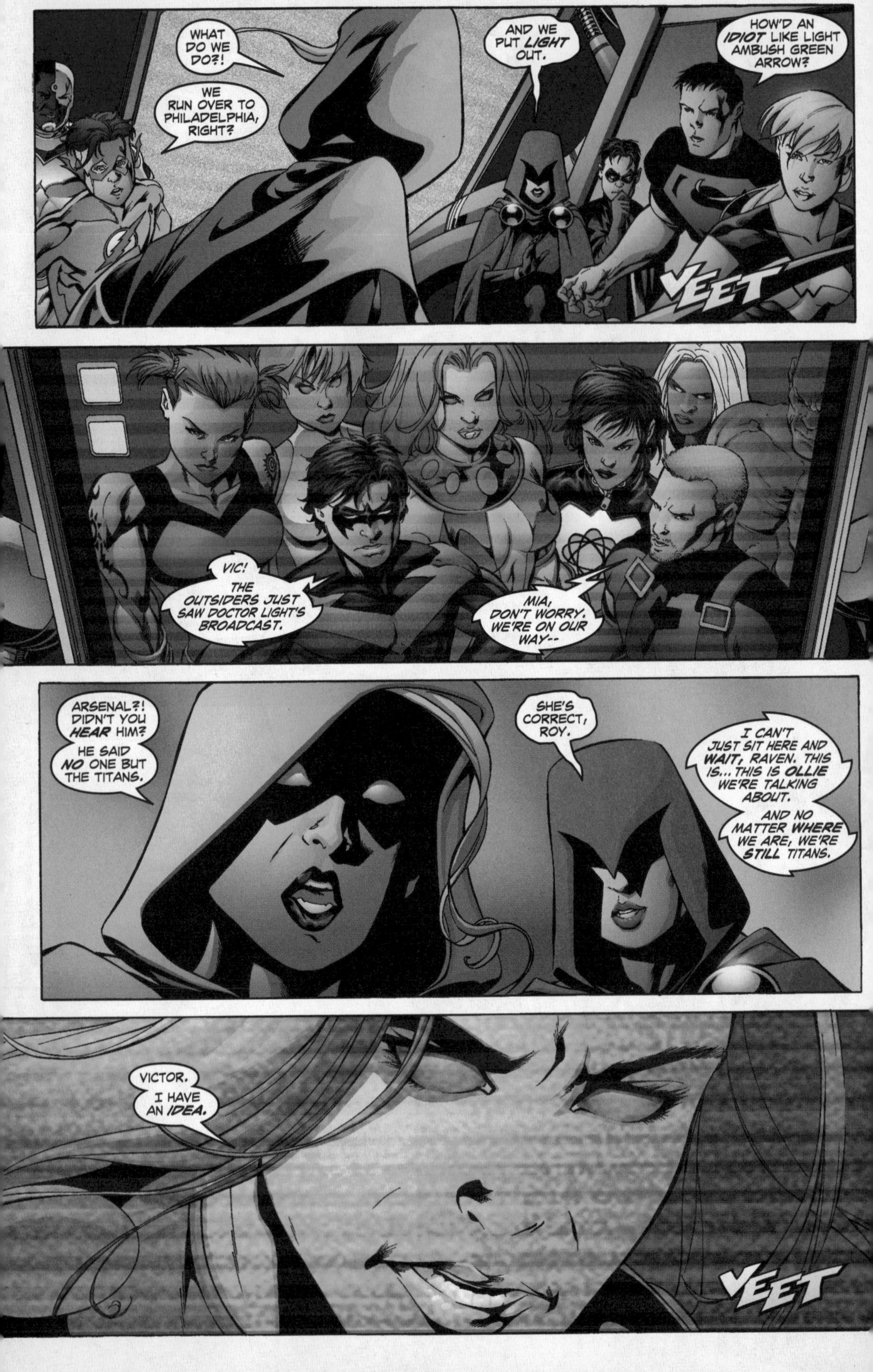
WHAT DO WE DO?!
WE RUN OVER TO PHILADELPHIA, RIGHT?
AND WE PUT LIGHT OUT.
HOW'D AN IDIOT LIKE LIGHT AMBUSH GREEN ARROW?
VEET
VIC! THE OUTSIDERS JUST SAW DOCTOR LIGHT'S BROADCAST.
MIA, DON'T WORRY. WE'RE ON OUR WAY--
ARSENAL?! DIDN'T YOU HEAR HIM? HE SAID NO ONE BUT THE TITANS.
SHE'S CORRECT, ROY.
I CAN'T JUST SIT HERE AND WAIT, RAVEN. THIS IS... THIS IS OLLIE WE'RE TALKING ABOUT.
AND NO MATTER WHERE WE ARE, WE'RE STILL TITANS.
VICTOR. I HAVE AN IDEA.
VEET

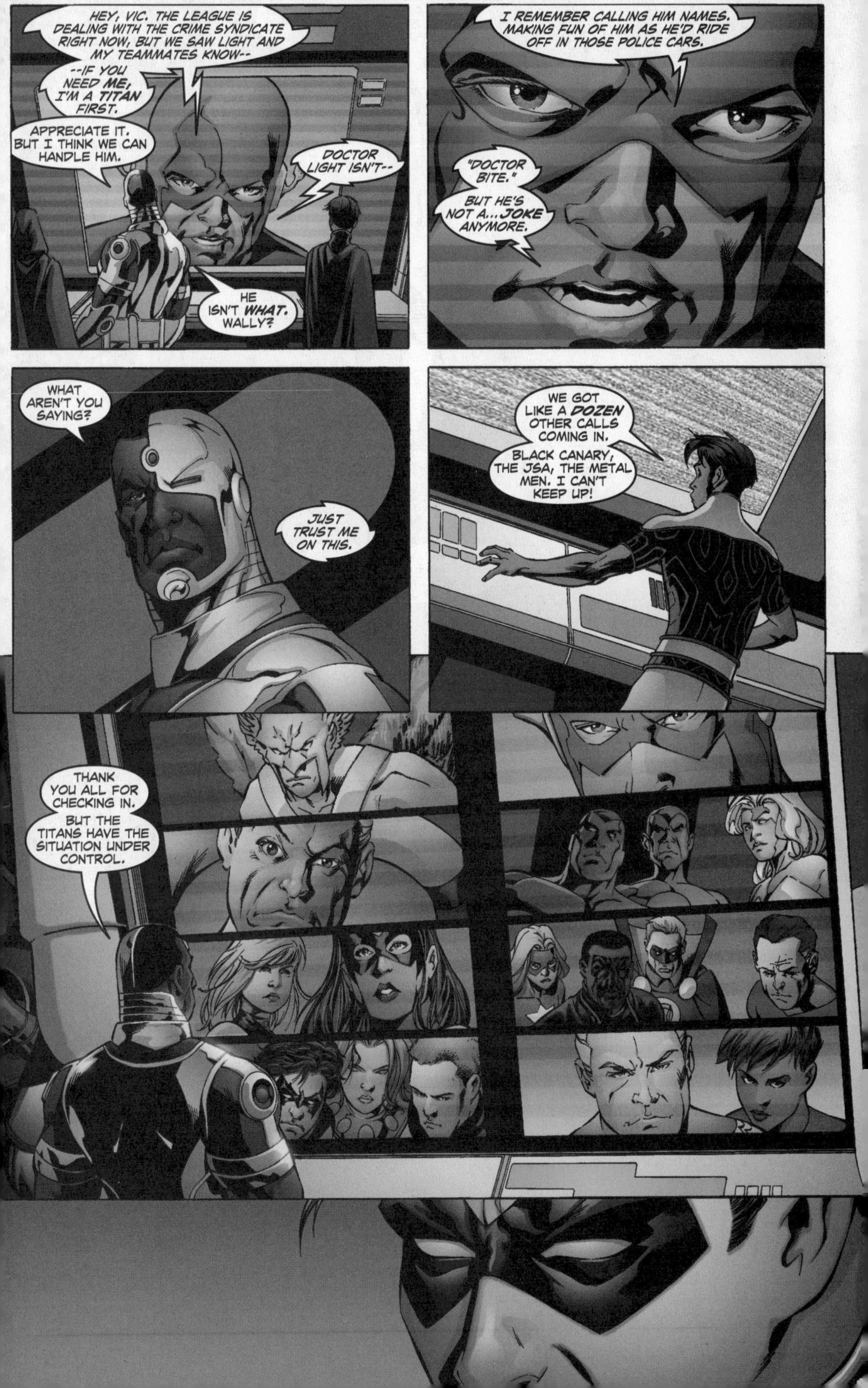

HEY, VIC. THE LEAGUE IS DEALING WITH THE CRIME SYNDICATE RIGHT NOW, BUT WE SAW LIGHT AND MY TEAMMATES KNOW--
--IF YOU NEED ME, I'M A TITAN FIRST.
APPRECIATE IT. BUT I THINK WE CAN HANDLE HIM.
DOCTOR LIGHT ISN'T--
HE ISN'T WHAT. WALLY?
I REMEMBER CALLING HIM NAMES. MAKING FUN OF HIM AS HE'D RIDE OFF IN THOSE POLICE CARS.
"DOCTOR BITE."
BUT HE'S NOT A...JOKE ANYMORE.
WHAT AREN'T YOU SAYING?
JUST TRUST ME ON THIS.
WE GOT LIKE A DOZEN OTHER CALLS COMING IN.
BLACK CANARY, THE JSA, THE METAL MEN. I CAN'T KEEP UP!
THANK YOU ALL FOR CHECKING IN.
BUT THE TITANS HAVE THE SITUATION UNDER CONTROL.

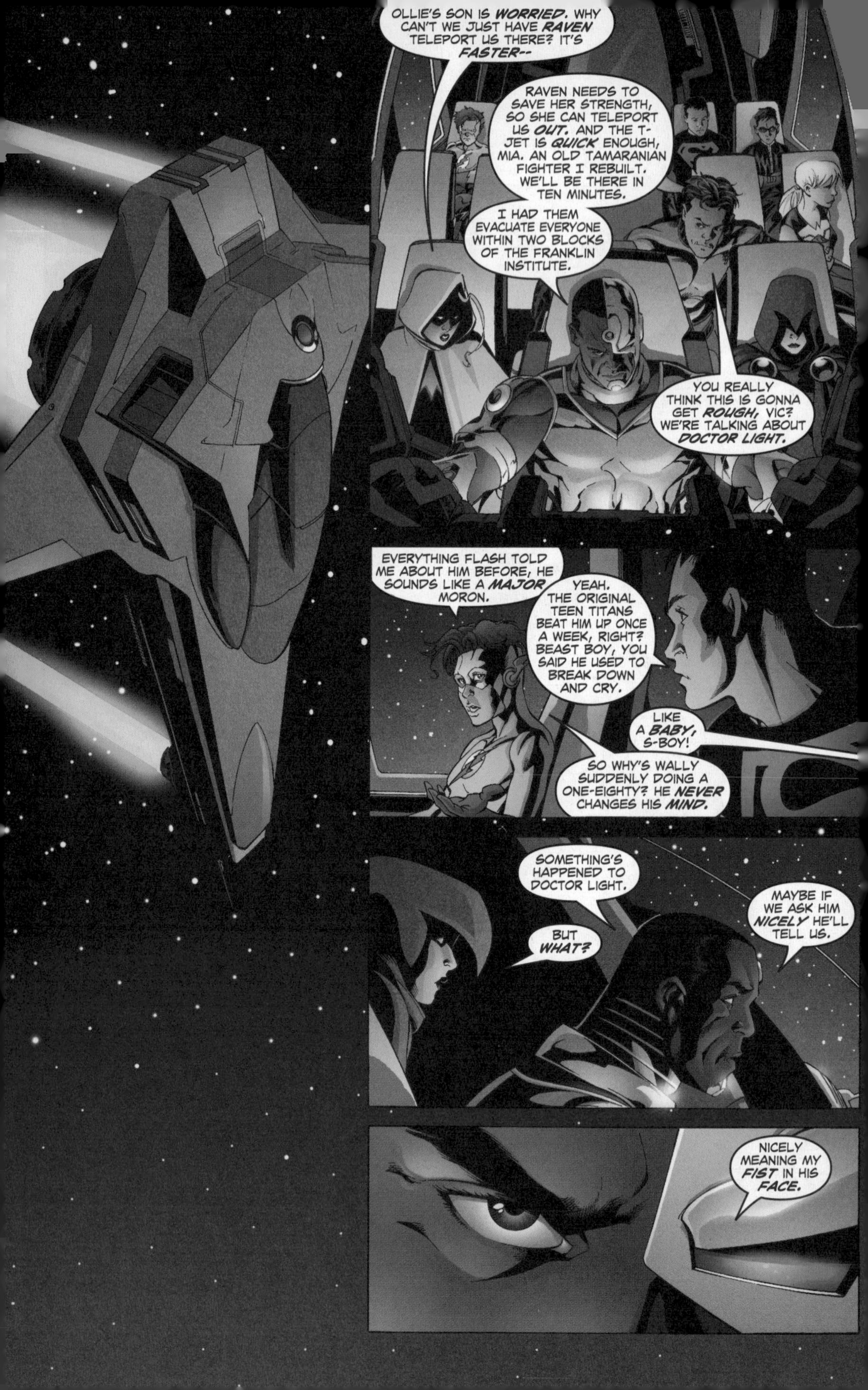

OLLIE'S SON IS WORRIED. WHY CAN'T WE JUST HAVE RAVEN TELEPORT US THERE? IT'S FASTER--
RAVEN NEEDS TO SAVE HER STRENGTH, SO SHE CAN TELEPORT US OUT. AND THE T-JET IS QUICK ENOUGH, MIA. AN OLD TAMARANIAN FIGHTER I REBUILT. WE'LL BE THERE IN TEN MINUTES.
I HAD THEM EVACUATE EVERYONE WITHIN TWO BLOCKS OF THE FRANKLIN INSTITUTE.
YOU REALLY THINK THIS IS GONNA GET ROUGH, VIC? WE'RE TALKING ABOUT DOCTOR LIGHT.
EVERYTHING FLASH TOLD ME ABOUT HIM BEFORE; HE SOUNDS LIKE A MAJOR MORON.
YEAH. THE ORIGINAL TEEN TITANS BEAT HIM UP ONCE A WEEK, RIGHT? BEAST BOY, YOU SAID HE USED TO BREAK DOWN AND CRY.
LIKE A BABY, S-BOY!
SO WHY'S WALLY SUDDENLY DOING A ONE-EIGHTY? HE NEVER CHANGES HIS MIND.
SOMETHING'S HAPPENED TO DOCTOR LIGHT.
BUT WHAT?
MAYBE IF WE ASK HIM NICELY HE'LL TELL US.
NICELY MEANING MY FIST IN HIS FACE.

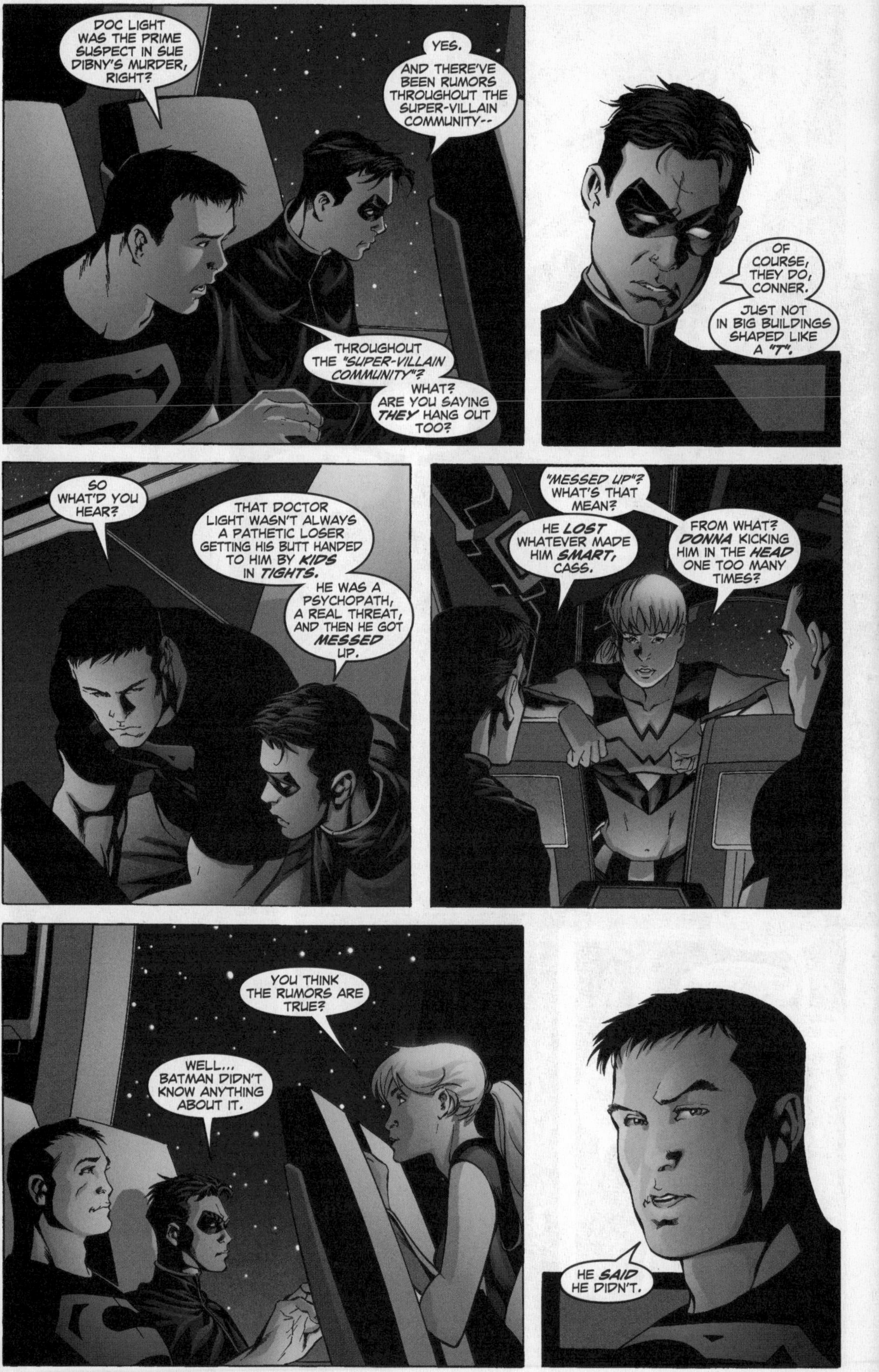
DOC LIGHT WAS THE PRIME SUSPECT IN SUE DIBNY'S MURDER, RIGHT?
YES.
AND THERE'VE BEEN RUMORS THROUGHOUT THE SUPER-VILLAIN COMMUNITY--
THROUGHOUT THE "SUPER-VILLAIN COMMUNITY"?
WHAT? ARE YOU SAYING THEY HANG OUT TOO?
OF COURSE, THEY DO, CONNER.
JUST NOT IN BIG BUILDINGS SHAPED LIKE A "T".
SO WHAT'D YOU HEAR?
THAT DOCTOR LIGHT WASN'T ALWAYS A PATHETIC LOSER GETTING HIS BUTT HANDED TO HIM BY KIDS IN TIGHTS.
HE WAS A PSYCHOPATH, A REAL THREAT, AND THEN HE GOT MESSED UP.
"MESSED UP"? WHAT'S THAT MEAN?
HE LOST WHATEVER MADE HIM SMART, CASS.
FROM WHAT? DONNA KICKING HIM IN THE HEAD ONE TOO MANY TIMES?
YOU THINK THE RUMORS ARE TRUE?
WELL... BATMAN DIDN'T KNOW ANYTHING ABOUT IT.
HE SAID HE DIDN'T.

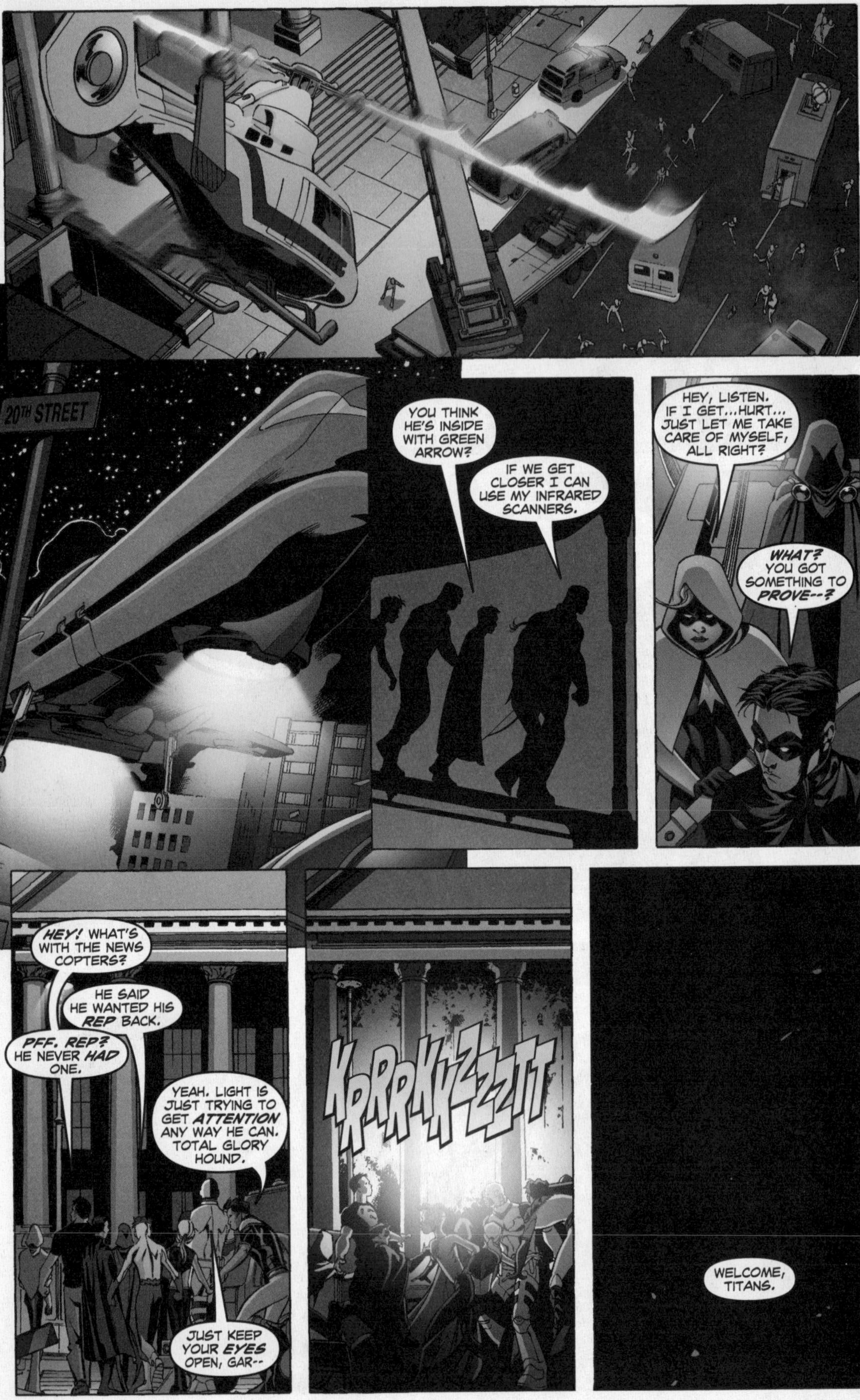
20TH STREET
YOU THINK HE'S INSIDE WITH GREEN ARROW?
IF WE GET CLOSER I CAN USE MY INFRARED SCANNERS.
HEY, LISTEN. IF I GET...HURT... JUST LET ME TAKE CARE OF MYSELF, ALL RIGHT?
WHAT? YOU GOT SOMETHING TO PROVE--?
HEY! WHAT'S WITH THE NEWS COPTERS?
HE SAID HE WANTED HIS REP BACK.
PFF. REP? HE NEVER HAD ONE.
YEAH. LIGHT IS JUST TRYING TO GET ATTENTION ANY WAY HE CAN. TOTAL GLORY HOUND.
JUST KEEP YOUR EYES OPEN, GAR--
KRRRKKZZZTT
WELCOME, TITANS.

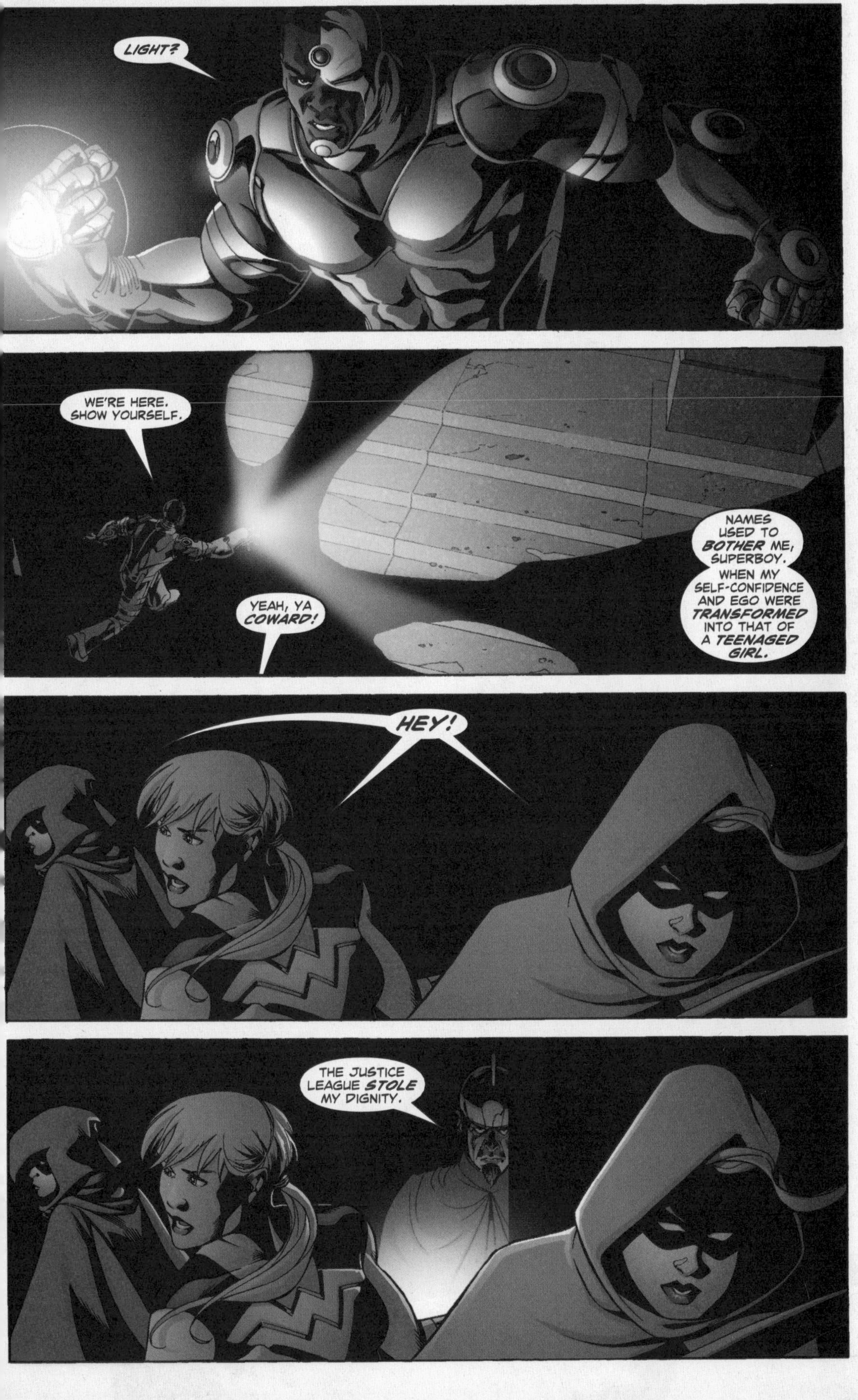
LIGHT?
WE'RE HERE. SHOW YOURSELF.
YEAH, YA COWARD!
NAMES USED TO BOTHER ME, SUPERBOY. WHEN MY SELF-CONFIDENCE AND EGO WERE TRANSFORMED INTO THAT OF A TEENAGED GIRL.
HEY!
THE JUSTICE LEAGUE STOLE MY DIGNITY.

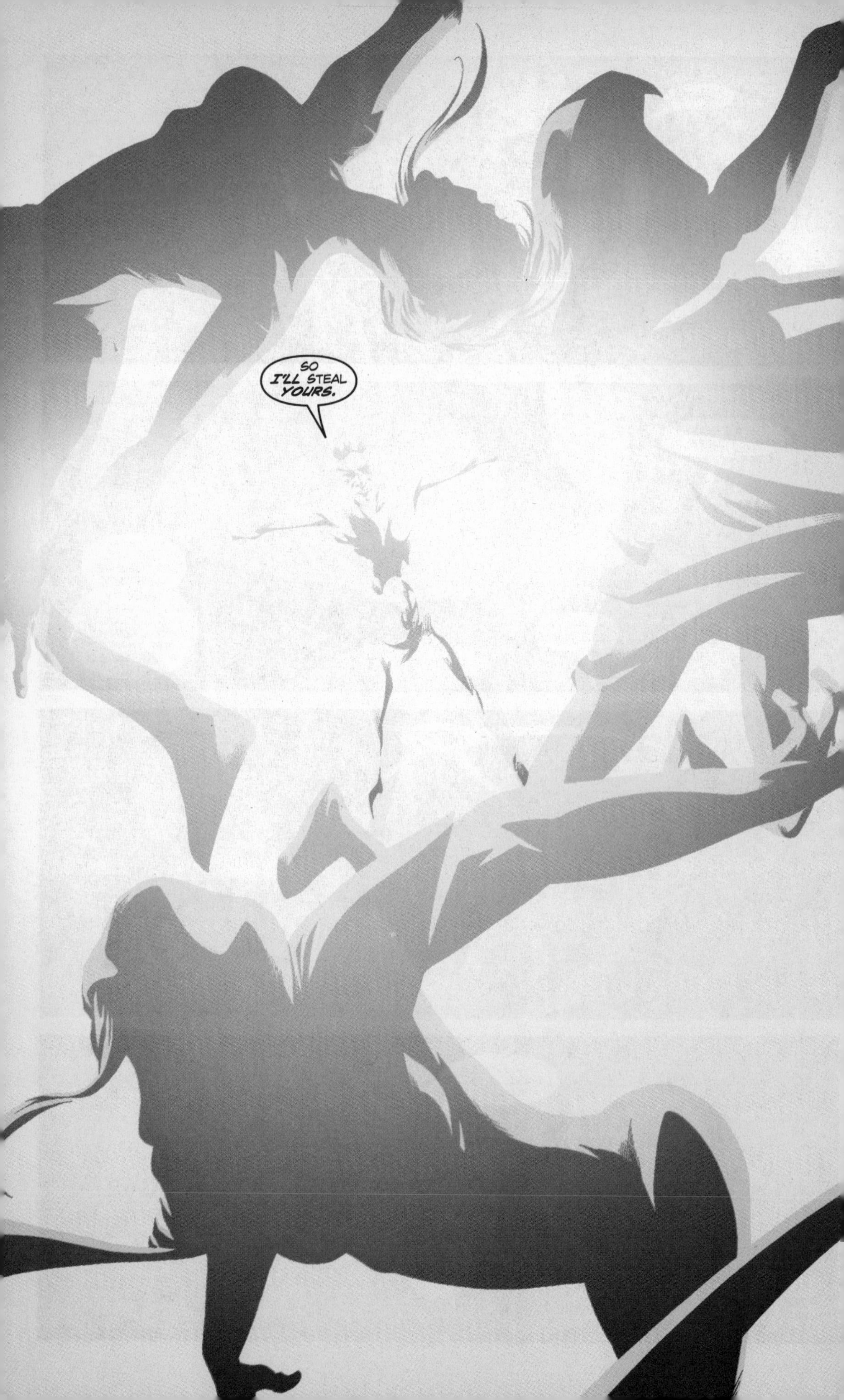
SO I'LL STEAL YOURS.

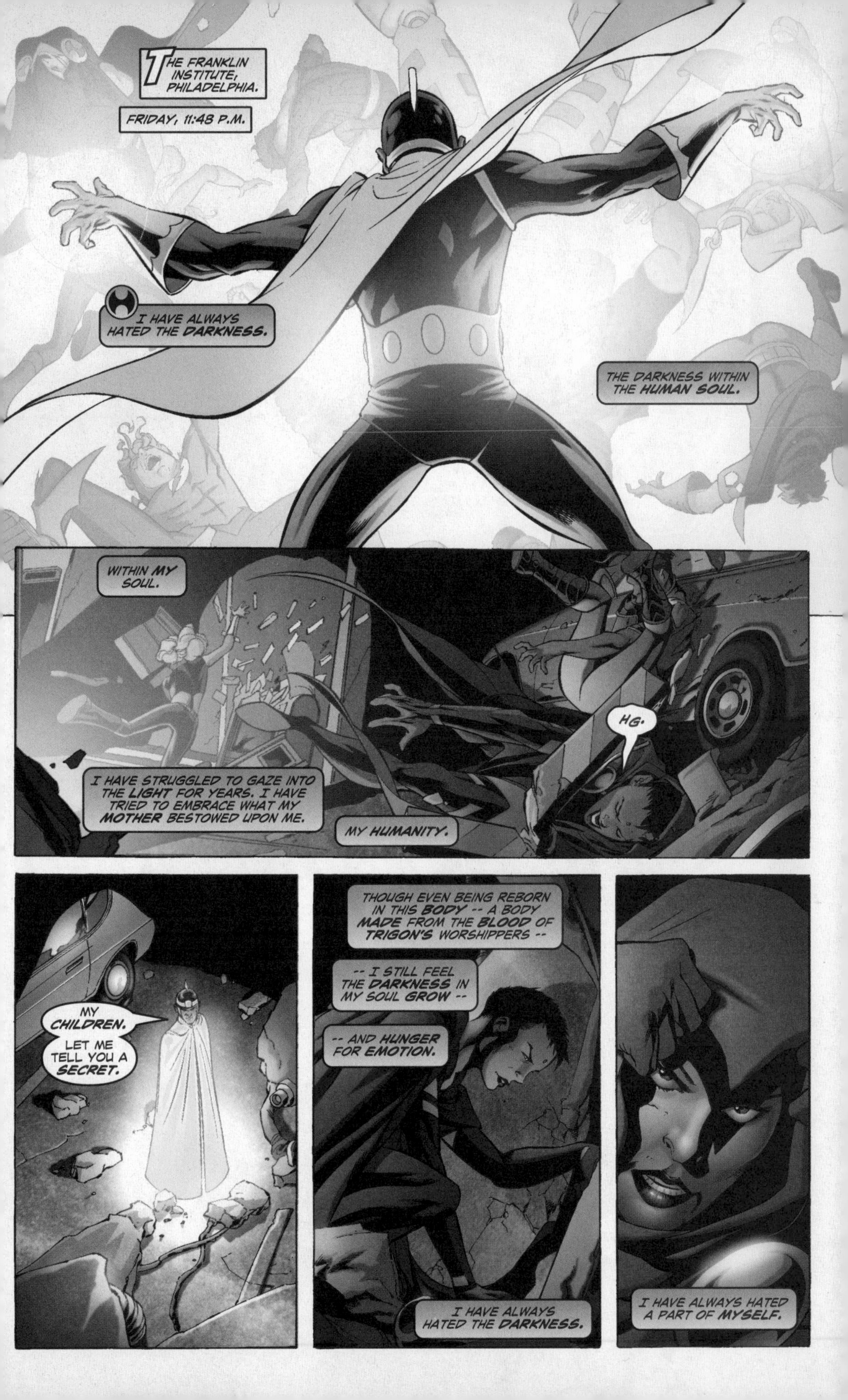
THE FRANKLIN INSTITUTE, PHILADELPHIA.
FRIDAY, 11:48 P.M.
I HAVE ALWAYS HATED THE DARKNESS.
THE DARKNESS WITHIN THE HUMAN SOUL.
WITHIN MY SOUL.
HG.
I HAVE STRUGGLED TO GAZE INTO THE LIGHT FOR YEARS. I HAVE TRIED TO EMBRACE WHAT MY MOTHER BESTOWED UPON ME.
MY HUMANITY.
MY CHILDREN.
LET ME TELL YOU A SECRET.
THOUGH EVEN BEING REBORN IN THIS BODY -- A BODY MADE FROM THE BLOOD OF TRIGON'S WORSHIPPERS --
-- I STILL FEEL THE DARKNESS IN MY SOUL GROW --
-- AND HUNGER FOR EMOTION.
I HAVE ALWAYS HATED THE DARKNESS.
I HAVE ALWAYS HATED A PART OF MYSELF.

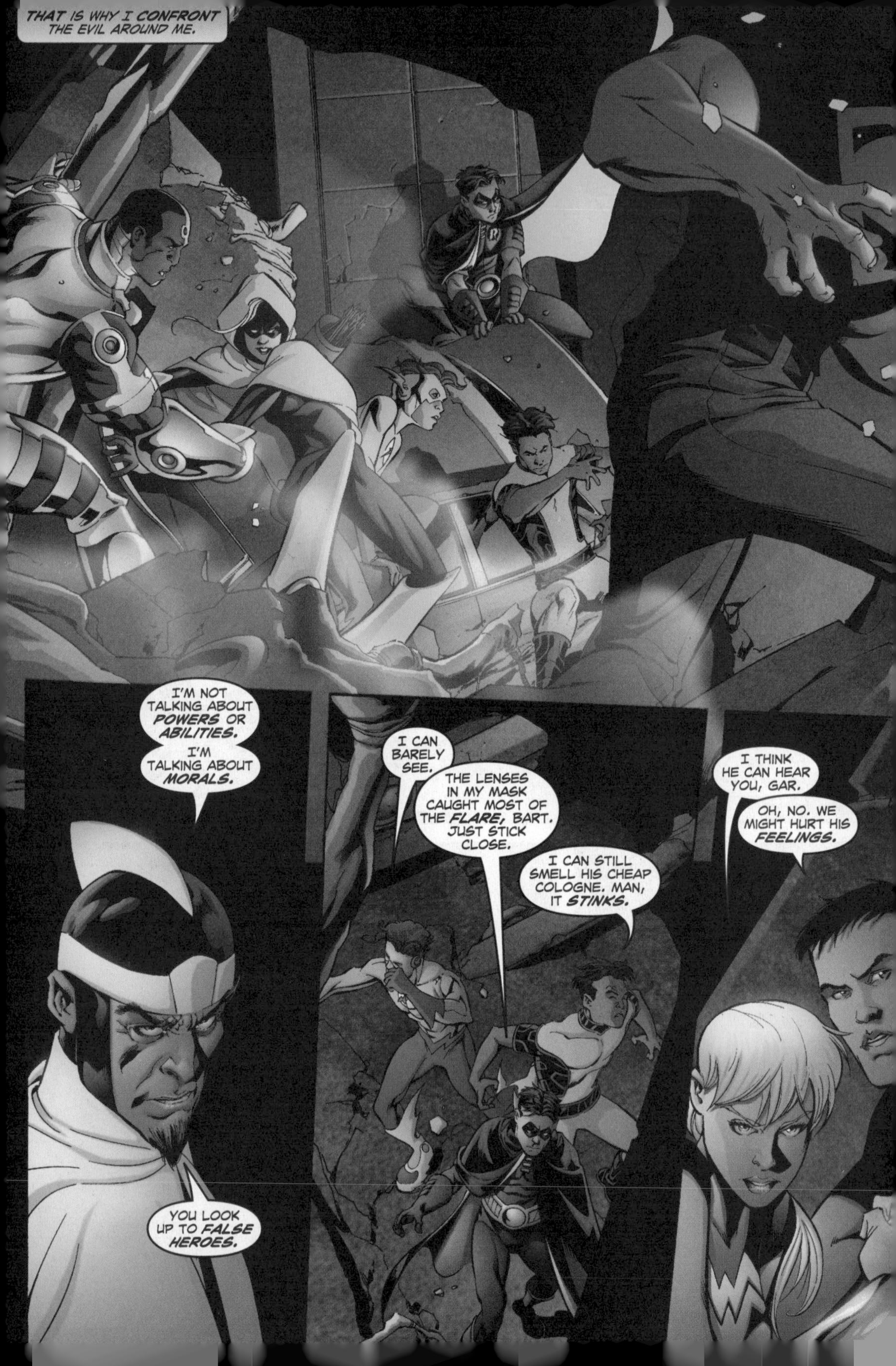
THAT IS WHY I CONFRONT THE EVIL AROUND ME.
I'M NOT TALKING ABOUT POWERS OR ABILITIES.
I'M TALKING ABOUT MORALS.
YOU LOOK UP TO FALSE HEROES.
I CAN BARELY SEE.
THE LENSES IN MY MASK CAUGHT MOST OF THE FLARE, BART. JUST STICK CLOSE.
I CAN STILL SMELL HIS CHEAP COLOGNE. MAN, IT STINKS.
I THINK HE CAN HEAR YOU, GAR.
OH, NO. WE MIGHT HURT HIS FEELINGS.

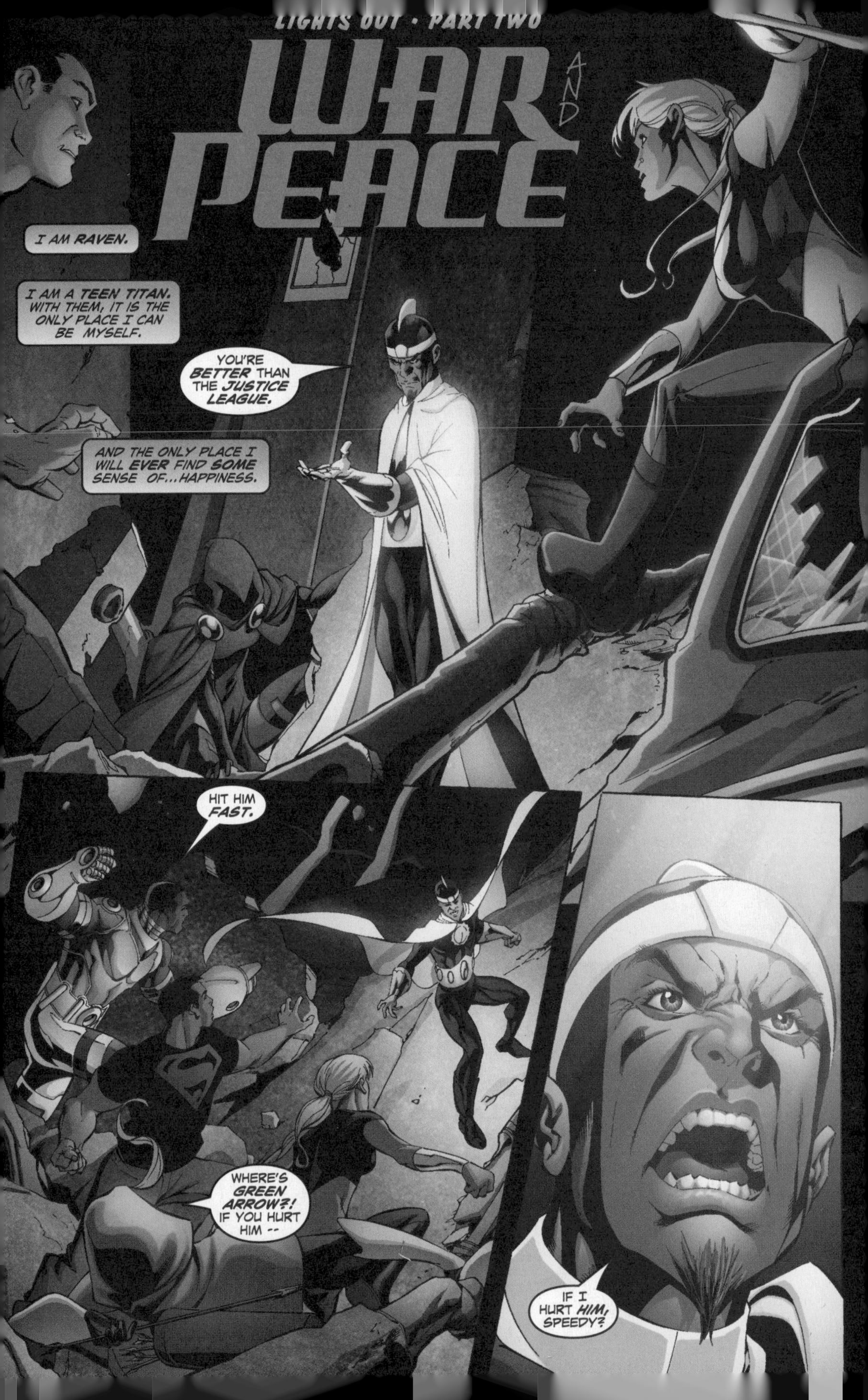
LIGHTS OUT • PART TWO
WAR AND PEACE
I AM RAVEN.
I AM A TEEN TITAN. WITH THEM, IT IS THE ONLY PLACE I CAN BE MYSELF.
YOU'RE BETTER THAN THE JUSTICE LEAGUE.
AND THE ONLY PLACE I WILL EVER FIND SOME SENSE OF... HAPPINESS.
HIT HIM FAST.
WHERE'S GREEN ARROW?! IF YOU HURT HIM --
IF I HURT HIM, SPEEDY?

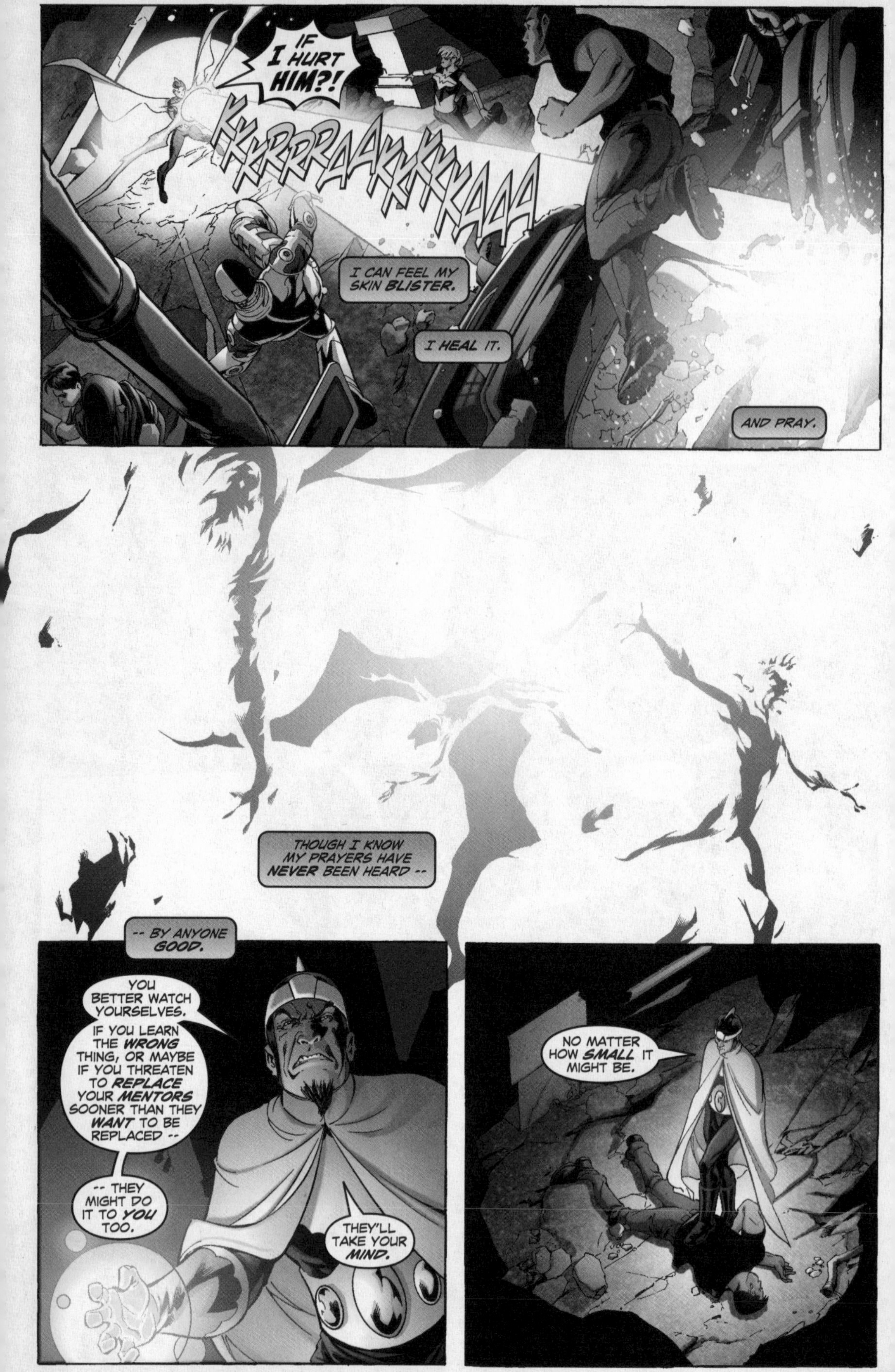

IF I HURT HIM?!
KKKRRRAAKKKKAAAA
I CAN FEEL MY SKIN BLISTER.
I HEAL IT.
AND PRAY.
THOUGH I KNOW MY PRAYERS HAVE NEVER BEEN HEARD --
-- BY ANYONE GOOD.
YOU BETTER WATCH YOURSELVES.
IF YOU LEARN THE WRONG THING, OR MAYBE IF YOU THREATEN TO REPLACE YOUR MENTORS SOONER THAN THEY WANT TO BE REPLACED --
-- THEY MIGHT DO IT TO YOU TOO.
THEY'LL TAKE YOUR MIND.
NO MATTER HOW SMALL IT MIGHT BE.

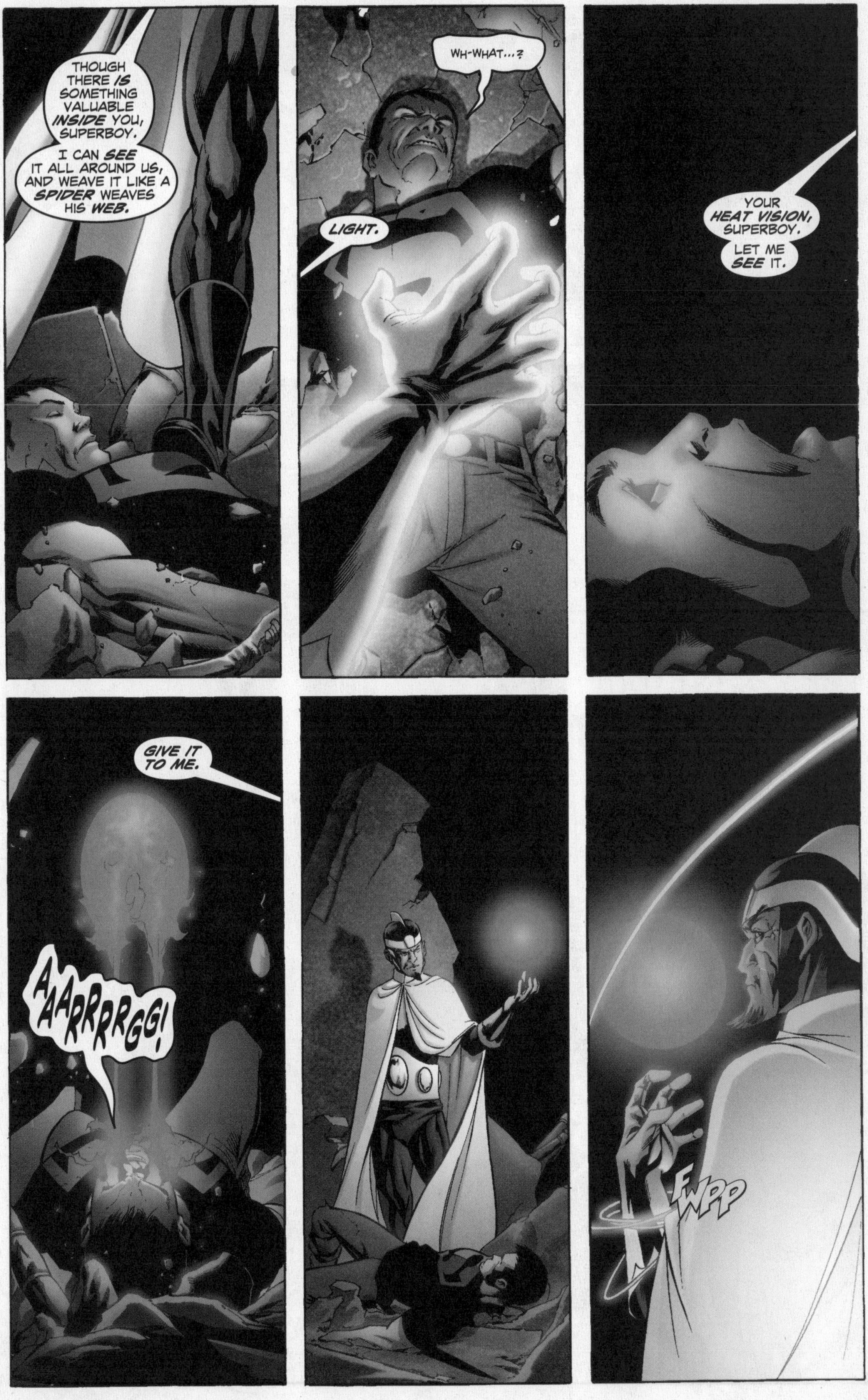
THOUGH THERE IS SOMETHING VALUABLE INSIDE YOU, SUPERBOY.
I CAN SEE IT ALL AROUND US, AND WEAVE IT LIKE A SPIDER WEAVES HIS WEB.
WH-WHAT...?
LIGHT.
YOUR HEAT VISION, SUPERBOY.
LET ME SEE IT.
GIVE IT TO ME.
AAARRRRGG!
FWPP

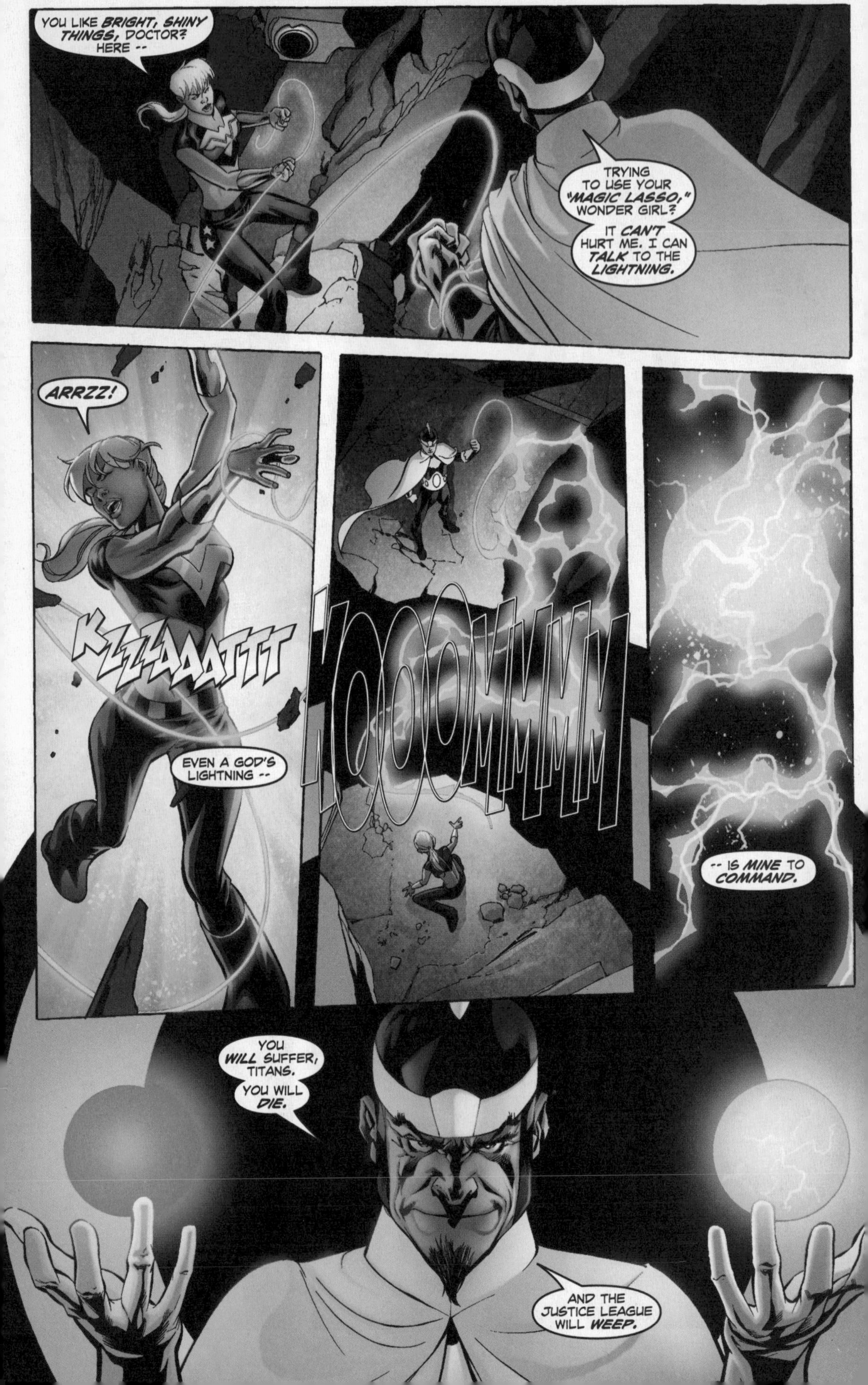
YOU LIKE BRIGHT, SHINY THINGS, DOCTOR? HERE --
TRYING TO USE YOUR "MAGIC LASSO," WONDER GIRL?
IT CAN'T HURT ME. I CAN TALK TO THE LIGHTNING.
ARRZZ!
KZZZAAATTT
EVEN A GOD'S LIGHTNING --
KOOOOMMMMMM
-- IS MINE TO COMMAND.
YOU WILL SUFFER, TITANS. YOU WILL DIE.
AND THE JUSTICE LEAGUE WILL WEEP.

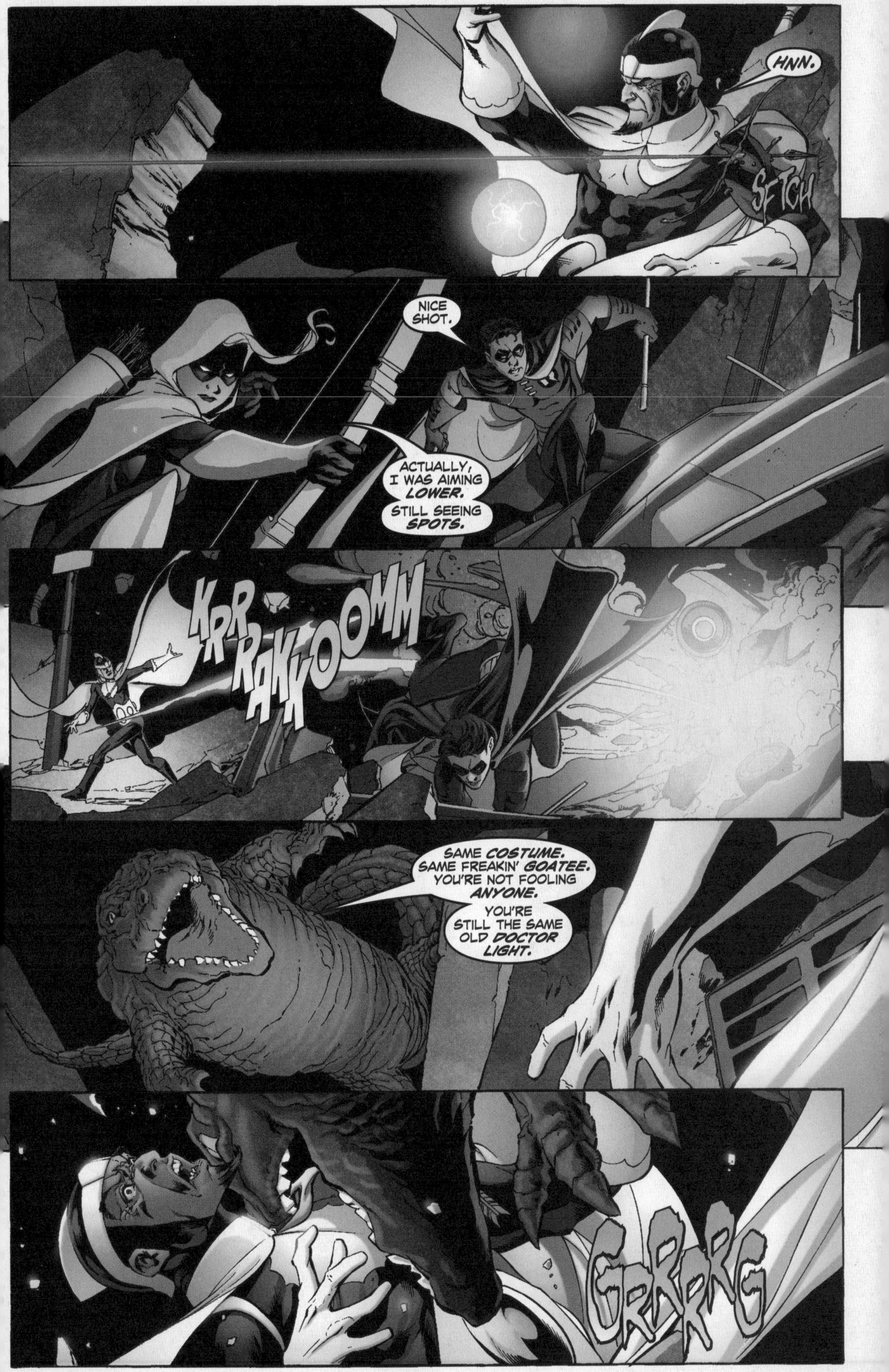
HNN.
SFTCH
NICE SHOT.
ACTUALLY, I WAS AIMING LOWER.
STILL SEEING SPOTS.
KRRRAKKOOMM
SAME COSTUME. SAME FREAKIN' GOATEE. YOU'RE NOT FOOLING ANYONE.
YOU'RE STILL THE SAME OLD DOCTOR LIGHT.
GRRRRG

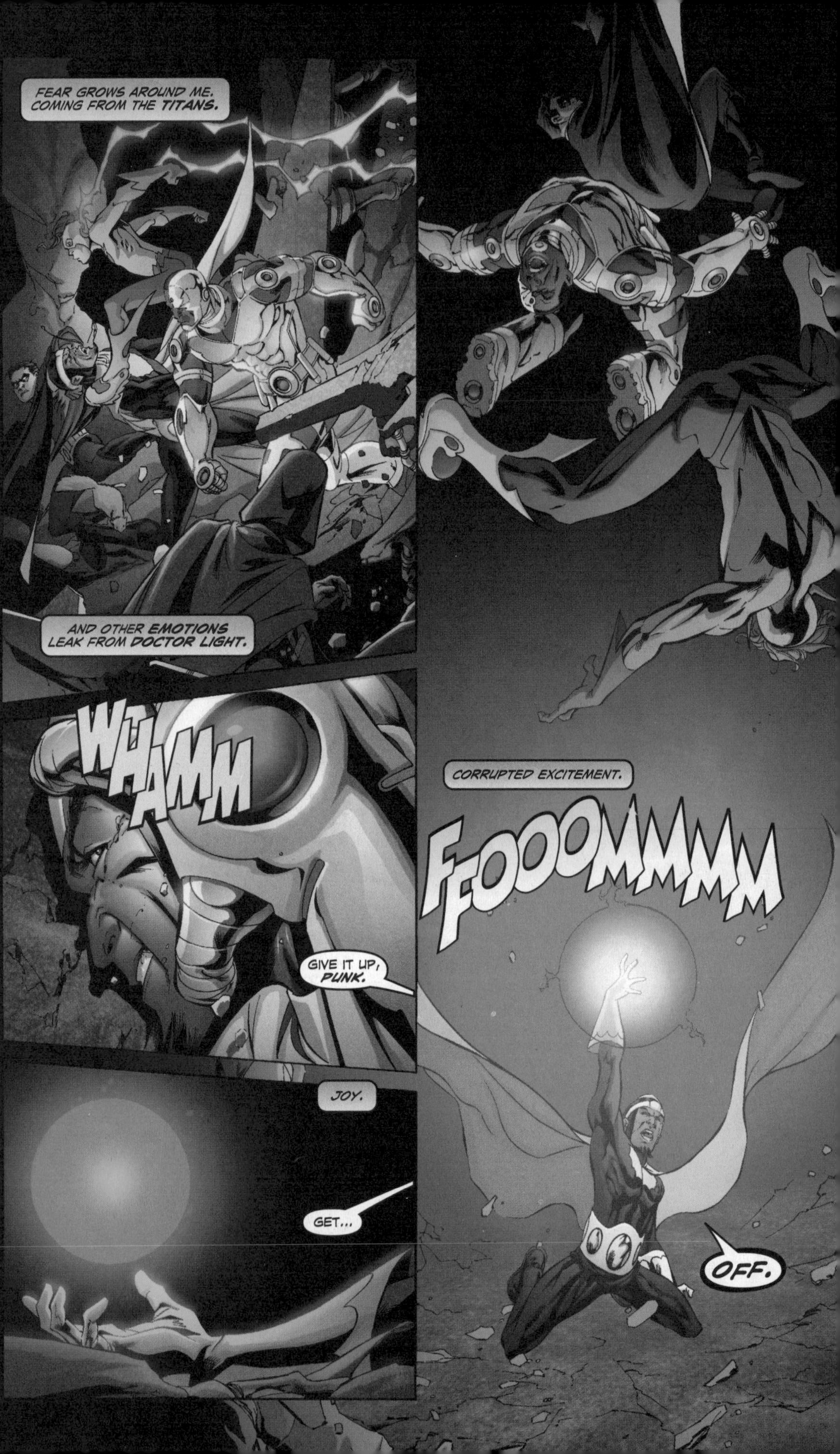
FEAR GROWS AROUND ME. COMING FROM THE TITANS.
AND OTHER EMOTIONS LEAK FROM DOCTOR LIGHT.
WHAMM
GIVE IT UP, PUNK.
JOY.
GET...
CORRUPTED EXCITEMENT.
FFOOOMMMMM
OFF.

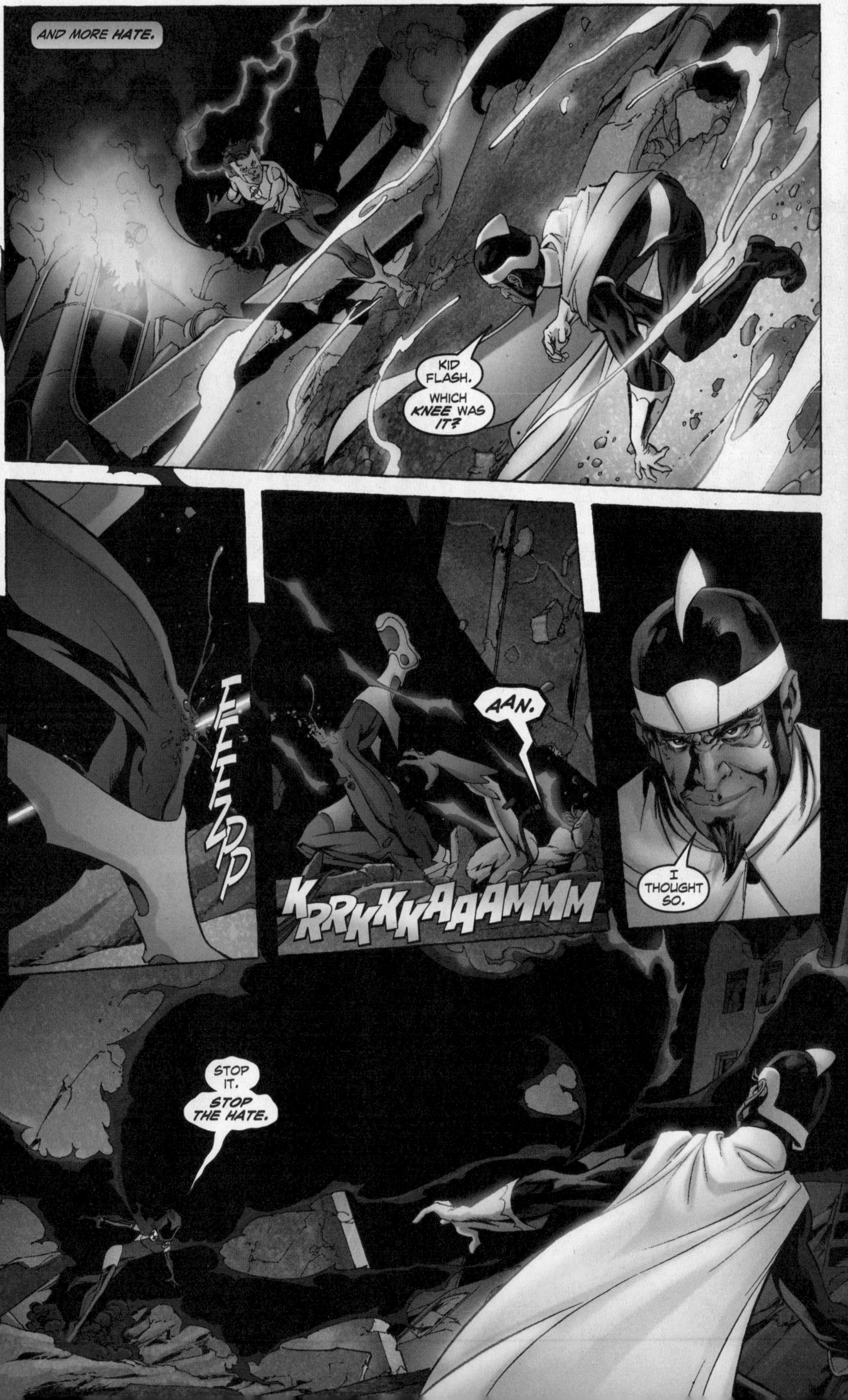
AND MORE HATE.
KID FLASH. WHICH KNEE WAS IT?
FEEEZPP
AAN.
KRRKKKAAAMMM
I THOUGHT SO.
STOP IT. STOP THE HATE.

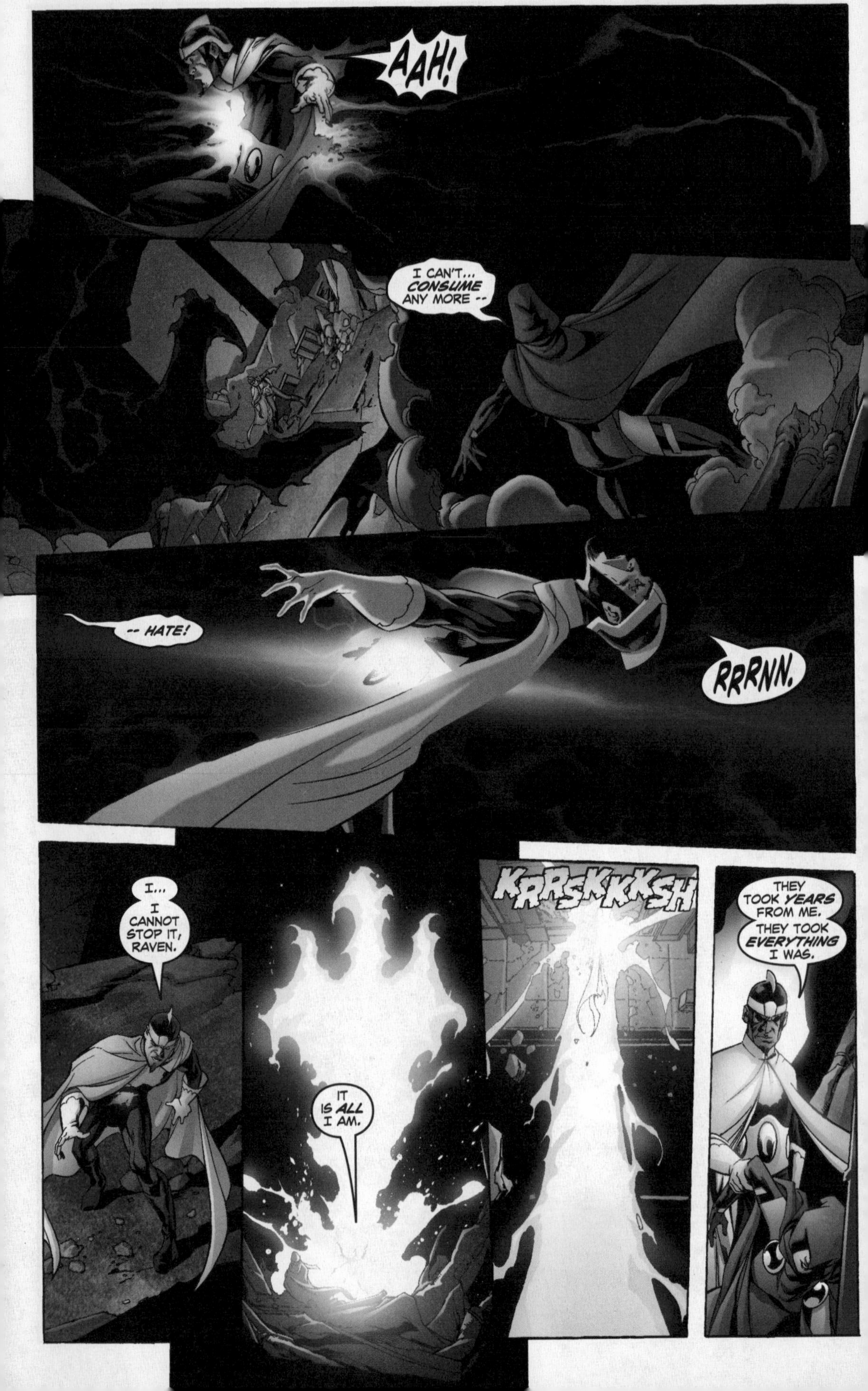
AAH!
I CAN'T... CONSUME ANY MORE --
-- HATE!
RRRNN.
I... I CANNOT STOP IT, RAVEN.
IT IS ALL I AM.
KRRSKKKSH
THEY TOOK YEARS FROM ME. THEY TOOK EVERYTHING I WAS.

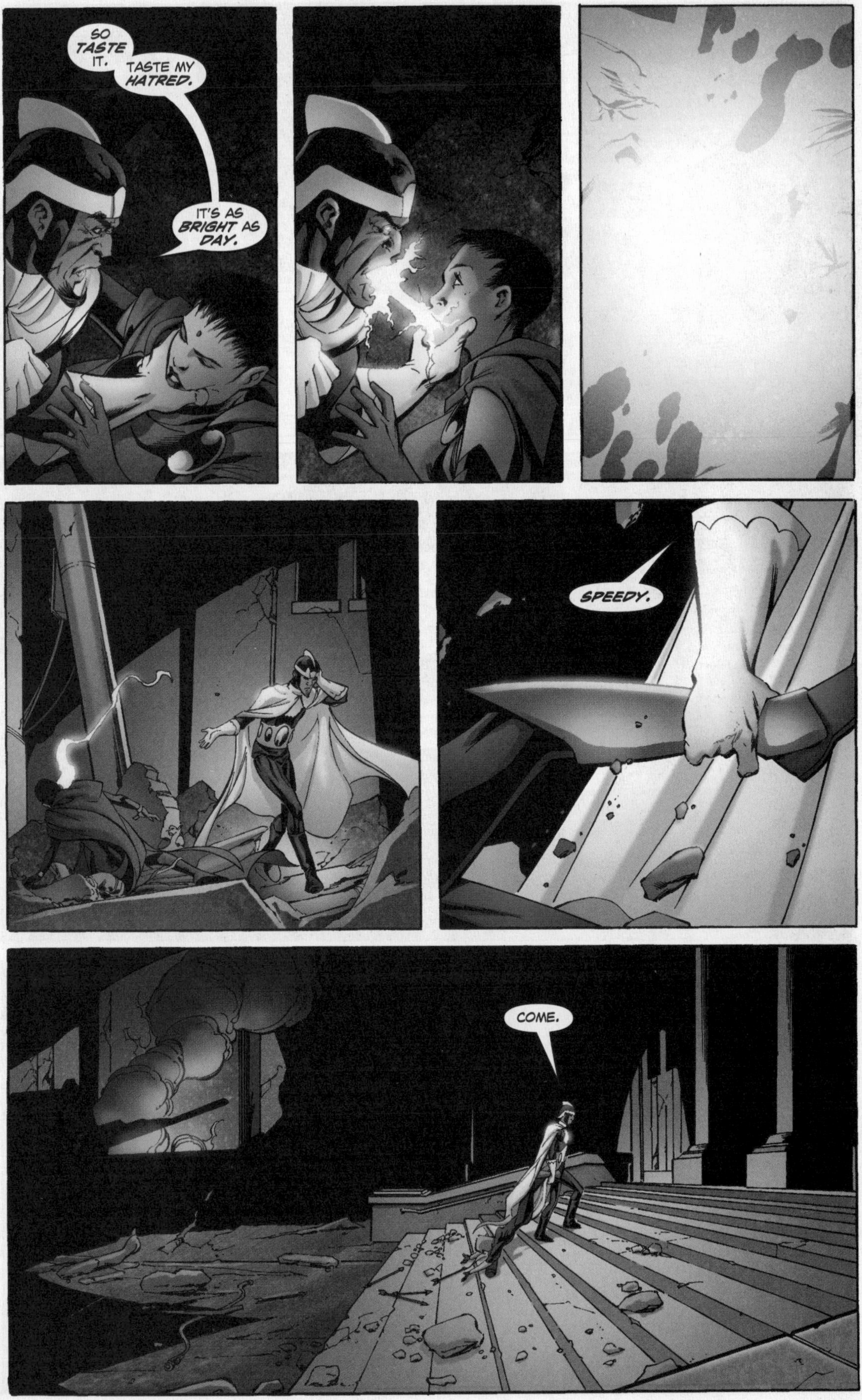
SO TASTE IT.
TASTE MY HATRED.
IT'S AS BRIGHT AS DAY.
SPEEDY.
COME.

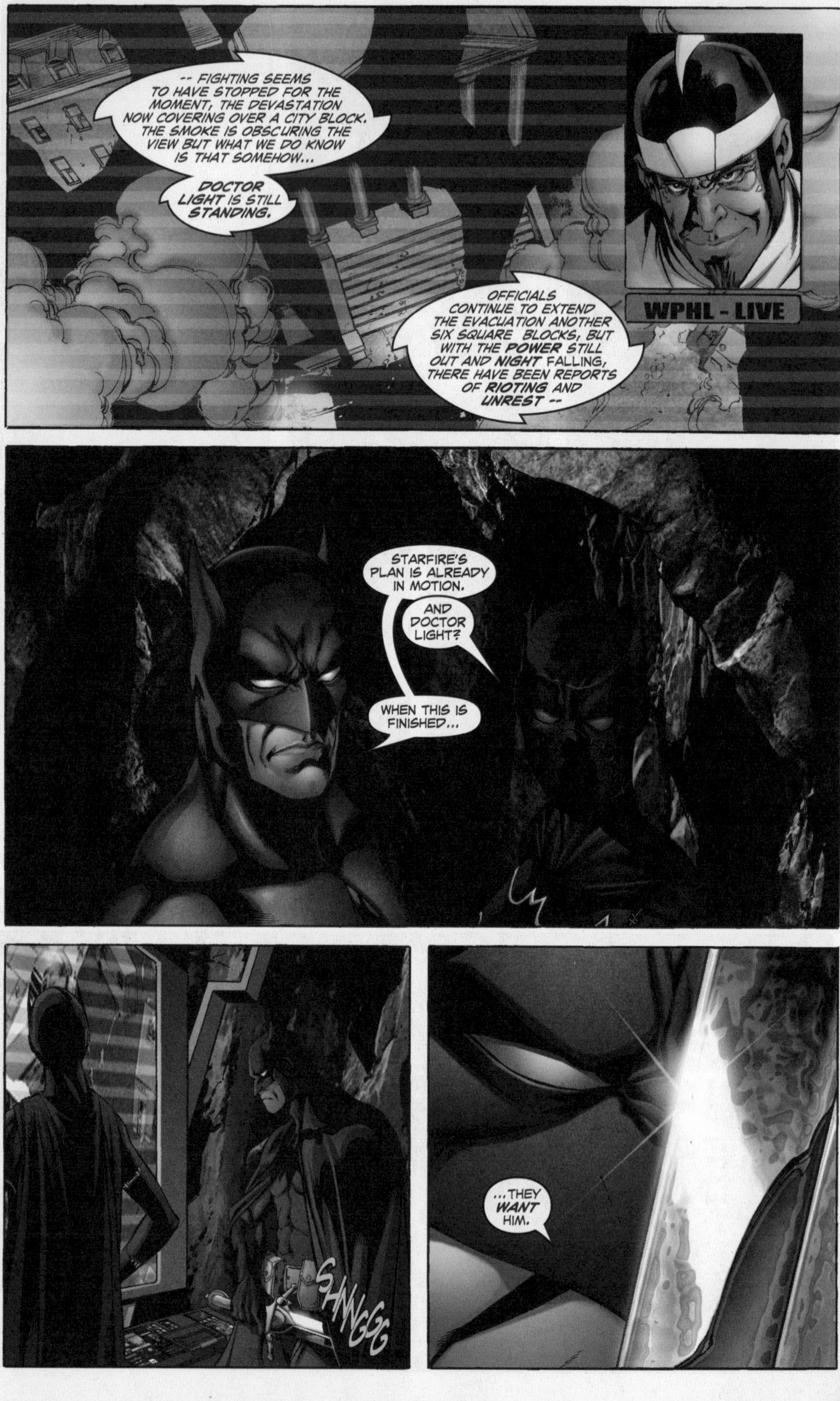
-- FIGHTING SEEMS TO HAVE STOPPED FOR THE MOMENT, THE DEVASTATION NOW COVERING OVER A CITY BLOCK. THE SMOKE IS OBSCURING THE VIEW BUT WHAT WE DO KNOW IS THAT SOMEHOW...
DOCTOR LIGHT IS STILL STANDING.
WPHL - LIVE
OFFICIALS CONTINUE TO EXTEND THE EVACUATION ANOTHER SIX SQUARE BLOCKS, BUT WITH THE POWER STILL OUT AND NIGHT FALLING, THERE HAVE BEEN REPORTS OF RIOTING AND UNREST --
STARFIRE'S PLAN IS ALREADY IN MOTION.
AND DOCTOR LIGHT?
WHEN THIS IS FINISHED...
SHNGGG
...THEY WANT HIM.

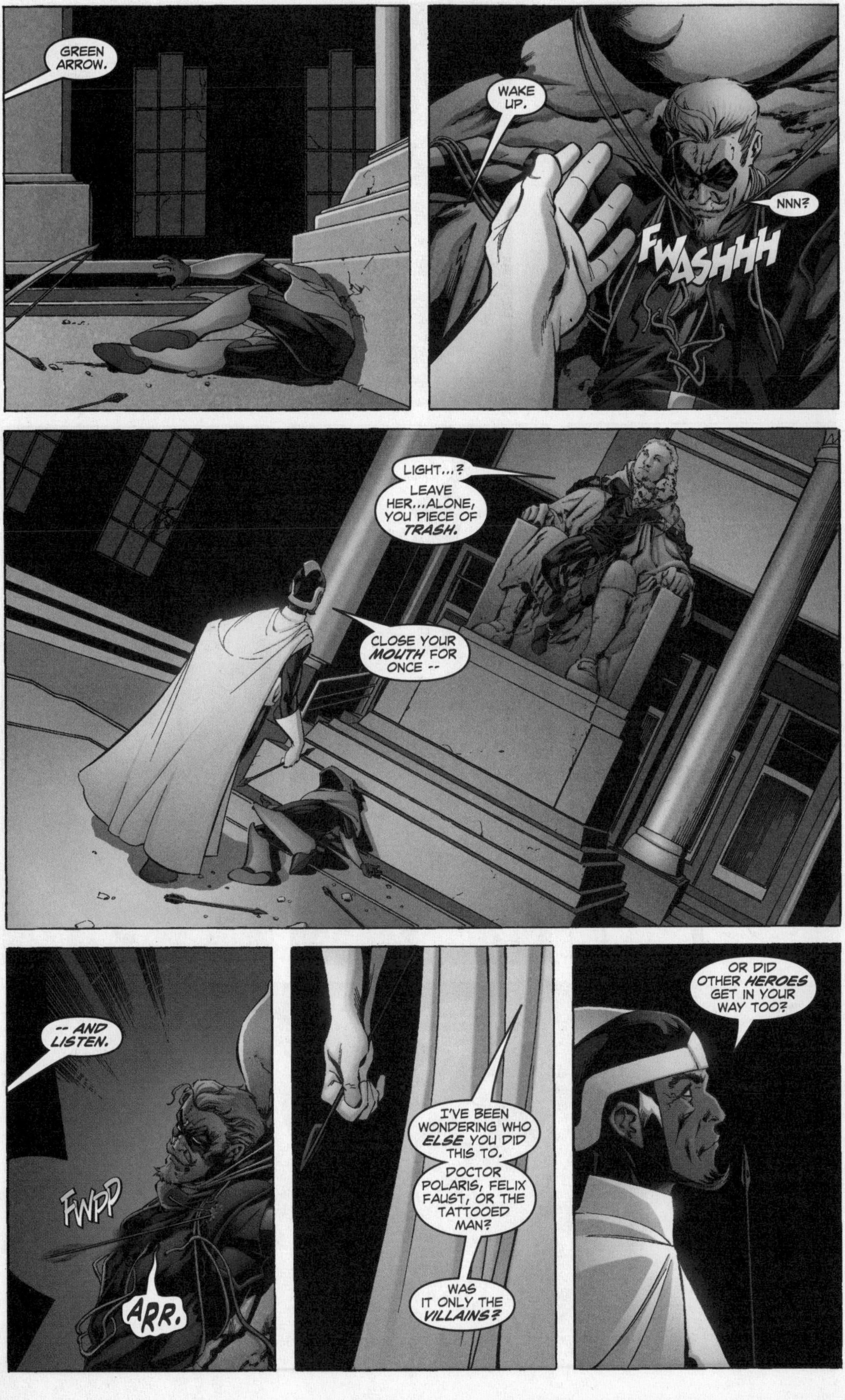
GREEN ARROW.
WAKE UP.
NNN?
FWASHHH
LIGHT...? LEAVE HER...ALONE, YOU PIECE OF TRASH.
CLOSE YOUR MOUTH FOR ONCE --
-- AND LISTEN.
FWPP
ARR.
I'VE BEEN WONDERING WHO ELSE YOU DID THIS TO.
DOCTOR POLARIS, FELIX FAUST, OR THE TATTOOED MAN?
WAS IT ONLY THE VILLAINS?
OR DID OTHER HEROES GET IN YOUR WAY TOO?

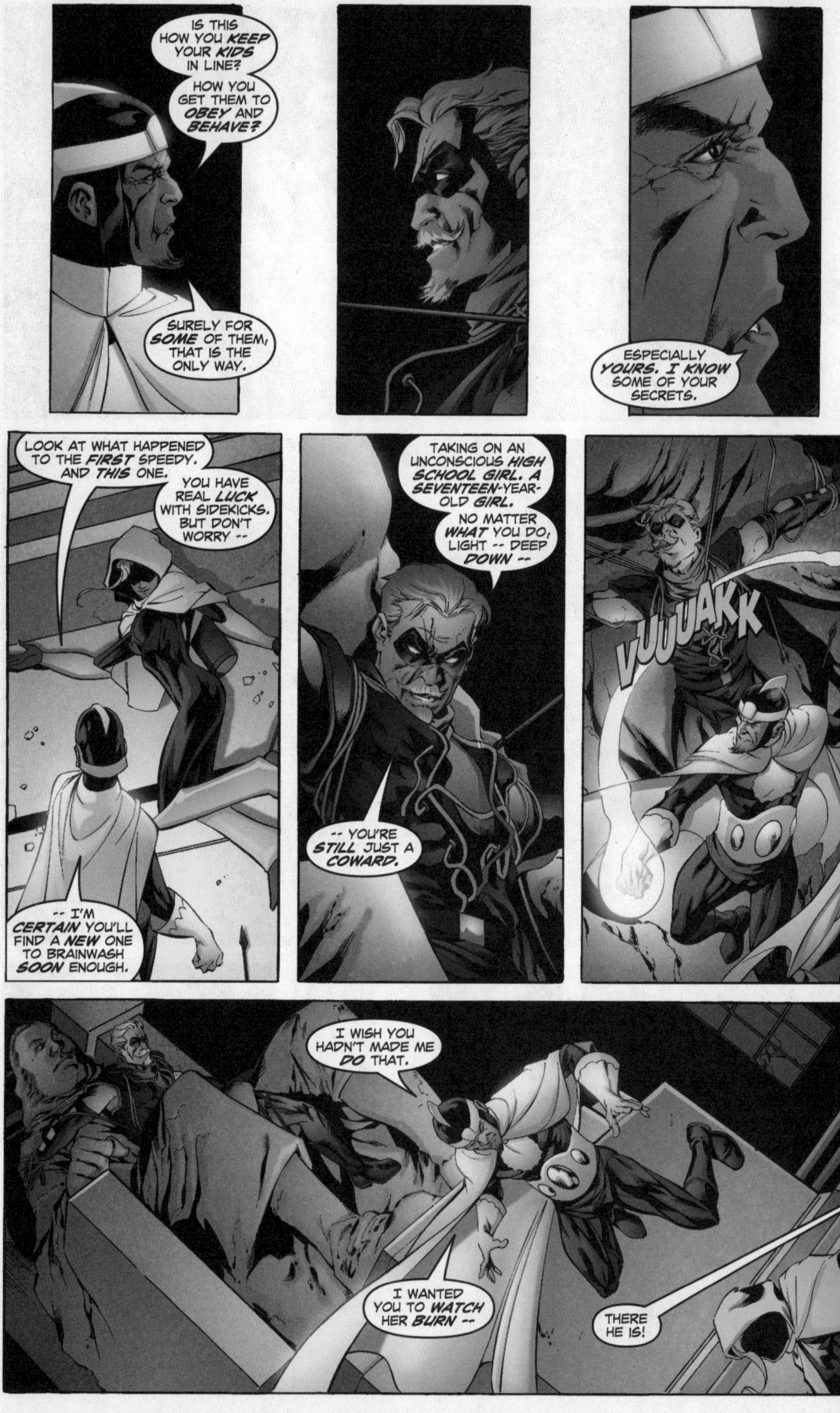
IS THIS HOW YOU KEEP YOUR KIDS IN LINE?
HOW YOU GET THEM TO OBEY AND BEHAVE?
SURELY FOR SOME OF THEM, THAT IS THE ONLY WAY.
ESPECIALLY YOURS. I KNOW SOME OF YOUR SECRETS.
LOOK AT WHAT HAPPENED TO THE FIRST SPEEDY. AND THIS ONE.
YOU HAVE REAL LUCK WITH SIDEKICKS. BUT DON'T WORRY --
-- I'M CERTAIN YOU'LL FIND A NEW ONE TO BRAINWASH SOON ENOUGH.
TAKING ON AN UNCONSCIOUS HIGH SCHOOL GIRL. A SEVENTEEN-YEAR-OLD GIRL.
NO MATTER WHAT YOU DO, LIGHT -- DEEP DOWN --
-- YOU'RE STILL JUST A COWARD.
VUUUAKK
I WISH YOU HADN'T MADE ME DO THAT.
I WANTED YOU TO WATCH HER BURN --
THERE HE IS!

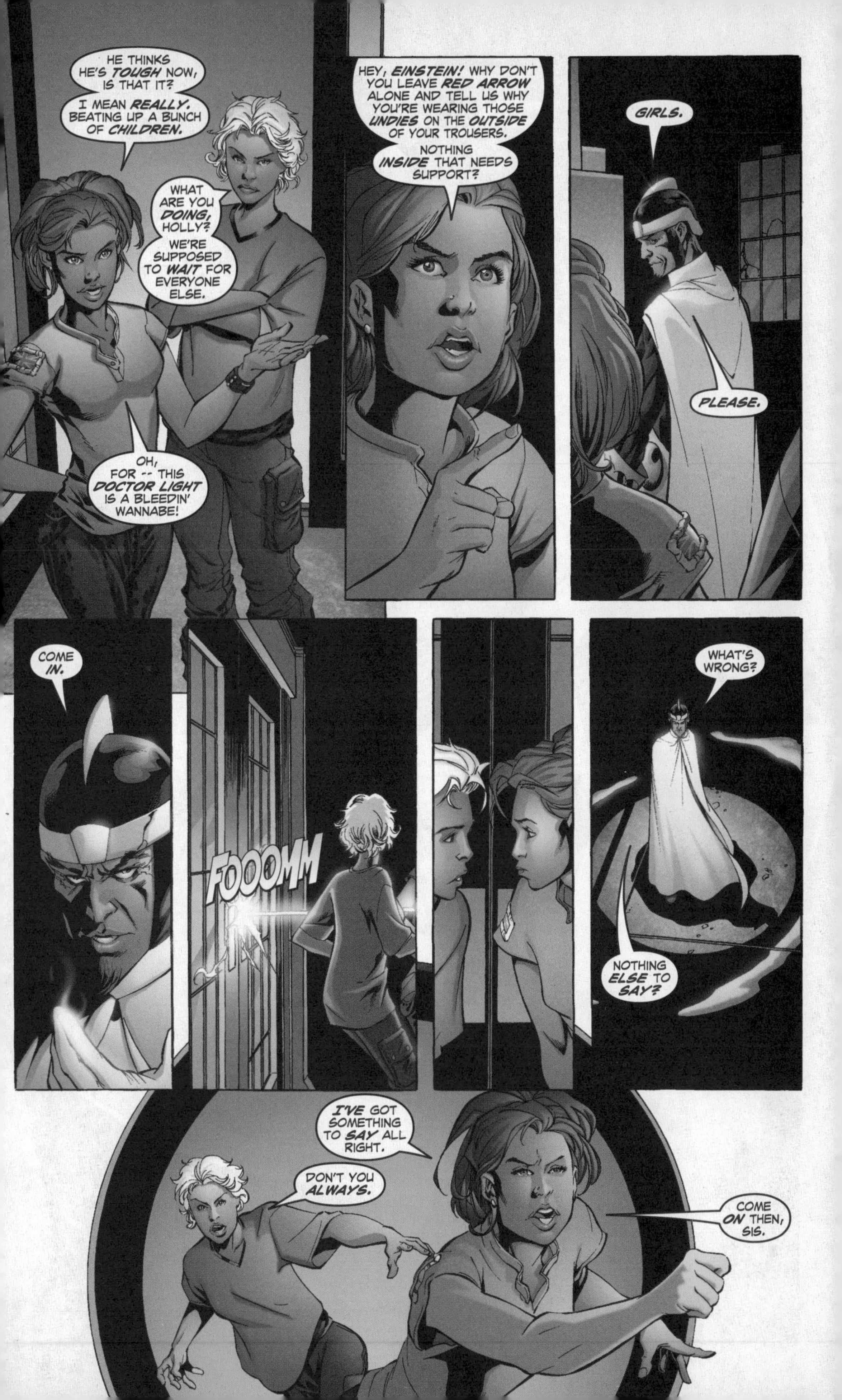
HE THINKS HE'S TOUGH NOW, IS THAT IT?
I MEAN REALLY. BEATING UP A BUNCH OF CHILDREN.
WHAT ARE YOU DOING, HOLLY?
WE'RE SUPPOSED TO WAIT FOR EVERYONE ELSE.
OH, FOR -- THIS DOCTOR LIGHT IS A BLEEDIN' WANNABE!
HEY, EINSTEIN! WHY DON'T YOU LEAVE RED ARROW ALONE AND TELL US WHY YOU'RE WEARING THOSE UNDIES ON THE OUTSIDE OF YOUR TROUSERS.
NOTHING INSIDE THAT NEEDS SUPPORT?
GIRLS.
PLEASE.
COME IN.
FOOOMM
WHAT'S WRONG?
NOTHING ELSE TO SAY?
I'VE GOT SOMETHING TO SAY ALL RIGHT.
DON'T YOU ALWAYS.
COME ON THEN, SIS.

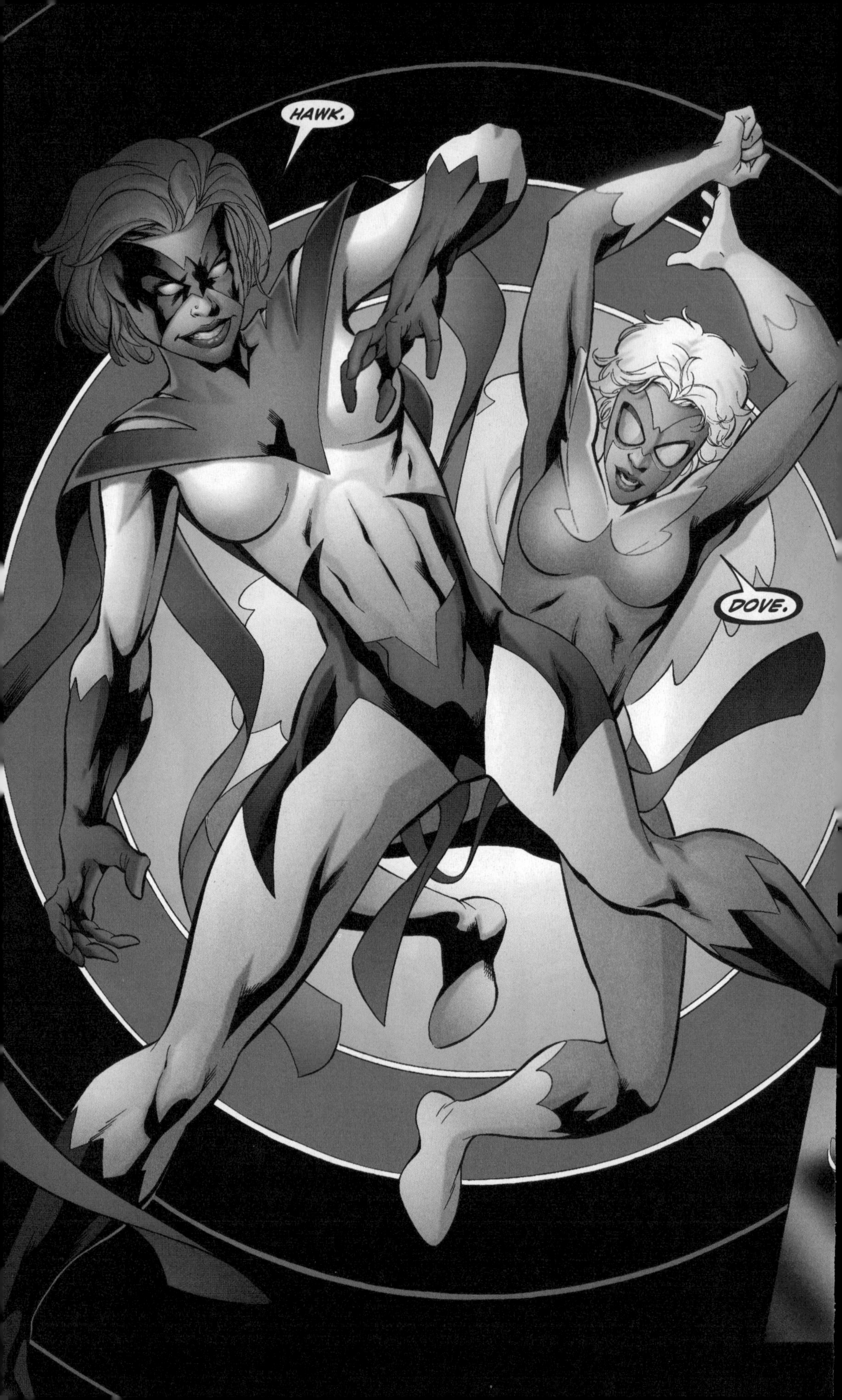
HAWK.
DOVE.

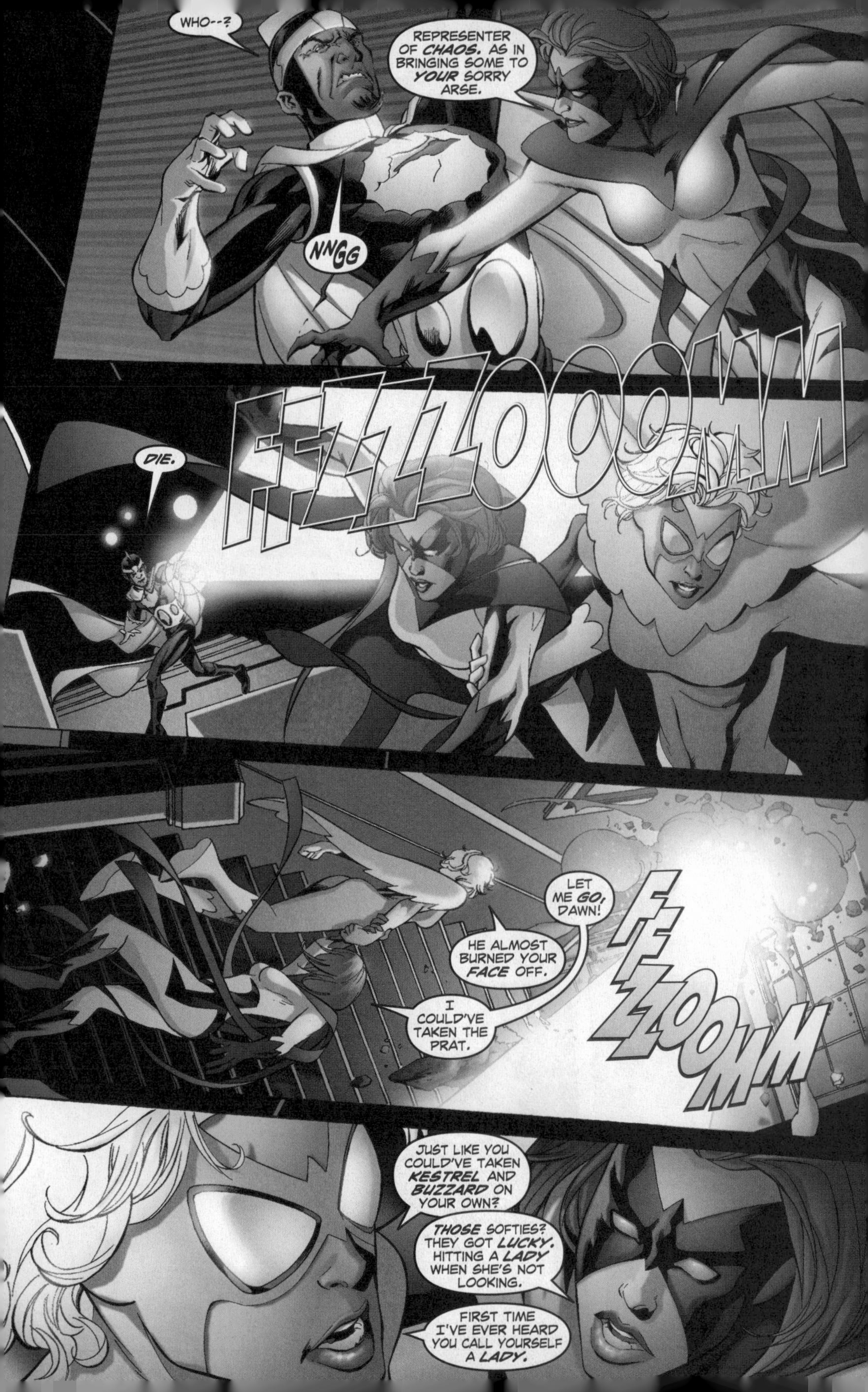
WHO--?
REPRESENTER OF CHAOS. AS IN BRINGING SOME TO YOUR SORRY ARSE.
NNGG
DIE.
FFZZZOOOOMM
LET ME GO, DAWN!
HE ALMOST BURNED YOUR FACE OFF.
I COULD'VE TAKEN THE PRAT.
FFZZOOMM
JUST LIKE YOU COULD'VE TAKEN KESTREL AND BUZZARD ON YOUR OWN?
THOSE SOFTIES? THEY GOT LUCKY. HITTING A LADY WHEN SHE'S NOT LOOKING.
FIRST TIME I'VE EVER HEARD YOU CALL YOURSELF A LADY.

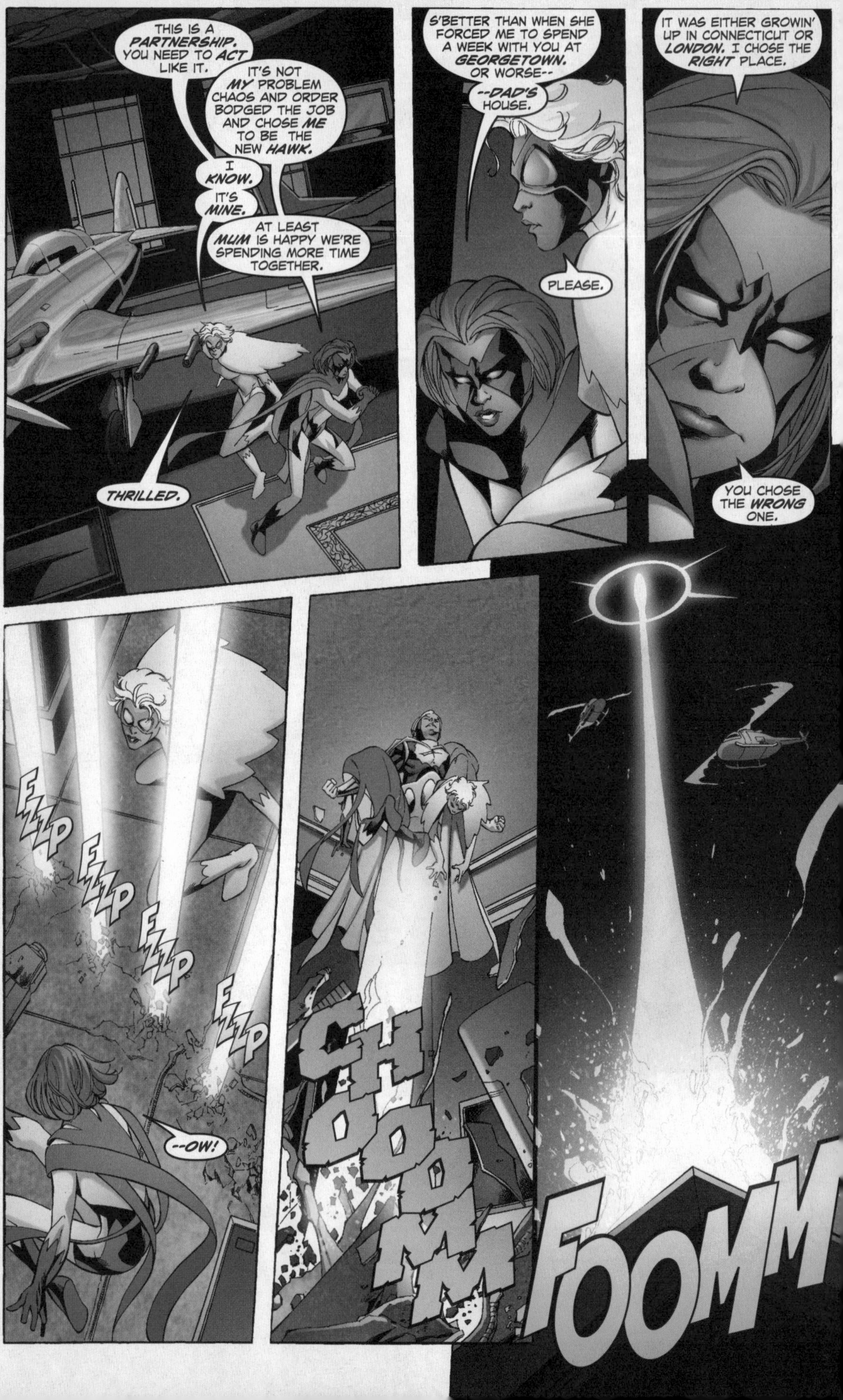
THIS IS A PARTNERSHIP. YOU NEED TO ACT LIKE IT.
IT'S NOT MY PROBLEM CHAOS AND ORDER BODGED THE JOB AND CHOSE ME TO BE THE NEW HAWK.
I KNOW.
IT'S MINE.
AT LEAST MUM IS HAPPY WE'RE SPENDING MORE TIME TOGETHER.
THRILLED.
S'BETTER THAN WHEN SHE FORCED ME TO SPEND A WEEK WITH YOU AT GEORGETOWN. OR WORSE--
--DAD'S HOUSE.
PLEASE.
IT WAS EITHER GROWIN' UP IN CONNECTICUT OR LONDON. I CHOSE THE RIGHT PLACE.
YOU CHOSE THE WRONG ONE.
FZZP
FZZP
FZZP
FZZP
--OW!
CHOOOOMM
FOOMM

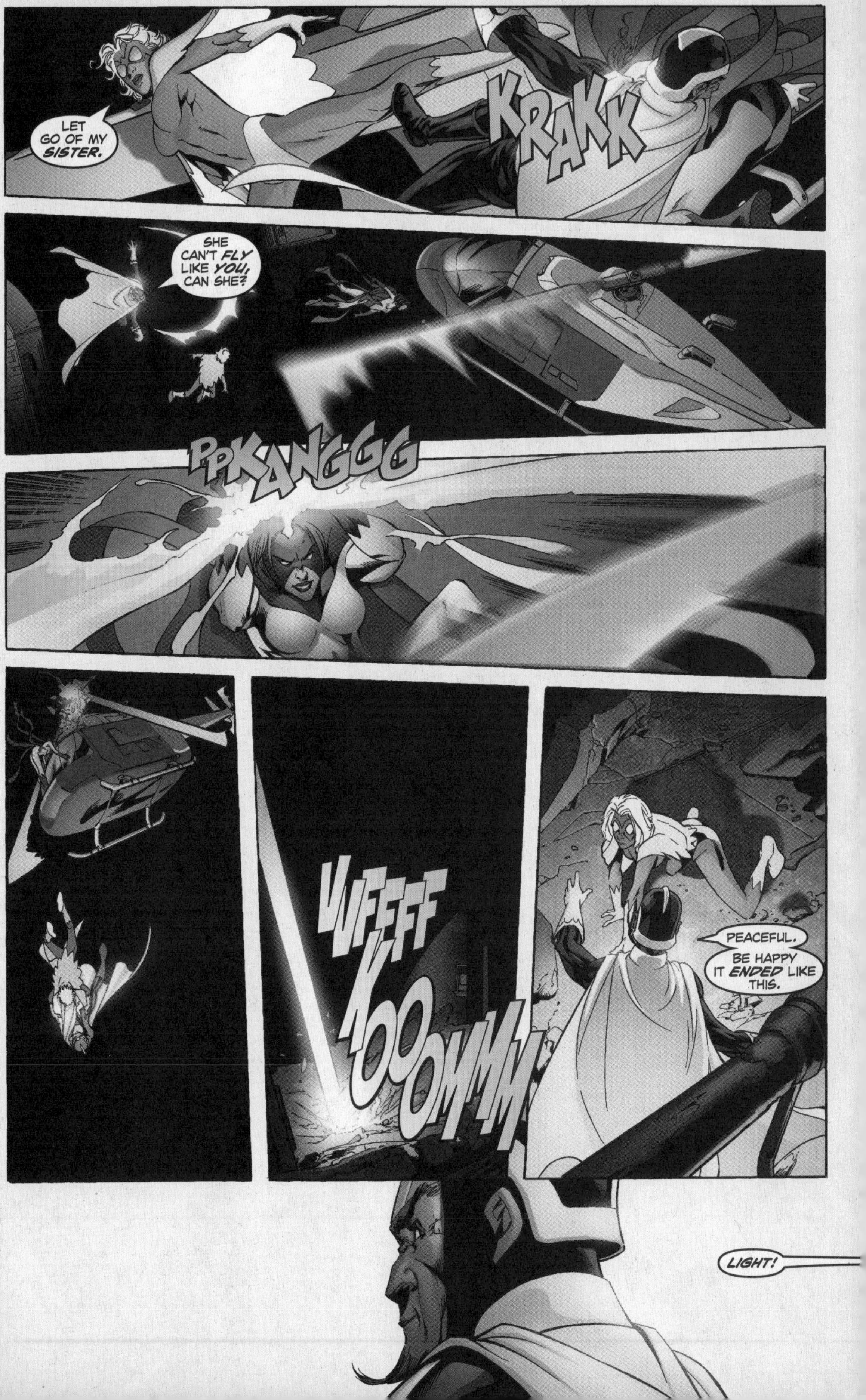

LET GO OF MY SISTER.
KRAKK
SHE CAN'T FLY LIKE YOU, CAN SHE?
PPKANGGG
VUFFFF KOOOMMM
PEACEFUL. BE HAPPY IT ENDED LIKE THIS.
LIGHT!

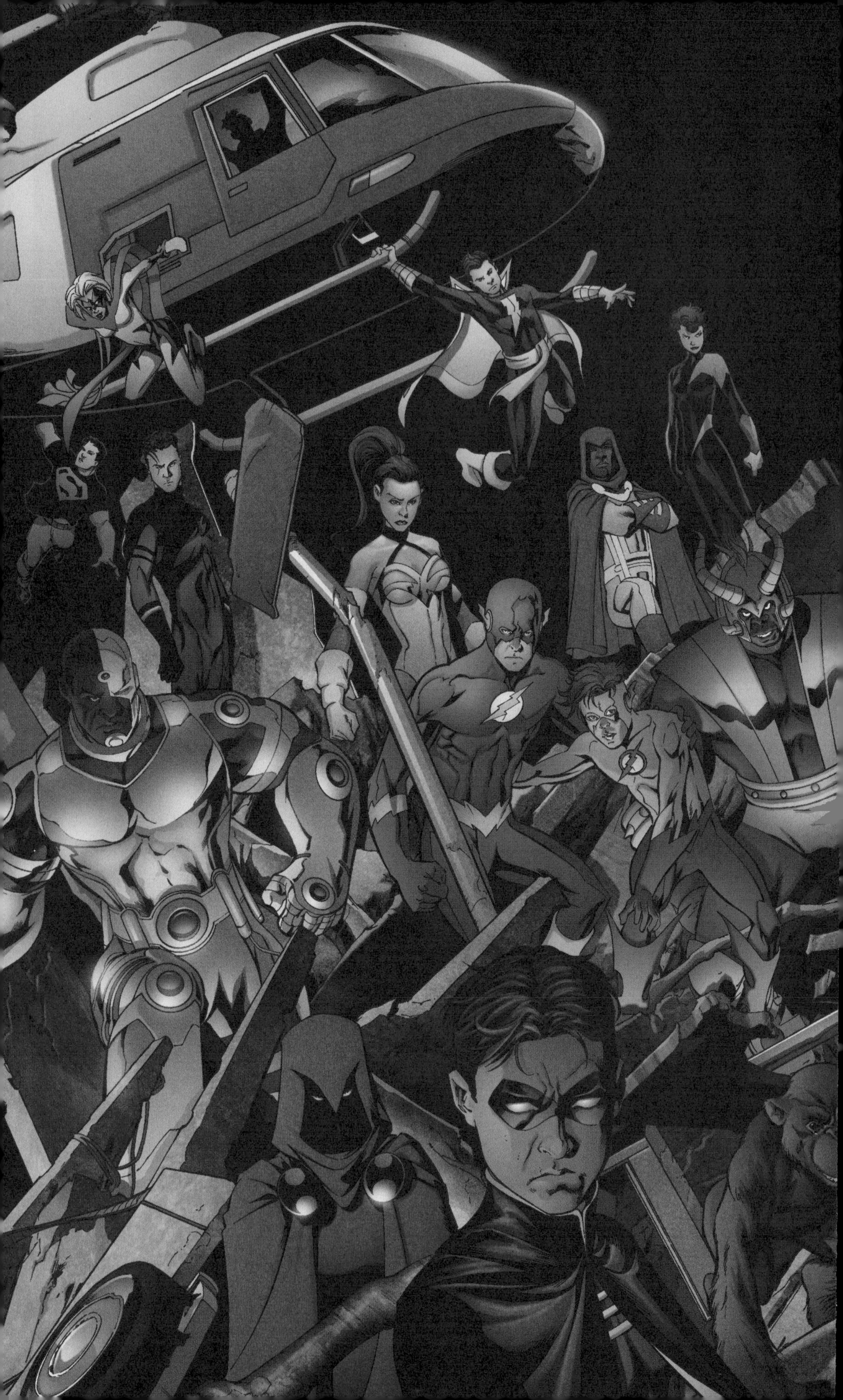

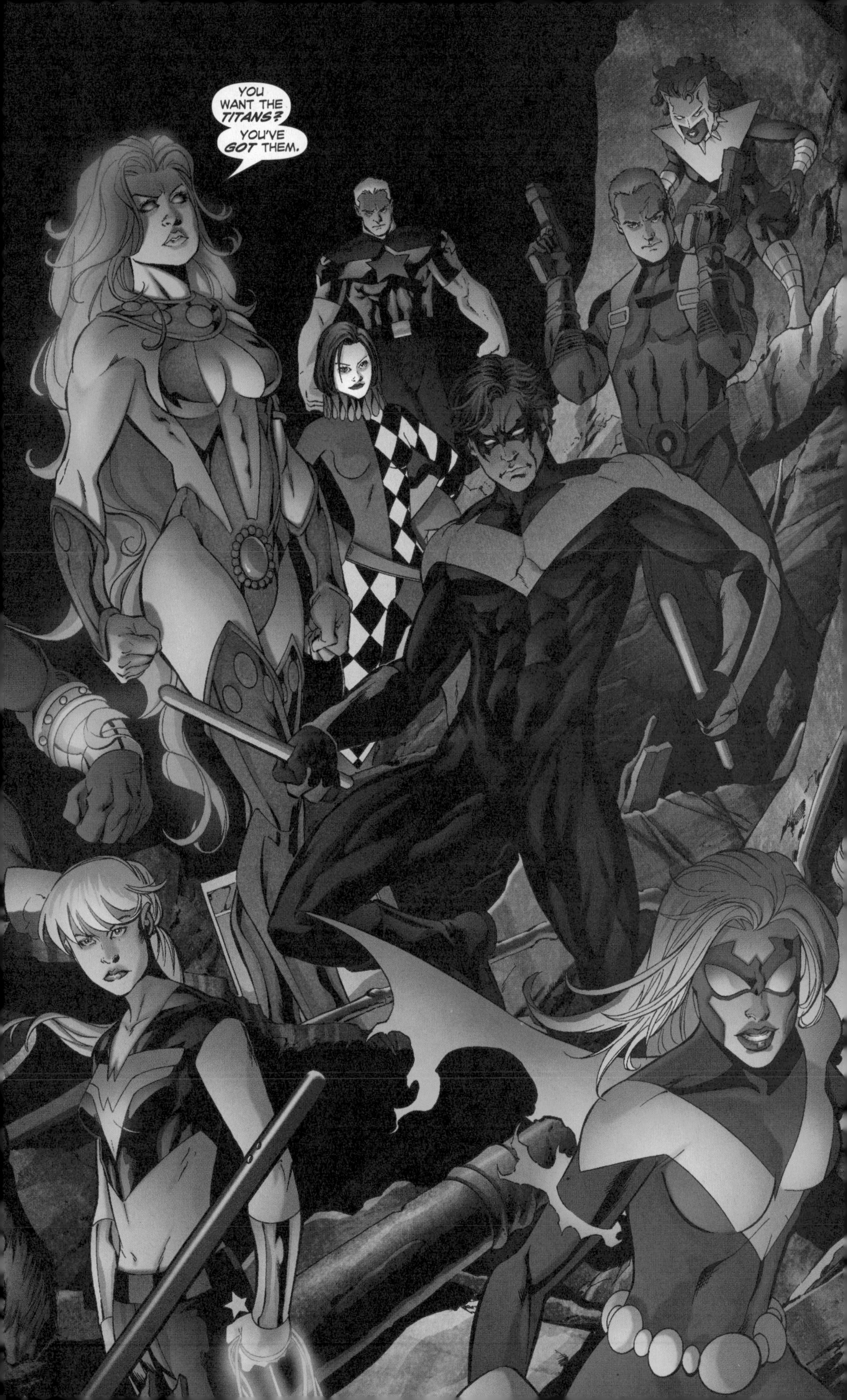
YOU WANT THE TITANS? YOU'VE GOT THEM.

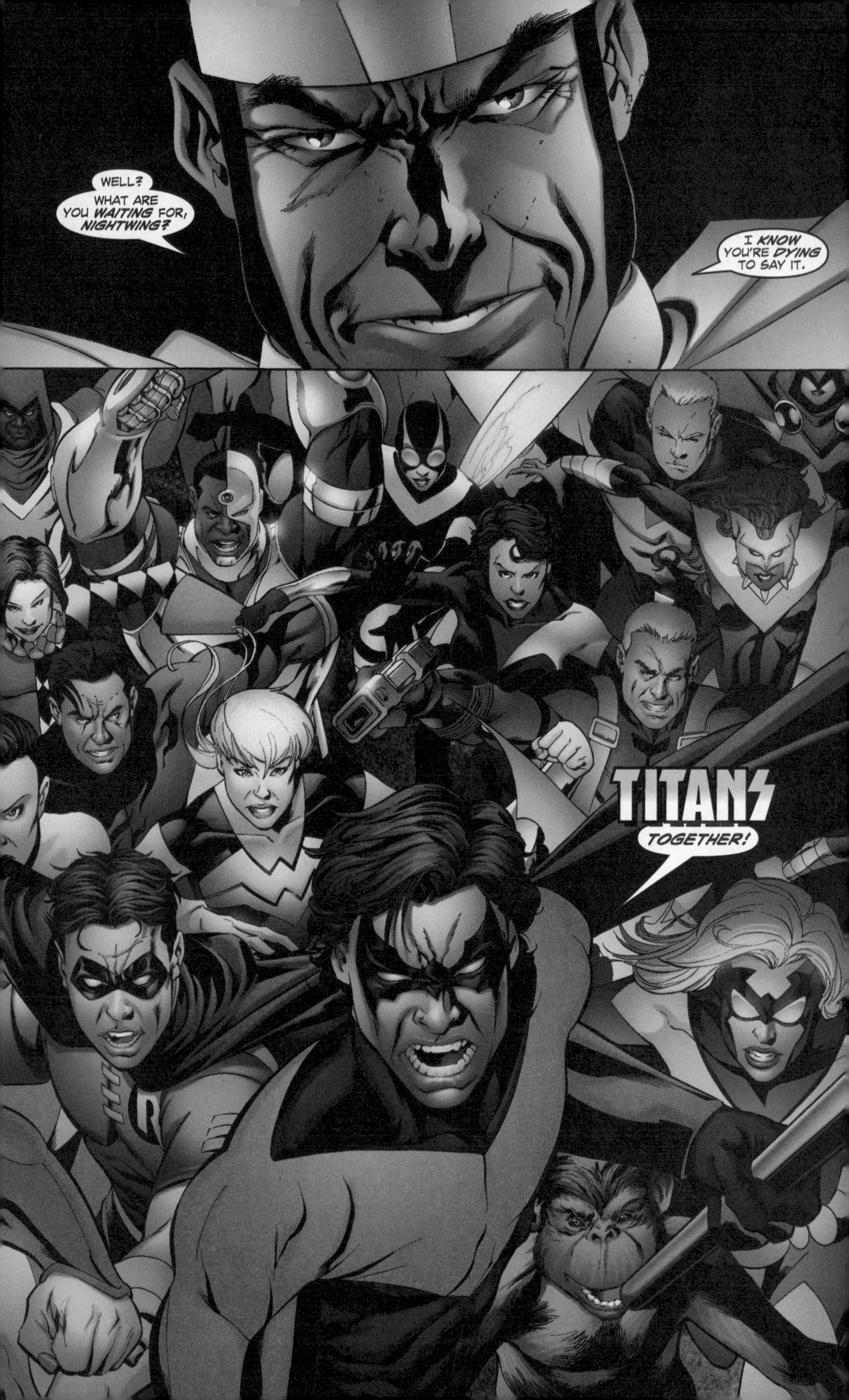
WELL? WHAT ARE YOU WAITING FOR, NIGHTWING?
I KNOW YOU'RE DYING TO SAY IT.
TITANS TOGETHER!

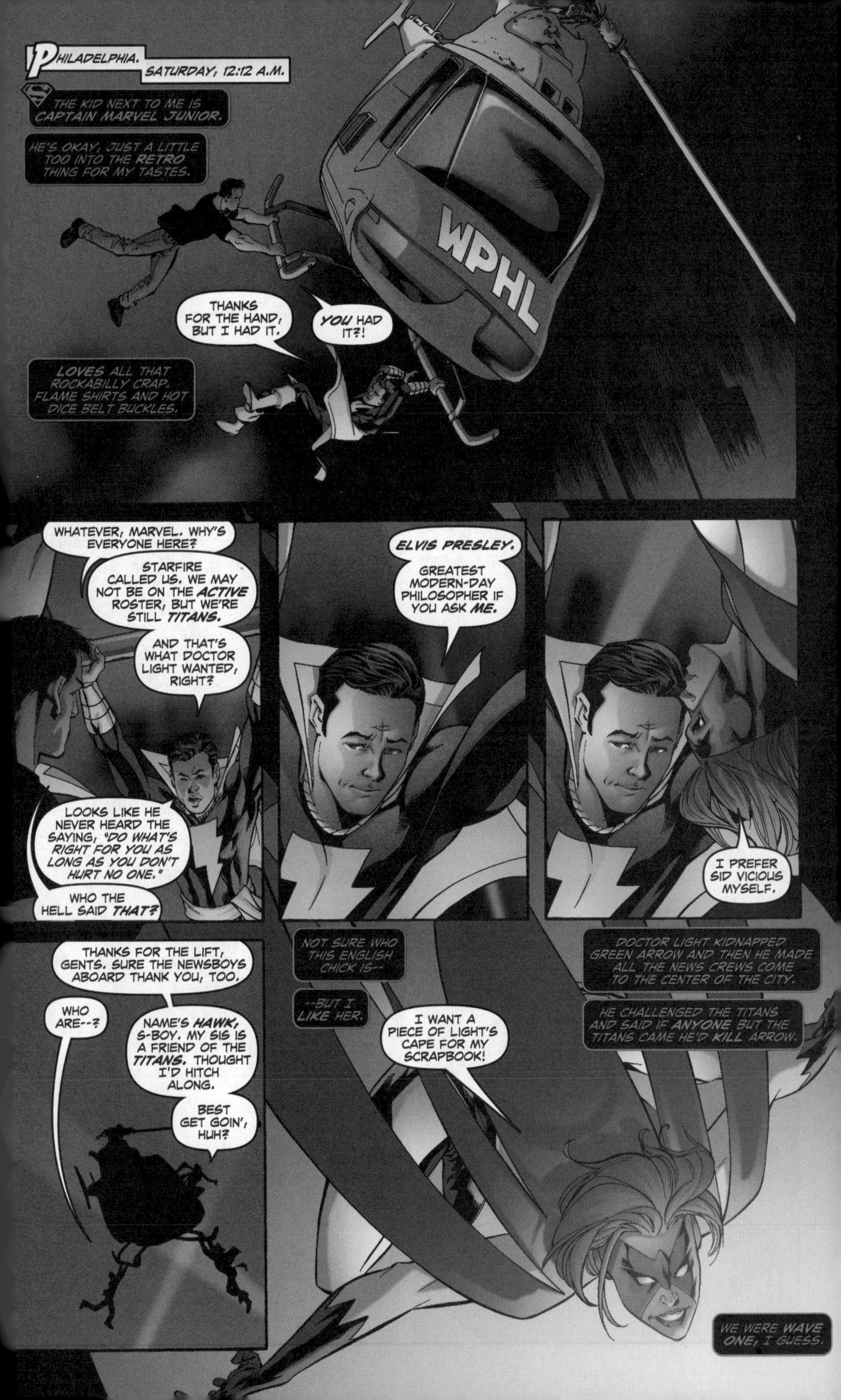
PHILADELPHIA.
SATURDAY, 12:12 A.M.
THE KID NEXT TO ME IS CAPTAIN MARVEL JUNIOR.
HE'S OKAY, JUST A LITTLE TOO INTO THE RETRO THING FOR MY TASTES.
THANKS FOR THE HAND, BUT I HAD IT.
YOU HAD IT?!
WPHL
LOVES ALL THAT ROCKABILLY CRAP. FLAME SHIRTS AND HOT DICE BELT BUCKLES.
WHATEVER, MARVEL. WHY'S EVERYONE HERE?
STARFIRE CALLED US. WE MAY NOT BE ON THE ACTIVE ROSTER, BUT WE'RE STILL TITANS.
AND THAT'S WHAT DOCTOR LIGHT WANTED, RIGHT?
LOOKS LIKE HE NEVER HEARD THE SAYING, "DO WHAT'S RIGHT FOR YOU AS LONG AS YOU DON'T HURT NO ONE."
WHO THE HELL SAID THAT?
ELVIS PRESLEY.
GREATEST MODERN-DAY PHILOSOPHER IF YOU ASK ME.
I PREFER SID VICIOUS MYSELF.
THANKS FOR THE LIFT, GENTS. SURE THE NEWSBOYS ABOARD THANK YOU, TOO.
WHO ARE--?
NAME'S HAWK, S-BOY. MY SIS IS A FRIEND OF THE TITANS. THOUGHT I'D HITCH ALONG.
BEST GET GOIN', HUH?
NOT SURE WHO THIS ENGLISH CHICK IS--
--BUT I LIKE HER.
I WANT A PIECE OF LIGHT'S CAPE FOR MY SCRAPBOOK!
DOCTOR LIGHT KIDNAPPED GREEN ARROW AND THEN HE MADE ALL THE NEWS CREWS COME TO THE CENTER OF THE CITY.
HE CHALLENGED THE TITANS AND SAID IF ANYONE BUT THE TITANS CAME HE'D KILL ARROW.
WE WERE WAVE ONE, I GUESS.

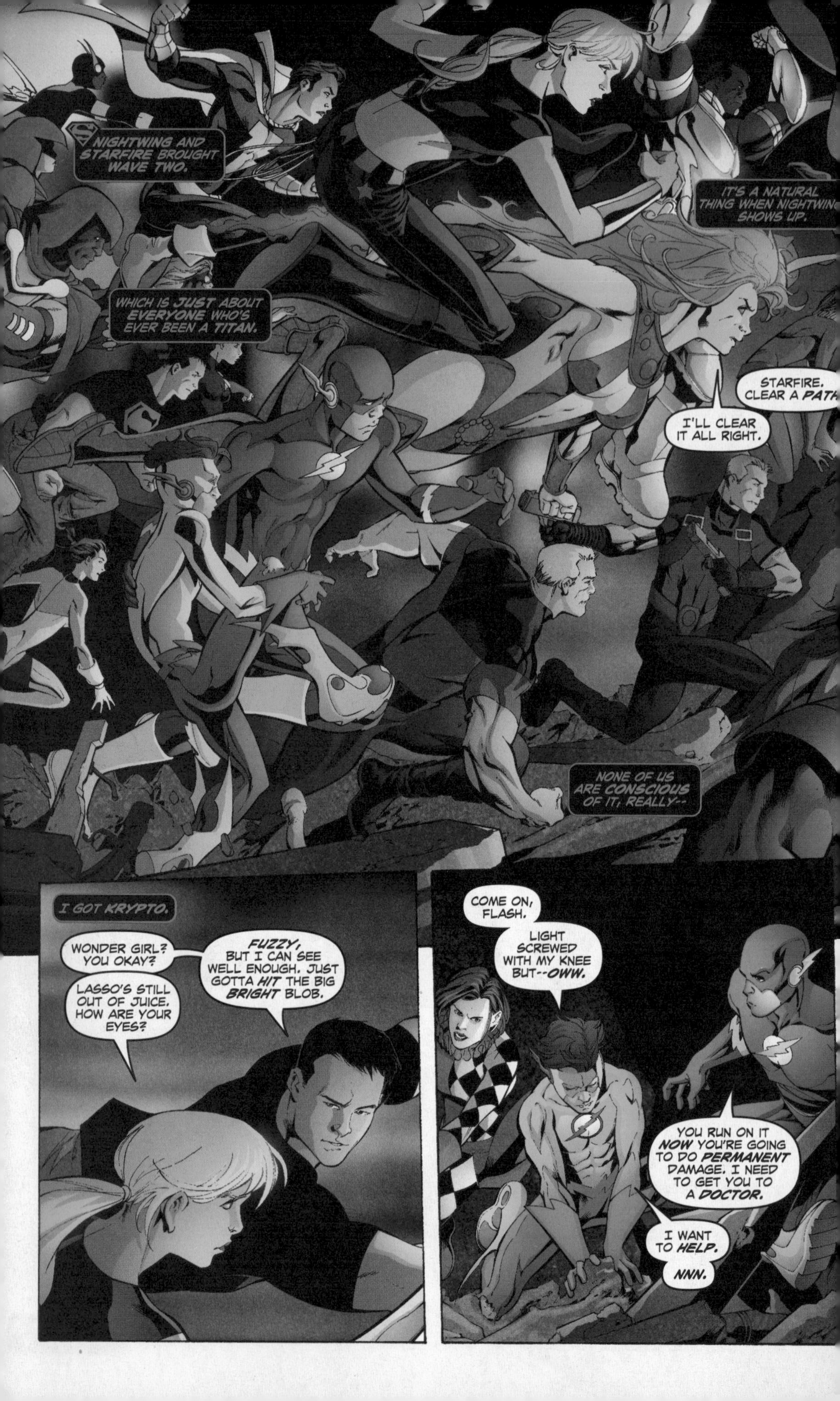
NIGHTWING AND STARFIRE BROUGHT WAVE TWO.
IT'S A NATURAL THING WHEN NIGHTWING SHOWS UP.
WHICH IS JUST ABOUT EVERYONE WHO'S EVER BEEN A TITAN.
STARFIRE. CLEAR A PATH
I'LL CLEAR IT ALL RIGHT.
NONE OF US ARE CONSCIOUS OF IT, REALLY--
I GOT KRYPTO.
WONDER GIRL? YOU OKAY?
FUZZY, BUT I CAN SEE WELL ENOUGH. JUST GOTTA HIT THE BIG BRIGHT BLOB.
LASSO'S STILL OUT OF JUICE. HOW ARE YOUR EYES?
COME ON, FLASH.
LIGHT SCREWED WITH MY KNEE BUT--OWW.
YOU RUN ON IT NOW YOU'RE GOING TO DO PERMANENT DAMAGE. I NEED TO GET YOU TO A DOCTOR.
I WANT TO HELP.
NNN.

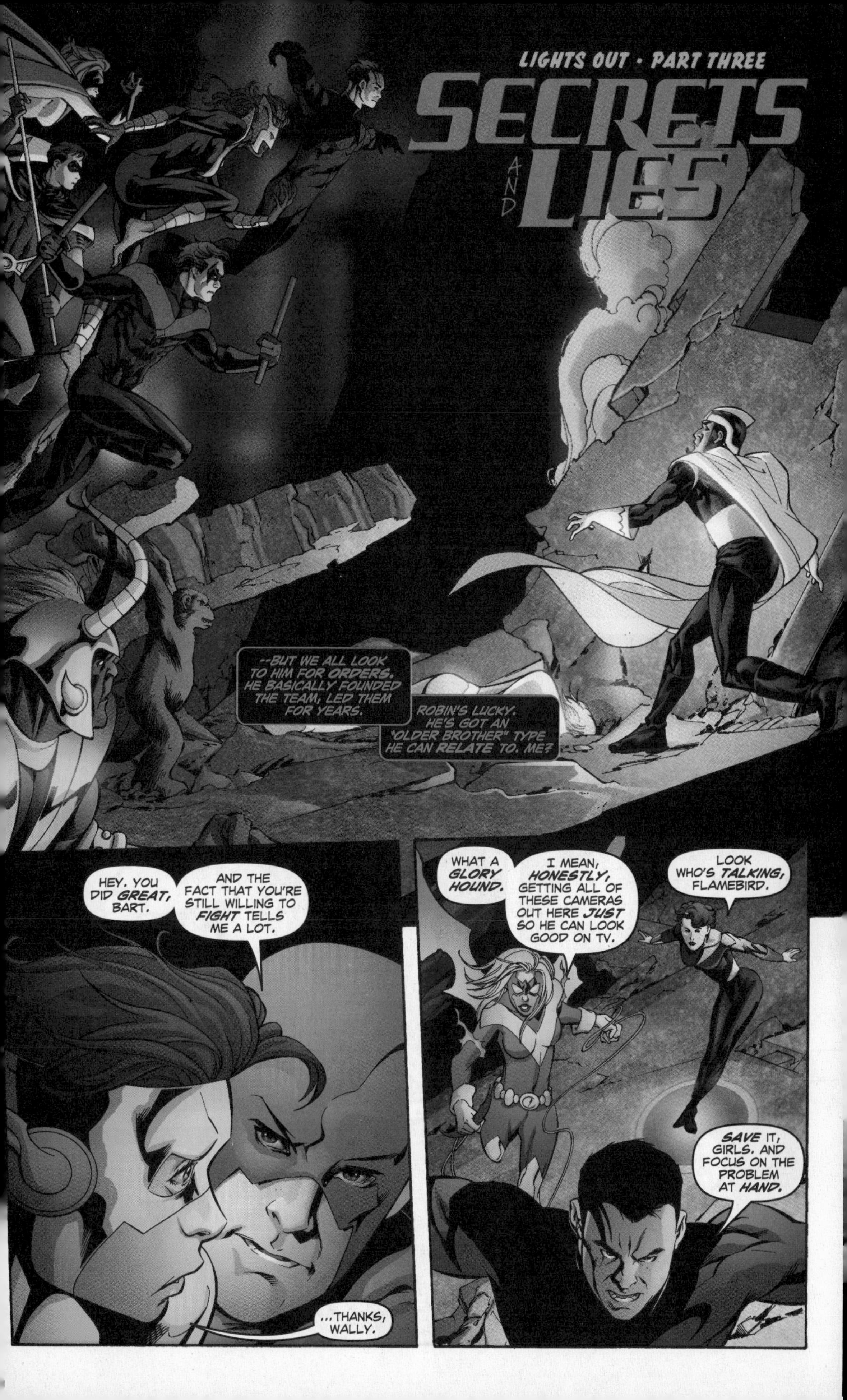
LIGHTS OUT · PART THREE
SECRETS AND LIES
--BUT WE ALL LOOK TO HIM FOR ORDERS. HE BASICALLY FOUNDED THE TEAM, LED THEM FOR YEARS.
ROBIN'S LUCKY. HE'S GOT AN "OLDER BROTHER" TYPE HE CAN RELATE TO. ME?
HEY. YOU DID GREAT, BART.
AND THE FACT THAT YOU'RE STILL WILLING TO FIGHT TELLS ME A LOT.
...THANKS, WALLY.
WHAT A GLORY HOUND.
I MEAN, HONESTLY, GETTING ALL OF THESE CAMERAS OUT HERE JUST SO HE CAN LOOK GOOD ON TV.
LOOK WHO'S TALKING, FLAMEBIRD.
SAVE IT, GIRLS. AND FOCUS ON THE PROBLEM AT HAND.

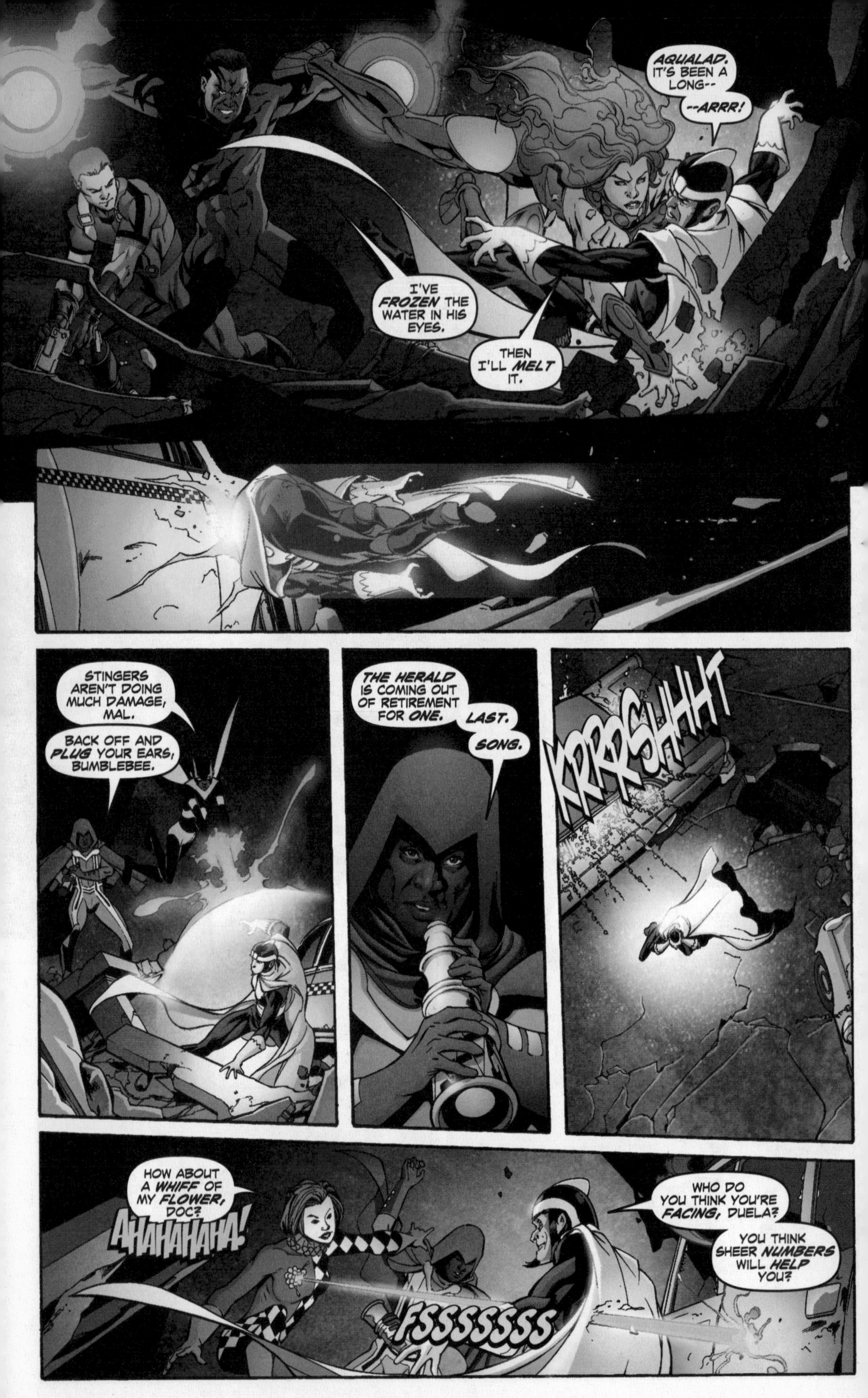
AQUALAD. IT'S BEEN A LONG--
--ARRR!
I'VE FROZEN THE WATER IN HIS EYES.
THEN I'LL MELT IT.
STINGERS AREN'T DOING MUCH DAMAGE, MAL.
BACK OFF AND PLUG YOUR EARS, BUMBLEBEE.
THE HERALD IS COMING OUT OF RETIREMENT FOR ONE.
LAST.
SONG.
KRRRSHHHT
HOW ABOUT A WHIFF OF MY FLOWER, DOC?
AHAHAHAHA!
WHO DO YOU THINK YOU'RE FACING, DUELA?
YOU THINK SHEER NUMBERS WILL HELP YOU?
FSSSSSSS

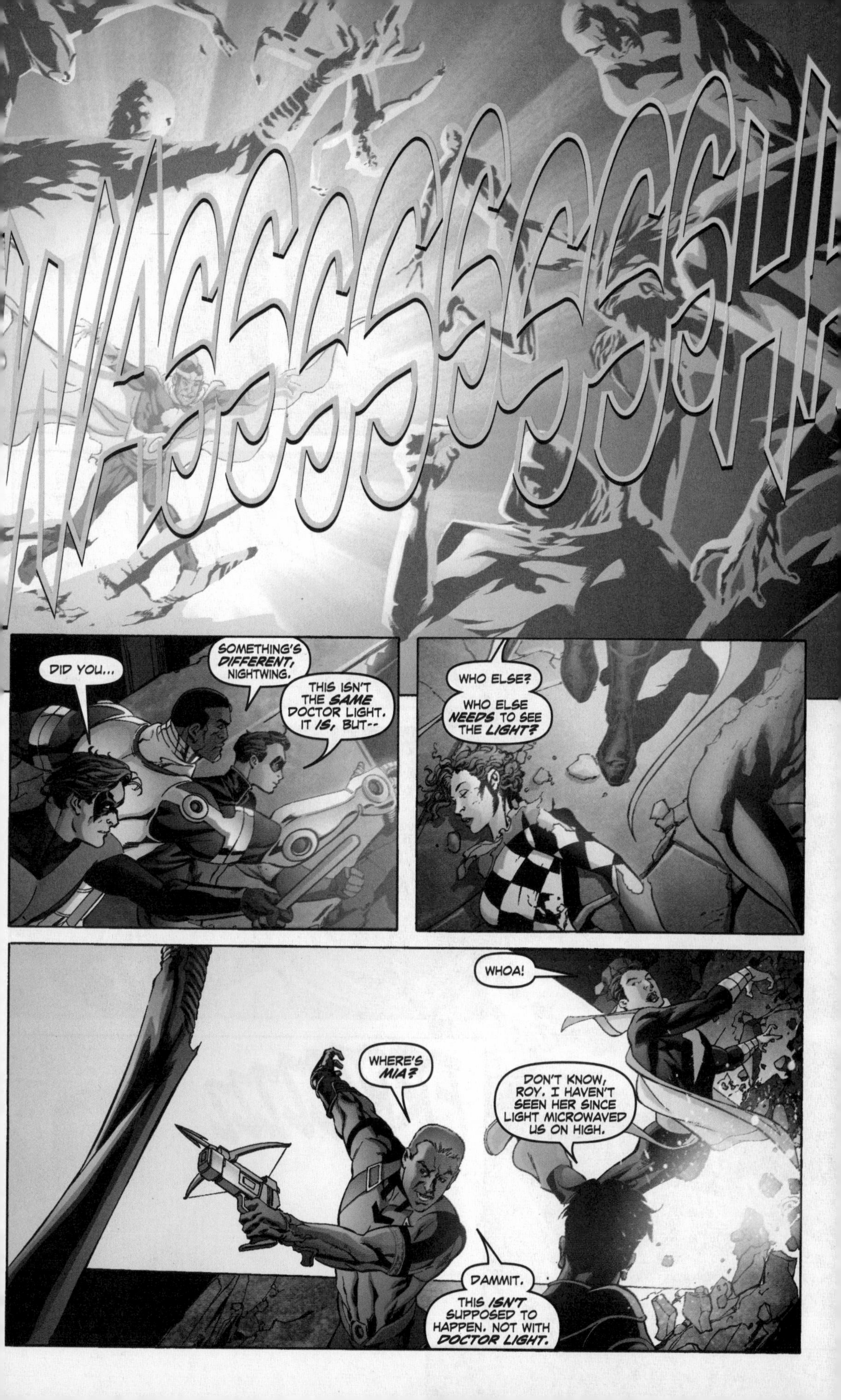
DID YOU...
SOMETHING'S DIFFERENT, NIGHTWING.
THIS ISN'T THE SAME DOCTOR LIGHT. IT IS, BUT--
WHO ELSE?
WHO ELSE NEEDS TO SEE THE LIGHT?
WHOA!
WHERE'S MIA?
DON'T KNOW, ROY. I HAVEN'T SEEN HER SINCE LIGHT MICROWAVED US ON HIGH.
DAMMIT.
THIS ISN'T SUPPOSED TO HAPPEN. NOT WITH DOCTOR LIGHT.

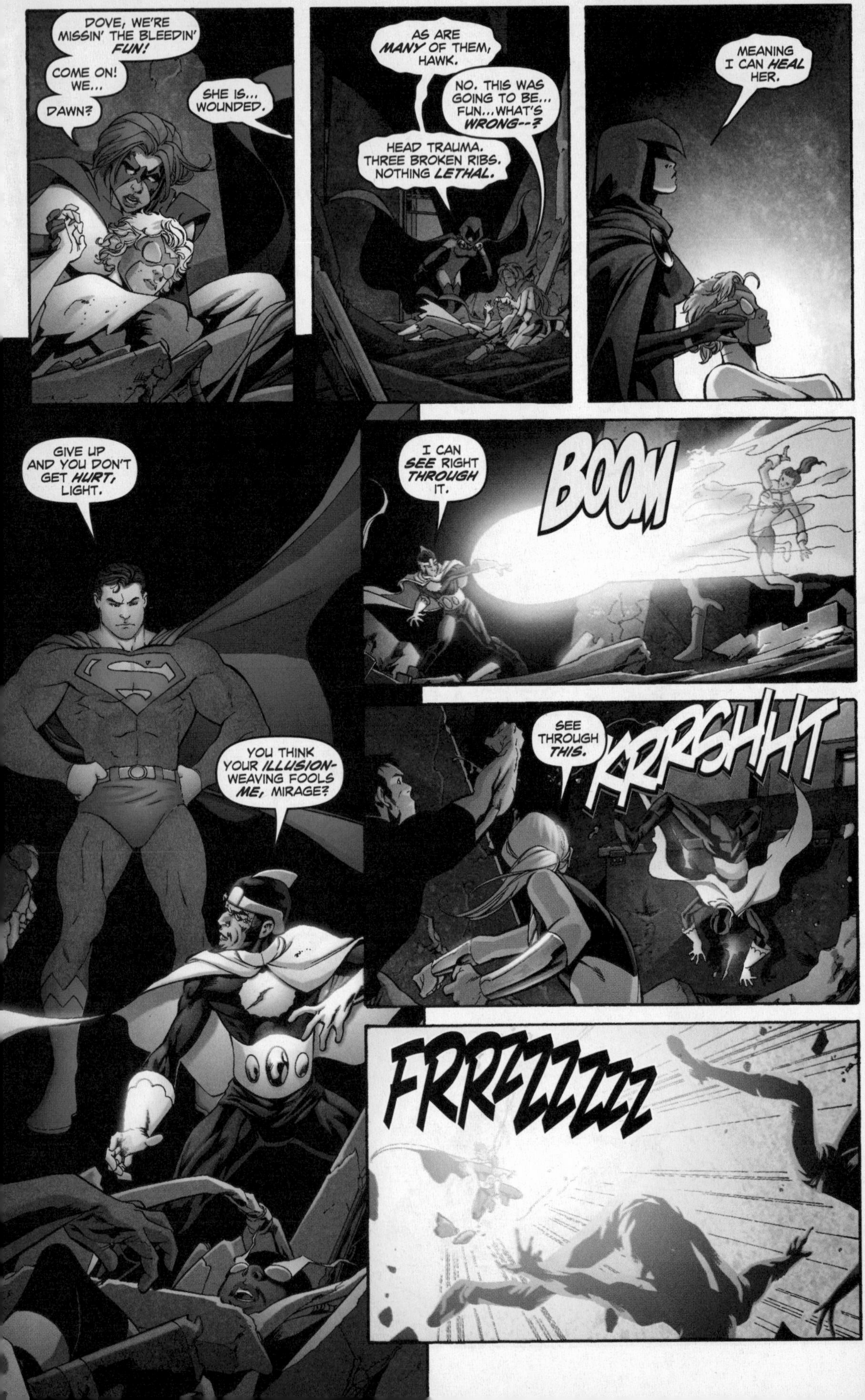

DOVE, WE'RE MISSIN' THE BLEEDIN' *FUN!*
COME ON! WE...
DAWN?
SHE IS... WOUNDED.
AS ARE *MANY* OF THEM, HAWK.
NO. THIS WAS GOING TO BE... FUN...WHAT'S *WRONG--?*
HEAD TRAUMA. THREE BROKEN RIBS. NOTHING *LETHAL.*
MEANING I CAN *HEAL* HER.
GIVE UP AND YOU DON'T GET *HURT,* LIGHT.
YOU THINK YOUR *ILLUSION-*WEAVING FOOLS *ME,* MIRAGE?
I CAN *SEE* RIGHT *THROUGH* IT.
BOOM
SEE THROUGH *THIS.*
KRRSHHT
FRRZZZZZZ

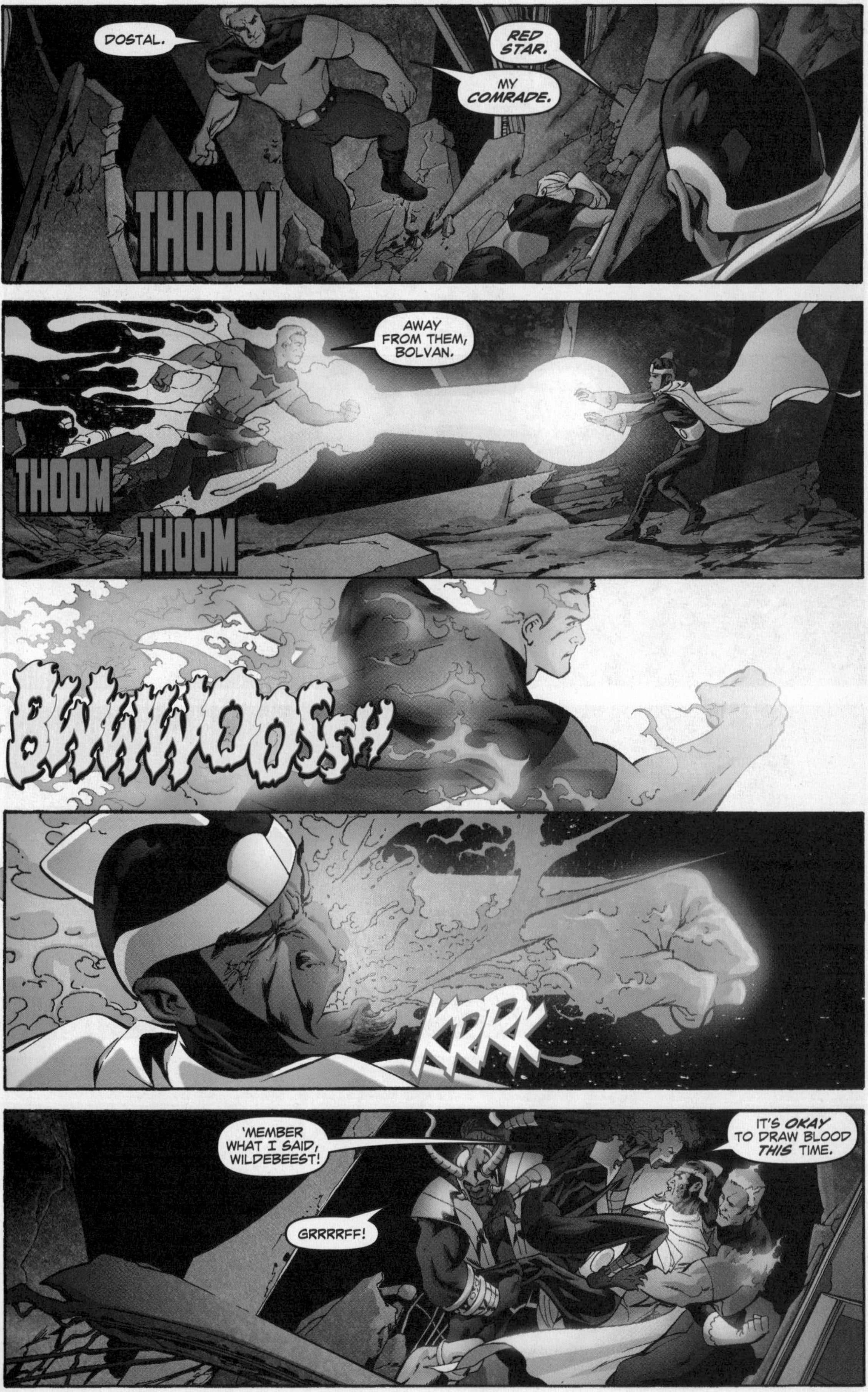
DOSTAL.
RED STAR.
MY COMRADE.
THOOM
AWAY FROM THEM, BOLVAN.
THOOM
THOOM
BWWOOSH
KRRK
'MEMBER WHAT I SAID, WILDEBEEST!
IT'S OKAY TO DRAW BLOOD THIS TIME.
GRRRRFF!

MORE.

GIVE HIM WHAT HE WANTS.

KRRRANK

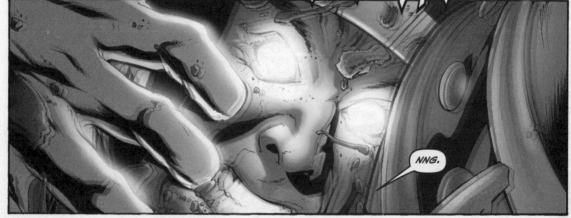

NNG.

IS IT GETTING *DARKER?*

HE'S *POWERING UP.* HE'S *SUCKING IN* ALL THE *AMBIENT LIGHT.*

TITANS! GET--

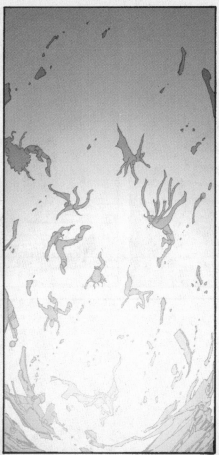

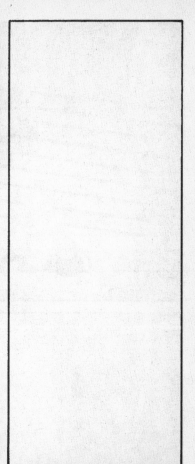

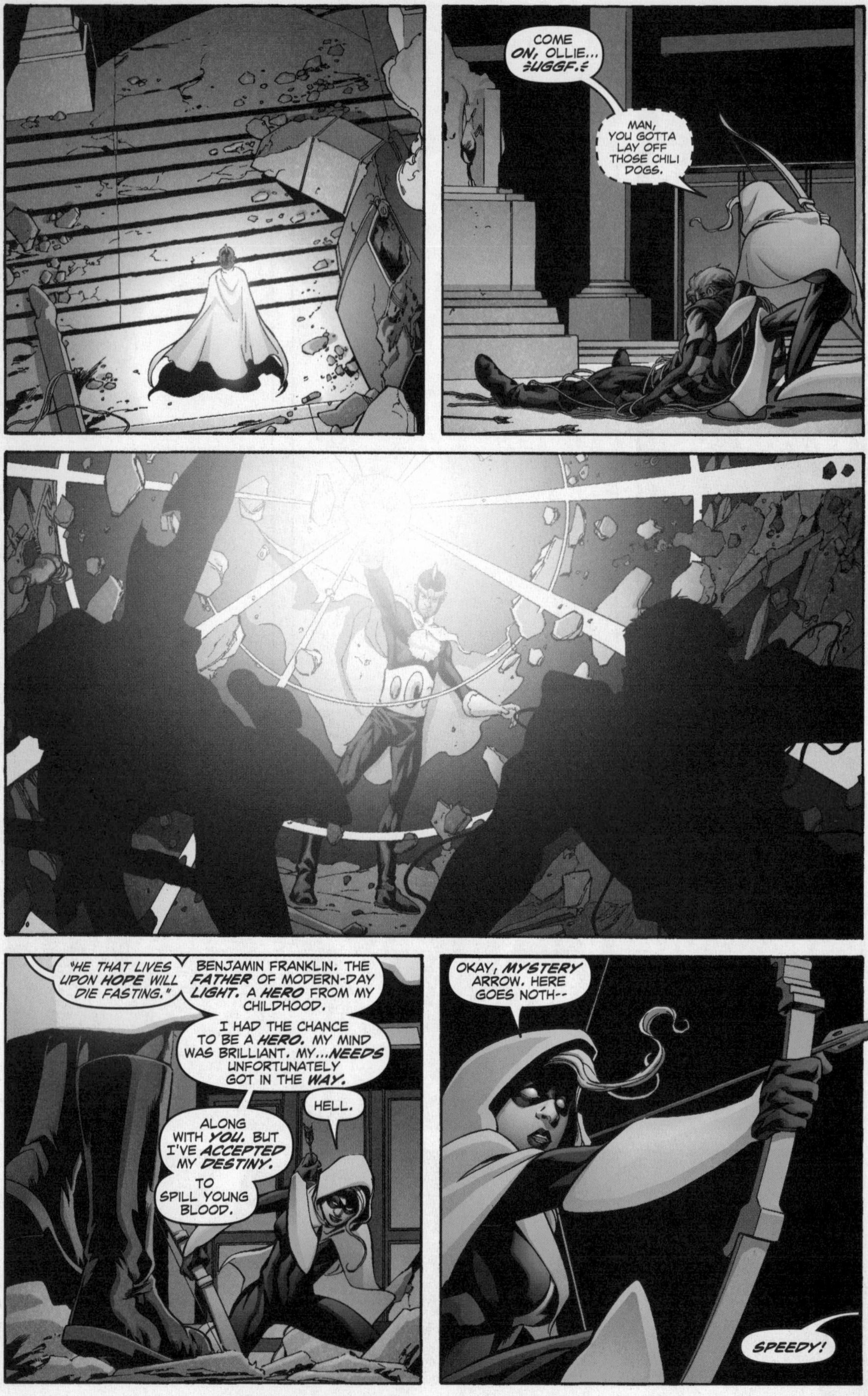
COME ON, OLLIE... UGGF.
MAN, YOU GOTTA LAY OFF THOSE CHILI DOGS.
"HE THAT LIVES UPON HOPE WILL DIE FASTING."
BENJAMIN FRANKLIN. THE FATHER OF MODERN-DAY LIGHT. A HERO FROM MY CHILDHOOD.
I HAD THE CHANCE TO BE A HERO. MY MIND WAS BRILLIANT. MY... NEEDS UNFORTUNATELY GOT IN THE WAY.
ALONG WITH YOU. BUT I'VE ACCEPTED MY DESTINY.
TO SPILL YOUNG BLOOD.
HELL.
OKAY, MYSTERY ARROW. HERE GOES NOTH--
SPEEDY!

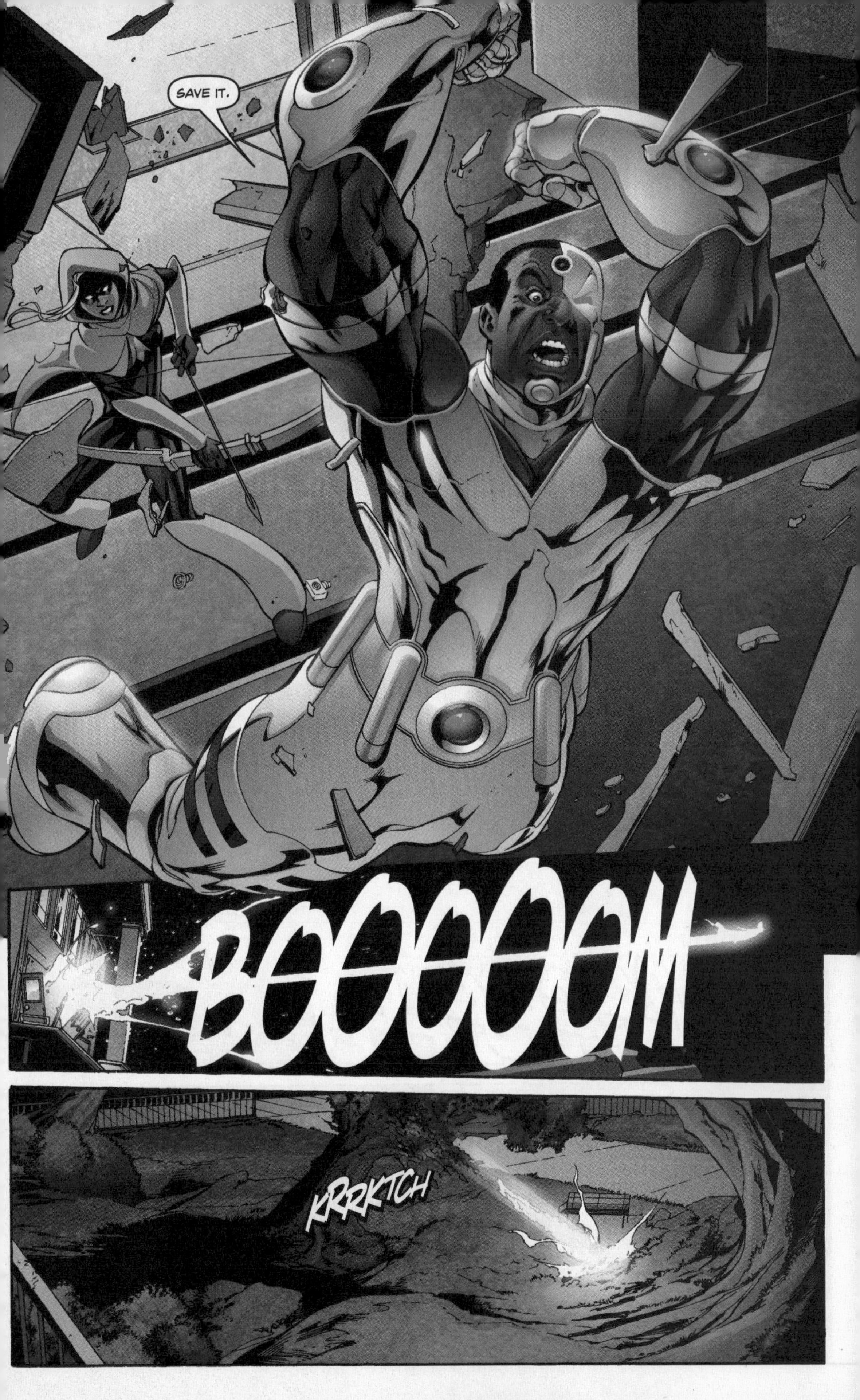
SAVE IT.
BOOOOOOM
KRRKTCH

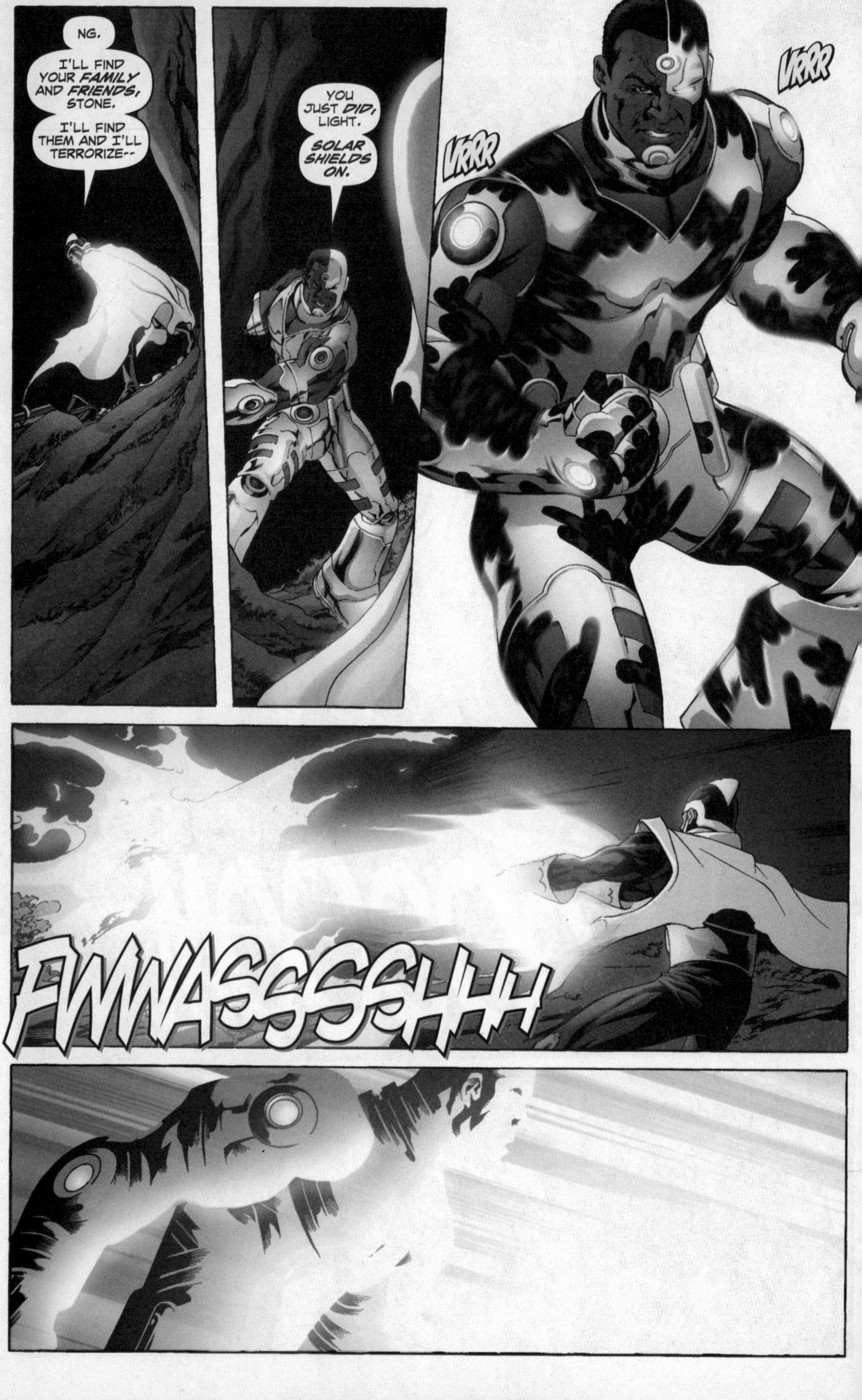
NG.
I'LL FIND YOUR FAMILY AND FRIENDS, STONE.
I'LL FIND THEM AND I'LL TERRORIZE--
YOU JUST DID, LIGHT.
SOLAR SHIELDS ON.
VRRR
VRRR
FWWASSSSHHH

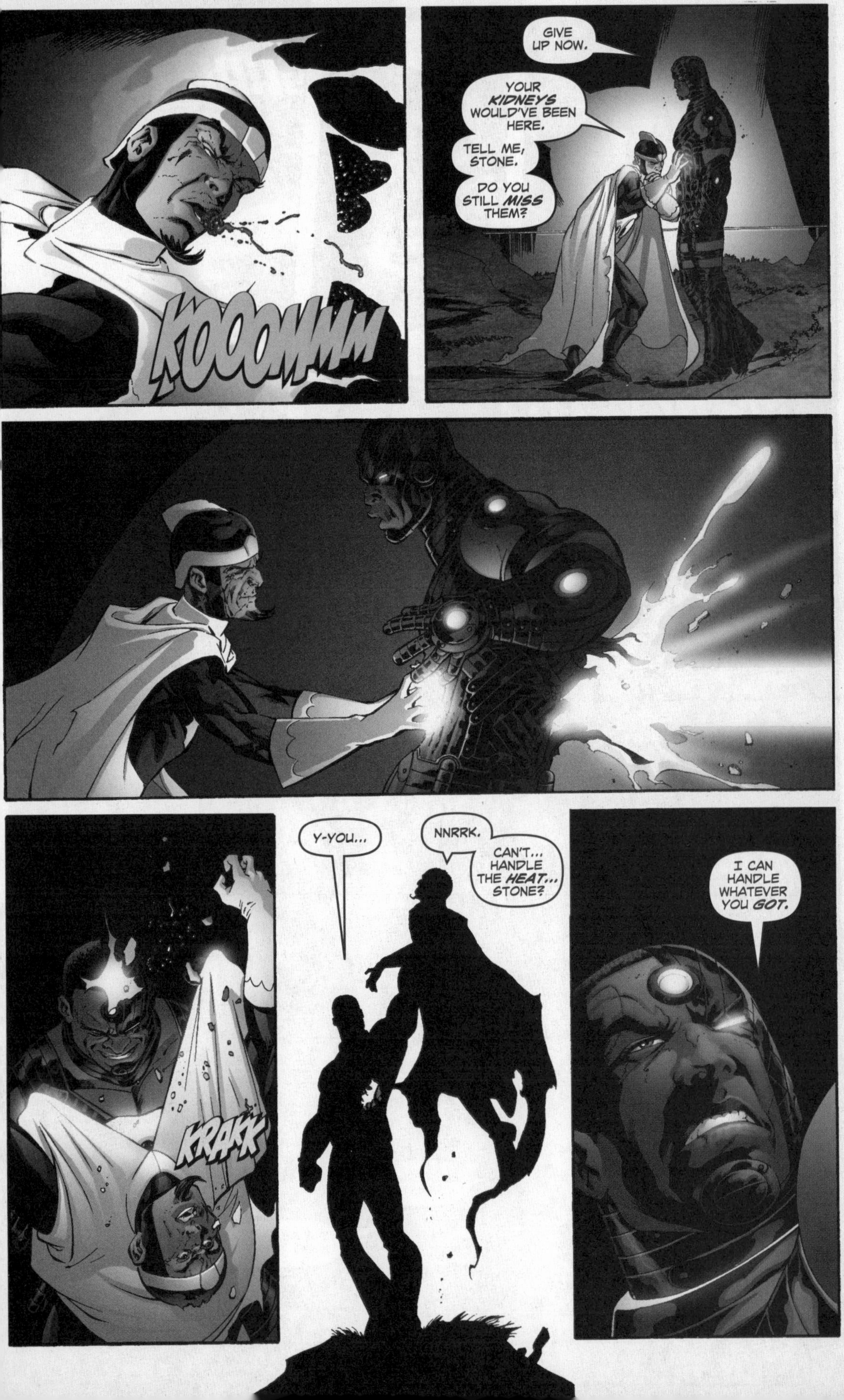
KOOOMMM
GIVE UP NOW.
YOUR KIDNEYS WOULD'VE BEEN HERE.
TELL ME, STONE.
DO YOU STILL MISS THEM?
KRAKK
Y-YOU...
NNRRK.
CAN'T... HANDLE THE HEAT... STONE?
I CAN HANDLE WHATEVER YOU GOT.

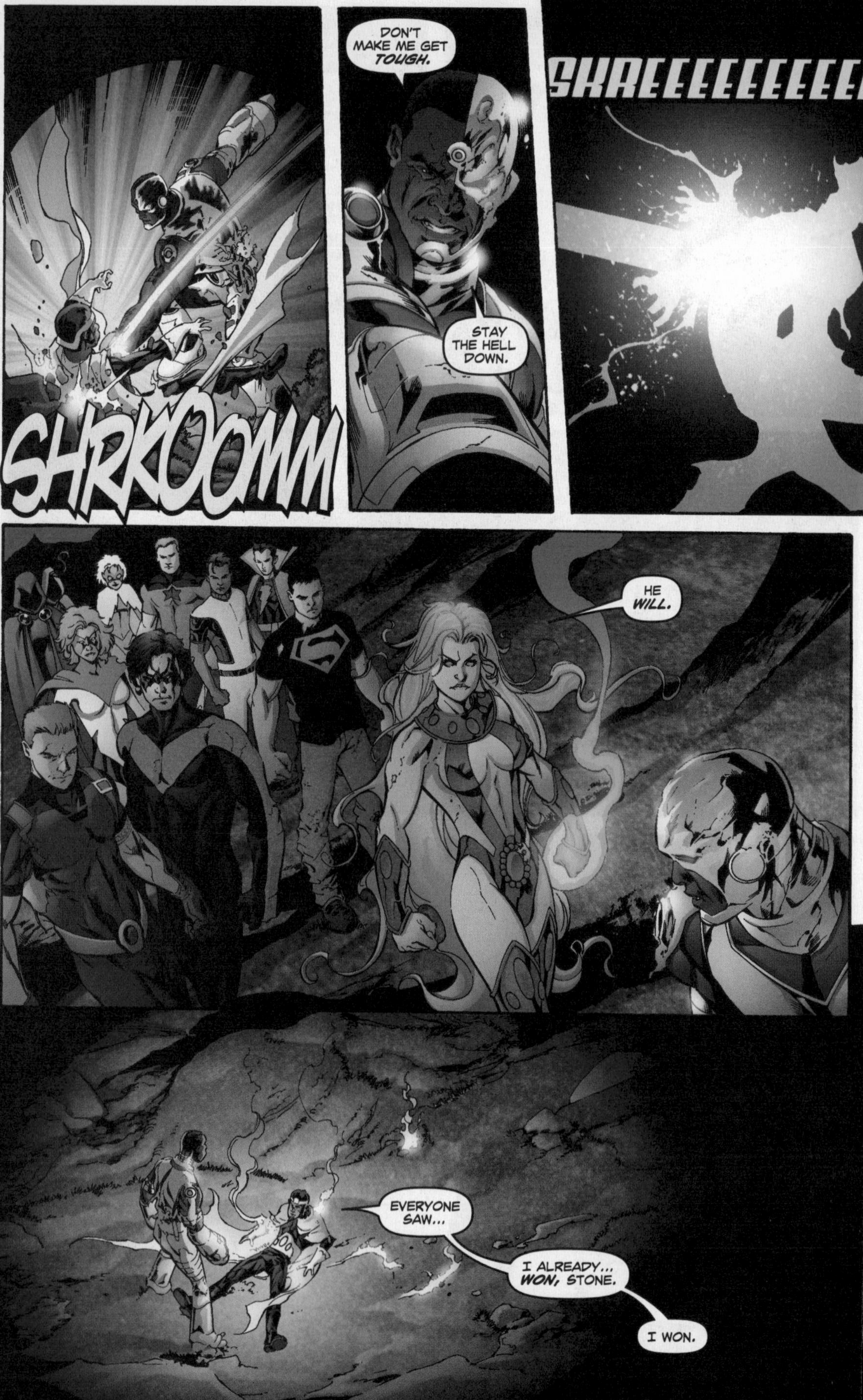
SHRKOOMM
DON'T MAKE ME GET TOUGH.
STAY THE HELL DOWN.
SKREEEEEEEEE
HE WILL.
EVERYONE SAW...
I ALREADY... WON, STONE.
I WON.

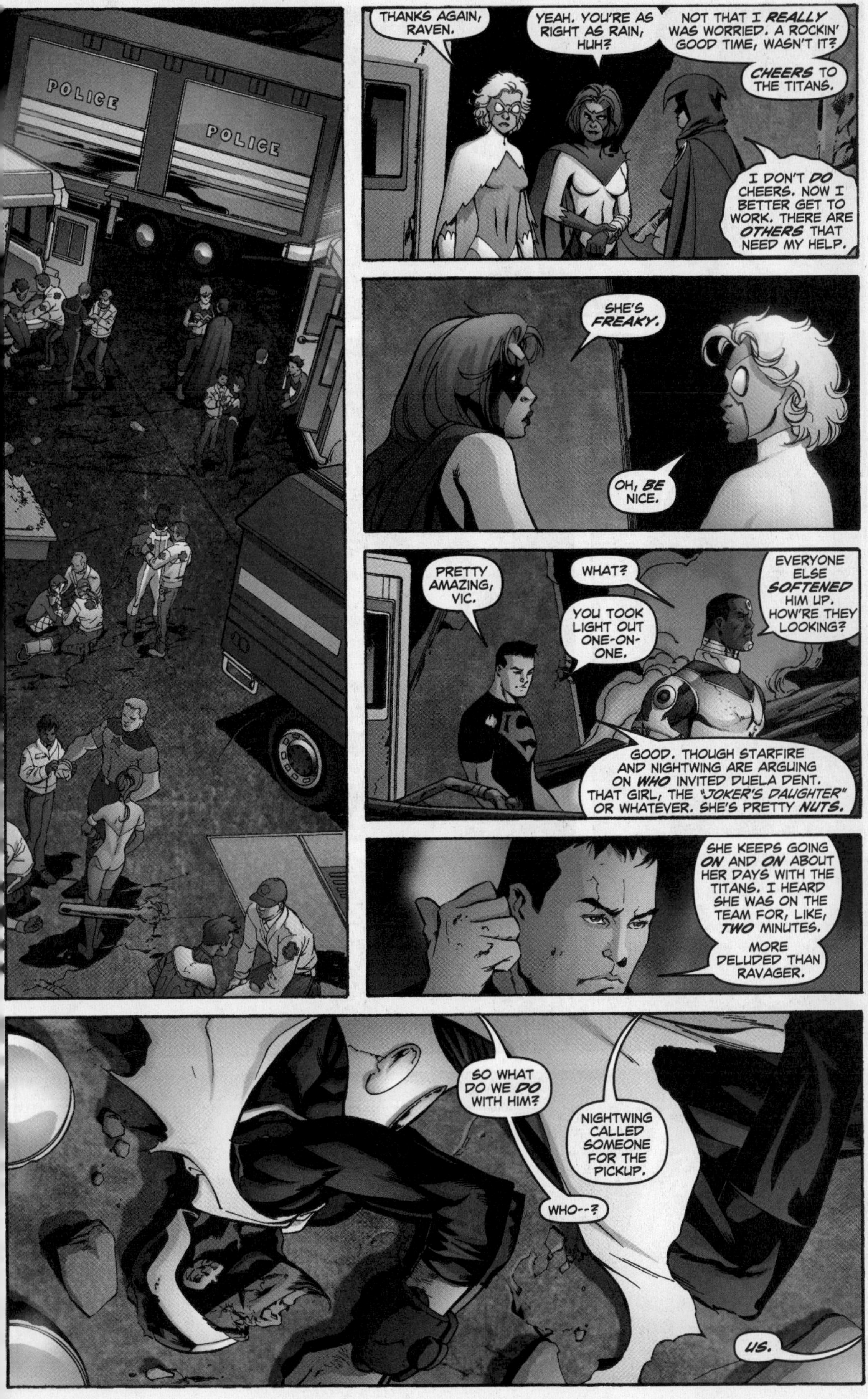
POLICE
POLICE
THANKS AGAIN, RAVEN.
YEAH. YOU'RE AS RIGHT AS RAIN, HUH?
NOT THAT I REALLY WAS WORRIED. A ROCKIN' GOOD TIME, WASN'T IT?
CHEERS TO THE TITANS.
I DON'T DO CHEERS. NOW I BETTER GET TO WORK. THERE ARE OTHERS THAT NEED MY HELP.
SHE'S FREAKY.
OH, BE NICE.
PRETTY AMAZING, VIC.
WHAT?
YOU TOOK LIGHT OUT ONE-ON-ONE.
EVERYONE ELSE SOFTENED HIM UP. HOW'RE THEY LOOKING?
GOOD. THOUGH STARFIRE AND NIGHTWING ARE ARGUING ON WHO INVITED DUELA DENT. THAT GIRL, THE "JOKER'S DAUGHTER" OR WHATEVER. SHE'S PRETTY NUTS.
SHE KEEPS GOING ON AND ON ABOUT HER DAYS WITH THE TITANS. I HEARD SHE WAS ON THE TEAM FOR, LIKE, TWO MINUTES.
MORE DELUDED THAN RAVAGER.
SO WHAT DO WE DO WITH HIM?
NIGHTWING CALLED SOMEONE FOR THE PICKUP.
WHO--?
US.

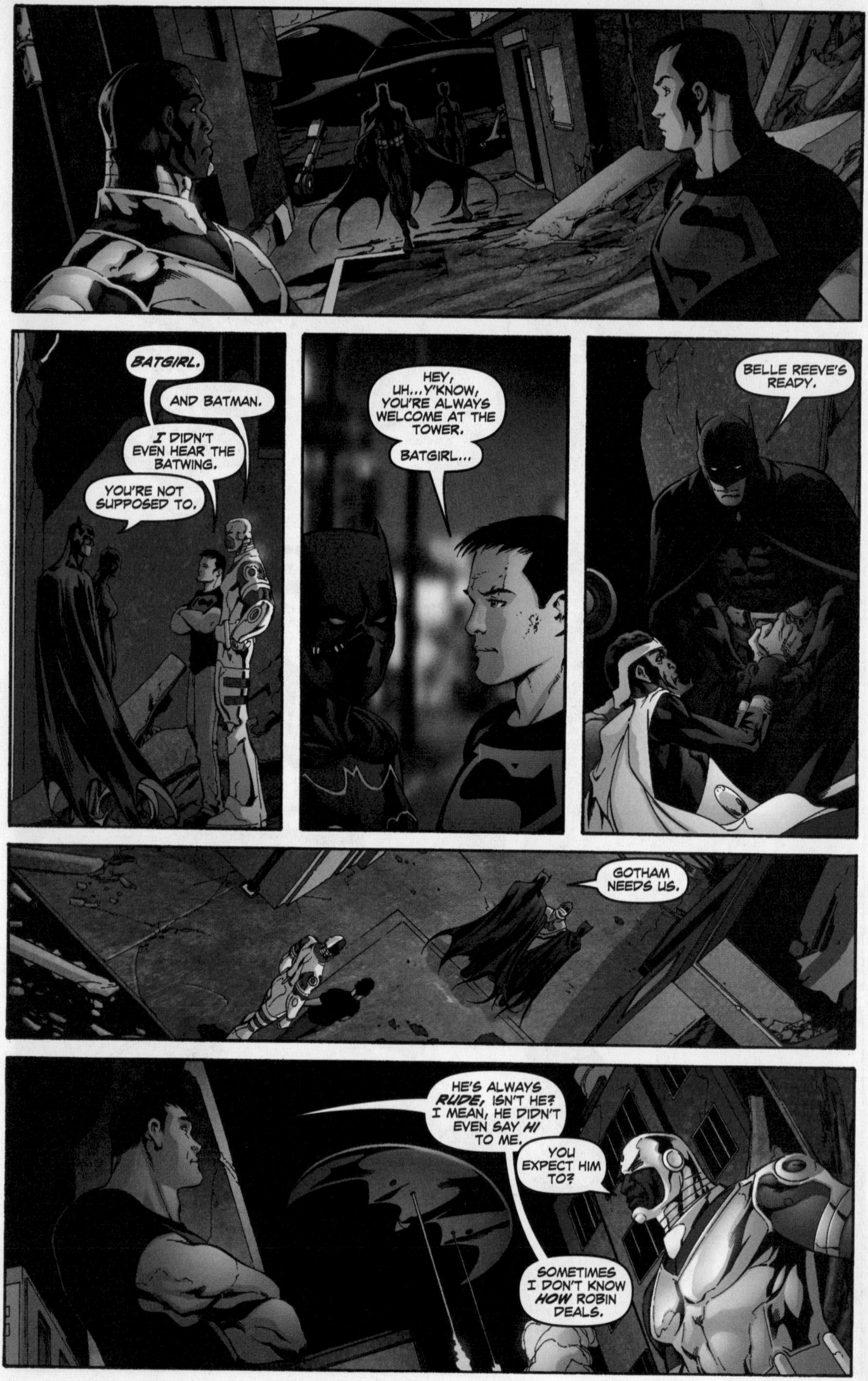

BATGIRL.
AND BATMAN.
I DIDN'T EVEN HEAR THE BATWING.
YOU'RE NOT SUPPOSED TO.
HEY, UH...Y'KNOW, YOU'RE ALWAYS WELCOME AT THE TOWER.
BATGIRL...
BELLE REEVE'S READY.
GOTHAM NEEDS US.
HE'S ALWAYS RUDE, ISN'T HE? I MEAN, HE DIDN'T EVEN SAY HI TO ME.
YOU EXPECT HIM TO?
SOMETIMES I DON'T KNOW HOW ROBIN DEALS.

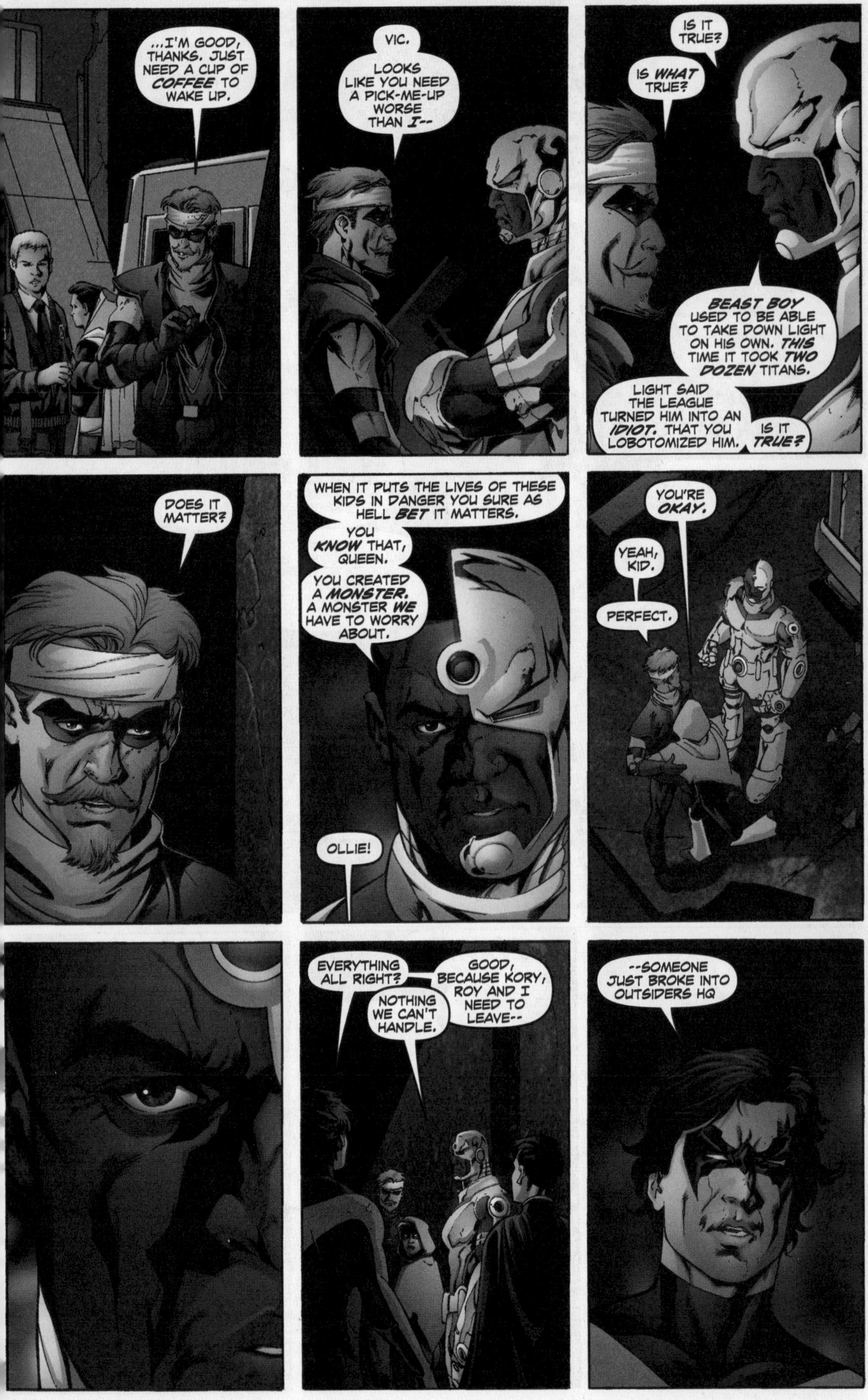
...I'M GOOD, THANKS. JUST NEED A CUP OF COFFEE TO WAKE UP.
VIC.
LOOKS LIKE YOU NEED A PICK-ME-UP WORSE THAN I--
IS IT TRUE?
IS WHAT TRUE?
BEAST BOY USED TO BE ABLE TO TAKE DOWN LIGHT ON HIS OWN. THIS TIME IT TOOK TWO DOZEN TITANS.
LIGHT SAID THE LEAGUE TURNED HIM INTO AN IDIOT. THAT YOU LOBOTOMIZED HIM.
IS IT TRUE?
DOES IT MATTER?
WHEN IT PUTS THE LIVES OF THESE KIDS IN DANGER YOU SURE AS HELL BET IT MATTERS.
YOU KNOW THAT, QUEEN.
YOU CREATED A MONSTER. A MONSTER WE HAVE TO WORRY ABOUT.
OLLIE!
YOU'RE OKAY.
YEAH, KID.
PERFECT.
EVERYTHING ALL RIGHT?
NOTHING WE CAN'T HANDLE.
GOOD, BECAUSE KORY, ROY AND I NEED TO LEAVE--
--SOMEONE JUST BROKE INTO OUTSIDERS HQ

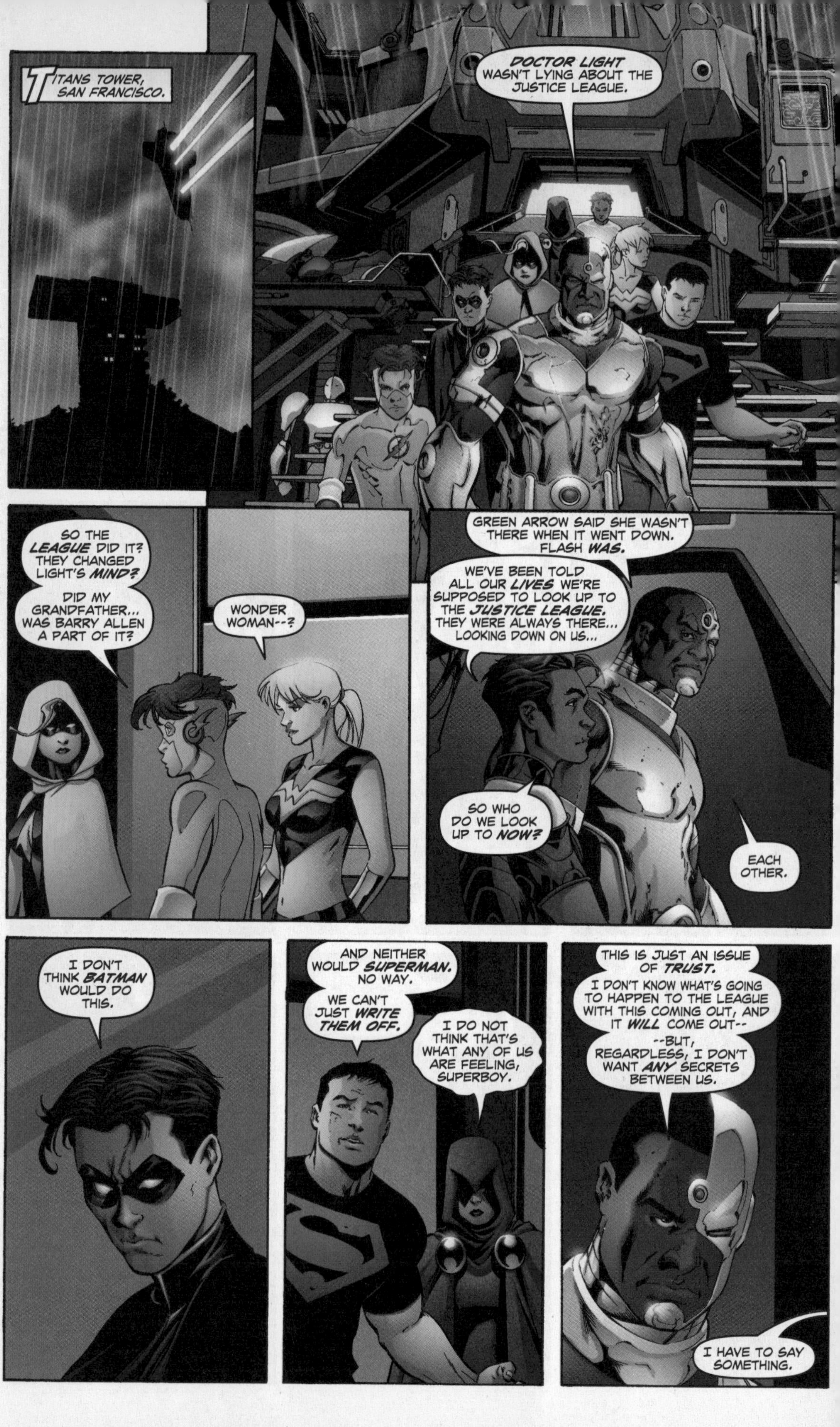
TITANS TOWER, SAN FRANCISCO.
DOCTOR LIGHT WASN'T LYING ABOUT THE JUSTICE LEAGUE.
SO THE LEAGUE DID IT? THEY CHANGED LIGHT'S MIND?
DID MY GRANDFATHER... WAS BARRY ALLEN A PART OF IT?
WONDER WOMAN--?
GREEN ARROW SAID SHE WASN'T THERE WHEN IT WENT DOWN. FLASH WAS.
WE'VE BEEN TOLD ALL OUR LIVES WE'RE SUPPOSED TO LOOK UP TO THE JUSTICE LEAGUE. THEY WERE ALWAYS THERE... LOOKING DOWN ON US...
SO WHO DO WE LOOK UP TO NOW?
EACH OTHER.
I DON'T THINK BATMAN WOULD DO THIS.
AND NEITHER WOULD SUPERMAN. NO WAY.
WE CAN'T JUST WRITE THEM OFF.
I DO NOT THINK THAT'S WHAT ANY OF US ARE FEELING, SUPERBOY.
THIS IS JUST AN ISSUE OF TRUST.
I DON'T KNOW WHAT'S GOING TO HAPPEN TO THE LEAGUE WITH THIS COMING OUT, AND IT WILL COME OUT--
--BUT, REGARDLESS, I DON'T WANT ANY SECRETS BETWEEN US.
I HAVE TO SAY SOMETHING.

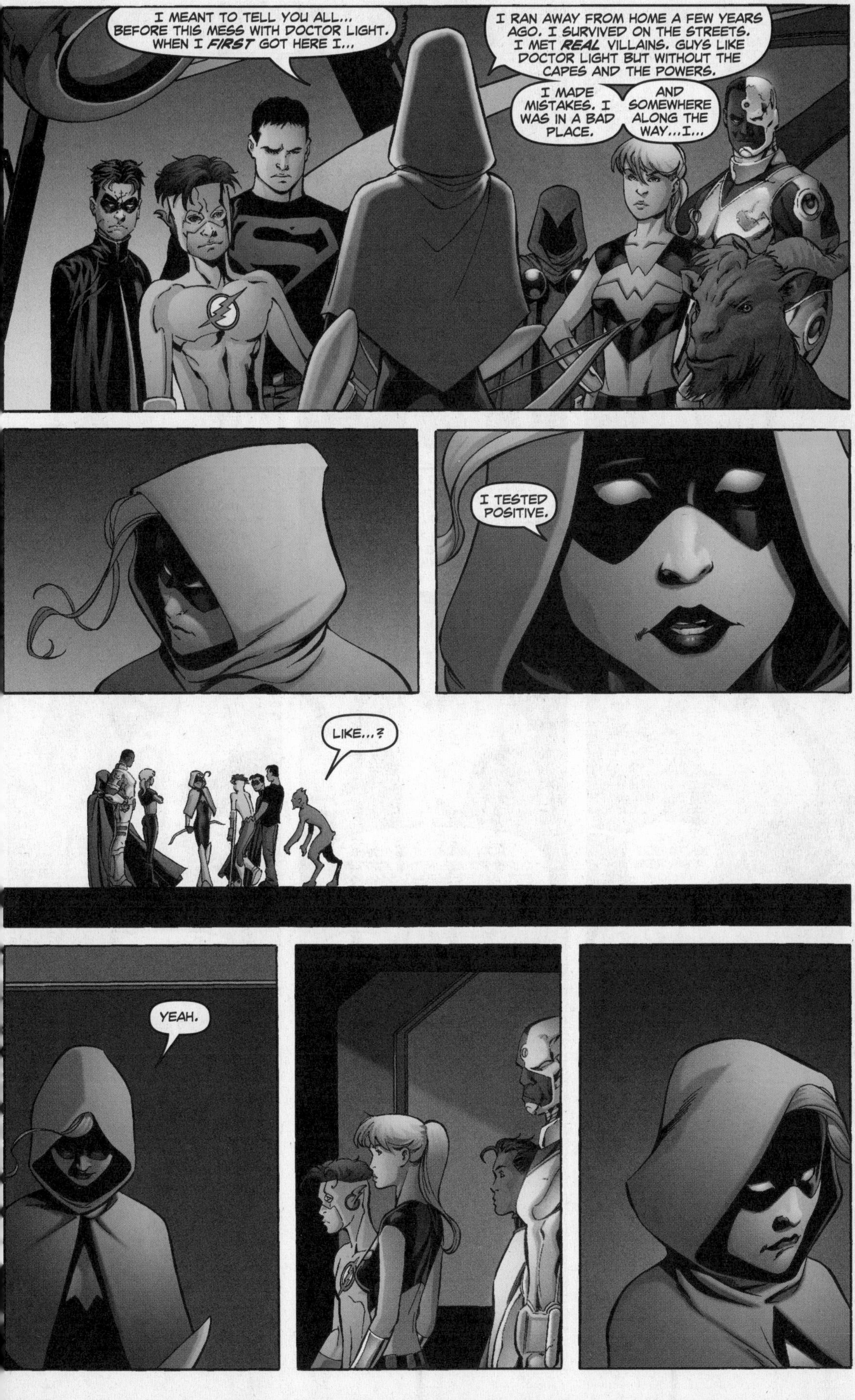
I MEANT TO TELL YOU ALL... BEFORE THIS MESS WITH DOCTOR LIGHT. WHEN I *FIRST* GOT HERE I...
I RAN AWAY FROM HOME A FEW YEARS AGO. I SURVIVED ON THE STREETS. I MET *REAL* VILLAINS. GUYS LIKE DOCTOR LIGHT BUT WITHOUT THE CAPES AND THE POWERS.
I MADE MISTAKES. I WAS IN A BAD PLACE.
AND SOMEWHERE ALONG THE WAY...I...
I TESTED POSITIVE.
LIKE...?
YEAH.

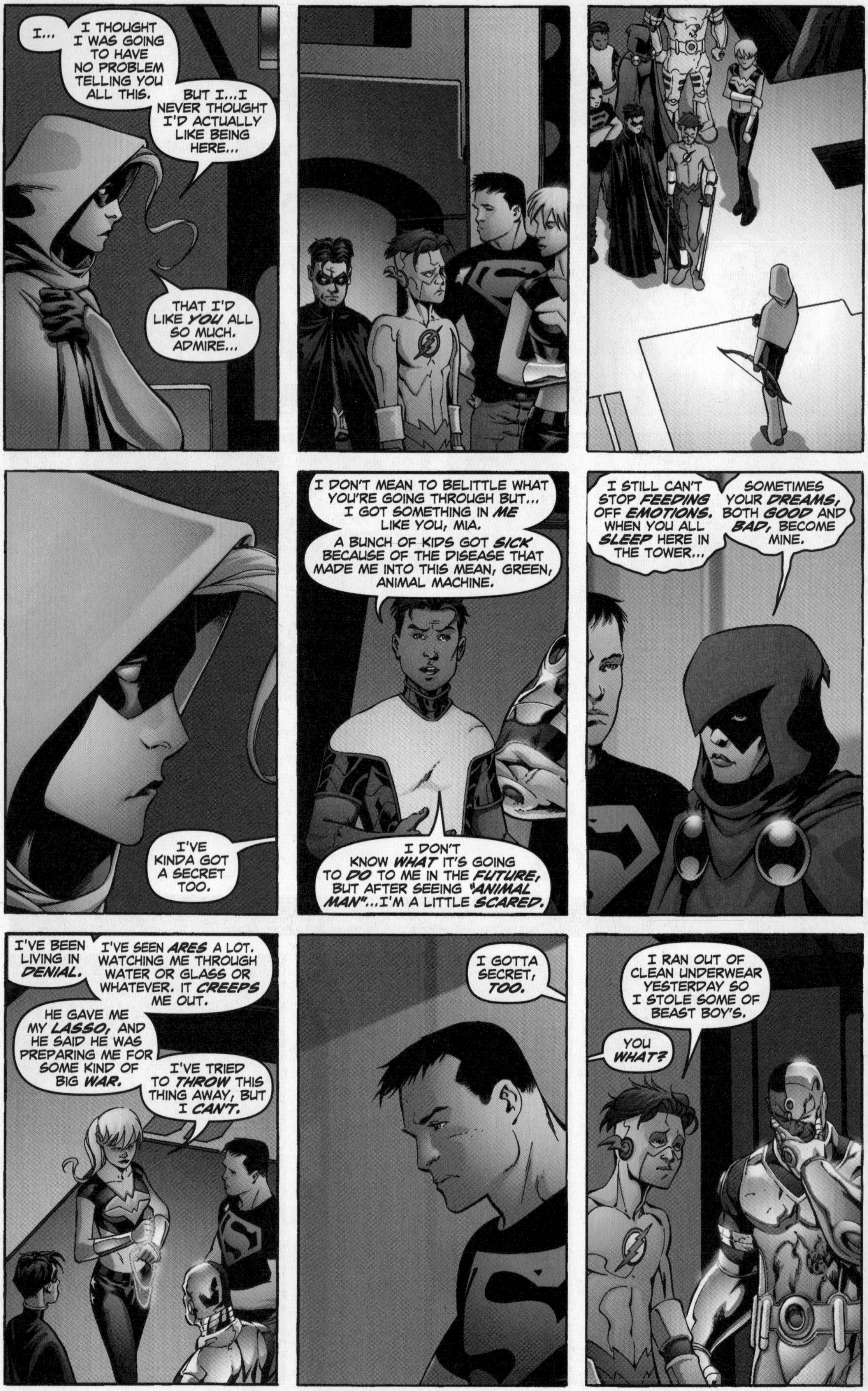
I...
I THOUGHT I WAS GOING TO HAVE NO PROBLEM TELLING YOU ALL THIS.
BUT I...I NEVER THOUGHT I'D ACTUALLY LIKE BEING HERE...
THAT I'D LIKE YOU ALL SO MUCH. ADMIRE...
I'VE KINDA GOT A SECRET TOO.
I DON'T MEAN TO BELITTLE WHAT YOU'RE GOING THROUGH BUT... I GOT SOMETHING IN ME LIKE YOU, MIA.
A BUNCH OF KIDS GOT SICK BECAUSE OF THE DISEASE THAT MADE ME INTO THIS MEAN, GREEN, ANIMAL MACHINE.
I DON'T KNOW WHAT IT'S GOING TO DO TO ME IN THE FUTURE, BUT AFTER SEEING "ANIMAL MAN"...I'M A LITTLE SCARED.
I STILL CAN'T STOP FEEDING OFF EMOTIONS. WHEN YOU ALL SLEEP HERE IN THE TOWER...
SOMETIMES YOUR DREAMS, BOTH GOOD AND BAD, BECOME MINE.
I'VE BEEN LIVING IN DENIAL.
I'VE SEEN ARES A LOT. WATCHING ME THROUGH WATER OR GLASS OR WHATEVER. IT CREEPS ME OUT.
HE GAVE ME MY LASSO, AND HE SAID HE WAS PREPARING ME FOR SOME KIND OF BIG WAR.
I'VE TRIED TO THROW THIS THING AWAY, BUT I CAN'T.
I GOTTA SECRET, TOO.
I RAN OUT OF CLEAN UNDERWEAR YESTERDAY SO I STOLE SOME OF BEAST BOY'S.
YOU WHAT?

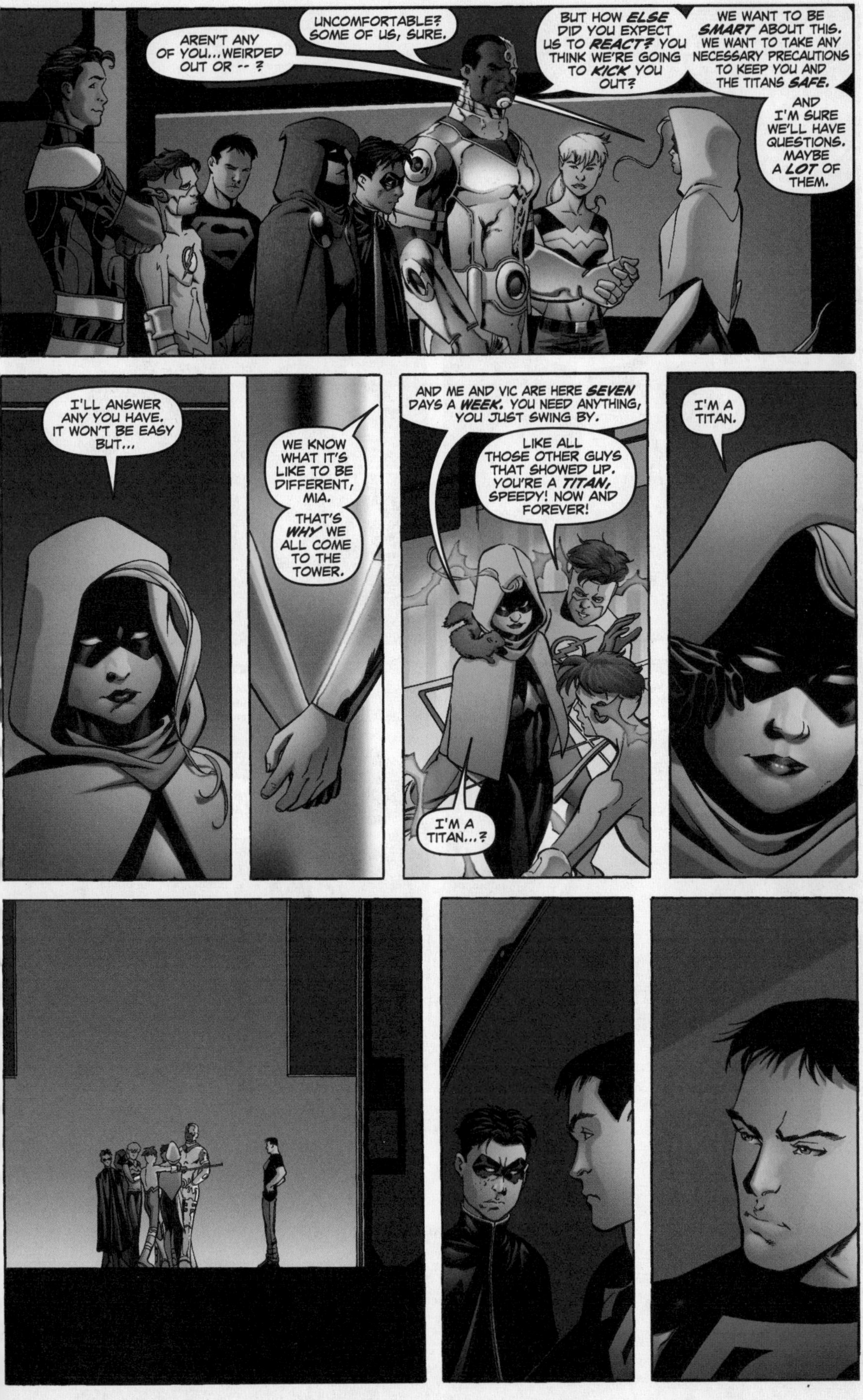

AREN'T ANY OF YOU...WEIRDED OUT OR -- ?
UNCOMFORTABLE? SOME OF US, SURE.
BUT HOW ELSE DID YOU EXPECT US TO REACT? YOU THINK WE'RE GOING TO KICK YOU OUT?
WE WANT TO BE SMART ABOUT THIS. WE WANT TO TAKE ANY NECESSARY PRECAUTIONS TO KEEP YOU AND THE TITANS SAFE.
AND I'M SURE WE'LL HAVE QUESTIONS. MAYBE A LOT OF THEM.
I'LL ANSWER ANY YOU HAVE. IT WON'T BE EASY BUT...
WE KNOW WHAT IT'S LIKE TO BE DIFFERENT, MIA.
THAT'S WHY WE ALL COME TO THE TOWER.
AND ME AND VIC ARE HERE SEVEN DAYS A WEEK. YOU NEED ANYTHING, YOU JUST SWING BY.
LIKE ALL THOSE OTHER GUYS THAT SHOWED UP. YOU'RE A TITAN, SPEEDY! NOW AND FOREVER!
I'M A TITAN...?
I'M A TITAN.

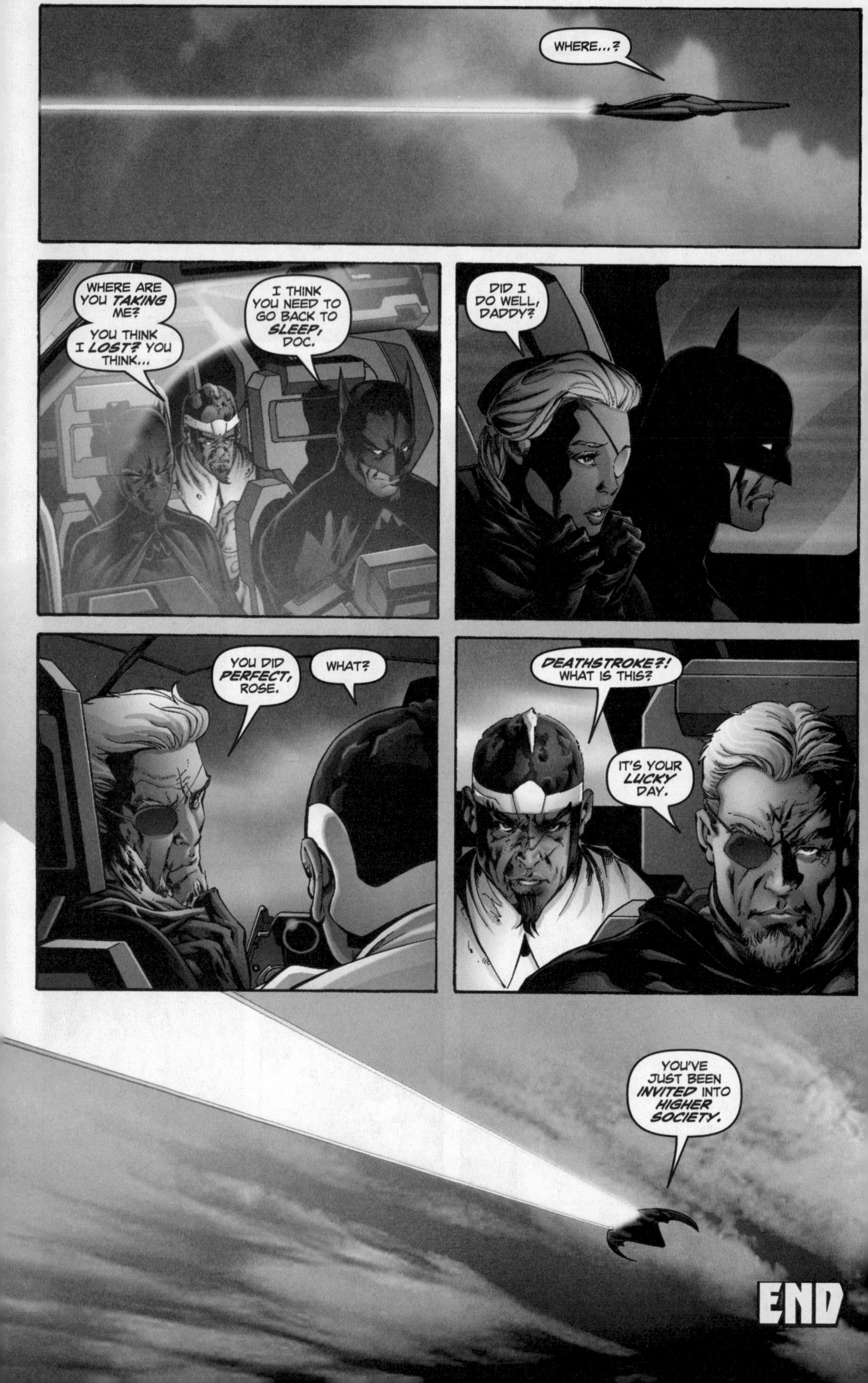
WHERE...?
WHERE ARE YOU TAKING ME?
YOU THINK I LOST? YOU THINK...
I THINK YOU NEED TO GO BACK TO SLEEP, DOC.
DID I DO WELL, DADDY?
YOU DID PERFECT, ROSE.
WHAT?
DEATHSTROKE?! WHAT IS THIS?
IT'S YOUR LUCKY DAY.
YOU'VE JUST BEEN INVITED INTO HIGHER SOCIETY.
END

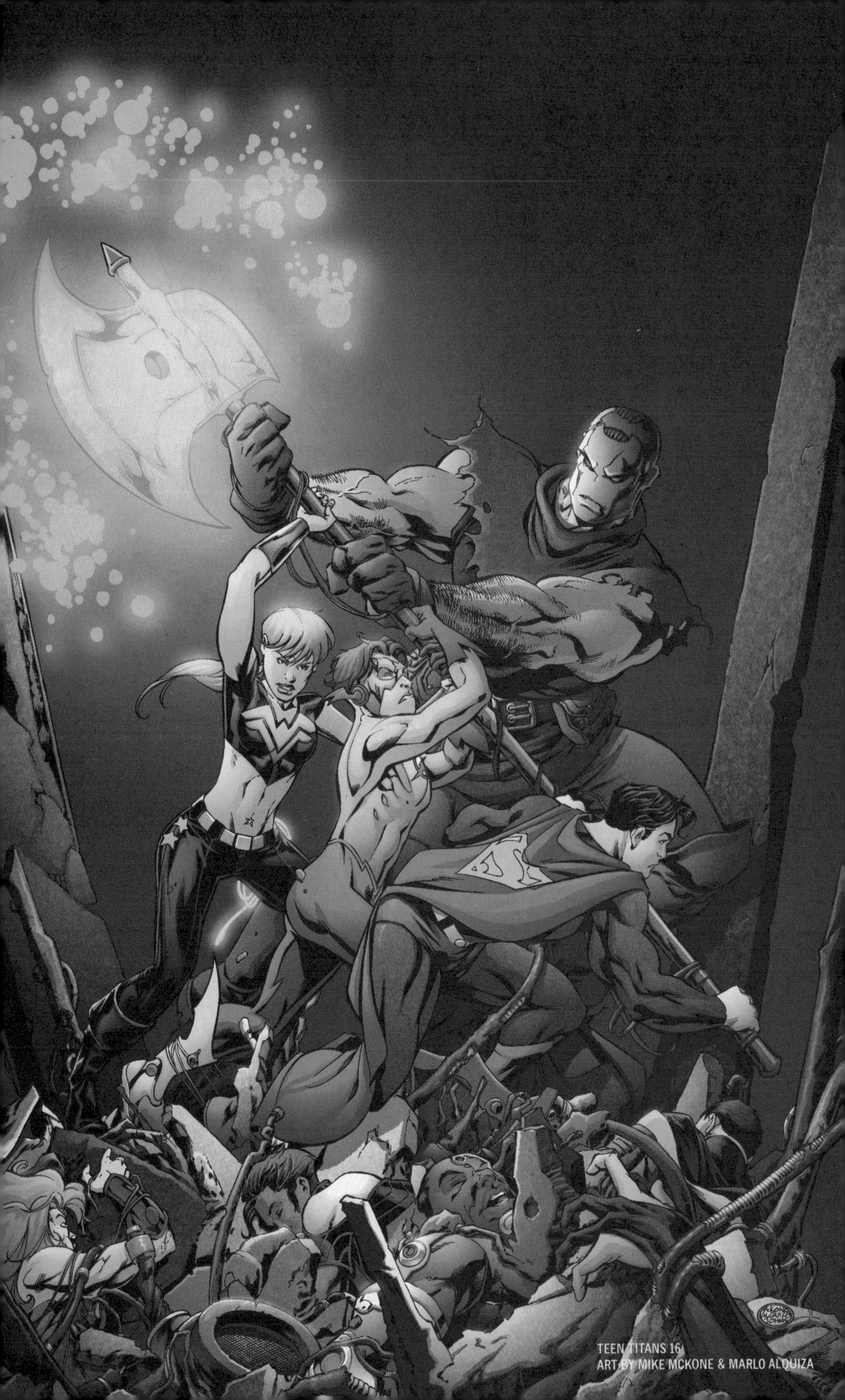

TEEN TITANS 16
ART BY MIKE MCKONE & MARLO ALQUIZA

TEEN TITANS/LEGION SPECIAL
ART BY PHIL JIMENEZ & ANDY LANNING

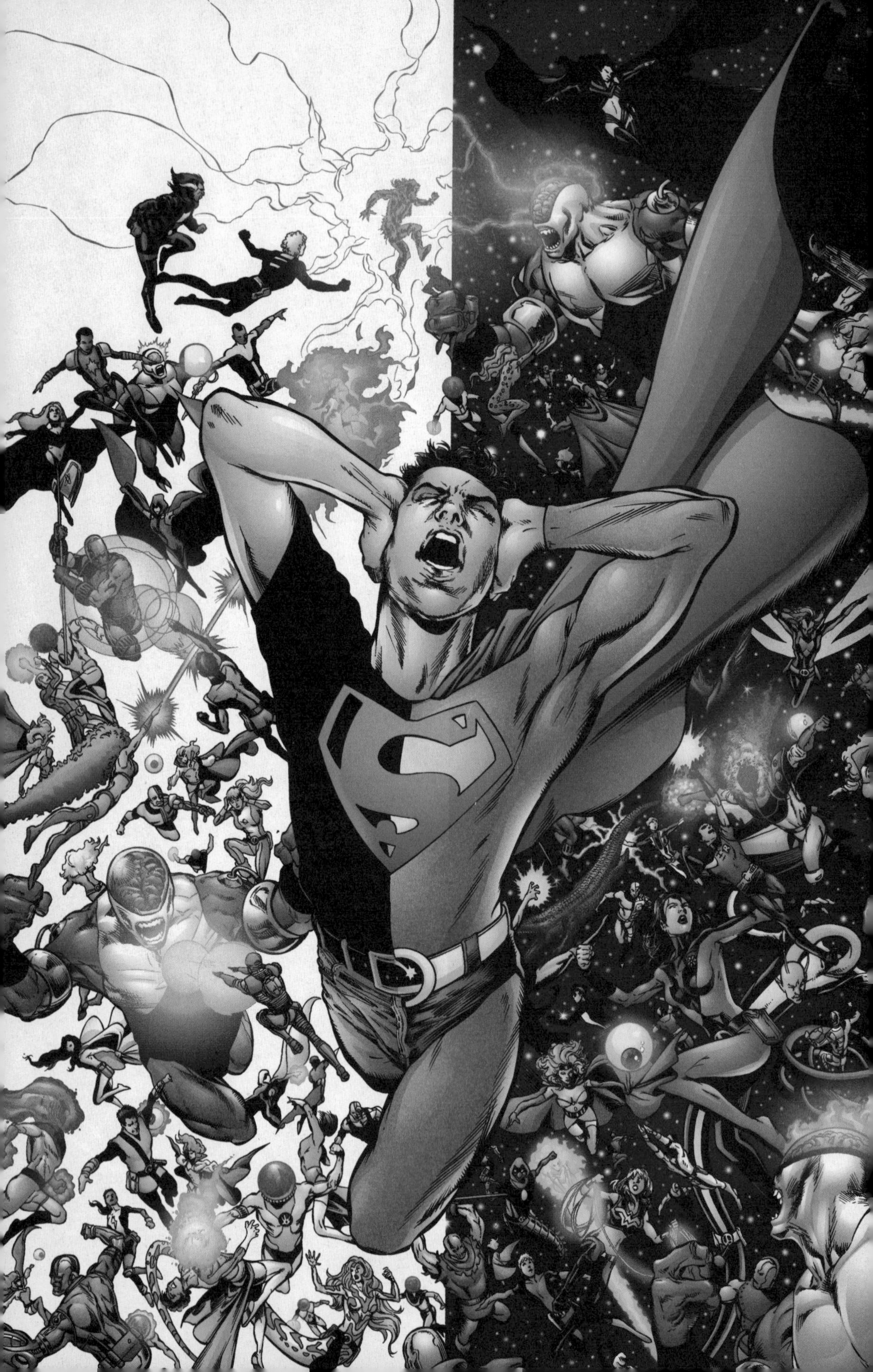

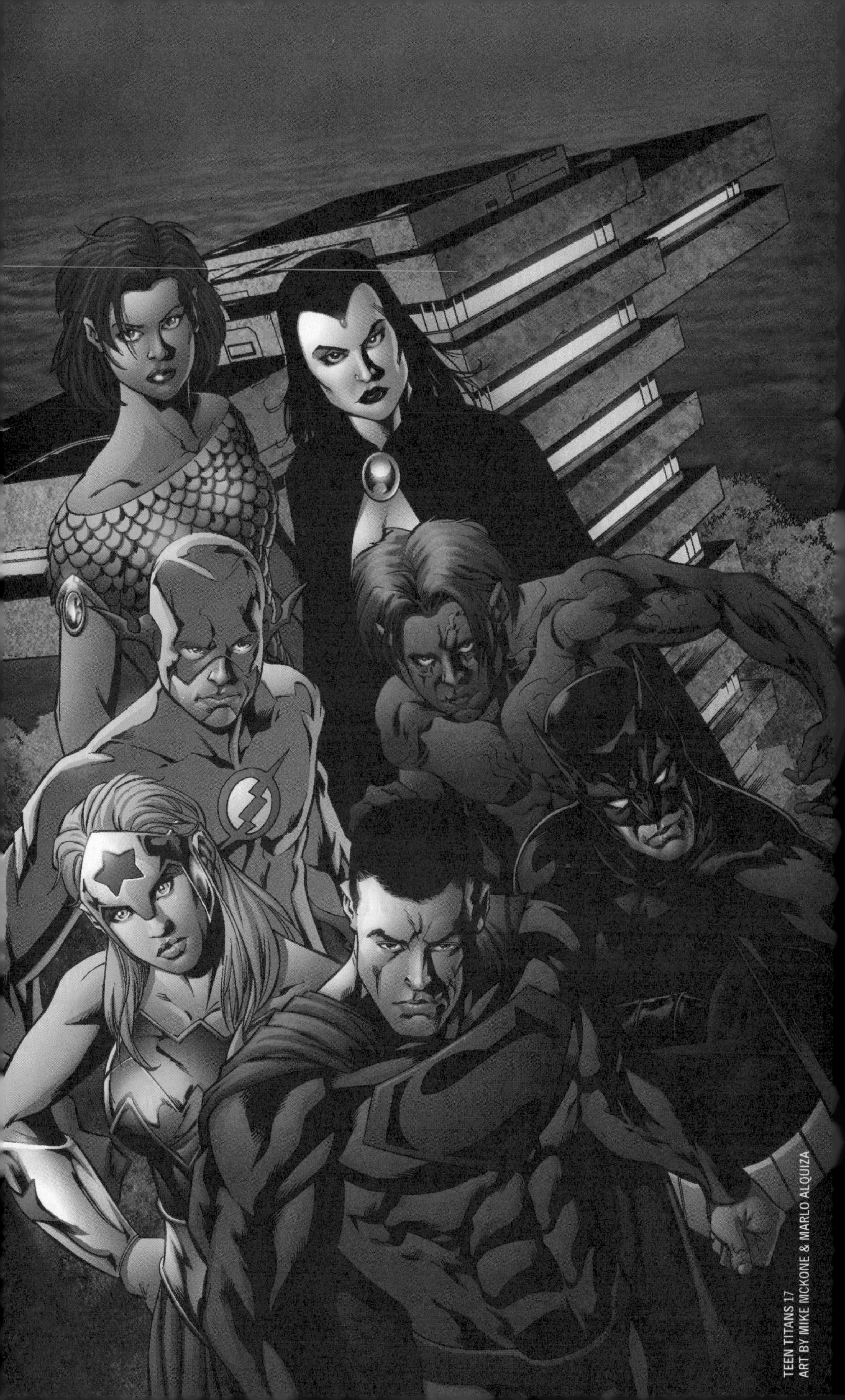

TEEN TITANS 17
ART BY MIKE MCKONE & MARLO ALQUIZA

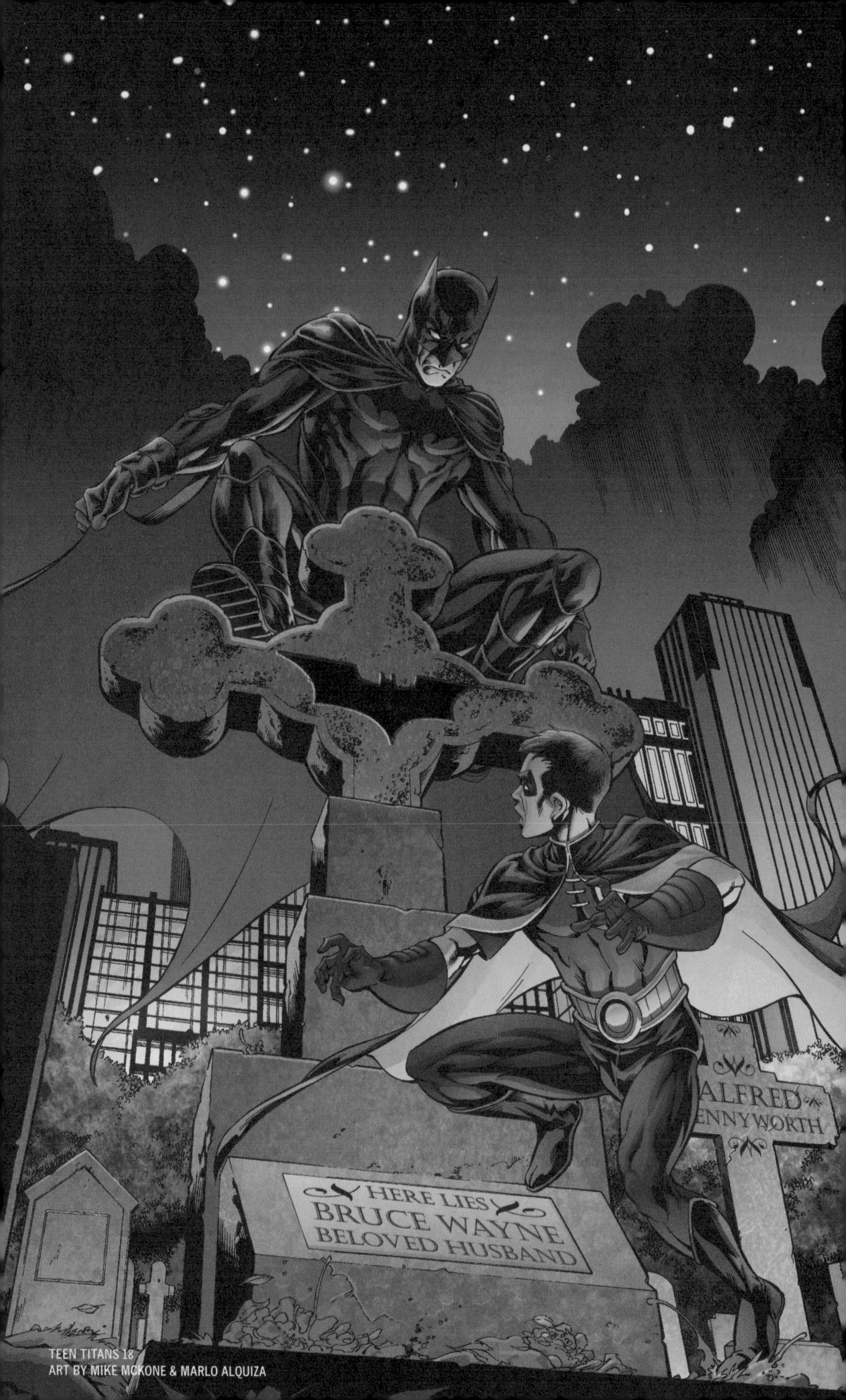
HERE LIES
BRUCE WAYNE
BELOVED HUSBAND
ALFRED
PENNYWORTH

TEEN TITANS 18
ART BY MIKE MCKONE & MARLO ALQUIZA

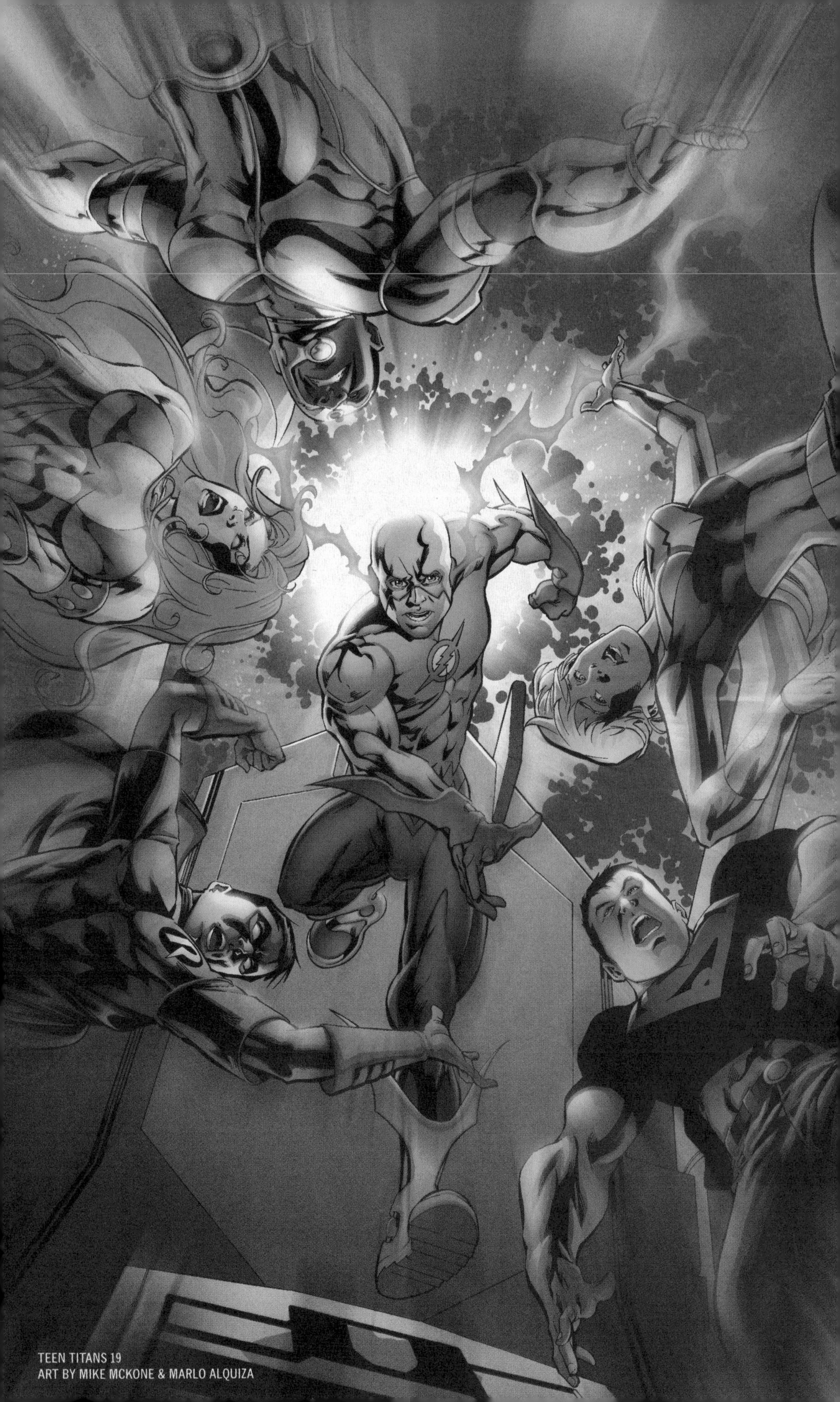

TEEN TITANS 19
ART BY MIKE MCKONE & MARLO ALQUIZA

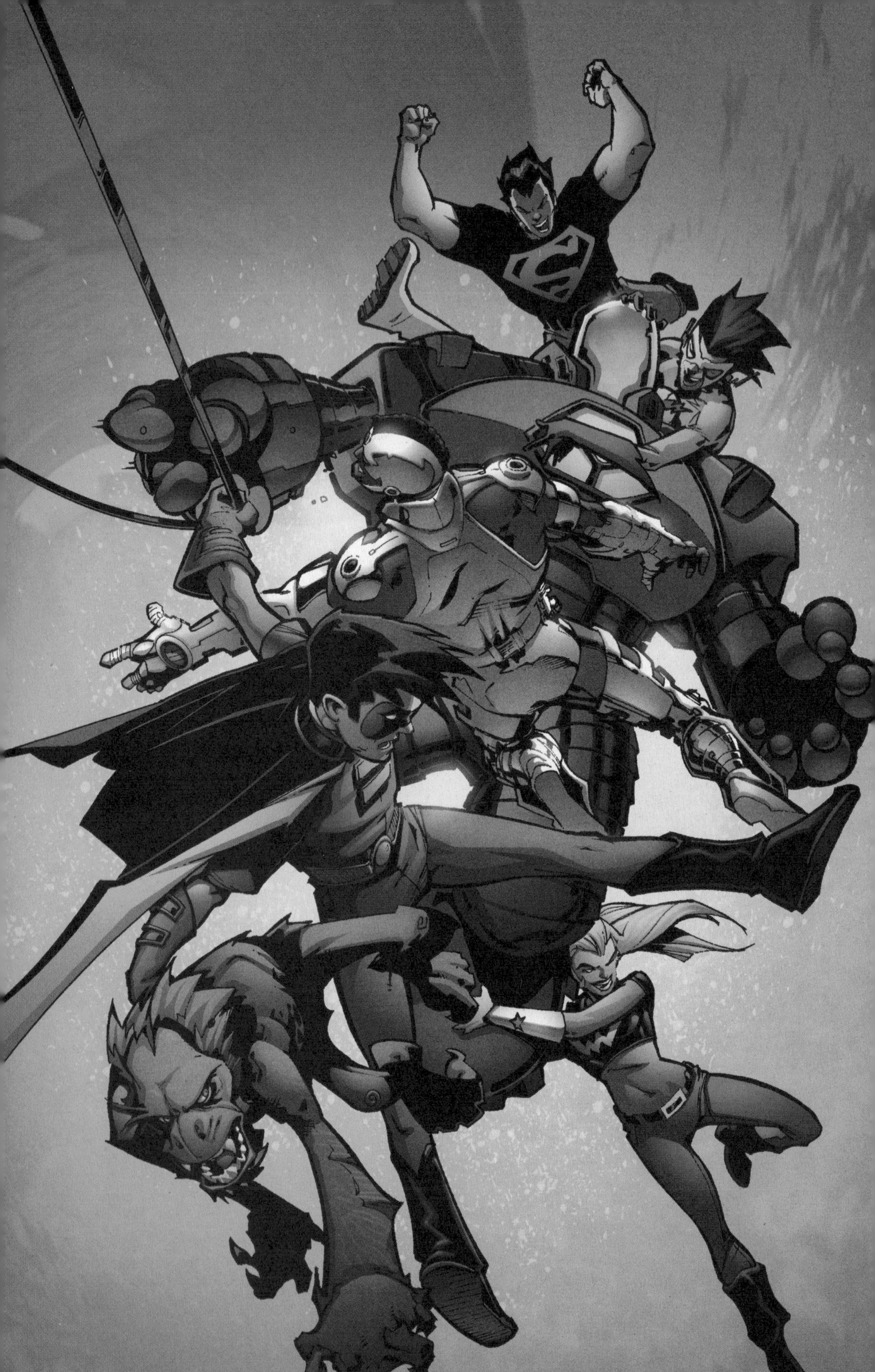

TEEN TITANS 20
ART BY DUNCAN ROULEAU

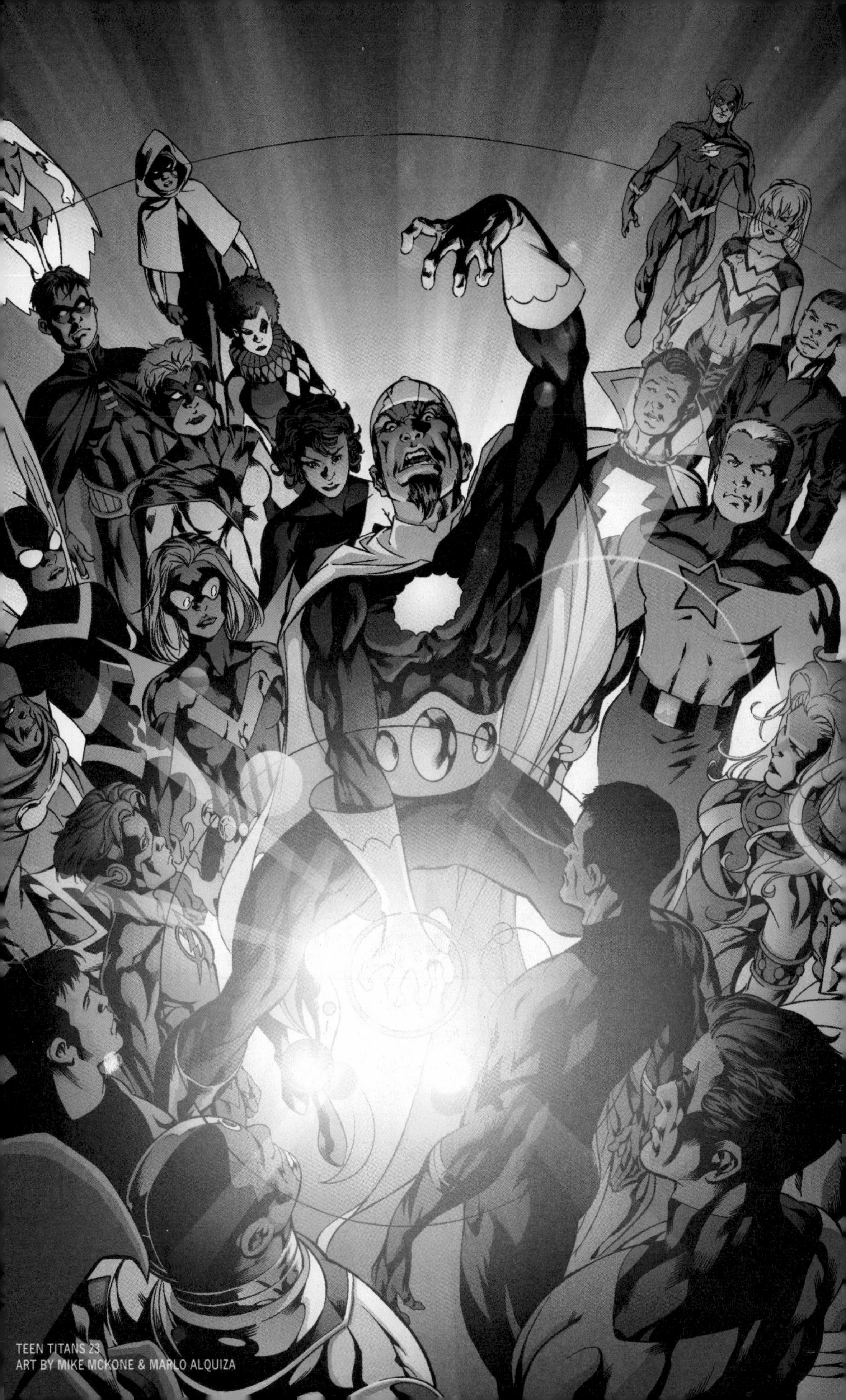

TEEN TITANS 23
ART BY MIKE MCKONE & MARLO ALQUIZA

DESIGNING THE FUTURE

Mike McKone got a rare chance to redesign the Teen Titans for a new generation, one ten years in the future. He relished the opportunity and proved both prolific and creative. From his files, here are some of the designs he envisioned for the team.

Left: A very rough composition for the future's Titans West, with the revised final at right.
Below: Robin becomes Batman, keeping the cape and cowl, but also retaining elements from his own uniform. Sleek and made for acrobatic battle, the outfit is more for a darker world than just the streets of Gotham.

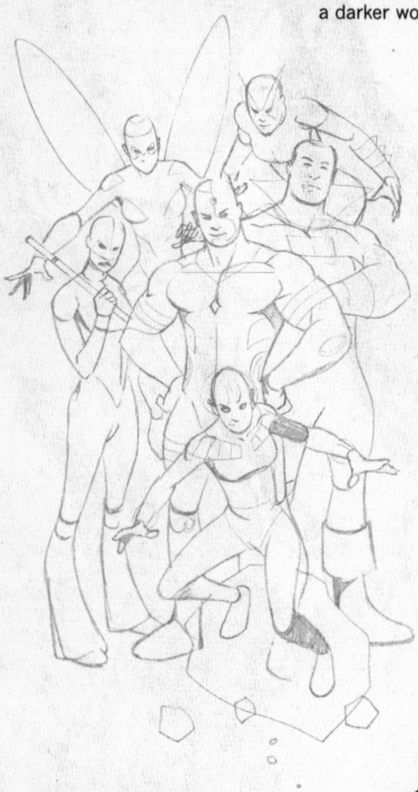

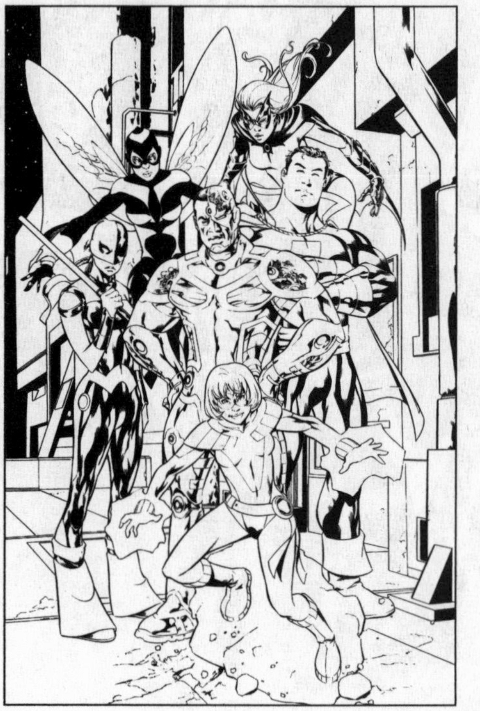

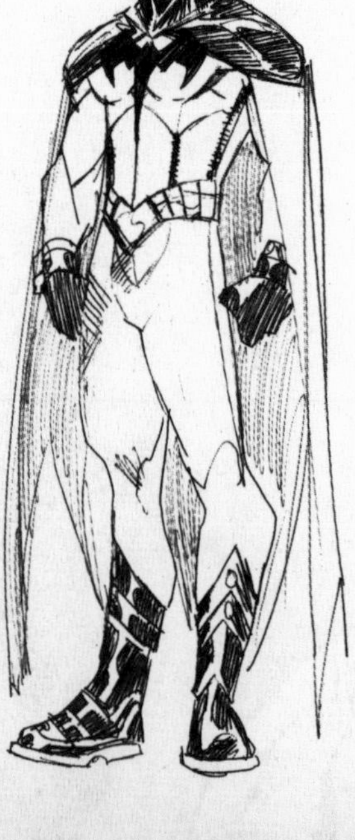

Clockwise from top left: Aquagirl joins the team at some point in the future and is seen here in a modified chain mail outfit. Next is a more mature Kid Flash, honoring the Flash legacy. Cassie in full Amazon armor. Superboy in an outfit familiar, but yet more militaristic. Raven, dark and moody as ever. Gar Logan as a more amorphous figure.

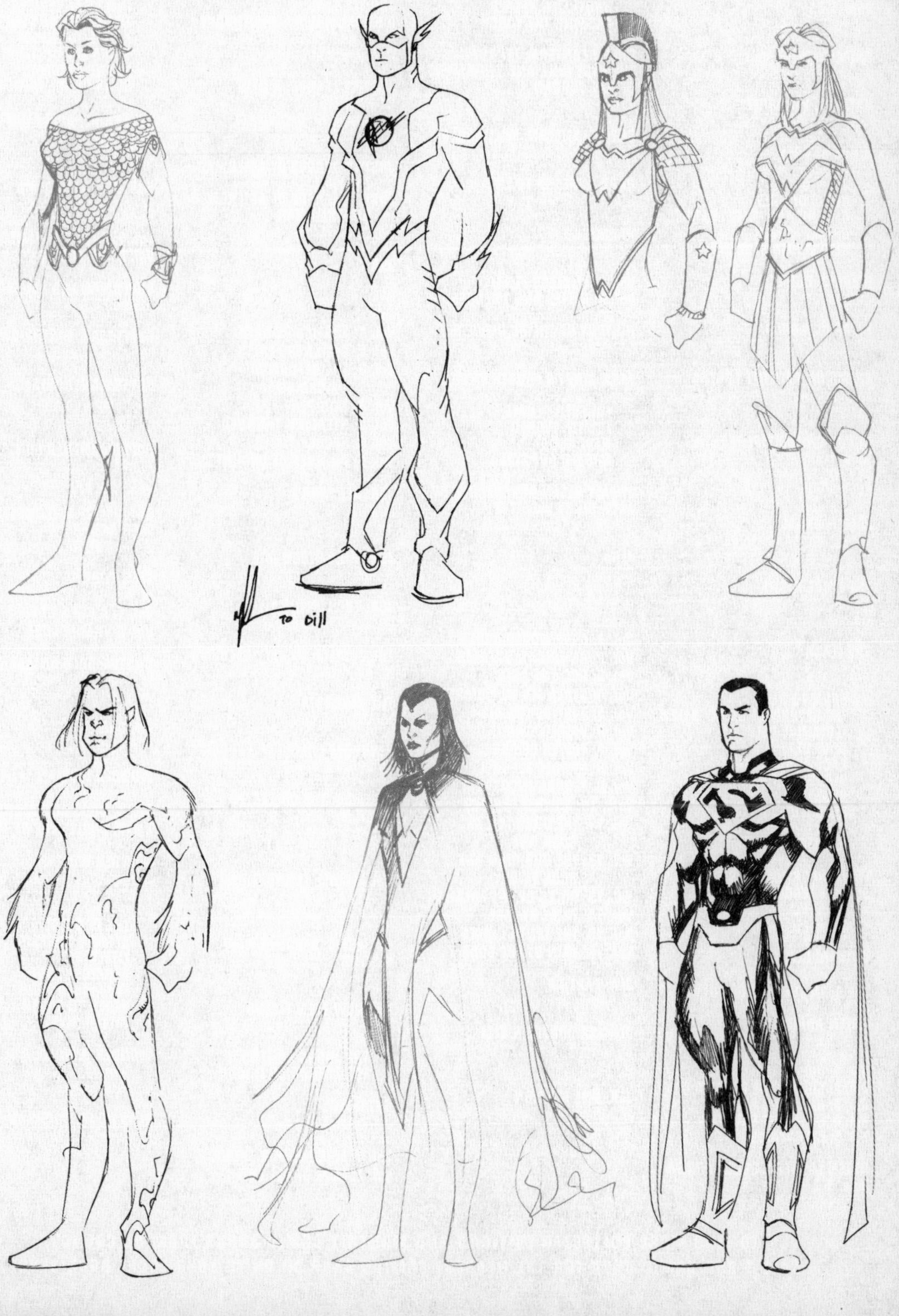

THE STARS OF THE DC UNIVERSE
CAN ALSO BE FOUND IN THESE BOOKS: